OTTOMAN SUNNISM

Edinburgh Studies on the Ottoman Empire
Series Editor: Kent F. Schull

Published and forthcoming titles

Migrating Texts: Circulating Translations around the Ottoman Mediterranean
Edited by Marilyn Booth

Ottoman Sunnism: New Perspectives
Edited by Vefa Erginbaş

The Politics of Armenian Migration to North America, 1885–1915: Sojourners, Smugglers and Dubious Citizens
David E. Gutman

The Kizilbash-Alevis in Ottoman Anatolia: Sufism, Politics and Community
Ayfer Karakaya-Stump

Çemberlitaş Hamami in Istanbul: The Biographical Memoir of a Turkish Bath
Nina Macaraig

Nineteenth-Century Local Governance in Ottoman Bulgaria: Politics in Provincial Councils
Safa Saraçoğlu

Prisons in the Late Ottoman Empire: Microcosms of Modernity
Kent F. Schull

Ruler Visibility and Popular Belonging in the Ottoman Empire
Darin Stephanov

Children and Childhood in the Ottoman Empire: From the Fourteenth to the Twentieth Centuries
Edited by Gulay Yilma and Fruma Zachs

edinburghuniversitypress.com/series/esoe

OTTOMAN SUNNISM

NEW PERSPECTIVES

Edited by Vefa Erginbaş

EDINBURGH
University Press

Edinburgh University Press is one of the leading university presses in the UK. We publish academic books and journals in our selected subject areas across the humanities and social sciences, combining cutting-edge scholarship with high editorial and production values to produce academic works of lasting importance. For more information visit our website: edinburghuniversitypress.com

© editorial matter and organisation Vefa Erginbaş, 2019, 2021
© the chapters their several authors, 2019, 2021

Edinburgh University Press Ltd
The Tun – Holyrood Road
12 (2f) Jackson's Entry
Edinburgh EH8 8PJ

First published in hardback by Edinburgh University Press 2019

Typeset in Jaghbuni by
Servis Filmsetting Ltd, Stockport, Cheshire

A CIP record for this book is available from the British Library

ISBN 978 1 4744 4331 9 (hardback)
ISBN 978 1 4744 4332 6 (paperback)
ISBN 978 1 4744 4333 3 (webready PDF)
ISBN 978 1 4744 4334 0 (epub)

The right of the contributors to be identified as authors of this work has been asserted in accordance with the Copyright, Designs and Patents Act 1988 and the Copyright and Related Rights Regulations 2003 (SI No. 2498).

Contents

Contributors vii
Acknowledgements xi
Note on Transliteration xiii

1. Introduction 1
   Vefa Erginbaş

2. The Rise of the 'Religion and State' Order:
   Re-confessionalisation of State and Society in the Early Modern
   Ottoman Empire 12
   Rıza Yıldırım

3. One Word, Many Implications: The Term '*Kızılbaş*' in the Early
   Modern Ottoman Context 47
   Ayşe Baltacıoğlu-Brammer

4. Reappraising Ottoman Religiosity in the Last Decades of the
   Sixteenth Century: Mustafa Darir's *Siret* and its Alid Content 71
   Vefa Erginbaş

5. Confessionalisation or a Quest for Order? A Comparative Look
   at Religion and State in the Seventeenth-century Ottoman,
   Russian and Habsburg Empires 90
   Yasir Yılmaz

6. From the *Hamzaviyye* to the *Melāmiyye*: Transformation of an
   Order in Seventeenth-century Istanbul 121
   F. Betül Yavuz

7. Fabricating the Great Mass: Heresy and Legitimate Plurality in
   Harputlu İshak Efendi's Polemics against the *Bektaşi* Order   146
   Benjamin Weineck

8. The Ottoman Policy of 'Correction of Belief(s)'   166
   Necati Alkan

9. Some Reflections on the Fluidity of Orthodoxy and Heterodoxy
   in an Ottoman Sunni Context   193
   John J. Curry

Bibliography   211
Index   247

Contributors

Necati Alkan is currently a research fellow at the University of Bamberg, Germany, where he is completing his second book in which he analyses the Nusayris (Alawis) in the late Ottoman state in the context of conversion to Protestantism and Sunni Islam. He received his MA in Islamic Studies and PhD in late Ottoman history both from University of Bochum in Germany. He has worked at universities in Germany, Turkey and Israel. His first book, *Dissent and Heterodoxy in the late Ottoman Empire: Reformers, Babis and Baha'is*, was published in 2008. He has published widely since, including articles in academic journals such as the *Bulletin of the School of Oriental and African Studies*, *Middle and Eastern Studies*.

Ayşe Baltacıoğlu-Brammer is currently an assistant professor in the Departments of History and Middle Eastern and Islamic Studies at New York University. She completed her PhD at the Ohio State University in 2016. She is a specialist in Middle Eastern history with a focus on the early modern Ottoman and Safavid empires. Her existing and forthcoming publications include articles in the *International Journal of Turkish Studies*, the *Journal of Turkish and Ottoman Studies* and chapters in various volumes, including *Rethinking 'Sunnitization' in the Ottoman Empire, c. 1450–c.1700*, edited by Tijana Krstić and Derin Terzioğlu, and *The Safavid World*, edited by Rudi Matthee.

John J. Curry is an Associate Professor in the Department of History, University of Nevada, Las Vegas, where he has taught since 2006. He graduated from the Ohio State University with a dual MA in History and Arabic Language (1998) and a PhD in History (2005). He specialises in the history of the early modern Ottoman Empire in particular, and in the history of the Islamic world and global history more generally. He is the author of *The Transformation of Muslim Mystical Thought in the Ottoman Empire: The Rise of the Halveti Order, 1350–1650* (Edinburgh University Press, 2010), a study of a major Ottoman religio-mystical brotherhood with branches throughout the Islamic world, in addition to a number of journal articles on various topics. He has also published an edited volume of studies on Sufism in the medieval and early modern Islamic world titled *Sufism and Society: Arrangements of the Mystical in the Muslim World 1200–1800* (co-edited with Erik S. Ohlander), to which he contributed both the introduction chapter and one of the twelve chapters in the volume.

Vefa Erginbaş is an Associate Professor of History at Providence College, Rhode Island. He received his BA from Bogazici University, Istanbul, MA from Sabanci University, Istanbul, and his doctorate from the Ohio State University in 2013. He studies Ottoman intellectual, cultural and social history in the early modern period. His articles and reviews have appeared in the *Journal of the Economic and Social History of the Orient*, *International Journal of Middle East Studies*, and *Journal of the Ottoman and Turkish Studies Association*. He has also contributed chapters in various edited volumes.

Benjamin Weineck works at the Department for the Study of Religion at the University of Bayreuth, Germany. After finishing his undergraduate degree in Near and Middle Eastern Studies in Mainz and Ankara, he obtained his MA in Ottoman Studies from Heidelberg University in 2013. He has recently finished his dissertation on *Kızılbaş*-Alevis and their relation to the Ottoman state, in the sixteenth–eighteenth centuries. His research interests include the history of the Alevis in Turkey and the Ottoman Empire, Ottoman religious, social and administrative history as well as contemporary Shiite religiosity. He is the editor, with Johannes Zimmermann, of the collective volume *Alevism between Standardisation and Plurality: Negotiating Texts, Sources, and Cultural Heritage*. Weineck's other publications also deal with historical as well as contemporary issues of Alevi and Shiite collective identity and religiosity and have appeared in various journals and edited volumes.

F. Betül Yavuz received her doctorate from Rice University, Religious Studies Department in 2013. Her research explores expressions of non-conformist Sufism in the Ottoman Empire in connection with the broader Islamic world. She is also interested in delineating concepts of heterodoxy as they relate to the collective expressions of religiosity in the early

Contributors

modern era. She is working on other articles exploring the rural and urban forms of mystical expression in the Bayrami–Melāmi texts during the seventeenth century.

Rıza Yıldırım is currently pursuing his second PhD at Emory University, Atlanta, Georgia. He received his first PhD in history from Bilkent University, Ankara, in 2008, studying the formative period of the *Kızılbaş*–Alevi tradition within the context of Ottoman–Safavid rivalry. After post-doctoral study at Harvard University (2008/9), he worked in the History Department of TOBB University of Economics and Technology, Ankara, as an associate professor of Ottoman history. He resigned from his position in 2016 to pursue his second PhD. His research interests lie in the history and religiosity of non-orthodox religious traditions in the Middle East, such as Alevis, Bektaşis, Akhis, Alawites and Ahl-i Haqq. He has published several books and articles on these subjects. His recent books include *Aleviliğin Doğuşu: Kızılbaş Sufiliğinin Toplumsal ve Siyasal Temelleri, 1300–1501* (2017) and *Geleneksel Alevilik: İnanç, İbadet, Kurumlar, Toplumsal Yapı, Kolektif Bellek* (2018).

Yasir Yılmaz is a Visiting Assistant Professor of History at Palacký University, Olomouc, and has recently completed a Guest Researcher term as a Richard Plaschka Fellow at the Austrian Academy of Sciences, Institute for Modern and Contemporary Historical Research, Vienna. His broad research and teaching interests encompass the histories of the Habsburg Monarchy, Ottoman Empire, and the Middle East and the relations between Muslim societies and Europe, with a current focus on Habsburg–Ottoman diplomacy. His publications have appeared in the *Austrian History Yearbook*, *Mediterranean Historical Review* and many edited volumes. Yılmaz is currently working on a book project concerning Habsburg and European diplomacy in Istanbul during the time of Grand Vizier Kara Mustafa Paşa (1676–83). He holds a PhD in history from Purdue University, West Lafayette, and an MA in history from Bilkent University, Ankara. He has formerly taught in the United States and Turkey.

Acknowledgements

The idea for the current volume came from a panel I organised at the Middle East Studies Association (MESA) Annual Conference in Denver, Colorado, 2015, titled 'Beyond Orthodoxy and Confessionalization: New Perspectives on Ottoman Sunnism'. After this panel, I approached Kent Schull, the current editor of the Edinburgh Series on the Ottoman Empire and the former editor of the *Journal of Ottoman and Turkish Studies Association* (*JOTSA*) with the idea of a special issue to be published on a future issue of *JOTSA*. Kent Schull kindly encouraged me to consider publishing an edited volume rather than a special journal issue, and thus the idea for the present volume was born. Therefore, my special thanks go to Kent Schull for not only his initial encouragement but also support for the publication of this volume within the Edinburgh Ottoman Series. I would like to express my special gratitude to my friend and colleague John Curry for not only agreeing to write the concluding chapter of the volume, but also going over each chapter and offering his revisions. I am also very thankful to Nicola Ramsey, the acquisitions editor for Edinburgh University Press and the anonymous reviewers for their feedback, which no doubt made the volume more complete.

During the process, many colleagues helped me with their comments and suggestions. I would like to thank Virginia Aksan, Guy Burak, Dana Sajdi and Gottfried Hagen for their assistance in this process. The contributors to the original panel at the MESA, Yasir Yılmaz, Selim Güngörürler, Aslıhan Gürbüzel, and Malissa Taylor, also deserve thanks for agreeing to be on that panel. My doctoral adviser, Jane Hathaway, graciously agreed to serve as both chair and discussant of the panel. I am very grateful, *Hocam*, for your support during the last thirteen years. The Department of History and Classics at Providence College, my chairs Raymond Sickenger and Margaret Manchester, and the Dean of Arts and Sciences Sheila Adamus-

Liotta, all deserve thanks for their support (both financial and personal) during my work at Providence College. I am indebted to the participants in this volume, especially Rıza Yıldırım and Ayşe Baltacıoğlu-Brammer who provided sample chapters during the proposal process, for not only agreeing to participate in this project but also bearing with me during the editing and publication process, and kindly responded to my revisions, inquiries and suggestions promptly. Finally, I am much obliged to my wife, Ebru, for her continuous encouragement and support. I dedicate this project to my first teacher, Vasfiye Mandacı, who instilled in me an undying love of learning. *Ellerinizden öperim öğretmenim!*

Note on Transliteration

I have generally followed the transliteration practice standardised by the *International Journal of Middle East Studies*. Personal and common names (unless there is ambiguity or they exist in an original version of a reference), as well as the words that can be found in Merriam Webster Dictionary's online edition (2019), that is, ulema, fatwa, mufti, qadi, sharia, waqf, taqiyah, timar, Shiite, etc. are not transliterated. The reader may find some inconsistencies especially in the rendering of Ottoman Turkish words as some of the authors prefer modern Turkish orthography as indicated on the *IJMES* transliteration chart. For instance, the long vowel which denotes possession as in Bektaşī is rendered Bektaşi, whereas words of Arabic origin such as Ḥurūfī are rendered with long vowels.

1
Introduction

Vefa Erginbaş

In 2022, we will mark the centenary of a series of articles by Fuad Köprülü in 1922, which were subsequently published under the title *Islam in Anatolia*.[1] Building on Köprülü's studies, some of which he wrote before the declaration of the Turkish Republic, modern historiography has focused on the nature of Islam's existence in Anatolia, the Balkans and the Arab provinces of the Ottoman Empire, both before and after the foundation of the empire. Köprülü penned these works as a response to Franz Babinger's[2] assertion that pre-Ottoman Anatolia was not Sunni, and in so doing laid out a framework that would define scholarly attitudes towards the nature of the relationship of Turks with Islam for decades. During the 1970s, some of these ideas were furthered by rightist intellectuals in Turkey who created the famed Turkish–Islamic synthesis, which proposes that Turks (especially Turkish dynasties) had been instrumental in the spread of Islam, and that no contradiction between the ancient beliefs of the Turks and Islam existed.[3] These intellectuals thus argued that Turkishness and Islam (or more accurately, Sunni Islam) are harmonious.

Putting aside the veracity of Köprülü's claims, most of which were formed under the emergence of the nationalist exuberance of the nascent Republic, additional views have expanded our knowledge significantly. Beginning with the work of pioneering intellectuals of the early Republican era such as Abdulbaki Gölpınarlı[4] and Ömer Lütfi Barkan,[5] various studies by Irene Mélikoff[6] and her students, such as Ahmet Yaşar Ocak,[7] as well as by influential Ottoman and late medieval historians like Suraiyya Faroqhi,[8] Ahmet Karamustafa,[9] Madeline Zilfi,[10] Cemal Kafadar[11] and Gülru Necipoğlu,[12] we have subsequently seen a new generation of brilliant scholars. Among these, Dina Legall,[13] John J. Curry,[14] Rıza Yıldırım,[15] Ayfer Karakaya-Stump,[16] Tijana Krstić,[17] Derin Terzioğlu,[18] Guy Burak,[19] Nabil al-Tikriti,[20] Stefan Winter,[21] Markus Dressler,[22]

Abdurahman Atçıl,[23] Sara Nur Yıldız[24] and Hüseyin Yılmaz[25] have all made valuable contributions to our understanding of Islam in the Ottoman context.[26] This not to say that there was ever a consensus among these scholars; however, each generation of intellectuals took up a different topical focus and aspect of this issue and studied it in depth. Though one would expect many more studies on a subject of this magnitude over the course of many decades, interest in studying Ottoman (or pre-Ottoman) Islamic society and culture has been sporadic and uneven. For a time, some scholars paid attention to the relationship between the state and religion, as Ocak's many studies illustrate. There has also been a more recent interest in Sufism and various Sufi orders, whether within the Sunni fold or not, as well as the role of ulema in their capacities as professors, preachers and judges. One could also argue that there has been a more concerted effort to understand *Bektaşi/Alevi* Islam, due to a combination of its mysterious and contested nature, its connections with the Ottoman Janissary and palace hierarchies, and its foundation as one of the largest religious minority groups in modern Turkey today.

What emerges from these studies as a whole has not yet reified into a coherent picture, but each provides a piece of the puzzle as to how we might eventually define 'Ottoman Islam'. But what do we mean by Ottoman Islam, or Ottoman Sunnism or any other such formulation? Is it a collective name for the religious policies that the Ottoman state upheld? Or does it refer to the religious culture that the subjects of this empire espoused? Answers to these questions are far from simple. The religious policy of the Ottoman state changed from one era to another (there is a vast gap between the cultures of the fourteenth and sixteenth centuries, for example), and sometimes from one consecutive sultan to another (as in the very different approaches of Bayezid II and Selim I). In their own phrasing, the Ottomans prided themselves on adhering to the norms of the *ehl-i sünnet ve'l cemaat*, but what this meant, and the strictness of their adherence varied across the centuries based upon the Sufi or scholarly affiliations and biases of each sultan. The Ottoman state also reacted intuitively and pragmatically in many cases: they relentlessly pursued *Kızılbaş* sympathisers in Anatolia during the emergence of the Safavid Empire,[27] but tolerated Yazidis and Nusayris in Syria and Lebanon in the following two centuries.[28] As for the religious culture experienced and lived by the masses, it is even more difficult to reach conclusions. Ottoman madrasas no doubt propagated certain elements of Sunni and Hanafi Islam, with the support of some of the Sufi orders; however, many other orders spread antinomian or Alid ideas. Therefore, a coherent vision of Islam as Ottoman subjects themselves experienced it is difficult to discern and

Introduction

resembles more a colourful diversity. Intermittent heresy trials in the sixteenth century, as well as the periodic state-sponsored efforts to suppress these groups from the sixteenth century onwards, clearly demonstrate this breach between 'desired' and 'actual' Sunnism.

In the past decade, a new generation of scholars has innovatively engaged with the question of how the Ottoman version of Islam evolved. This new generation of scholars has tried to locate the Ottomans within the Eurasian trend of confessionalisation, which began in the fourteenth century and peaked in either the sixteenth or early seventeenth century. According to these scholars, the Ottomans were not unique or exceptional in their historical trajectory; they followed similar paths to their European and Asian rivals in undertaking a process of defining and defending what they deemed as the orthodox practice of their religion. Accordingly, the concept of 'confessionalisation' thereby provides a useful line of inquiry to those who find it helpful to study religion in the Ottoman Empire in a comparative perspective.

In its original usage in European historiography, 'confessionalisation' refers to a rapprochement between the state and the church in the era following the Reformation, and was marked by efforts to create unified confessions and religious practices. But is it analytically sound and methodologically helpful to import this term into the study of the Ottoman religious context? While the term can be useful to identify elements of the institutionalisation of Sunnism in the Ottoman Empire as enforced by the state through an alliance with state-sponsored actors, such as the ulema, it also carries the danger of overemphasising the state's role in this process. Even though the official religious policy of any given state is undoubtedly significant for understanding the religious proclivities of any given group, the process of confession-building often more resembles a negotiation than coercion. Therefore, however we choose to define Ottoman Islam as a concept, it is best to understand it as a continuing (and cumulative) process shaped by many agents and trends, as suggested by Derin Terzioğlu. These agents and trends may not always coalesce with each other, keeping in mind Shahab Ahmed's idea of 'coherent contradiction' as a reality in Muslim religious expression,[29] the inability to define a coherent whole need not suggest confusion or cacophony; instead, it shows a resilient presence of religious diversity that most Ottomans did not find unusual.

The impetus for this volume emerged out of the context of the 'confessionalisation' debate and aims to contribute a new line of thought to it by problematising, revising and contextualising various notions that relate to various facets of Ottoman Islam. Most chapters in this collection, in one way or another, engage with this debate. Indeed, the 'confessionalisation' debate provides ammunition for productive discussion and has produced some provocative comparative insights. The chapters in this study offer much-needed nuances in the study of Ottoman religion and showcase the complex approaches various Ottoman actors took towards it. The chapters cover most of the historical span of the empire, except the eighteenth century. There are not many studies on eighteenth-century Ottoman religiosity even though this century offers a wide venue for research, and important developments in this century must be placed in their religious context. Ali Yaycıoğlu's recent study is a fine attempt to remedy this problem.[30] At least one study in this volume offers a comparative approach that includes the Ottomans in conjunction with the Habsburg and Russian monarchies. Several others examine how the Ottoman approach compares with the Safavid case. Two of the chapters are historiographical and provide new conceptualisations and a revisionist approach. The chapters collectively refer to political, social and cultural aspects of Ottoman religious life, and use a variety of sources ranging from state archives, court registers and documents, unpublished manuscript sources, and Sufi treatises. Even though the volume tilts towards the period before 1700, inclusion of two chapters covering the nineteenth century is especially important in providing a link to the last century of empire, a period in which studies on the nature of Ottoman Islam are scanty compared with earlier periods.[31]

To immediately engage the confessionalisation debate, Rıza Yıldırım opens the first chapter by carefully examining the historiography to determine the usefulness of the concept of 'confessionalisation' in the Ottoman context. After extended treatment of the usage of this concept in the recent literature, the author examines the gradual transformation of the Ottoman state ideology from what he calls as the 'dynastic law-based Turco-Mongolian polity' to a 'religious law-based Islamic polity'. Yıldırım challenges the idea that the Ottoman version of confessionalisation was an extension of the Mediterranean-wide confessionalisation process, and proposes to detach it from European notions of the concept. He argues that the origins of this process were Islamic rather than Mediterranean. He acknowledges that elements of this concept can be useful in describing the universal rapprochement between state, religion and society across Islamic Eurasia, but argues that this process began a lot earlier in the Islamic world than in Europe. In contrast, in the Islamic world this process began in the fifteenth century via a return to the Perso-Islamic caliphal model after an interruption over two centuries of Turco-Mongolian invasions and climaxed in the middle of the sixteenth century.[32] Thanks to this change in the political culture, states and confessions drew closer to each other. The author suggests a recalibration of the confessionalisation term

Introduction

and labels the transformation of the religio-political order under Ottoman rule as 're-confessionalisation', given its return to the classical caliphal model.

In the next chapter, Baltacıoğlu-Brammer takes up the issue of the usage of the term '*Kızılbaş*' in the Ottoman sources between the 1480s and 1650s. Inspired by a similar article by Shahzad Bashir, which dealt with the use of the term '*Kızılbaş*' in Iran, the author argues that Ottomanists have defined this term within a rather limited ethno-religious context as a way to reflect the position of Ottoman judges and jurists. These groups espoused a specific point of view that defined the *Kızılbaş* as 'heretics' to be suppressed and used the term to justify their persecution. However, Baltacıoğlu-Brammer argues that Ottoman sources used the term in a much more nuanced manner. Whereas earlier Ottoman sources used the term pretty much in a literal sense until the late fifteenth century, later sources came to differentiate between *Kızılbaş*-born subjects of the empire, *Kızılbaş* converts and the *Kızılbaş* subjects of the Safavid Empire. In the end, the term acquired different meanings reflecting the Ottoman authorities' relationship with the Safavids with regard to issues of taxation or migration. By the nineteenth century, it had become a pejorative term for the Turkish- or Kurdish-speaking Shiites of Anatolia. Baltacıoğlu-Brammer bases her conclusions on government decrees, religious rulings and court chronicles in regard to their respective rhetorical aspects and the contexts in which they were written. By exploring these previously ignored variances in the usage of the term *Kızılbaş*, the author reveals that fluid cultural, religious, regional and political identities were attached to it in the early modern era.

In the following chapter, I study closely what is often considered to be the most famous biography of Muhammad ever disseminated in the Ottoman Empire, Mustafa Darir's *Siretü'n-Nebi*. Through an examination of its sources, main themes and the role played by Ali b. Abu Talib in the work, we can assess how Alid narratives influenced religious and cultural productions in the Ottoman Empire, and how these narratives could be received and reproduced in a Sunni context. According to the conventional view of the trajectory of Ottoman religious history, the Ottomans solidified their Sunni identity in the sixteenth century, when they openly clashed with the Safavids and their *Kızılbaş* sympathisers in Anatolia. Within the empire, they initiated an unprecedented religious campaign by either destroying or taming non-conformist groups and their adherents who did not follow proper religious doctrine and praxis. In this chapter, I argue that the historiographical emphasis on an increasing Sunnification of Ottoman religious life at the state level has obscured our understanding of what being a Sunni really meant in the broader Ottoman social context of the sixteenth century. Instead, Sunnism, as it evolved in the Ottoman Empire up to this point, had a strong *ahl al-bayti*st bent to it. *Ahl al-bayti*sm is a reverence among Sunnis towards the family of Muhammad and his descendants, including the Twelve Imams, and as a result, a reverence for Ali b. Abu Talib was never unusual in Sunni Islam in its Ottoman context. This chapter argues that with the impact of cross-sectarian fertilisation in the Islamic world introduced by the Mongol invasions and the increasing role of Alid Sufism, *ahl al-bayti*sm made significant advances in Sunni communities. This infiltration of *ahl al-bayti*sm very much influenced the confessional ambiguity of the early Ottomans. As a result, the *Siretü'n-Nebi* is permeated by strong Alid overtones, due to the primary source for its compilation: the later medieval author al-Bakri. The sponsorship of this expensive production by Sultan Murad III at the end of the sixteenth century displays the continuing influence and strength of Alid narratives among the Sunni Ottoman population, including those at the top of the political hierarchy.

The next two chapters deal with the seventeenth-century context. In the first, Yasir Yılmaz extends his inquiry beyond the Ottoman domains to encompass the broader European context. His chapter puts religious developments in the seventeenth-century Ottoman Empire in a comparative perspective by acknowledging the similarity between the Ottoman, Habsburg and Russian monarchies in their religious policies of the period. However, Yılmaz takes a different approach by urging us not to deem these similarities as part of a European-wide confessionalisation effort. He is also critical of the approach that boasts the idea that Ottoman history makes sense only when placed in the European context. Yılmaz's chapter does not intend to turn the confessionalisation approach into a mere strawman; rather, he questions the applicability of this paradigm to Ottomanist scholarship by emphasising what was different in the Ottoman case in comparison with the Russian and Habsburg empires. Yılmaz also points out that scholars who utilise confessionalisation terminology in Ottomanist scholarship borrowed original usage from Schilling and Reinhard but ignore a vibrant debate that followed in the European historiography. Yılmaz argues that over the course of the seventeenth century, charismatic scholars, pietistic preachers and religious functionaries, including patriarchs and court confessors in the Ottoman Empire, Russian tsardom and Habsburg Monarchy competed and cooperated with their governments for influence over subjects about the proper forms of religious practice. In due course, he posits, their interaction about spiritual matters evolved into a struggle over decision-making processes. In Istanbul, Moscow and

Introduction

Vienna, pietistic Muslim preachers (*Kadızadeli*s), reformist Orthodox patriarchs and Catholic Habsburg monarchs became involved in efforts to define and enforce what they considered to be genuine and authentic religious practice. In the Ottoman and Russian cases, these preachers and religious functionaries openly competed (and sometimes cooperated) with state authorities in defining religious policy. In the Habsburg case, on the other hand, Catholic monarchs themselves became proselytisers in a mission to convert Protestant princes in their territories. What was the primary motivation behind these conflicts, competition and cooperation between the state and religious groups? Was it a religious zeal that united them all? Yılmaz's answer is that it was not. Instead, what was at stake was stability and order, and how best to preserve them. Therefore, the religious changes in the seventeenth century were not the result of heightened spiritual awareness or pietistic concerns, but an imperial impulse on the part of early modern empires to impose their terms upon a variety of populations, officials, princes and scholars.

In the second of the seventeenth-century chapters, Betül Yavuz takes us into the enigmatic world of Ottoman Sufi orders in the form of the *Melāmetiyye*, which was born as a problematic and unruly branch of the otherwise Sunni-oriented *Bayramiyye* order. *Melāmis* were active mostly in small Ottoman towns until they began appearing more extensively in the religious scene of the Ottoman capital in the seventeenth century. At this time, Yavuz argues, they habilitated their image from low-class Sufi deviants to a respected and refined religious group. Yavuz argues that this evolution marks an interesting episode in Ottoman religious history which we should not overlook. The author searches for the dynamics of this transformation through studying the life and oeuvre of Sarı Abdullah (d. 1665). Yavuz argues that Sarı Abdullah was the central figure who helped the rehabilitation of the *Melāmi* order into the urbane Sufi milieu that had developed by the seventeenth century in the Ottoman capital. She contends that subsequent generations of the *Melāmi* community relied heavily on Abdullah's vision to place the order in the long Sufi tradition. Abdullah was instrumental in creating an interpretive toolbox that provided the intellectuals and followers of the order with a novel way to present their beliefs and traditions. Through this process, Yavuz argues the order came to be included within the Sufi networks acceptable in the Ottoman Sunni tradition. In particular, the tweaking and articulation of the concept of *melāmet* were very significant in this process. In a way, the transformation of the image of the order represents perfectly the negotiated process of creating an Ottoman Sunni identity.

The final two chapters jump ahead to the nineteenth century, which is important because studies on nineteenth-century conceptions of Ottoman Sunnism are less frequently undertaken than for previous centuries. This century was marked by three significant developments in regard to religion in the Ottoman Empire: the abolition of the *Bektaşi* order, along with the Janissary corps; the *Tanzīmāt* and *Iṣlāhāt* reforms, which opened the way for a more equal representation of non-Muslim communities in the empire; and rising concerns about the Ottoman sultan as caliph, and ideas of pan-Islamic unity espoused by the regime of Sultan Abdülhamid II and its supporters. Therefore, the nineteenth century provides scholars with critical developments that allow us to explore religious changes in the Ottoman Empire, and Benjamin Weineck's and Necati Alkan's chapters aim to contribute to filling this gap.

In his chapter on Harputlu İshak Efendi's text about the *Bektaşi*s, Weineck draws our attention to the two different versions of the text, and how each version tells us divergent stories about the context and anxieties that surround the period in which they were published. His chapter examines the politico-theological universe of İshak Efendi as a late Ottoman scholar. Even though he wrote his text almost half a century after the abolition of the order, İshak's text is a fascinating work of religious polemics. İshak drew a complex picture of who would be among the saved in the hereafter, and developed subtle demarcations between various non-Sunni groups like Nusayris, Twelver Shiites and the *Bektaşi*s in this continuum. While the Twelvers might be saved, the *Bektaşi*s had no such chance. Weineck argues that İshak's interpretations provide a distinctive approach to the evolution of a 'Muslim plurality'. He studies İshak's work against the backdrop of the late nineteenth-century political evolution of the Ottoman Empire, and by studying the nuances in İshak's imagination of who belonged to the saved versus the non-saved, his chapter encourages us to go beyond traditional notions of 'orthodox' ulema and 'heterodox' groups. As a result, Weineck's analysis uncovers an outlook of late Ottoman Sunnism as being 'intentionally fabricated, in continuous flux, and contingent'.

The second of the nineteenth-century chapters deals with the neglected concept of 'correction of beliefs' (*taṣḥīḥ-i i'tikād*) and its historical trajectory. Necati Alkan argues that Mahmud II's administration used this concept in the context of the persecution of *Bektaşi*s during the first half of the nineteenth century, and he compares the application of this policy with the similar strategy of Abdülhamid II, who applied it to non-Sunni Islamic sects such as the Turkish or Kurdish Alevis, the Nusayris in Syria, the Shiites in Iraq, and the Yezidis in eastern Anatolia. Alkan argues that the Hamidian regime attempted to 'civilise' these non-conformist groups and bring them into the Sunni fold by finely tuning their beliefs. Utilising

Introduction

extensive state archives as well as chronicles of the period, Alkan artfully demonstrates how this concept evolved, beginning in the eighteenth century when it was invoked in the context of taming groups such as the Abkhaz and Circassians, and, later, Caucasian tribes. During the tumultuous reign of Mahmud II, Ottoman administrators and scholars made use of this term as an official policy to correct the beliefs of the *Bektaşi*s both before and after the prohibition of their order. But, like Yılmaz's study of the seventeenth century, Alkan attributes Mahmud II's efforts at taming the *Bektaşi*s not to religious zeal, but to imperial anxieties. Mahmud II was concerned with the preservation of order and entrenching his policies of centralisation. During Abdülhamid's reign, on the other hand, Alkan argues there were more concerted efforts to utilise this policy towards various groups in Iraq and eastern Anatolia. The intellectuals of the age saw sectarianism as a significant roadblock to the unity of Muslims and offered missionary work to correct the 'corrupt beliefs' of these groups. Alkan concludes that the concept of *taṣḥīḥ-i i'tiḳād* replaced the more widely-used 'commanding the right and forbidding wrong' of earlier centuries, and became a political tool to 'civilise' those groups they considered to be outside the Sunni fold with an eye towards centralisation efforts and a desire for pan-Islamic unity.

In the final chapter of the collection, John Curry takes up the challenging but equally rewarding task of synthesising the findings of the volume. He outlines rather aptly the main ideas of each chapter, puts them in their proper contexts, points out alternative and critical directions, and offers future venues for scholarly research. Curry warmly welcomes crucial interventions of each chapter and concludes that these studies demonstrate more than anything else the multivalency of Ottoman Sunnism and the difficulty attached to monolithic and rigid renderings of it. He also reminds readers to assess Ottoman Islam as an organic part of the society in which it was practised rather than from the perspectives of a post-Enlightenment materialist viewpoint.

The studies in this volume collectively testify to the need to understand the evolution of Ottoman Sunnism in its complexity and divergent trajectories. Granted, the chapters in the volume mostly cover the heartlands of the Ottoman Empire (Anatolia and the Balkans) and do not discuss the relationship of Ottoman Sunnism to non-Muslim communities and issues such as conversion. Future scholarly endeavours should pay attention to these issues. The current volume is a modest but necessary contribution to the study of Ottoman Islam; the editor and the contributors hope that students and scholars of not only Ottoman but also social and religious history in general benefit from the approaches and findings outlined here.

Notes

1. Köprülüzāde Mehmed Fuad, 'Anadolu'da İslamiyet', I, pp. 281–311; II, pp. 385–420; III, pp. 457–86. For a more recent edition of this book, see Mehmet Fuad Köprülü, *Anadolu'da İslamiyet*.
2. Babinger, 'Der Islam in Kleinasien', pp. 126–52. This article was translated into Turkish shortly: Babinger, 'Anadolu'da İslamiyet', pp. 188–221.
3. Kafesoğlu, *Türk-İslam Sentezi*. For an excellent treatment discussing how Köprülü's ideas were born in the context of the early Turkish Republic and its nationalistic framework, see Yıldırım, 'Büyüklüğün Büyümeye Set Çekmesi', pp. 357–98; Yıldırım, 'Anadolu'da İslamiyet: Gaziler Çağında', pp. 93–124. See also Dressler, 'How to Conceptualize Inner-Islamic Plurality', pp. 241–60. See also Balcı, 'From Nationalization of Islam', pp. 82–107; Balcı, 'The Rise and Fall of Nine Lights', pp. 145–60.
4. Gölpinarli's works are too many to count here. For a list of his important works, see Yazıcı, 'Gölpınarlı Abdülbaki'.
5. Especially his seminal article, Barkan, 'Osmanlı imparatorluğunda bir iskān', pp. 279–353.
6. These are too many to list here, but see especially Mélikoff, *Sur les traces du soufisme turc*; Mélikoff, *Hadji Bektach*.
7. Again, too numerous to list, but see especially Ocak, *XIII. Yüzyılda Anadolu'da Baba Resul*; Ocak, *Islam-Türk inançlarında*; Ocak, *Türkiye'de tarihin saptırılması sürecinde Türk Sufiliğine bakışlar*; Ocak, *Alevi ve Bektaşi İnançlarının*; Ocak, *Osmanlı Toplumunda Mülhidler ve Zındıklar*; Ocak, *Türkler, Türkiye ve İslam*; Ocak, *Perspectives and Reflections*; Ocak, *Osmanlı Toplumunda Tasavvuf ve Sufiler*; Ocak, *Osmanlı İmparatorluğu'nda Marjinal Sufilik*.
8. See especially Faroqhi, *Pilgrims and Sultans*; Faroqhi, *Der Bektaschi-Orden*.
9. Karamustafa, *God's Unruly Friends*.
10. Zilfi, *Politics of Piety*.
11. Kafadar, *Between Two Worlds*.
12. Necipoğlu, *The Age of Sinan*.
13. Le Gall, *A Culture of Sufism*.
14. Curry, *The Transformation of Muslim Mystical Thought*.
15. See especially Yıldırım, *Aleviliğin Doğuşu* and various articles.
16. Karakaya-Stump, *Vefailik, Bektaşilik, Kızılbaşlık*.
17. Krstić, *Contested Conversions*; Krstić, 'Illuminated by the Light'; Krstić, 'From *Shahāda* to *'Aqīda'*; Krstić, 'State and Religion, "Sunnitization"'.
18. Terzioğlu, 'How to Conceptualize Ottoman Sunnitization'; Terzioğlu, 'Where 'İlm-i Ḥāl Meets Catechism'.
19. Burak, *The Second Formation of Islamic Law*; Burak, 'Faith, Law and Empire'.
20. al-Tikriti, 'Kalam in the Service of State'; al-Tikriti, 'Ibn-i Kemal's Confessionalism'.

Introduction

21. Winter, *A History of the 'Alawis*; Winter, *The Shiites of Lebanon*.
22. Dressler, *Writing Religion*.
23. Atçıl, *Scholars and Sultans*.
24. Two collected volumes: Peacock and Yıldız, *Islamic Literature and Intellectual Life*; Peacock, De Nicola and Yıldız, *Islam and Christianity in Medieval Anatolia*.
25. Yılmaz, *Caliphate Redefined*.
26. This list is not intended to be comprehensive; it serves only to display the variety and extent of the existing scholarship on the topic. It is obviously biased towards the studies in Turkish, English, French and German, and it would be helpful to compile a bibliography of studies in other languages, especially Bulgarian, Arabic and Persian.
27. Ocak, *Osmanlı Toplumunda Mülhidler ve Zındıklar*; Imber, 'Persecution of Ottoman Shiites'.
28. Winter, *Shiites of Lebanon*.
29. Ahmed, *What is Islam?*
30. Yaycıoğlu, 'Guarding Traditions and Laws'.
31. See Berkes, *The Development of Secularism*; Karpat, *The Politicization of Islam*; Deringil, *The Well-Protected Domains*; Deringil, *Conversion and Apostasy*.
32. For a similar argument, see Yılmaz, *Caliphate Redefined*.

2

The Rise of the 'Religion and State' Order: Re-confessionalisation of State and Society in the Early Modern Ottoman Empire

Rıza Yıldırım[1]

Introduction

As opposed to the Orientalist notion that the Orient has its own particular history, culture, and religion, recent scholarship has attempted to integrate Ottoman history into broader world history. Accordingly, some historians have tended to study the sixteenth- and seventeenth-century Ottoman Empire as a part of the early modern world, especially of Eurasia and in particular of Europe.[2] Instead of drawing clear-cut religious and cultural boundaries that separate the West and the East, these scholars have considered the Ottomans as active participants of global and regional economic and cultural systems. Leaving the old-fashioned amplification of differences between Christians and Muslims, and uniqueness of Ottoman civilisation, this new scholarship has suggested that ideological, religious, cultural, economic, and political interactions and similarities were far more than previously recognised. Scholars have further argued that especially the Mediterranean basin constituted a cultural, economic and ideological unity, which transcended religious boundaries between Muslims, Christians and Jews. Therefore, ideological, cultural, economic and political trends exercised great influence across the Mediterranean world, or even globally as some other scholars have suggested.[3]

As a part of this overarching trend in Ottoman historiography, some scholars have suggested approaching religious developments in the sixteenth- and seventeenth-century Ottoman Empire from the perspective of confessionalisation, a conceptual category that has been developed to examine religious and political developments in post-Reformation Europe. Scholars such as Tijana Krstić, Derin Terzioğlu and Guy Burak have suggested that the concept of confessionalisation might be a useful heuristic device to think through early modern Ottoman history, especially when examining different aspects of changes in public and popular religiosities as well as in political ideologies. Overarching assumptions that govern this newly arising scholarship are: (1) the early modern era of world history had common traits across the Mediterranean basin, and even Eurasia; (2) major ideological, political, economic and social trends were transnational, especially within the Mediterranean basin; (3) confessionalisation was the benchmark of the early modern period; and (4) the formation of Ottoman orthodoxy in the sixteenth and seventeenth centuries appeared as a part of this greater Mediterranean-wide trend.

Though opening fruitful avenues of debate, this transnational approach has sweeping generalisations, which create difficulties in accommodating many peculiarities of Ottoman history into the broader theoretical framework. Precisely because of this reason, the 'confessional approach' to Ottoman history has two obvious problems. First, as I will discuss below, the inventors of the paradigm argue that the 'age of confessionalism' in European history was the era between 1550 and 1660. Meanwhile, the development of Ottoman orthodoxy had started by the mid-fifteenth century and was already in the process of formation by the mid-sixteenth century, that is, before the so-called 'age of confessionalism' had started. If we take confessionalisation as a Mediterranean-wide phenomenon and analyse Ottoman 'Sunnitization' within it, how can we explain this one-century lag between Ottoman and European 'confessionalisations'? Another significant difference between the two 'confessionalisations', which the scholarship mentioned above does not address, regards some basic characteristics of Islam and Christianity. As scholars of confessionalisation in Europe acknowledge, the primary result of the confessionalisation process – that is, the confessional state that emerged out of the merging of religion, state and society – was a new phenomenon in European history. On the other hand, Sunni Islam has a long history of the intertwining of state and religion in the sense that religion served as the legal basis of the socio-political order. Islam, as a religion comprising all aspects of life, including politics and law, had already taken its mature form as *madhhabs* long before the sixteenth century. Therefore, as opposed to the European case, the formation of Ottoman Sunni orthodoxy was by no means a creation of a new confession, but a readoption of the already formed Sunni (-Hanafi) Islam with certain readjustments.

This chapter concurs with the basic idea that as a conceptual tool, the paradigm of confessionalisation can be useful to understand religious developments in the early modern Islamic world, especially in the Ottoman Empire. Nonetheless, it suggests a recalibration of the paradigm in accordance with the peculiar dynamics of the latter. I agree with the idea that the phenomenon of rapprochement of state, religion and society emerged as a universal trend in the early modern Islamic world, and the concept of confessionalisation is useful for analysing this phenomenon. However, the Ottoman version of confessionalisation had started during the first half of the fifteenth century, had become unambiguously clear by the mid-sixteenth century and climaxed by the mid-seventeenth century. Therefore, any chronological synchronisation with European history does not work well. To better understand this underlying change in the Ottoman state and society, we should instead look at socio-political dynamics of the Islamic world. In my view, the fifteenth century marks a return to Perso-Islamic caliphal polity after two centuries of Turko-Mongolian interruption.[4] It was because of this sea change in political culture that states and religious confessions (or sects) became increasingly close, eventually creating official religions or a conception of orthodoxy. After a discussion of the literature on the confessionalisation paradigm, first on its original sense in European history, and then its adoption to the Ottoman historiography, this chapter examines the transformation of state–religion relations in the Ottoman world between the mid-fifteenth and the mid-seventeenth centuries. It suggests that a recalibrated concept of confessionalisation would be far more useful for conceptualising the re-formation of the Ottoman religio-political order during this period, which might instead be called 're-confessionalisation' tied to a previous caliphal model.

The Confessionalisation Paradigm

Confessionalisation as a conceptual tool to approach early modern history was first coined in the late 1970s almost simultaneously by Heinz Schilling and Wolfgang Reinhard.[5] It was developed partly as a response to the Weberian idea of a Calvinist monopoly on modernism, arguing that other confessions (Catholicism and Lutheranism) too could change and progress, and partly against the socio-economic approach to historical progress claiming that religion and culture equally served to lead Europe to modernity. Schilling considers the confessionalism that occurred between the mid-sixteenth and mid-seventeenth centuries as uniquely European. According to him, despite significant overlaps between religious and secular spaces in medieval Europe, there was a strong sense of dualism of church and state. This duality blurred during the post-Reformation period where state, church and society drew increasingly closer, a process that ended up in the creation of three main confessions with distinct doctrines, rituals, spiritualities and popular cultures. The process that was initiated by the doctrinal schism and that was driven by ecclesiastical forces soon joined with political and social dynamics and eventually created distinct religious, cultural, political, social and territorial blocs.[6] Theological differences that the Reformation created were complemented by political and social differentiation between confessional blocs as well as intra-confessional harmonisation and unification. These changes signified both a distinctionalisation of confessions and coherence within a confession.[7] Hence, confessionalisation refers to 'Reformation of Life' that complemented the 'Reformation of Doctrine'.[8]

Schilling and Reinhard deem confessionalism to be the driving force that shaped European history between 1550 and 1660; a period they called the 'Confessional Age'. According to them, confessionalisation refers to a fundamental social transformation, a comprehensive religious–political–social–cultural process that included purification of faith, ideological correction, harmonising and uniting religion and disciplining society through schooling and coercion.[9] This process was disciplinary, centralising and integrative:

> Confessionalization was not solely a religious process. It was a social, cultural, and political process as well. On the religious level, confessionalization involved not only the emergence of distinct and opposed doctrines and rituals, be the (re)imposition of ecclesiastical discipline on both the clergy and the laity. On the social level, confessionalization involved efforts to 'Christianize' everyday life, and to bring individual conduct into line with Biblical law, a campaign in which church and state often joined hands. On the cultural level, confessionalization involved efforts to suppress popular 'superstitions' and to impose a new, more fully 'Christian' ethos. Finally, on the political level, confessionalization meant a deepening of the alliance between church and state and tightening of the relationship between confessional and 'national' identity.[10]

According to Schilling, confessionalisation signifies a fundamental process of society that runs parallel to the rise of the early modern state and the formation of the early modern society of disciplined subjects which gave way to the rise of modern nations.[11] Two watermarks of confessionalisation were (1) the integration of state, church and society on an unprecedented scale, and (2) the aspiration to consolidate territorial boundaries of the three confessions and consequently the territorial structure of the early modern state. Confessionalism was closely related to the process of early modern state-building in many aspects: it fostered institutionalisation, state control over the public spheres that were previously under church control (such as education), social discipline and territorialisation. As opposed to its role as a universally unifying factor, religion now became a divisive one between different states. In the meantime, it functioned as a unifying force within the boundaries of the confessional state and fostered the formation of social solidarity via religious uniformity. Confessional allegiance, political loyalty and the means of citizenship became intimately tied to each other. Consequently, it gave rise to modern nation-states.[12]

Reformation and the accompanying confessionalisation was also a process of religious and cultural rationalisation. Keith Thomas has argued in his study on sixteenth- and seventeenth-century England that distinction between magic and religion was not clear-cut before the sixteenth century.[13] Duffy has made similar arguments in his much-quoted study on late medieval England. According to him, medieval Christianity was an amalgam of magic and faith; superstition and magic were tolerated or even sanctioned by the Church.[14] In the same vein, John Bossy has argued that, after 1400, the practical, effective and corporately social religion of medieval Catholicism gave way to a more theorised, spiritualised and individualised Christianity of which Protestantism and Catholicism represented two different versions.[15] Recent scholarship on the Reformation argues that post-Reformation Europe was no less religious or Christian than medieval Europe. What happened instead was the rationalisation and individualisation of the Christian faith.[16] According to Gorski, the Reformation was a transition from a magical, ritual and communal religion to an ethical, intellectual and individual one. Magical religions signify a religiosity in which individual believers seek divine intervention using rituals, whereas ethical religions seek divine intervention by proper conduct and individual supplication.[17]

An essential aspect of the confessional age was the significant change in scope, aim and practitioners of the educational system. Spearheaded by Lutheran reformists, education was now considered to be the primary means by which to cultivate the right beliefs and dispositions in resonance with the true faith.[18] Since the Reformation was not only about creating a new faith but also about creating a new society, education for reformists was, before everything else, an instrument to shape society through indoctrinating each individual; it was considered to be the most effective means to achieve 'a spiritual renewal of state, society, and individual'.[19] In accordance with Luther's idea of the 'priesthood of all believers', education was aimed at society at large. The spread of literacy among the masses opened the channels of indoctrination to control and shape the religious and civic behaviours of the people, hence, made it possible to achieve a great measure of uniformity of belief and practice. Another significant consequence was the growing influence of secular bureaucracy on the educational system. The fusion of ecclesiastical and secular bureaucracy, a yardstick of the confessional age, was first and most effectively realised in the educational system. Eventually, the state would hold the upper hand in this symbiotic coalition, which laid the ground for political intervention in religious matters, on the one hand, and for sacralisation of the political authority, on the other. For example, the *Small Catechism*, which was used as the primary text of Lutheran confessionalisation, sanctifies the temporal ruler as God's agent to supervise the 'external' government that is to be ruled according to the secular law, while limiting the jurisdiction of religious authority to spiritual matters.[20]

To sum up, the confessionalisation paradigm consist of the following elements: (1) rapprochement of the state and the church; (2) shaping and disciplining of society at large through education; (3) rationalisation of religion and routinisation of the leadership (charisma); (4) instalment of state authority upon the church and the bureaucratisation of religious institutions and clergy; (5) the rise of confessional blocs as religious, political, territorial and cultural units; and (6) the individualisation and spiritualisation of religion.

'Confessional' Approaches to Early Modern Ottoman History

Tijana Krstić suggests that we should regard general religious trends in the early modern Ottoman and Safavid empires as a part of greater Mediterranean-wide confessionalisation that watermarked the historiography of post-Reformation Europe.[21] She argues that, 'Contrary to the established historiography, which views this process as exclusively European ... confessionalization encompassed the contemporary Ottoman and Safavid Empires as well, where it gave rise to the formation of Sunni and Shiite Muslim confessional and territorial blocks'.[22] According to her, as a broader early modern phenomenon, confessionalisation created a transnational religious polarisation across three great empires (Safavid–Shii, Ottoman–Sunni and Habsburg–Christian). This was catalysed particularly by political rivalries and intense traffic of people and ideas that was born thanks to the boom in long-distance trade. Focusing on conversion narratives from the fifteenth to the seventeenth centuries, she argues that millenarianism and confessionalisation were central in the political culture of both the Ottoman and the Safavid empires in the sixteenth and seventeenth centuries.[23] Resonating with the Protestant Reformation, she claims, we observe in the Ottoman Empire a heightened sensitivity to return to original sources, the centrality of scripture, and concerted efforts to draw boundaries of the true faith. Similarly, she deems the legislative activities of Ebussuud Efendi in the Ottoman Empire and Ali Karaki in the

Ottoman Sunnism

Safavid Empire as an unprecedented sacralisation of the ruler, a process of 'theologisation' of political discourse that eventually established an essential link between the imperial sovereignty and religious orthodoxy:

> This latter goal was achieved through different processes of social disciplining such as the promulgation of a new criminal law code that policed the boundaries of orthodoxy and public morality, the promotion of mosque worship through the imposition of new fines for irregular attendance, the construction of an unprecedented number of mosques in order to stabilize mosque congregations and monitor them easily, etc. These measures closely corresponded in spirit to those taking place in Carlo Borromeo's Milan or the Habsburg lands in the aftermath of the Council of Trent (1545–1563), aimed at establishing an 'orthodox' Catholic community ... The principle of *cuius regio, eius religio* [whose realm, his religion] was therefore upheld in the Ottoman and Safavid Empires as well, while the debates over spiritual authority in the Muslim community, correct ritual, and even original text of the Qur'an began to be debated in the language reminiscent of the Catholic–Protestant and Muslim–Christian polemics.[24]

According to Krstić, these efforts at harmonising and unifying Islamic religiosity across the empire emerged as part of the 'Mediterranean-wide age of confessional and imperial polarization in the sixteenth and seventeenth centuries'.[25] In general, scholars warmly welcomed this idea. Krstić's central argument that the concept of confessionalisation would help us better understand the religious and political developments in the early modern Ottoman and Safavid empires is useful. However, Krstić's approach needs some correctives. First, her periodisation of Ottoman confessionalisation remains unclear. On one occasion she says that the project of Sunnitisation and social disciplining of the empire began in the mid-sixteenth century.[26] Yet she states on the next page that the 'age of confessionalism' in the Ottoman Empire lasted from the 1450s to the 1690s.[27] Secondly, her overall discussion presumes a simultaneity between the 'confessionalisation' of the Ottoman Empire and that of Europe. However, most changes in the religious and political spheres of the Ottoman Empire that she lists as manifestations of confessionalisation took place before the mid-sixteenth century, when the so-called 'confessional age' had just begun in Europe. If we talk about a religio-political transformation in the Ottoman world that is to be explained by confessionalisation, this transformation took place roughly between the mid-fifteenth and mid-seventeenth centuries. Therefore, it is hardly possible to claim simultaneity between these two developments.

A significant contribution to the debate came from Derin Terzioğlu, who resorted to a wider set of historical sources to test the usefulness of the concept of confessionalisation in the Ottoman context. Agreeing with Krstić, she deems the 'Ottoman confessionalisation' to be a corollary to the state-building process, during which Ottoman religious and political authorities refashioned attitudes and behaviours of the empire's Muslim subjects in conformity with the principles of Sunni Islam.[28] In another essay, Terzioğlu has attempted to explain changing features of Ottoman Sunnism via the confessionalisation paradigm.[29] Opposing the conservative view of timeless, normative and unchanging Sunnism, she argues that both the doctrine and practice of Sunni Islam was in constant evolution through the Ottoman era. She argues that, closely linked with evolving imperial politics and state-building processes, Ottoman Sunnism was also 'confessionalised'.[30] Departing from Krstić, Terzioğlu stretches the period of confessionalisation to a broader time interval; this process, according to her, began before the onset of the Ottoman–Safavid rivalry and ended with the resolution of the Sufism debate and the demise of the *Kadızadeli* movement in the 1680s.[31] She acknowledges that during the late medieval period confessional allegiances were softened and boundaries were blurred by the effect of various developments, such as the spread of Sufism, the flourishing of *Ahl-i Bayt* veneration and, above all, a non-sectarian Mongol polity. In the early sixteenth century, however, a Sunni orthodoxy emerged in the Ottoman Empire, partly as a legitimising response to the Safavid challenge, and partly as a result of the rise of Islamic literacy and ulema empowerment.[32] As a consequence, 'a greater expectation of confessional exactitude in matters of doctrine and ritual as well as a heightened concern with social discipline in the broadest sense were characteristic of Ottoman Sunnism by the late 16th and early 17th century'.[33]

Elsewhere, Terzioğlu examines *'ilm-i hāl*s, simple guidebooks for the essentials of religion that emerged in the fourteenth century and became most popular in the seventeenth century, as markers of confessionalisation. According to her, *'ilm-i hāl*s were aimed from the beginning at lay people who were unfamiliar with details of religion. However, there is a significant difference between early *'ilm-i hāl*s and those written by the mid-sixteenth century. Early *'ilm-i hāl*s aimed partly at teaching basics of Islam to new converts in the Balkans. Later *'ilm-i hāl*s, on the other hand, appealed primarily to Muslim lay people to guide them to pure Islam. Terzioğlu sees a direct link between the culmination of *'ilm-i hāl* writing and the onslaught of the Ottoman Sunnitisation project against the Safavids in the sixteenth century, as well as the rise of sharia-minded piety in the seventeenth century.[34] She compares the function of *'ilm-i hāl* in Ottoman society with the function of catechism in the Protestant and Catholic confessionalisation of the mid-sixteenth century. Similar to parish priests' periodical teaching sessions for members of local communities, *'ilm-i hāl*s assumed a role in measuring and indoctrinating the true rite for lay people who had no chance to get a proper religious education.[35] Terzioğlu also suggests that a significant transition to a sharia-grounded, this-world-oriented and austere Islamic piety among the Ottoman Muslim urbanites after the sixteenth century resonates with the shift from magical-ritual to rational-ethical religiosity in Reformation Europe.[36]

Guy Burak has contributed to the debate with his studies on the Hanafi doctrine of Islamic law in the Ottoman Empire. According to Burak, by the fifteen century onward certain readjustments of the Hanafi tradition can be explained within the broader paradigm of confessionalism, which was marked by the infusion of religious rhetoric into the process of state and social formation, on the one hand, and the self-proclamation of rulers as the guardians of the orthodoxy of their respective religions, on the other. Assuming that legal institutions and actors – such as legal courts, inquisition tribunals and legislators – had played a decisive role in the processes of state and social formation, Burak focuses particularly on the role of jurisconsults (mufti) in negotiation and ultimate articulation of the orthodoxy during the Ottoman 'age of confessionalisation', which stretched from the fifteenth to the seventeenth century. Through hierarchisation and institutionalisation of the ulema, the Ottoman dynasty intervened in formulating the doctrine of the Hanafi School of law in an unprecedented manner. Officially appointed jurisconsults played a central role in the articulation of the new doctrine of law, as well as its promulgation across the empire. As a case study of the Ottoman confessionalisation, Burak examines the development of the legal concept of 'renewal of faith', which was an Ottoman invention of the late fifteenth century.[37]

Similarly, Nabil al-Tikriti considers religious developments in the sixteenth-century Ottoman Empire as a part of the Mediterranean-wide phenomenon of confessionalisation. He suggests re-examining Ibn Kamal's legal decisions, especially his treatise on the *Kızılbaş*, as examples of confessionalisation.[38]

On the other hand, some studies have raised serious criticism against the application of the confessionalisation paradigm in Ottoman historiography. Arguing that Sunnitisation was not a wholesale process that comprised all segments of Ottoman society, they have suggested a rather pluralist look at the religious attitudes and practices across the empire during the so-called 'confessional age'. For example, through a study of world histories written in the Ottoman Empire during this period, Vefa Erginbaş has made a compelling case against the confessionalisation approach. Erginbaş focuses on five important litterateurs from the sixteenth century and scrutinises their narration of key events and personalities in early Islamic history that became the perennial reference points for later Sunni–Shiite sectarian dispute. His examination shows that a strong Alid tinge as well as an interest in the lives and exalted status of the Twelve Imams were maintained in the writings of some prominent Ottoman intellectuals such as Lami Çelebi (d. 1532), Muslihuddin Lari (d. late sixteenth century), Mustafa Cenabi (d. late sixteenth century) and Mustafa 'Ali (d. 1600). Based on this controversial data in the writings of these unmistakably 'Sunni' and 'Ottoman' intellectuals of the 'confessional age', Erginbaş concludes that there was not a monolithic Sunnism in the Ottoman Empire, but conspicuously different interpretations in different social segments. It is true that a state-sponsored Sunnitisation process had already been set in motion by the mid-fifteenth century and continued unabated into the sixteenth and seventieth centuries. Nonetheless, the pace and quality of Sunnitisation occurred quite differently among various groups, even among different branches of the ulema class. Although some scholars who attached themselves to prestigious positions in the bureaucracy advocated and cultivated a narrow-minded and strict form of Sunnism, others, especially those who had strong Sufi affiliations, continued to include reverence of Ali b. Abu Talib and his offspring within the essentials of the true religion. In order to make a clear-cut distinction with Twelver or Ismai'ili Shiism, which was universally refuted by the Ottoman intelligentsia, Erginbaş prefers to use the concept of '*Ahl al-Baytism*'[39] to explain this particular form of confessional ambiguity, which allowed an amorphous sectarian position that he calls '*Ahl al-Baytist* Sunnism' to exist side by side with a staunchly anti-Shiite official Sunnism.[40]

Another critic of the confessionalisation paradigm as it is adopted by Ottoman historiography is Marc David Baer. In his review of Krstić's book,[41] Baer raised strong objections to the former's understanding and conceptualisation of the concept. Basing his argument on the idea that 'Confessionalization is not an applicable heuristic device for understanding contemporary developments in the Ottoman and Safavid empires',[42] Baer categorically opposes Krstić's vision. According to Baer, historical evidence does not substantiate the argument that the Ottoman and Safavid empires went through a process of confessionalisation similar to that in post-Reformation Europe. He criticises Krstić for confusing the process of empire-building, which includes centralisation and bureaucratisation, with confessionalisation, which refers essentially to the creation of uniform faiths.

The Resurgence of the Neo-Caliphal Polity

One of the most crucial differences between Ottoman and European confessionalisation is that, unlike the case in Europe, Ottomans did not create a brand-new confession. On the contrary, Islam appeared as a religion of law from its earlier phases. Sharia as an outcome of juristic speculations reached its maturity at least two centuries before the emergence of the Ottoman Empire.[43] Therefore, what happened in the Ottoman case was not a creation of a state-affiliated 'national' confession, as it was in Europe, but rather a reconciliation of the state and sharia, which had been effectively distanced during the Mongol and the immediate post-Mongol era. One should note, however, that in the course of this rapprochement, both the state and the religion underwent a substantial transformation. One should also keep in mind that the Ottoman re-confessionalisation started one century earlier than the European confessionalisation.

Yet much of the above-summarised characteristics, except for individualisation and spiritualisation of the faith and schooling society at large, are unmistakably visible in the early modern Ottoman Empire. Indeed, it is widely accepted among historians that during the first half of the sixteenth century the Ottoman state refashioned its identity as the defender of sharia against 'infidels' and 'heretics'. Accordingly, enforcement of Sunni orthodoxy became an official policy. Most historians have further argued that the Ottoman regime created an official religion in the sixteenth century that is often called 'Ottoman Sunnism'.[44] Elaborating on the concept, I will argue that four interrelated developments were particularly influential in shaping Ottoman Sunnism: (1) the formation of the Ottoman ulema class, which was unprecedentedly bureaucratised and state-dependent; (2) the creation of a particularly Ottoman version of the Hanafi *madhhab*; (3) heightened sensitivity to assert boundaries of religion; and (4) an increasing state control of public religiosity.[45]

Formation of the Imperial Learned Hierarchy

The Ottomans reorganised the ulema class between the mid-fifteenth and late sixteenth centuries according to a highly centralised and hierarchical model. During the formative period (1300–1453), the burgeoning ulema class was overwhelmed by immigrant scholars who were trained in Anatolia, Syria, Egypt and Iran. First-generation Ottoman scholars such as Şeyh Bedreddin (d. 1412) and Şemseddin Fenari (d. 1431) continued to obtain their training in the classical centres of Islamic learning, before settling in Ottoman towns.[46] It was only after the mid-fifteenth century that the growing number of scholars that had graduated from Ottoman madrasas created a relatively self-sufficient system.[47] The rise of the Ottoman learned class in the second half of the fifteenth century coincided with the centralisation of education and the ascendancy of the state monopoly on both training and employment mechanisms. Two developments were particularly important for the centralisation and bureaucratisation of madrasas: (1) the harmonisation of curricula across the main provinces; and (2) the creation of the control mechanisms for waqf revenues which financially supported madrasas.[48] The institutionalisation of the educational system in a centrally organised hierarchy has found its official expression in the first known law code of the empire that was promulgated towards the end of Mehmed II's reign in 1481.[49] According to this law code, at the top of this thoroughly bureaucratised and pyramid structured body of scholars was the chief mufti[50] and two *kadıaskers*, who were in charge of the appointment of madrasa professors (*müderris*), jurists (qadi) and jurisconsults (mufti), as well as supervising appointments of trustees of religious endowments.

Traditionally, ulema's responsibility in Islamic societies was triadic: juridical (*qaḍa*), jurisprudential (*ifta*), and educational (*tadris*).[51] A career in governmental bureaucracy had never been the usual track to advancement for a madrasa graduate that it became in the late fifteenth- and sixteenth-century Ottoman Empire.[52] Even after the mid-sixteenth century, when some specialised branches of the bureaucracy, such as financial departments, developed their own training systems, scholars continued to be assigned to scribal and financial offices.[53] The careers of many scholars from the mid-fifteenth century included service in government offices such as scribal, chancery, military and treasury.[54] This fact alone shows clearly how the educational system was integrated into the state apparatus. As a matter of fact, by the mid-fifteenth century at the latest, Ottoman madrasas were oriented towards training scholars to fulfil educational, judicial and governmental functions across the empire. Abdurrahman Atçıl estimates the number of government-affiliated ulema to be as many as 1,500–2,000 people in 1523. This number, as well as the number of madrasas, further increased in the course of the sixteenth century.[55]

Such an empire-wide bureaucratisation within a strict hierarchy stripped the ulema class of its financial and intellectual autonomy, leaving them vulnerable to dictates of the state. Eventually, the whole body of the ulema class, which had always assumed public services in Islamic societies but never became an intimate branch of state institutions, evolved into a bureaucratic organ of the Ottoman state apparatus; likewise, scholars turned into civil servants of the sultan. As opposed to the previous system, in which scholars were able to find positions in a decentralised and relatively competitive market sustained by myriad independent waqfs, the new regulations rendered obsolete those scholars who did not adopt to the newly institutionalised system of appointments. Consequently, the guardianship of religion, a role the ulema had assumed since the early Umayyad period, was now subjugated to a more pressing mission: developing an administrative system and legitimising and propagating the sultan's rule. It was within this political atmosphere and intellectual climate that the state-employed ulema reinterpreted Islamic law and created the Ottoman way of Hanafi *madhhab*.

Rise of the Ottoman-Hanafi Madhhab

The benchmark of 'Ottoman Sunnism' was the emergence of a 'distinctively Ottoman Hanafism'[56] as the official *madhhab*, which reached its maturity in the course of the sixteenth century. The formation of the Ottoman official *madhhab* was a corollary to a complex set of developments which included empire-building, territorial expansion, sectarian strife, urbanisation, ideological reorientation and restructuring of the learned class. Scholars usually distinguish Ottoman Hanafism with its unprecedented degree of uniformity and state monopoly on jurisprudential processes.

All schools of Islamic law, including Hanafism, emerged as a series of legal rulings and judicial sentences by individual jurists. Therefore, the legal corpus of the Hanafi *madhhab*, like the others, was a plethora of rulings and opinions on various matters.[57] As practitioners of sharia, qadis were entitled to choose among many legal opinions that had emerged within the *madhhab*, or even to apply their own independent reasoning if they were qualified. Therefore, qadis enjoyed extensive discretionary power in implementing sharia, a process which continuously enhanced the diversity within the *madhhab*, not to mention variations between different *madhhab*s.[58] As for state interference in religious law, pre-Ottoman *madhhab*s were markedly attentive to restricting sovereigns' right to manipulate jurisprudential processes.[59]

As Peters has pointed out, Ottomans reformed this modus operandi of sharia; through refashioning the Hanafi *madhhab*, they created a system of law which was homogeneous, uniform, universal and predictable across the empire. First, they declared the Hanafi *madhhab* to be the official law of the state, made its application compulsory in the core provinces of Anatolia and the Balkans, and deemed it superior to the other *madhhab*s in the Arab provinces. Second, a uniformity of opinions was created by establishing a hierarchy of authority within the *madhhab*.[60] Third, they developed a central administrative system that tightly controlled practitioners and interpreters of the law, that is, qadis and muftis. Since qadis and muftis were the perpetual creators and the carriers of Islamic law, bureaucratisation and centralisation of their education and appointments were perhaps the most important steps in the creation of an official Ottoman *madhhab*.

Traditionally, muftis had acted essentially independently though they might have acquired local or governmental posts.[61] It was this informality of the mufti that invested the whole process of jurisprudence with a great deal of autonomy vis-à-vis the state.[62] By the rise of the imperial learned hierarchy, however, the Ottoman state had established a monopoly over jurisprudential mechanisms by dint of the chief mufti[63] and the provincial muftis, all of whom were appointed by and incorporated into the central bureaucracy.[64] Finally, the marriage of religion and the state invested the sultans with unprecedented authority over the qadis and jurisprudential processes, and as a result, the discretionary sphere of the qadis, which was previously quite wide, was narrowed down by the imposition of limited opinions by the state. The same was true for the interpretive and legislative mechanisms, that is, the functioning of the mufti or jurisconsult.[65]

Crucial to understanding the peculiarity of the official Ottoman *madhhab* is the fusion of sultanic law (*'örf*) and religious law to an unprecedented extent, that is, the unification of religious and political order into the same ideological framework.[66] Originally, the only sources of legislation and jurisprudence were scripture and the Prophetic tradition. During the Mongol and post-Mongol period, *töre* or *yasak* was introduced as a second source of law in Islamicate governments, which took its mature form in *kānūn* in the Ottoman Empire. As Imber has noted, 'Unlike the sharia, which was the law of a religious community, the *kānūn* was the law of an Empire.'[67]

Uriel Heyd argues on the authority of Tursun Bey, the historian of Mehmed II, that in the Ottoman Empire there was a clear distinction between secular law and sacred law. The former was based on the customary practices and the will of the sultan and called *siyāset-i sultānī* or *yasagh-i pādishāhī*. According to Tursun Bey, this law was necessary to maintain the order of the apparent world (*zāhir*). But there was a higher law which maintained not only the apparent world but also the hidden world (*bātin*). In Islam, this is called sharia, and the institutor or legislator of sharia was the Prophet (on behalf of God). While *yasagh-i pādishāhī* was necessary for maintaining the social order, sharia was necessary for the moral perfection of men.[68] The rationale of customary law was explained in preambles of *kānūnnāmas* as follows: in time, fraud and crime increased to such an extent that the guardians of sharia could not solve all disputes. Hence, the coercive regulations of rulers became necessary. Eventually, *siyāset-i sultāni* was conceptualised within sharia, not as a separate entity.[69]

The religious validity of separate secular law has been debated among Islamic scholars. Some scholars like Ibn Khaldun rejected its legality, while others considered *'örf* or custom valid on matters that are not dealt with by sharia; some even considered it as the fifth source of the law.[70] According to the second opinion, the sultan's authority of legislation becomes crucial especially in the field of criminal law. As the legitimate political authority (*'ulu'l-amr*), the sultan was entitled to impose punishment for administrative or political reasons (*siyaseten*). This extra-canonical authority of ruler was conceptualised as *siyāsa shar'iyya*.[71] According to Muslim jurists, these extra-sharia regulations that are imposed by rulers were to be applied and administered by secular judges, the *wāli al-mazālim* or *wāli al-jarā'im*.[72] Therefore, the jurisprudential field of *siyāsa shar'iyya* was considered complementary to sharia, some even claimed it to be a part of sharia. As Heyd has argued, the Ottoman *kānūn* was grounded on the concept of *siyāsa shar'iyya* that had been elaborated by early Muslim legists.[73] However, in the Ottoman Empire, the careful distinction between *siyāsa shar'iyya* and sharia had become increasingly blurred by the mid sixteenth century. Kınalızade Ali Efendi, a leading member of the ulema class who served as *kadıasker* under Suleyman I and Selim II, wrote that there is only one valid law, the divine sharia, which included *siyāsa*.[74]

The narrowly circumscribed penal law in sharia was based on the concepts of the rights of God (*haqq* Allah) and the rights of human beings (*haqq ademī*). Therefore, the concept of crimes against society or the state was not addressed. Over time, as the need to regulate the public sphere grew, a third category was added to the legal concept of right, that is, *haqq al-saltana* or the right of the state. As we see in al-Mawardi, this third category was generally considered to be inferior to the original Qur'anic ones.[75] Nonetheless, this concept provided the legal basis for rulings of sultans in a vast area of public law. In Muslim societies, qadis administered only the divine law, while matters of *siyāsa shar'iyya* were adjudicated by government officials such as governors or military commanders. In the Ottoman Empire, this two-tier administration of justice gradually changed in the sixteenth century. The scope of the qadi courts was comprised mostly of matters regarding secular law (*kānūn*). Sharia and *siyāsa shar'iyya* were inextricably merged not only in theory but also in practice.[76]

As Repp has noted, *kānūn* legislation covered three main areas. First, it regulated governmental affairs such as the regulation of the court, army, taxation, land regime and the relationships between individuals and the state. These affairs were fairly widely accepted as having been left untouched by sharia, hence, they were considered a legitimate legislative sphere of the ruler for the public interest. Second, and less obviously outside the bounds of sharia, was criminal law. Third, Ottoman sultans intervened in controversial issues of sharia to secure uniformity of religious practice across the realm by throwing the weight of the state behind certain opinions. This intervention paved the way for sultanic legislation on matters of sharia.[77] In theory, *kānūn* was supposed to operate within the legislative sphere where sharia has no say. In practice, however, it was not so easy to draw lines of separation; hence, there was always a tension between the two types of law and their protagonists, that is, administrative cadres and the ulema.[78] By the same token, *kānūn* could not supersede or contradict sharia; it was instead to amplify and supplement it. As a famous ruling of Ebussuud declared, 'There can be no decree of [the] sultan ordering something that is illegal according to sharia'.[79] Again, this was not always the case in practice. If sharia had *de jure* superiority, *kānūn* enjoyed *de facto* supremacy.

Before the fifteenth century, the scope and practitioners of these two laws, that is, *yasak* and sharia, were conspicuously separated from each other. By the mid-fifteenth century onwards, these two systems of law increasingly intermingled. It is important to note that in the Ottoman case, the creators, interpreters, practitioners and guardians of both laws were madrasa-educated scholars. Sharia and sultanic law were reconciled through muftis' fatwas; they were practised by qadis as the administrators of justice, and the supply of muftis and qadis for the imperial system was provided by professors running the empire-wide madrasas. One should note that there was a high degree of fluidity between these three branches that created and sustained the Ottoman legal system. It was quite usual for a scholar to practise each of them in different parts of his career, or to hold joint positions (mufti–*müderris*, qadi–*müderris* mufti–qadi) at the same time.[80]

Indeed, the idea of sharia–*kānūn* conciliation, or the unification of state and religion, was epitomised in the office of qadi. The Ottoman qadi was one of two key officials representing the sultan in the provinces (the other being the governor). As such, his duty and authority to administer justice were broadly defined in the classical Ottoman system in a way that covered a whole range of governmental activities such as practising sharia, supervising tax registrations and collections, validating every kind of transaction and acting as notary, etc.[81] Judicial decrees and notarial acts derived their authority from two sources: Hanafi juristic tradition and the sultan.[82] Yet, in practice, the legal opinions of muftis, which reflect Hanafi tradition, were not binding on qadis whereas the sultan's orders were.[83] As the conflation of sharia and *kānūn* increased, the distinction between these two fields of law became increasingly obscure. On the one hand, this merging invested sultanic law with an unprecedented breadth and power vis-à-vis sharia; on the other hand, the sphere of sharia was considered so broad that it included everything. In any case, state and religious affairs were entangled inseparably.[84]

As for the jurisprudence and legislation, the principal religio-legal device that was used to open up rooms for the emergence of the Ottoman Sunnism was the fatwa, the legal opinion, which were issued by the jurisconsults of various ranks in the pyramidal hierarchy, from the chief mufti (*şeyhülislam*) down to the local muftis in towns.[85] Typically, the spheres of *kānūn* and sharia were separated, and the people in charge of issuing their jurisprudence were different. The shaykh al-Islam was the institutional head of sharia jurisprudence, while the *Nişancı*, who was also called the 'mufti of *kānūn*', was the chief bureaucrat who supervised the customary law. In theory, fatwas derived their legitimacy solely from the tradition of Hanafi jurisprudence. However, in practice, the ulema class was functioning as part of the bureaucracy.[86] Therefore, the notion of independence from real politics was more or less fiction.[87] Due to the enthusiastic support of Ebussuud, the two spheres of law increasingly overlapped under Suleyman I. Ebussuud became the first chief jurist who unequivocally issued legal opinions on matters of customary law (*fetāvā-yi kānūniye*); these rulings were based on *kānūn* or decrees of the sultan.[88] As Heyd noted, 'the Ottoman shaykh al-Islam and other muftis regarded themselves as being authorized to issue legal opinions not only with regard to the rules of the religious law but also on points of State law as laid down in *kānūn*, firmans, capitulations, etc.'.[89] These fatwas relating to non-sharia matters such as land regime, fiscal questions and state regulations were based on references to *kānūn*s and sultanic decrees.

Asserting the Boundaries of Religion

Attitudes towards the issue of apostasy are a good mirror for reflecting how this state-tied ulema refashioned long-lasting legal opinions according to the pressing needs of politics. The question was widely discussed by early jurists, and a universal consensus was reached by the tenth century, according to which apostasy was considered as a break from the community[90] that requires the death penalty. However, the legal ways and procedures of deciding what constituted apostasy remained controversial. The founders of the Hanafi and Shafi'i schools assumed a somewhat lenient attitude towards apostates. According to al-Shafi'i's fundamental opinion, an apostate is not subject to capital punishment unless he or she publicly announces his or her apostasy and does not accept repentance.[91] Al-Shafi'i's position was adopted by the early Hanafi jurists as well and remained the mainstream in the Shafi'i and Hanafi tradition until the beginning of the eleventh century.[92]

The sectarian situation in the Islamic world changed drastically in the tenth century with the rise of the Fatimid Ismai'ili state in Egypt (initially in North Africa) and the Twelver Buyid dynasty at the centre of the Sunni world. It was in this conjucture of the politico-religious schism of the Islamic ecumene that some prominent Shafi'i jurists, such as al-Mawardi (d. 1058), al-Juwayni (d. 1085) and his student al-Ghazali (d. 1111), reformulated the legal procedures for deciding apostasy. Their effort was a direct extension of the anti-Ismai'ili fight of the caliph and, subsequently, his Seljuq patrons. In this political context, the adjudication of apostasy became the primary means to fight heresy. These jurists abandoned the principle of public renunciation and repentance and declared that it is enough to see outward signs to judge one's apostasy. Once unbelief is sufficiently established, the judge must issue a death penalty without giving the supposed apostate a chance to repent.[93] Al-Ghazali was well aware of the fact that his opinion was not in line with the practice of the Prophet, who rejected the judgement of hypocrites (*munāfiqūn*) according to their inward confession and instead accepted them as members of the community. To tackle this problem, he distinguished between apostasy of 'ordinary people', who should be judged according to the older precedents, and members of heretical movements (such as Ismai'ili *dā'is*), who must be treated according to the new opinion.[94] Separating himself from the earlier jurists, he argued that 'the consideration in all these cases should be the increase of ruler's benefit'.[95]

Al-Ghazali's path was further broadened by the Ottoman ulema. To back the Ottomans' political/military campaign against the Safavids, the Ottoman ulema expanded upon his legal opinion with extreme interpretations. They not only decided that outward signs of apostasy were enough to subject an individual to capital punishment, against al-Shafi'i's grounding opinion but in line with al-Ghazali's, but also multiplied those 'signs of apostasy'. They included in the list contested acts such as wearing red headgear, bowing to one's leader, cursing the first three caliphs and A'isha, and consuming alcohol, among others. When it comes to state intervention in adjudicating apostasy, the Ottoman ulema's opinions went beyond the sphere outlined by al-Ghazali, thereby granting sultanic law the legitimacy to serve as a source of jurisprudence.

The Ottoman ulema's politically minded and extreme opinion on the issue of apostasy is epitomised in two treatises by Mufti Hamza and Ibn Kamal, as well as in several fatwas by Ebussuud.[96] However, an 'official' legal opinion seems to have started to flourish earlier. Nabil al-Tikriti's study on a treatise by Prince Korkud (d. 1513) on the boundaries of belief and apostasy, which was allegedly written in 1508, shows that the concept of state interference in the adjudication of some politically delicate religious issues, like apostasy, had already been well-established among Ottoman learned circles. Korkud follows al-Ghazali's interpretation in deeming outward signs to be sufficient for the verdict of apostasy. He provides a long list of these signs, such as wearing certain clothing that is reserved for non-Muslims, treating the Qur'an and other sacred texts with disrespect, bowing down to idols (he does not include bowing down to kings), sacrificing animals in someone's name, claiming false prophethood, practising sorcery, denial of Muhammad's prophecy, intentional abandonment of communal prayer, and abuse of texts which support religion (e.g., texts of legal sciences, speculative theology, hadith, etc.).[97]

The legal invention of the 'renewal of faith' by the late fifteenth century also supports the idea that the notorious *Kızılbaş* fatwas were not the beginning but rather the climax of the development of the Ottoman official jurisdiction of apostasy. Guy Burak has argued that by the late fifteenth century Ottoman jurists had invented the legal concept of 'renewal of faith' (*tecdīd-i īmān*), which signifies return to the community after a temporary excommunication. As opposed to their Hanafi predecessors, they also tightened the link between internal faith and external works,[98] and expanded the list of actions that constituted signs of unbelief far beyond the limited list recorded in Sunni heresy literature.[99] Burak argues that the rise of the apostasy issue to prominence in a new form should be read against the socio-religious and political background of the fifteenth century, in which increased conversions and the rising Safavid challenge forced scholars to develop a legal mechanism to cultivate and differentiate the categories of orthodoxy and heterodoxy. To this end, they redrew boundaries between the true faith and heresy using the muftis' rulings (fatwa).

Fatwas regarding apostasy, which were now reformulated within the framework of the concept of 'renewal of faith', functioned as the spearhead of this process of drawing boundaries. Similarly, state-employed ulema turned adjudication of apostasy into a principal ideological and institutional weapon in the struggle against heresy. Muftis enumerated the various ways in which one could depart the abode of faith, with fatwas used not only as a legal basis to persecute those subjects whose heresy was established, but also as the Sword of Damocles to dissuade those people who had a tendency towards heresy. Numerous fatwas from the late fifteenth to the seventeenth centuries listed acts and utterances that would break one's bond with the faithful community. In addition to the abovementioned actions, they declared highly controversial deeds as signs of apostasy, such as disparaging muftis' decisions, disrespecting learned hierarchy, disdaining juridical processes and reviling possessors of religious knowledge.[100] Obviously against the Shiite menace from the Safavid front, reviling the first three caliphs and prominent companions of the Prophet is included in the list as a sign of apostasy. Even some contested figures of early Islamic history, who had been obviously disdained in many religious texts from medieval Anatolia, were shielded by the protection of apostasy fatwas. For example, Sun'ullah Efendi, who served as the chief jurisconsult during the late sixteenth and early seventeenth centuries, ruled in favour of imposing punitive measures (ta'zīr) against those who reviled the Umayyad caliph Mu'awiya.[101] Even more controversially, some scholars declared that loyalty to the Ottoman state was included in the articles of faith, hence, a betrayal of Ottoman authority was a heresy. For example, the chief jurisconsult Esad Efendi (d. 1625) issued a fatwa declaring supporters of the rebel Abaza Mehmed Pasha apostates, and stated that they must renew their faith and marriages.[102] Likewise, another chief jurisconsult Yahya Efendi (d. 1643) ruled that praising the Safavid Shah Abbas was a sign of apostasy and required renewal of faith and marriage.[103]

It is not an exaggeration to argue that the primary function of the state-sponsored ulema had become the development of a religious discourse to legitimise the sovereignty claims of the sultan.[104] The issue of apostasy provides us with a litmus test that reflects the Ottoman ulema's state-centred reinterpretation of Islamic law according to the expectations of the sultan. Their invention of the legal concept of 'renewal of faith' marked the culmination of a legal trend in Islamic history, a process that was conditioned and fostered by the broader phenomenon of religion and state rapprochement, if not fusion. It is important to note that, as Burak has rightfully underlined, the official view on apostasy was not initially appropriated by non-appointed Syrian Arab ulema who preferred to pursue the traditional lenient approach regarding the issue.[105] But once they joined the hierarchical body of Ottoman ulema, they too started to follow the official opinion in their fatwas as they lost their intellectual autonomy.[106]

This trend of change in legal opinions on apostasy should be regarded as a sign of the wholesale reformulation of religion within the increasing rapprochement of the ulema and the state. In the formative period of Islamic theology and law, religious scholars maintained a substantial degree of independence from political authorities.[107] As they lost their autonomy in later periods, legal opinions on politically delicate issues gained more and more political taints. Furthermore, during the first three centuries, apostasy was not understood as a matter of the inner plurality of Islam, except perhaps during the temporary *Ridda* wars in the immediate aftermath of the Prophet's death. Therefore it did not pose a serious political threat to the government. By the rise of Shiite powers as political entities, however, the situation changed drastically. The question of apostasy now became the main conceptual device to draw boundaries of the true faithful community within Islam. As a result, adjudication of apostasy turned into inquisition trials to fight heresy. In the context of Sunni–Shiite conflict, al-Ghazali's decisive reformulation redefined the means of drawing the boundaries of the faithful community and led to a watershed moment in the development of Islamic orthodoxy.[108] In many aspects, the formation of the Ottoman ulema class four centuries after al-Ghazali, and that of subsequent Ottoman Sunnism, signifies the ultimate culmination of state and religion convergence in Islamic history. As a result, strident state supervision over jurisprudence processes and imperial control over sharia practices harnessed 'the justifying power of sharia norms to state interests'.[109] More importantly, the acceptance of the *'örf* as a source for a legal decision on religious issues invested the state with the capacity to influence the ideological content of the ulema's work, that is, guarding and continually reinterpreting religion.

Disciplining Public Religiosity

State interference in the regulation of religion was extended to public religiosity as well. Clauses regulating the fines to be imposed upon habitual absentees from the five daily prayers were inserted in the penal codes most probably by the time of Mehmed II (d. 1481). The related article recorded in the law code which was drafted under Suleyman I reads as follows:

> Furthermore, in every [town-]quarter and in every village, those who do not perform the ritual prayers shall be examined and severely chastised; and a fine of one *akçe* shall be collected for [every] two strokes. And [attendance at] the Friday prayer service is compulsory. [A person] who neglects [it] or intentionally violates his fast [in the month of Ramadan] shall be severely punished; after he has been chastised, a fine of one *akçe* shall be collected for [every] two strokes.[110]

Rise of the 'Religion and State' Order

We have evidence showing that these laws were imposed widely upon society, even in villages. Already during the reign of Mehmed II the office of *namazcı* had been initiated for surveillance and enforcement of the people's participation in daily prayers. An imperial decree dated 1476 orders governors, qadis and heads of policing forces in the province of Rum to compel everybody to attend the five daily congregational prayers and to punish those who do not obey. Obviously decreed by Mehmet II, the firman first summarises an earlier hearing from the region that people of cities, towns and villages in the province were not following the prescriptions of the Qur'an and the Sunna of the Prophet; they were not observing the prayers (*namaz*), as well as leaving mosques in ruins. The sultan then states that since it is his duty 'to command the right and to forbid the wrong', he has appointed a certain person as '*namaz mahmādī* –نمز محمادي', whose duty is to investigate those people who do not observe prayers, force them to pray and to punish those who insist on disobedience. He then orders the governors (*sanjak begleri*), qadis and heads of policing forces (*subaşılar*) to provide this person with every kind of help in order to establish firmly the sharia in the province so that 'the religion of Islam shall perfectly shine, Muslims shall live in prosperity, and they shall pray for the continuity of the *devlet* of the Sultan and for the increase of his majesty'.[111]

Similar imperial orders and legislation were issued during the reign of Suleyman I, such as the imperial degree in 1537 that ordered the construction of Friday mosques in towns and masjid in every village. Another firman in 1546 instructs local officials to force villagers to participate in the five daily prayers in mosques.[112] This imperial order was addressed to the qadi of Vize province in Rumelia, ordering him to investigate the situation of mosques and masjids, and their attendees, in the village of Ibri and other villages around. It starts with a summary of an earlier report submitted to the Sublime Court, according to which, most of the masjids in the villages of Vize had been ruined, their imams were not qualified, and most of the villagers were not attending the daily five communal prayers. The sultan then orders the qadi to investigate the situation properly, to warn those absentees to congregational prayers and to punish those who insist on not attending prayers in masjids, to have the attendees restore the ruined masjids, and to appoint qualified imams who can read the Holy Qur'an properly. At the end of the firman, Suleyman warns the qadi to deal with this issue in person, not to appoint a *namazcı* to investigate and to prosecute these absentees, for that was already in place.[113]

Ebussuud's fatwas cover the requirement to construct masjids in every village and Friday mosques in every town that lacked one. Several imperial decrees and fatwas also regulated compulsory attendance to congregational prayers. In an undated fatwa, which was from after 1537 (since the fatwa refers to an imperial firman issued in that year), Ebussuud rules that those who do not observe congregational prayers in villages should be punished.[114] As Necipoğlu observes, Ebussuud issued several fatwas determining legal punishment for those who abandon congregational prayers in masjids. In one of them, where he was asked about the measure that should be taken if the people of a village abandon their prayers as a group, he rules that they must renew their faith and marriage since they temporarily became apostates. Another fatwa declares that denying the necessity of congregational prayer in the masjid is an act of apostasy and those people who insist on that must be vigorously punished and then executed.[115]

These imperial orders and rulings are just a few examples among many others. We have convincing evidence showing that these orders were not just prescribed on paper but executed seriously. For example, in 1566, a citadel commander was fired, arrested and dispatched to Istanbul simply because he stopped performing regular prayers.[116] Similarly, in 1588, Sultan Murad III declared a general firman ordering everyone to occupy themselves with the public ceremonies observing the commemorative night of the Prophet's birth (*mevlid*).[117]

Closely related to the enforcement of the five daily prayers in masjids and the Friday prayers, the number of mosques increased drastically during the reign of Suleyman I. Mosques became the most conspicuous Islamic symbol in the cityscape and the socio-religious nucleus of neighbourhoods. A register surveying Istanbul's waqf in 1546 shows that most of the neighbourhoods of the city (219 in total) were named after the persons who had built masjids or mosques.[118] Contemporary Ottoman writers boasted about the proliferation of mosques in the empire's flourishing cities as they considered this to be a sign of Ottoman patronage of orthodox Islam. The sixteenth-century writer Mevlana Isa, for example, interpreted this development as indicative of the sultan's being the prophesied 'renewer of the religion' in the tenth century of the Islamic era.[119]

As Necipoğlu has noted in detail, the transformation of the Ottoman polity from a Turko-Mongolian tribal confederacy to a sharia-based bureaucratic state is well reflected in the architectural styles of mosques. During the early period, Ottoman mosques were intended to be a complex of masjid and convent, and, accordingly, they were built in a T-shape. Until the conquest of Istanbul, each sultan built one or more of these T-shaped convent-masjids in capital cities; many others were built in provinces under the patronage of viziers and feudal lords. These convent-masjids were entrusted to Sufi shaykhs who propagated a flexible popular religiosity, quite different from the rigidly structured Sunni orthodoxy that would be enforced by the late fifteenth century. It is no coincidence that the first sultan who built a big Friday mosque combined with a grand complex was Mehmed II (d. 1481); this represented his vision of centralised empire as opposed to the decentralised ghazi confederacy. As Necipoğlu has noted, connected to the rising imperial vision and 'with the growing emphasis on religious orthodoxy, T-shaped convent-masjids and Friday mosques with flanking guest-rooms fell out of favor'.[120]

It was not only the architecture of mosques that changed but also the activities in them. Convent-masjids also functioned as gathering places and Sufi lodges (*zāwiya*) in which *dhikr* ceremonies and other 'non-orthodox' rituals were practised. As a part of monopolising public religiosity, the religious space of mosques was strictly regulated. A fatwa included in a late fifteenth-century compendium called *Hulviyāt-i Shāhī* (*Royal Sweetmeats*) forbids the people from forming circles in Friday mosques and reciting epics or stories.[121] In a similar fatwa, Ebussuud strictly forbids forming circles and chanting and dancing in mosques, which were common practices of Sufi groups, ruling that those shaykhs who insisted that these acts are licit forms of worship would become apostates and should be executed. Likewise, if a Sufi-minded preacher publicly preaches that the ulema cannot fathom the inner mysteries of religion, he would become a heretic and should be executed.[122] The project of implementing orthodoxy across the empire entailed the close control and disciplining of mosques as the epitome of public religious spaces. Those Sufis who preached ideas that fell outside the fold of the designated orthodoxy became subject to rigorous inquisition and harsh punishments. Several shaykhs and even scholars were executed on the accusation of heresy.[123]

As İnalcık has noted, these reforms were signs of a shift towards a more conservative, sharia-minded state that was bitterly resented by the Turkoman tribes of Anatolia who were supporters of the Turko-Mongolian polity.[124] In other words, all of these measures to enhance the state's grab on the religious practices across the empire, which aimed at creating a uniform orthodoxy, were clear manifestations of the fundamental sea-change in the socio-political order, that is, from the Turko-Mongolian polity to the Perso-Islamic caliphal model.

According to the theorists of the confessionalisation paradigm, a benchmark of confessionalisation was disciplining society through enforcement of a uniform set of religious beliefs and practices. The idea of 'social disciplining' by shaping public religiosity is clearly visible in the Ottoman case. From this perspective, the heightened pressure during the reign of

Suleyman I on the subjects to make them participate in communal prayers should be seen as a marker of the culmination of 'social disciplining' that had started by the mid-fifteenth century.[125] The evidence leaves no doubt that the Ottoman administration not only crafted an official orthodoxy but also imposed it upon society at large through various means, among which controlling and disciplining the sacred space of the mosque and the masjid was the most prominent and efficient. Mosques and masjids were the principal platforms where official propaganda and the ordinary people met. Because educational institutions were serving only a limited and selective population, and the activities of the Sufi lodges were hard to monitor.

The 'Religion and State' Order

Most scholars agree that state and ulema cooperation escalated during the reign of Mehmed II and climaxed under Suleyman the Lawgiver (d. 1556). As Cornell Fleischer has noted, a significant regulatory impetus in the Ottoman governmental system surfaced in the 1530s and 1540s. This period saw an intensified effort towards compilation, codification and regularisation of imperial ordinances, as well as their universalisation and reconciliation with the dictates of sharia.[126] In particular, the work of Ebussuud marked the culmination of this conciliation process, which eventually merged sultanic law and the sharia into one legal framework. His adjudications in governmental issues such as the tax system, land regime and fiscal problems successfully incorporated sultanic law in religious law, and hence sanctioned them as a part of sharia.[127] Nev'izāde Atā'ī (d. 1635) notes his and his predecessor Kemalpaşazade's efforts to harmonise the two laws as follows: 'Truly the effects of their *ijtihād*s was the harmonization of the Ottoman *kānūn* with the noble sharia and the ordering of religious and state affairs on the best possible basis.'[128]

Ebussuud combined two previously separate forms of authority, that is, religious and temporal, in the person of Suleyman I as the universal caliph of Sunni Islam.[129] Holding the two sovereignties, Suleyman I and his descendants claimed themselves to be the heirs of the early Islamic caliphs.[130] His exalted personality as a source of the now combined law (religious plus sultanic) is best reflected in his regnal title 'Lawgiver'. Accordingly, contemporary writers depicted him as the ideal Muslim ruler who was extremely prudent in matters of sharia.[131] Ebussuud designated Suleyman I in the *Kānūnnāme of Buda* as the one 'who makes smooth the path for the precepts of the manifest sharia ... [and who] makes manifest the Exalted Word of God.'[132] He was, hence, the expounder of the signs of sharia. In short, as Imber concludes, as the caliph, he was depicted as the interpreter and executor of God's law.¹³³ As a matter of fact, Ottoman sultans used 'caliph' as titular title as early as 1421. However, it was Suleyman I who claimed not only the title but also the office of the caliphate with its implications of religious authority and universal sovereignty. According to Imber, redressing the Ottoman sultan in the image of the caliph, hence invoking the theory of the caliphate, was engineered by the ulema, especially by Ebussuud, simply to justify the sweeping extension of the ruler's authority especially on matters of sharia.¹³⁴

As sultans were now considered new caliphs, sharia gained increasingly more weight in the functioning of the state vis-à-vis progressive overshadowing of the *kānūn* as a distinct space of legislation. A *fermān* of Mustafa II (1695–1703) declared that 'in *fermān* and decrees all matters shall henceforth be based on the firm support of the noble sharia only ... and warnings are given against the coupling of the [terms] noble sharia and kanun'.¹³⁵ Another outcome of the dominance of sharia in state affairs was the inclusion of muftis' fatwas in the seventeenth-century *Kānūnnāme-i Cedīd*.¹³⁶ However, this does not necessarily mean that the state became totally submissive to the religiously minded legislation of the ulema. Quite the contrary, the *de jure* ascendancy of sharia in governmental affairs brought *de facto* state control over religion. As Imber notes, 'in adopting the title of Caliph, the Sultan was laying claim to authority over the interpretation and implementation of sharia which is very much wider than the strictly limited powers which the Hanafi jurists accord the ruler'.¹³⁷ The controversy over cash waqfs is perhaps one of the best examples showing how the state bent and harnessed sharia. Cash waqfs contradicted sharia because they incurred interest. Chief Mufti Çivizāde issued a ruling banning them; that cost him his post however. His successor Ebussuud abrogated the fatwa in cooperation with the sultan.¹³⁸

Connected to the ascendance of sharia in Ottoman public discourse, unwavering adherence to Sunni Islam replaced *ghaza* ideology as the primary ground of the legitimacy claims of the sultans. For example, the twenty qualities that the court historian Talikizade listed in his work, written in 1593–4, as signifying the superiority of the Ottoman dynasty do not include reference to the *ghaza* mission of the sultan. Instead, they all relate to Islamic universalism, such as (1) being the universal protector and exemplifier of Sunni Islam; (2) having the most developed governmental system and formidable military power; (3) representing universal cosmopolitan Islamic civilisation; and (4) having wealthy resources.¹³⁹

The Turko-Mongolian concept of legitimacy and frontier political culture was abandoned and replaced with this new vision of universal Sunni rule. As argued earlier, the process of religio-political transformation that had started by the reign of Mehmed II and culminated during the reign of Suleyman signifies a fundamental transition in the Ottoman political system. The course of this century saw the demise of the post-Mongol political culture while the pre-Mongol caliphal model resurged. The new polity found its best expression in the Ottoman political discourse of '*dīn u devlet*' or 'religion and state'.[140] This 'neo-caliphal polity' unified religious and political authorities in the same person, the caliph. The unification of *kānūn* and sharia was epitomised in the person of Sultan Suleyman the Magnificent, who later became the archetype of the Ottoman sultans. Once religion intermingled with the vision of the political order, being an observant and good Muslim and having political allegiance to the regime, that is the established socio-political and religious order (*dīn u devlet*), were perceived as being indistinguishable. Therefore, political dissent was envisioned as the most visible marker of heresy.[141] By the same token, disrespectful or disparaging attitudes against the learned hierarchy, which was now positioned as the ideological guardians of the order, were formulated as acts of apostasy.

Conclusion

Students of Ottoman history almost universally accept that both the structure of statecraft and the nature of Islamic religiosity underwent a substantial transformation during the early modern period. At the core of this transformation lay the rapprochement between the state and religion, and their subsequent fusion. This synthesis was formulated in the Ottoman notion of the '*dīn u devlet*' order. One aspect of such a sea-change in political culture was the shift in the legal basis of the state apparatus from *yasa* to Islamic law, while the other was the creation of a state-dependent religion which is now called 'Ottoman Sunnism'. Over the last decade, scholars have attempted to interpret this change in the religio-political order of the empire within the framework of Mediterranean-wide transnational trends, and have suggested examining these religious, political and social developments as a part of the broader confessionalisation process that was the benchmark of the early modern world. In this chapter, I contribute to this growing debate by demonstrating that some features of the confessionalisation paradigm can be applied to Ottoman history. As a conceptual category and heuristic device, confessionalisation is helpful to examine socio-political and religious developments in the early modern Ottoman world. However, my approach differs from current approaches in two substantial aspects: first, I take issue with the argument that Ottoman confessionalisation was just a part of the Mediterranean-wide (some say

Rise of the 'Religion and State' Order

Eurasian-wide) confessionalisation that created the three confessions (Catholicism, Lutheranism and Calvinism) along with the respective confessional states in Europe. Rather, I argue that we must talk about an Islamic version of confessionalisation, which surfaced one century before the emergence of the European confessionalisation. The underlying reasons for confessionalisation in this context were 'Islamic' rather than 'Mediterranean'. In the Islamic world, the fifteenth century was an era of transition and transformation in many respects, the most important among them being a sea-change in the concept of the socio-political order. Throughout this century, the Turko-Mongolian polity, which had governed the central and eastern Islamicate world since the collapse of the Abbasid caliphate in 1258, ebbed, while sharia-based bureaucratic government models were on the rise. This happened hand in hand with the gradual receding of nomadic-tribal Turkic elements from the political scene. Since the Turko-Mongolian government system operated on the basis of dynastic law, during the Mongol and post-Mongol era religion relatively withdrew from the political sphere. By the ebb of the Turko-Mongolian polity, religion and the state re-converged as had been the case in the classical caliphate. This resurgence of the caliphal polity brings me to my second divergence from the current works on confessionalisation. I argue that confessionalisation in the Ottoman case fundamentally differs from the European experience in the sense that, as opposed to the latter, there was no creation of a new confession in the Ottoman Empire. It was rather the resurgence of already well-established confessional structure (i.e., *madhhab*s) in the political sphere. Therefore, I call this process 're-confessionalisation' after the model of the classical caliphate, which was already a confessional state of its own kind long before the Christian Reformation.

Notes

1. I would like to offer my special thanks to Guy Burak, Vefa Erginbaş, Tijana Krstić, Kaya Şahin, Baki Tezcan and Fikret Yılmaz for their valuable comments and constructive suggestions on earlier drafts of this chapter. It goes without saying, nonetheless, that its shortcomings belong to the author.
2. For the concept of 'early modern' as a trans-religious, trans-regional and transnational category, see Goldstone, 'The Problem'. For approaches with stress on Eurasian unity, see Subrahmanyam, 'Connected Histories'; Şahin, *Empire and Power*. For studies of Ottoman history as a part of early modern Europe, see Goffman, *The Ottoman Empire*; Aksan and Goffman, *Early Modern Ottomans*; Orbay, *The Sultan's Portrait*; Dursteler, *Venetians in Constantinople*.

3. For example, Cornell Fleischer has argued that in the second half of the fifteenth century and the first half of the sixteenth century, millenarian expectations moulded the political culture equally in the Ottoman, Safavid and Habsburg worlds, as well as the other parts of Europe. See Fleischer, 'The Lawgiver as Messiah'; Fleischer, 'Mahdi and Millennium'; Fleischer, 'Shadows of Shadows'. Subrahmanyam carried Fleischer's idea one step further by arguing that millenarianism was actually a linchpin of early modern religious and political culture worldwide. See Subrahmanyam, 'Turning the Stones Over'.
4. For my preliminary discussion of this fundamental shift in Islamicate polity, see Yildirim, 'The Rise of the Safavids'.
5. Reinhard, 'Gegenreformation als Modernisierung'; Schilling, *Konfessionskonflikt und Staatsbildung*. For a brief discussion of the concept and its reception by the broader scholarly community, see Brady, 'Confessionalization'; Boettcher, 'Confessionalization'.
6. Schilling, 'Confessionalization', p. 29.
7. Gorski, 'Historicizing', p. 155.
8. Schilling, 'Confessionalization', p. 236.
9. Ibid., pp. 232–3.
10. Gorski, 'Historicizing', p. 152.
11. Schilling, 'Confessionalization', p. 209.
12. MacCulloch, Laven and Duffy, 'Recent Trends'.
13. Thomas, *Religion*, p. 33.
14. Duffy, *The Stripping of the Altars*, p. 278.
15. Bossy, *Christianity in the West*.
16. Gorski, 'Historicizing', pp. 139, 148.
17. Ibid., p. 148.
18. Strauss, *Luther's House of Learning*, p. 2.
19. Ibid., p. 8.
20. Quoted and cited in ibid., pp. 12–13.
21. Krstić, 'Illuminated by the Light'; Krstić, *Contested Conversions*.
22. Krstić, 'Illuminated by the Light', p. 37.
23. Ibid., p. 40; Krstić, *Contested Conversions*, pp. 13–14.
24. Krstić, 'Illuminated by the Light', pp. 51–2.
25. Ibid., p. 63.
26. Krstić, *Contested Conversions*, p. 14.
27. Ibid., p. 15.
28. Terzioğlu, 'Sufis in the Age of State-building', p. 87.
29. Terzioğlu, 'How to Conceptualize Ottoman Sunnitization'.
30. Ibid., p. 305.
31. Terzioğlu, 'Where 'Ilm-i Ḥāl Meets Catechism', pp. 322–3. To explain the rise of confessionalisation, she calls attention to the growth of Ottoman state power, the flourishing of towns and the revival of trade, in addition to ideological stimuli. See Terzioğlu, 'Sufis in the Age of State-building', p. 90.

Rise of the 'Religion and State' Order

32. Terzioğlu, 'Where 'İlm-i Ḥāl Meets Catechism', p. 309.
33. Ibid., p. 318.
34. Ibid., pp. 82–7. For an earlier study of fifteenth-century religious guidebooks for laypeople, which are broadly considered *'ilm- hāl*, see Krstić, *Contested Conversions*, pp. 16–37. An interesting observation on these guidebooks would be the shift of focus from the emphasis on true doctrine in the fifteenth-century *'ilm-i ḥāl*s to the emphasis on truth and its legal obligations in those from the later periods.
35. Terzioğlu, 'Where 'İlm-i Ḥāl Meets Catechism', pp. 102, 109–10.
36. Ibid., pp. 112–13.
37. Burak, 'Faith, Law and Empire'.
38. al-Tikriti, 'Ibn Kamal's Confessionalism'.
39. The concept was first introduced by R. D. McChesney to distinguish Alid-oriented religiosity that is harboured within the fold of Sunni Islam from doctrinal Shiism. See McChesney, *Waqf in Central Asia*.
40. Erginbaş, 'Problematizing Ottoman Sunnism'. For a more detailed examination of *Ahl-i Bayti*sm in Ottoman literary sources, see Erginbaş, 'The Appropriation of Islamic History'.
41. Baer, 'Book Review'.
42. Ibid., p. 392.
43. Imber, *Ebu's-su'ud*, p. 51.
44. Ocak, *Osmanlı Toplumunda*; Ocak, 'Islam in the Ottoman Empire'; Necipoğlu, *The Age of Sinan*, pp. 27–70.
45. Compare Burak, *The Second Formation of Islamic Law*, pp. 1–20.
46. For the early Ottoman madrasas, see Bilge, *İlk Osmanlı*.
47. There are numerous studies on the emergence of the 'Ottoman' learned class. For a summary account of literature, see Atçıl, *Scholars and Sultans*, pp. 32–45.
48. Normally Islamic law bans any interference with the operation of waqfs, which is stipulated solely by the waqf deed. Nonetheless, by the reign of Mehmed II, the Ottoman government had developed several devices and methods that invested the central administration with the capacity to oversee appointments and function of waqf institutions, see Atçıl, *Scholars and Sultans*, pp. 155–61; see also Ahmed and Filipovic, 'The Sultan's Syllabus'; Baltacı, *XV–XVI. Yüzyıllarda*.
49. Özcan, *Kānūnnāme*, pp. 5–12.
50. For the functions of the chief mufti in classical Islamic societies, see Bulliet, 'The Shaikh al-Islām'.
51. The classic study on the formation of the Ottoman ulema class is Repp, *The Mufti of Istanbul*. For a general study of the ulema class and their functions in the Ottoman Empire, see Uzunçarşılı, *İlmiye Teşkilatı*. For a recent reassessment of the formation of the Ottoman ulema class between the mid-fifteenth and the late sixteenth centuries, see Atçıl, *Scholars and Sultans*; see also Baki Tezcan, 'Ottoman Mevali'.

52. Atçıl, 'The Route'.
53. Atçıl, *Scholars and Sultans*, p. 175.
54. For some examples, see Fleischer, *Bureaucrat and Intellectual*, pp. 217–24; see also Atçıl, *Scholars and Sultans*, pp. 100–1.
55. Atçıl, *Scholars and Sultans*, pp. 57, 145–6. For Ottoman ulema in the seventeenth and eighteenth centuries, see Zilfi, 'Elite Circulation'; Zilfi, *Politics of Piety*; Zilfi, 'The Ottoman Ulema'; Uğur, *The Ottoman 'Ulema*.
56. Peters, 'What does It Mean', p. 147.
57. On the formation of Islamic law, see Hallaq, *The Origin*; Hallaq, *Sharīah*.
58. Burak, *The Second Formation of Islamic Law*, pp. 6–10.
59. Jackson, *Islamic Law*, p. xv.
60. Guy Burak underlines the importance of novel genealogy books (*tabaqāt*) that emerged by the early sixteenth century in establishing a hierarchy of authorities and uniformity of opinions within the Hanafi *madhhab*. Not surprisingly, the first serious work of this kind was written by the Chief Mufti Kemalpaşazade (d. 1534), who was one of the key leading actors of Ottoman 'Sunnitization'. See Burak, *The Second Formation of Islamic Law*, pp. 65–7.
61. Calder, *Islamic Jurisprudence*, pp. 128–9.
62. Devin Stewart has shown how in Mamluk Egypt and Syria this autonomous system had become institutionalised in a 'civil' manner. Within this system the authority to issue legal opinions was granted by an already established scholar to his student through a licence (*ijāza*), which was almost the same as the process of granting permission to teach and usually issued together. See Stewart, 'The Doctorate'.
63. This office was established as the head of the bureaucratised learned class, which was also designed as 'the supreme office in the Ottoman judicial hierarchy' and 'the chief source of juristic authority in the empire'. See Imber, *Ebu's-su'ud*, p. 7.
64. Burak, *The Second Formation of Islamic Law*, pp. 38–58. Burak notes that from the reign of Bayezid II teachers in the important madrasas founded by members of the royal family in major cities served as local muftis. See ibid., p. 40.
65. Peters, 'What does It Mean', pp. 147–58. For the authority ascribed to political leaders in the Hanafi *madhhab*, see Johansen, 'Secular and Religious Elements'.
66. It has been argued that Ebussuud's legal opinions marked the culmination of the conciliation between sultanic and religious law. See Imber, *Ebu's-su'ud*; also consider İnalcık, 'Suleyman the Lawgiver'; Abou el-Haj, 'Aspects of the Legitimation of Ottoman Rule'; Burak, *The Second Formation of Islamic Law*.
67. Imber, *Ebu's-su'ud*, p. 24.
68. Heyd, *Studies in Old Ottoman Criminal Law*, pp. 169–70.
69. Ibid., p. 176.

70. Ibid., p. 183.
71. One should remember that the term *siyāsa* originally had the general sense of punitive action falling outside the scope of sharia. In the Ottoman context, it came to have the primary meaning of capital punishment. It was only in the nineteenth century, when European concepts of government were introduced into the Islamic world, that the term acquired the sense of 'politics'. See Imber, *Ebu's-su'ud*, p. 98.
72. Heyd, *Studies in Old Ottoman Criminal Law*, pp. 198–9.
73. Ibid., p. 201.
74. Ibid., p. 203.
75. Ibid., p. 206.
76. For the functioning of provincial qadi courts, see Ergene, *Local Court*; Jennings, 'Kadi, Court'; Winter, 'Ottoman Qādīs'.
77. Repp, 'Qānūn and Sharī'a', pp. 124–5. For a more detailed examination of the scope of the Ottoman kanun, see Imber, *Ebu's-su'ud,* pp. 40–51.
78. Repp, 'Qānūn and Sharī'a', p. 128.
79. Quoted in Heyd, *Studies in Old Ottoman Criminal Law*, p. 180.
80. For some examples, see Atçıl, *Scholars and Sultans*, pp. 165–6.
81. Gradeva, 'A Kadi Court'.
82. Imber, *Ebu's-su'ud*, p. 55.
83. Repp, 'Qānūn and Sharī'a', pp. 138–9.
84. For further discussion, see Gerber, *State, Society, and Law*.
85. Ibid., pp. 71–111; Burak, 'Faith, Law and Empire'.
86. Heyd, 'Some Aspects'.
87. Imber, *Ebu's-su'ud*, p. 58.
88. Heyd, *Studies in Old Ottoman Criminal Law*, pp. 174–5.
89. Ibid., p. 189.
90. As Josef van Ess has noted, membership in the community was the oldest expression of Islamic soteriology. See Van Ess, *Theologie und Gesellschaft*, p. 613 ff.
91. Griffel, 'Toleration and Exclusion'. Al-Shaf'i's position was mostly maintained by leading jurists of the Hanafi, Maliki and Hanbali schools. For more reading on the question of apostasy, see Peters and De Rries, 'Apostasy in Islam'; Ahmad, 'Conversion from Islam'; Heffening, 'Murtadd'; Hallaq, 'Apostasy'; Isutzu, *The Concept of Belief*; Johansen, 'Apostasy as Objective'.
92. Griffel, 'Toleration and Exclusion', p. 349; Burak, 'Faith, Law and Empire', p. 6.
93. Griffel, 'Toleration and Exclusion', p. 353.
94. Ibid., p. 353.
95. Quoted in ibid., p. 353.
96. These texts have been studied by many scholars for different purposes. See Tekindağ, 'Yeni Kaynak'; Eberhard, *Osmanische Polemik*; Üstün, 'Heresy and Legitimacy', pp. 35–49; Yıldırım, 'Turkomans'; Atçıl, 'The Safavid

Threat'. Abussud's oft-cited fatwa collection was published in Düzdağ, *Şeyhülislam Ebussuud Efendi Fetvaları*.
97. al-Tikriti, 'Ibn Kalam's Confessionalism'.
98. The Hanafi and Maturidi schools dissociate faith and works, arguing that works do not increase or annul faith which is a matter of inner assertion. See, for example, Madelung, 'Early Doctrine'.
99. Burak, 'Faith, Law and Empire', pp. 2–3.
100. Ibid., pp. 8–9. These acts of apostasy relating to disrespect for the absolute religious authority of the learned hierarchy are particularly important for they clearly reflect the idea of the 'religion and state' ideological structure. As Barkan has pointed out, questioning the validity of religious rulings by the imperial ulema class, epitomised in the person of the shaykh al-islam, was considered a major transgression against the religio-political order. See Barkan, 'Caractère religieux', p. 36.
101. Sun'ullah Efendi, *Fetāvā*, 96r. For Ottoman attitudes towards Muawiya and his son Yazid, see Erginbaş 'Reading Ottoman Sunnism'.
102. Es'ad Efendi, *Fatāvā*, 48v, cited in Burak, 'Faith, Law and Empire', p. 10.
103. Yahya Efendi, *Fetāvā*, 95r, cited in Burak, 'Faith, Law and Empire', p. 10.
104. For example, Colin Imber has argued that they expanded the Ottoman sovereignty discourse over the concept of *ghaza* or holy war against the enemies of Islam. To this end, the conformist ulema of the sixteenth century reinterpreted the foundational ethos of the principality in accordance with the new universalist claims and ideological needs of the empire. Imber argued that the *ghaza* emphasis in the Ottoman discourse of sovereignty was picked in the first half of the sixteenth century and then waned by its end. Imber, 'Frozen Legitimacy'; Imber, 'Ideals and Legitimation'.
105. For criticisms of the ulema of the Arab provinces against Ottoman official legal opinions, see Rafeq, 'The Opposition'.
106. Burak, 'Faith, Law and Empire', pp. 11–14. Similar to Burak's conclusion, Helen Pfeifer's study shows that non-appointed ulema of sixteenth-century Damascus maintained a certain degree of autonomy against the central government and its official religious opinions. See Pfeifer, 'Encounter after the Conquest'.
107. See, for example, Watt, *The Formative Period*, p. 268.
108. Omid Safi shows how the Saljuq power and great Shafi'i scholars, including al-Ghazali, cooperated to defeat the Ismai'li challenge, and how they created a Sunni orthodoxy in the process. See Safi, *The Politics of Knowledge*.
109. al-Tikriti, 'Ibn Kalam's Confessionalism', p. 149.
110. Heyd, *Studies in Old Ottoman Criminal Law*, p. 122.
111. Lugal and Erzi, *Fatih Devrine Ait*, pp. 94–5.
112. Demir, 'Kanunī Sultan'.
113. Ibid., pp. 52–3.
114. Cited and quoted in Necipoğlu, *The Age of Sinan*, p. 48.
115. Ibid., pp. 48–9.

Rise of the 'Religion and State' Order

116. Demir, 'Kanunī Sultan', p. 49.
117. Selānikī, *Tārih-i Selānikī*, pp. 237–8.
118. Ibid., p. 47.
119. Necipoğlu, *The Age of Sinan*, p. 34.
120. Ibid., p. 52.
121. Ibid., pp. 52–3.
122. Several fatwas of Ebussuud on this issue are cited and quoted in ibid., p. 53.
123. For a thorough analysis of these religiously sanctioned executions in response to the accusation of apostasy, see Ocak, *Osmanlı Toplumunda Zındıklar ve Mülhidler*.
124. İnalcık, 'State and Ideology', p.81.
125. For a discussion of measures to ensure regular attendance at mosques during the reign of Suleyman, see Necipoğlu, *The Age of Sinan*, pp. 47–58.
126. Fleischer, 'The Lawgiver as Messiah', p. 167.
127. Imber, *Ebu's-su'ud*, p. 24.
128. Quoted in Repp, 'Qānūn and Sharī'a', p. 134.
129. İnalcık, 'Islamization'. There are many controversial issues that show how Ebussuud harnessed sharia to the benefit of the state. One good example is his unrelenting attitude on the question of 'cash waqf'. Although earning interest is clearly banned by Islamic law, he issued numerous fatwas in support of cash waqfs on the basis of its widespread practice and public benefit. See Mandaville, 'Usurious Piety'.
130. Imber, *Ebu's-su'ud*, pp. 99–111. For instance, Lutfī Paşa proclaims, in his painstaking effort to prove Suleyman I's rightful caliphate, that he was the 'Imam of the Age' who stands in the place of the Prophet. See Gibb, 'Lutfī Paşa', p. 288. Gibb truthfully underlines the role of slave-origin statesmen in amplifying Suleyman I's power.
131. Necipoğlu, *The Age of Sinan*, p. 28. For the rise of the ruler image, combining religious and secular authority, in the personality of Suleyman I, see Yılmaz, 'The Sultan and the Sultanate'.
132. Barkan, *Kanunlar*, p. 296.
133. Imber, *Ebu's-su'ud*, p. 76.
134. Ibid., p. 98. Imber discusses how the Ottoman concept of the neo-caliphate differed in some important senses from the classical sense of the office. It is important to note that Ottoman inventions all facilitated the sultan's intervention in the sphere of sharia. See ibid., pp. 98–101. One big obstacle in the classical theory of the caliphate that undermined the Ottoman claim was the prerequisite of having Quraysh descent in order to become a caliph. Sulyman I's grand vizier and son-in-law Lutfī Paşa composed a treatise to refute this argument, claiming that Quraysh descent was not a necessary qualification for the caliphate, therefore the Ottoman sultan was the rightful caliph. For a broader discussion, see Gibb, 'Lutfī Paşa', pp. 287–95.
135. Heyd, *Studies in Old Ottoman Criminal Law*, p. 155.
136. Repp, 'Qānūn and Sharī'a', p. 133.

137. Imber, *Ebu's-su'ud*, p. 76.
138. Repp, 'Qānūn and Sharī'a', pp. 139–41.
139. Necipoğlu, *The Age of Sinan*, p. 30.
140. For a good discussion of this concept, see Ocak, *Osmanlı Toplumunda Mülhidler ve Zındıklar*.
141. Compare Melis, 'A Seventeenth-Century Hanafi Treatise'.

3

One Word, Many Implications: The Term *'Kızılbaş'* in the Early Modern Ottoman Context

*Ayşe Baltacıoğlu-Brammer**

Introduction

In the gradual crystallisation of the Safavids from a non-sectarian Sufi order into a Shiite religio-political movement, Shaykh Haydar (d. 1485), the father of Shah Ismail (d. 1524), developed a distinctive identifier in the form of a twelve-gored crimson headpiece symbolising the adherents' allegiance to the Twelve Shiite imams and to the Safavid shaykhs/shahs as their spiritual and political leaders.[1] This twelve-folded piece of felt, called *kızıl taj/tac* (meaning 'red crown' in Turkish), with a stiff baton around which the turban was wound, eventually became a source of pride and honour, as well as a mark of religious and political loyalty among the followers and sympathisers of the Safavid movement, called Kizilbash/ *Kızılbaş* ('red head' in Turkish), most of whom were inhabitants of the Anatolian peninsula, Iraq and western Iran.[2]

By the 1470s and 1480s, this highly symbolic headpiece began to appear in contemporary sources (both Persianate and non-Persianate), such as an Armenian colophon from the late 1480s and a chronicle dated around 1490 from Fadlullah Ruzbihan Khunji (d. 1519), a staunch anti-Safavid, anti-Shiite intellectual from Isfahan, titled *Tarekh-e Alam Ara-ye Amini*.[3] While Ottoman official records began to refer the sympathisers of the Safavids (both Ottoman and non-Ottoman) as the 'Sufis of Ardabil' (*Erdebil sufileri*) as early as the late fifteenth century, without any reference to their sectarian identity, the earliest appearance of the term *Kızılbaş* dates back to the early 1510s, more than three decades after the first appearance of the symbolic headpiece. This also corresponds with the first Safavid-led rebellion in the Ottoman realm (the Shah Kulu Rebellion in 1511) and the inauguration of the reign of Sultan Selim I (r. 1512–20), who radically changed the nature of the relationship between the Ottoman and Safavid courts with extremely harsh policies against the *Kızılbaş* population in Anatolia, and launched the first major military conflict (the Battle of Chaldiran) shortly after this in 1514. Thereafter the term '*Kızılbaş*' appeared quite often in religious rulings, official edicts and provincial reports, and served as the literal and symbolic label for Ottoman and non-Ottoman sympathisers of the Safavid court, who allegedly held strong heretical beliefs and political and military commitments against Istanbul.

With the end of Selim I's reign in 1520, the relationship between the Ottomans and Safavids became highly convoluted, with increasing political, religious and economic interactions between the two courts, as well as diplomatic intricacies. Within this environment, a series of wars between the two sides were followed by three major peace treaties,[4] whilst the Safavids implemented a meticulous propaganda campaign within the Ottoman realm to convert Ottoman subjects to become sympathisers of the Safavid religio-political establishment as taxpayers, soldiers and, ultimately, subjects. From the early 1520s to the mid-seventeenth century (when the *Kızılbaş* ultimately lost its significance for the Safavid court upon its completion of the gradual transformation to a purist Imami Shiism and the replacement of the *Kızılbaş* emirs and soldiers with Georgian/Caucasian *ghulām*s, elite slave-soldiers), the term '*Kızılbaş*' held its primary meaning as 'rebellious heretic', as well as various new connotations and implications, which were not automatically associated with confessional identity and/or connections with the Safavid court.

Despite the complexity of the relationships among the three major actors in the region (i.e., the Ottoman and Safavid courts, with the *Kızılbaş* population in between), as well as the multifarious connotations and implications attached to the term *Kızılbaş* during this long period, the general tenor of Ottoman historiography created and perpetuated a narrowly defined ethno-religious and political framework, according to which individuals inherited their *Kızılbaş* identity, often against their will. The underlying assumption in these academic and, in some cases, popular works has been that each and every *Kızılbaş* mentioned in early modern Ottoman sources was a 'Turkish-speaking rebellious heretic subject' of the empire who was in close contact with the Safavid court against Istanbul's interests. The initial advocates of this narrative were Turkish nationalist historians of the 1930s and 1940s, who argued that one could not become *Kızılbaş* because being *Kızılbaş* was about pedigree, not conversion.[5] According to the later representatives of this approach, some of whom held high-ranking administrative positions in various Turkish governments, the *Kızılbaş* were always the greatest enemy of the Ottomans because of

One Word, Many Implications

their 'betrayal' of the Ottoman state and its ultimate goal of creating 'one great Turkish Empire that would have encompassed an area from Central Asia to the Balkans'.[6] Furthermore, this approach has reinforced the idea of a static position in describing the relationship between Istanbul and its *Kızılbaş* subjects, based on the policy of continual persecution of the latter by the Ottoman central authority and its agents, while neglecting any alternative policy the state may have developed (both at the central and provincial levels) in this interplay.

Pushing back against this essentialist approach, a few recent studies have successfully challenged this distorted narrative's domination. In doing so, they focused on various aspects of the complex relationship not only between the Ottoman Empire and its *Kızılbaş* subjects, but also between the Safavids and the various *Kızılbaş* populations of the region, ultimately problematising and contextualising Ottoman Sunnism and its non-linear history. For example, Vefa Erginbaş has successfully challenged the long-held historiographical position that 'state-sponsored Sunnism' was the only version of Sunnism in the Ottoman domains,[7] while Stefan Winter has meticulously demonstrated the importance of heterogeneity and pragmatism as the two leading factors determining Istanbul's approach towards its Shiite population, rather than confessional zealotry.[8] Analysing when and why the Ottoman sources began to use the term '*Kızılbaş*', as well as the ways in which religious and political actors used this term in nuanced and often conflicting contexts in the following decades, is a necessary addition for the new corpus of literature on this topic not only for understanding the Empire's largest and best-documented religious 'minority' but also for contextualising the debates about orthodoxy and heterodoxy within the framework of the early modern Ottoman state and society. Furthermore, taking into account the religio-political background of authors and the contexts in which the sources were written is essential to comprehend the Ottomans' perception of sectarian, political and regional identities within the broader scope of the formation of states, loyalties and sectarianisms in the early modern era and beyond.[9]

This chapter aims to explore the origins, as well as the often neglected variances, in the meaning of the term '*Kızılbaş*' within the context of early modern Ottoman literature (defined here as the period from the late fifteenth century to the mid-seventeenth century). I argue that Ottoman central authorities began to refer to the sympathisers (both Ottoman and non-Ottoman) of the Safavid court as '*Kızılbaş*' immediately before the reign of Sultan Selim I, who changed the nature of the relationship between Istanbul and the Safavid court with open military engagements and economic sanctions. In this earlier context, the term '*Kızılbaş*' provided the negative labelling that the Ottoman central authority required to identify and pursue the enemy of the 'religion and state' (*dīn ü devlet*), given that the geopolitical legitimacy of Istanbul was at stake with the rapid emergence and expansion of the Safavid state on its eastern frontier. As Guy Burak has cogently argued, this period also corresponds with the Ottoman adoption of the Hanafi sect (*madhhab/mezhep*) as the official school of law under the aegis of the office of the chief mufti (or *shaikh al-islam/şeyhülislam*), bridging the gap between religious and sultanic laws.[10] Therefore, Ottoman policymakers, more often than not, disguised their non-religious concerns with increasingly sectarian rhetoric provided by various influential members of the same religious elite group.

But in the wake of this foundational period, I also argue that after the short reign of Selim I, the Ottoman court embraced a more complex approach to both its *Kızılbaş* subjects and its rival, the Safavids. In this subsequent era, the term *Kızılbaş* carried different, and in many cases, conflicting meanings depending on the context, as well as the genre of the documents making these references. These documents include imperial chancery records (*mühimme defterleri*), edicts (*fermāns*), religious rulings (*fatwas*), chronicles and polemical literature, each of which targeted different audiences for different purposes. Therefore, a meticulous examination of the origins and use of the term *Kızılbaş* in the early modern Ottoman context reveals a significant fluidity in terms of the loyalties of various groups, along with their religious, regional and political identities, which have often been assumed to be non-existent during the so-called 'age of confessionalisation' in the Middle East.

First Appearance(s) – First Meaning(s)

As opposed to the older historiographical position's long-lasting emphasis on sectarianism as the core element that defined the Ottoman–Safavid relationship, the religious dichotomy between an alleged 'Ottoman Sunnism' and 'Safavid Shiism' was a product, rather than a cause, of the geopolitical and economic rivalry between the two actors.[11] It was the politicisation and the militarisation of the Safavid movement as a powerful rival on the eastern frontier of the Ottoman Empire, not the ultimate Shiite character of the Safaviyya Sufi order (and, subsequently, the Safavid state), that initially shifted Ottoman authorities' attention to the Safavids and their propaganda activities in Anatolia and Iraq.[12] While the evolution of the Shiitisation, politicisation and militarisation of the Safaviyya order began in the late fourteenth or early fifteenth century, its progression accelerated under the leadership of Shaykh Junayd (d. 1460), who switched the order's tactics from recruiting supporters within the urban setting of Ardabil in northwestern Iran and its surrounding hinterlands to the broader context of rural Anatolia, through ambitious strategies that employed an increasing network of followers and disciples, ultimately transforming the order's strategic outlook.[13] As mentioned above, his son, Shaykh Haydar, saw the tactical importance of symbolism within the burgeoning movement, and in the 1460s and 1470s introduced and promoted the *Qizil tāj/Kızıl tac* as the main symbol marking its wearers (and owners without wearing it) as the core constituency of his religio-political movement in the region. However, even given a growing Shiite emphasis and its expansion into territories within the Ottoman sphere of influence, the order initially did not pose a real threat to Ottoman central authority. The central lodge of the order in Ardabil continued to receive an annual payment, *çerāğ akçesi* (literally, the 'candle coin/money')[14] from the Ottoman capital, and surviving records show that leading contemporary Ottoman religious scholars regarded the order and its leaders as highly respected figures.[15]

Within this context, contemporary Ottoman chronicles, which include Neşri's *Cihannüma* (1485), Tursun Bey's *Tarih-i Ebu'l-Feth* (c. 1490s) and Oruç Bey's *Tevarih-i Ali Osman* (1503), along with other surviving official documents, do not mention Shaykh Haydar and his increasing group of supporters, and do not use the term *Kızılbaş* even when discussing the rivalry between Ottoman Sultan Mehmed II (r. 1451–81) and Uzun Hasan (d. 1478), who was close to the Safavid family through marriage alliances with both Junayd and Haydar, and granted them political and military favours in the Akkoyunlu state.[16]

There is, however, one critical exception to these chronicles. Derviş Ahmet Aşıki, or Aşıkpaşazade (d. 1484 or 1502), in his *Tevarih-i Ali Osman*, gives a short account of Shaykh Junayd's travels to Anatolia, where he describes the Ottoman authorities' unease with his motivations, as well as Shah Ismail's increased popularity and his insistence on 'heresy', noting that:

> then another son of Haydar came to the world whose name was Ismail. [His followers] called him (*şāh*) for curing their sick. The ones in the Anatolian Peninsula were not the people of Sunna (*ehl-i sünnet*) ... they would not perform *salāt* and they would not fast either. And they would frequently employ heretical speech (*rafża mute'allik kelimāt*), their heresy (*rafż*) was apparent.[17]

Yet despite the useful details in his account, Aşıkpaşazade glosses over Shaykh Haydar when referencing the conflict between him and the Shirwan Shah[18] and does not use the term *Kızılbaş* or *kızıl tac*. It is also important to note that the twenty-third chapter of his account, where he mentions the two shayhks – Junayd and Haydar – and Shah Ismail and their 'heresy', is an addition at the end of the account, rather than being a part of his chronological narrative. While there is disagreement over when Aşıkpaşazade actually died – was it before or after the rise of Shah Ismail? – it is more than likely that this section was added – by someone other than Aşıkpaşazade – to the account after Shah Ismail's declaration of himself as the head of the Shiite Safavid Empire in 1501, when he had positioned himself as the main rival to the Ottoman Empire.[19]

On the other hand, a collection of official orders dating from 1501 occasionally warn various local authorities about the followers of Ardabil (*Erdebil sufileri*), be they Ottoman or non-Ottoman, who migrated – or were caught while migrating – to the Safavid realm. These orders labelled them as *ehl-i fesād* (corrupted people) and asked local authorities to capture them to collect fines (based on their status in the order) and, in some cases, to execute them. However, they make neither reference to the confessional identities of these people, nor do they use the term *Kızılbaş*.[20] Thus, even by the beginning of the sixteenth century, the lack of the term *Kızılbaş*, or indeed any reference to the Shiite nature of the Safaviyya religio-political movement for the period between the 1470s and early 1500s, can be interpreted as another indication of the lack of the long-assumed sectarian nature of the tension between the Ottomans and the Safavids. As such, these accounts indicate a primarily political (and fiscal) character of the relationship between the two sides in the early decades of the conflict.

Both Shah Ismail's ascension to the Safavid throne in 1499 and his declaration of Shiism as the official state religion in 1501 have rightfully been considered as turning points in the history of the Islamic world. However, regarding the term *Kızılbaş*, the relative silence of the Ottoman sources continued for at least a decade after Ismail's coronation. Ottoman expansion into eastern and southeastern Anatolia, a region where Ismail himself had longstanding connections through engaging in military campaigns, organising gatherings with his supporters, and encouraging the locals for conversions and migrations, led to the Shah Kulu Rebellion in 1511, and although it was put down by the Ottomans soon after, it was this event that laid the foundation for the Ottoman state to connect the term '*Kızılbaş*' with their new rival to the east. Accordingly, Selim I's accession to the Ottoman throne in 1512 led to a more militarised response, particularly in the contested regions between the two states.[21] Given this context, the term *Kızılbaş* began to appear in Ottoman sources regularly thereafter. In so doing, the term kept its initial definition of being the supporters of the 'heretic' Shah Ismail in northwestern Iran and also the frontier regions of central and eastern Anatolia, the majority of whom were Ottoman subjects.

One Word, Many Implications

The earliest Ottoman source that employed the term was the report of a certain Ali b. Abdülkerim,[22] which was submitted to the Ottoman court shortly after Selim's accession to the throne in 1512. While not much is known about the report's author, the report itself provides us with vivid details about whom the author thought wore the *kızıl taj*:

> then a cruel infidel [i.e., Shah Ismail] showed up wearing a **red hat** and becoming an enemy of the scholars, monotheists, Muslims, and Sunnis (*ehl-i 'ilme ve ehl-i tevḥīde ve ehl-i Islām ve Sünnilere 'aduvv olub*), fighting against them wrongfully. He named the red-hat the *taj*, perish the thought that it be a crown (*ḥāşā ki tac ola*).[23]

Later in the report, Abdülkerim uses the term '*Kızılbaş*' for those who were 'acting against the Sunna under the command of Shah Ismail' in eastern parts of the empire, probably meaning both the Ottomans and non-Ottomans.

It was also within this increasingly sectarian milieu where the genre of fatwa, or religious ruling, started to become a common way of addressing the issue of the Safavid threat with the term *Kızılbaş*.[24] The qadi of Istanbul, Nureddin Hamza Sarıgürz (d. 1521), for instance, issued the first Ottoman fatwa in 1514 directly mentioning the *Kızılbaş* as a group of heretics, whose destruction was a religious duty upon the 'Sultan of Islam' (i.e., Selim I):

> Muslim people! Note that this group of *Kızılbaş* [*şol tā'ife-i Kızılbaş ki*] whose leader is Isma'il, the son of Ardabil, disregards the sharia and Sunna of our Prophet the religion of Islam, the knowledge of religion and the incontestable Qur'an. They claim that the things forbidden by Allah are legal; they offend the mighty Qur'an ... aim to abolish the law and the religion of our Prophet ... for this clear and evident reason we, in the presence of my humble self and of the other scholars of Islam, have, by general consensus and by order of the law and after consultation with our books, issued a *fatwa* that the [members of the above-]mentioned group are infidels and heretics. To kill them and to destroy their communities is an implicit and essential obligation for all Muslims ... the sultan of Islam is authorized to kill their men and distribute their property, women, and children among the defenders of religion.[25]

It is notable that Sarıgürz's fatwa was rather vague in terms of differentiating Ottoman *Kızılbaş* from non-Ottoman *Kızılbaş*, for the following years brought a trend in which it was noticeably clearer if the term *Kızılbaş* was limited to Ottoman subjects with obvious sympathy towards the Safavid religio-political leaders or to the *Kızılbaş* living beyond the Ottoman frontier. Kemalpaşazade (d. 1534), a renowned Ottoman poet, religious scholar, historian and *şeyhülislam*, while emphasising the 'ungodliness' of the *Kızılbaş* and their increasing numbers in eastern Anatolia and western Iran, for instance, stated:

> A storm of disorder erupted in the East and shook the earth. Peace abandoned the land of the Arab and the Persian, and the Turk and the Daylamite. A pervert suddenly emerging from Erzincan climbed the castle of ungodliness and reached the peak, and in the heart of Azerbaijan the **Kızılbaş** blossomed like tulips. The head of this group of the wicked, Shah Ismail the shaykh of Ardabil, followed the path of ungodliness, declared the forbidden permissible, and *invited the masses overtly to his heresy. He spread the Shiite sect's tainted belief and fooled the common people with his tricks.* He went too far in loving Ali and too far in cursing the first [three] caliphs.[26]

Kemalpaşazade was more direct at identifying the increasing popularity of the movement among Ottoman subjects and recognising the threat they posed to the Ottoman state. His language towards the *Kızılbaş*, however, was more moderate, as he stressed the locals' 'gullibility' rather than assume the 'ill-intention' associated with the *Kızılbaş* that one sees in Sarıgürz's fatwa.[27] Furthermore, for Sarıgürz, the *Kızılbaş*, along with anyone else (be they Ottoman or non-Ottoman) who helped the Safavids, deserved 'the keen sword of the sultan', and he refused the right of repentance for them. Yet in Kemalpaşazade's view, while fighting against the *Kızılbaş* was a more crucial duty for the Ottoman sultan than 'fighting against the unbeliever enemies', he meant only the *Kızılbaş* living outside Ottoman territories. Proof of this lies in the fact that Kemalpaşazade identified specific non-Ottoman territories to clarify where the Safavids emerged and had spread rapidly.[28]

Complication of the Term: 1520s–1630s

The period between the 1520s and the 1630s signifies two major dynamics for the Ottoman–Safavid relationship and the use of the term '*Kızılbaş*'. By the 1520s, Ottoman dominance over Anatolia, greater Syria and Iraq was nearly complete following a series of conquests and policies of gradual centralisation. On the other hand, the Safavid court intensified its religio-political propaganda efforts in the very same region with their own strategies that recognised their inability to compete militarily with the Ottomans in their attempts to gain a foothold in the region.

This period also marked a visible differentiation between Safavid subjects (i.e., *Acem*) and the politically and religiously pro-Safavid inhabitants of the region (i.e., *Kızılbaş*) in the sources. This differentiation also recognised that there were subjects of Safavid Iran who may or may not have had clear attachments to the Safavid court.[29] While the Safavid

One Word, Many Implications

subjects, who did not show any overt attempt to undermine the Ottoman political and fiscal legitimacy concerns in the region, were usually labelled as *Acem* (an old term in Arabic referring to non-Arabic speakers, mainly Iranians), the politically and religiously active Ottoman and Iranian followers of the Safavids were labelled as *Kızılbaş*. For example, a series of official documents from Bursa, dating from the sixteenth century, noticeably distinguishes the Persian merchants (*Acem bezirgānları*) travelling to Bursa from various parts of Safavid Iran from the *Kızılbaş* (be they Ottoman or Safavid), portraying the latter negatively as they were to be caught and punished with lashings, exile to remote regions or long prison terms.[30]

Within this environment, a pragmatic and generally ad hoc use of the term '*Kızılbaş*' became more common, where the specific implementation depended on local administrative realities, the nature of the relationship between Istanbul and the Safavid capital, as well as the genre and the audience of a specific document. While confessional concerns and motivations retained their significance for the Ottoman political and religious authorities in determining the way sources employed the term, pragmatism and causality were also central factors. The flexibility and pragmatism of the empire must be particularly emphasised, because this era provides us with many cases in which it is nearly impossible to pinpoint a long-lasting and ideological motivation behind the identification of an individual (or a group) by Ottoman officials as *Kızılbaş*, other than the goal of accommodation or as part of the concerns of day-to-day politics.[31]

While acknowledging the added layers of complexity and the relative arbitrariness in the use of the term *Kızılbaş*, which makes simple classifications difficult to achieve, we can still point out three major categories of definition attributed to it by the Ottoman central authority in this period. These three categories reflected various combinations of policies contingent upon the political, confessional, geographical and also fiscal dynamics of specific chronological periods and/or regions.

The Kızılbaş as 'Heretic Followers of the Safavid Shah'

The first category of *Kızılbaş* in this period consisted of sympathisers of the Safavid court regardless of their subject-hood, be it Ottoman or Safavid. After the Safavids became a political threat, particularly along the eastern border of the empire, employment of its non-Safavid disciples against the Ottoman central authority led to an immediate shift in Istanbul that can be summarised as first to stop, and then to reverse pro-Safavid activities.[32] While Istanbul adopted various methods in this process, the term 'Kızılbaş' became a part of the increasingly sectarian narrative, particularly when it connoted the justification of the suppression of the 'wicked population'. As such, for instance, Kemalpaşazade (d. 1536), while serving Suleyman I (r. 1520–66) as the *şeyhülislam,* stated that the '*Kızılbaş* emerged at the core of the state and did not leave any place untouched' ('*ol mülkün temelinde Kızılbaş ẓahir oldu ... elin uzatmaduk yir komadı*').[33] In another letter in a similar vein, Sheikh Bali Efendi (d. 1552),[34] a prominent member of the Ottoman ulema, advised Grand Vizier Rüstem Pasha (r. 1544–53, 1555–61) to exterminate the entire *Kızılbaş* population, both Safavid and Ottoman, sparing only children, due to their outward heresy.[35]

The close connection between being a *mülḥīd* (or heretic) and a *Kızılbaş* was also perpetuated during this period, particularly before and during the periods of wars with the Safavids. Well-known fatwas of Ottoman *şeyhülislams*, including Sadullah Sadi Efendi (d. 1539), Ebussuud Efendi (d. 1574) and Kadızade Ahmet Şemseddin Efendi (d. 1580), served as the necessary tools for justifying Istanbul's oppressive actions taken against not just the subjects or soldiers of the neighbouring Safavids, but also the empire's own subjects. At the outset, most of these religious elites, using significantly more sectarian language than the official orders sent to the provinces, declared any type of activity backed by the Safavids to be 'sinful' and insisted that any person who became *Kızılbaş* would be considered a *rāfiẓī*, or apostate, and that his or her property would be confiscated and their women and children enslaved.[36]

Ebussuud Efendi (d. 1574) became a particularly common reference point with numerous fatwas in the following decades, in which he eliminated the *Kızılbaş* from any legal definition of the Muslim community, calling them 'nothing but infidels, spilling whose blood was an obligation for the guardian of Muslims', or the 'upholder of Sunni orthodoxy', that is, the Ottoman sultan.[37] While some of his rulings do not clarify if he means only the Safavid subjects in employing the term *Kızılbaş*, certain specific fatwas about the religio-legal position of the *Kızılbaş* and the necessary punitive actions to be taken against them openly target the Ottoman *Kızılbaş*:

> According to Imam Malik, Imam Shafi'i, Imam Ahmed b. Hanbal, Imam Leys ibn Sa'd, Imam Ishak b. Raheviyye, and the large majority of the religious scholars, at their execution, their [the *Kızılbaş*] repentance is never accepted and their belief is not acknowledged, thus they are executed by beheading ... However, [those who live] in cities and villages with trustful conduct in appearance in order to be immune to actions and punishments [of the Ottoman state], whose appearance testifies to their truthfulness, are not subjected to

punishments and executions ... it is more crucial to fight against this group [the ones who hide their true identity] rather than varying other unbelievers.[38]

It is important to note that, in addition to this clear differentiation between Ottoman and non-Ottoman *Kızılbaş*, Ebussuud makes a reference to the long-lasting Shiite practice of taqiyah, or dissimulation, and the importance of detecting it, without using the term itself.[39]

In the following decades, official decrees echoing the rulings and polemics of Sarıgürz, Kemalpaşazade and Ebussuud were issued to target the *Kızılbaş* as the 'heretic enemy of the religion and state'.[40] However, in many cases non-sectarian (mostly geopolitical and fiscal) concerns were behind the specific orders targeting a *Kızılbaş* individual or a group, even though on paper the state targeted a 'religious heretic'. For instance, according to an imperial order sent to Erzurum in 1578, the number of the *Kızılbaş* in the region had become impossible to handle, leading Istanbul to order their deportation to Cyprus.[41] However, we must note that the Ottoman central authority in this period was trying to repopulate Cyprus after its conquest in 1570 from Venice and similar orders around the same time were sent to various other parts of the empire asking local authorities to send specific populations to Cyprus.[42]

Moreover, in other cases, Ottoman policymakers labelled subjects (mainly, but not limited to, the Shiites of Greater Syria) as *Kızılbaş* as a legal device in order to justify official violence aimed at more ordinary situations such as brigandage and tax evasion, rather than on account of heretical beliefs.[43] In the eyes of the Ottoman authorities, the *Kızılbaş* who paid taxes to the Safavid shahs and sought to migrate to Safavid Iran represented the loss of a critical part of the empire's revenue-producing workforce, and various orders were sent to the provinces to closely watch these subjects of the empire. As a consequence, seventeen out of the thirty-three orders in the imperial registries (*Mühimme Defterleri*) for the years 1570 and 1571 mention *Kızılbaş* individuals and groups specifically when ordering governors to catch anyone providing financial support to either the shah's court or to the centre of the order in Ardabil.[44] In addition, the local authorities were also held responsible for confiscating the money and any type of valuables that the Kızılbaş had been sending to the Safavid shahs. In a similar vein, the status of *Kızılbaş* property saw a similar fate, as it changed from being legally protected to being subject to confiscation in specific cases where the owner was allegedly in contact with the Safavid court.[45] These examples indicate that the term *Kızılbaş* often did not serve to root out theological deviance, but to pursue political and fiscal agendas of the state.

Another Ottoman effort to counter Safavid propaganda was to disseminate the idea that the *Kızılbaş* were different from Twelver Shiites. Various accounts, including fatwas and polemical literature, served this purpose particularly due to the former's significance and power across the empire. For instance, Ebussuud Efendi, in a mid-sixteenth century fatwa, ruled that the *Kızılbaş* were not Shiites and thus it was lawful to kill them on the grounds of heresy, while the same was not true of other Shiite sects because they were of the 'seventy-three legitimate sects' of Islam.[46] One should, however, note the ambiguity of the statutory fatwa, which in fact left it to the discretion of local Ottoman officials to decide who fell into the category of *Kızılbaş* or Shiite. As mentioned above, these authorities could thus use the framework of these religious rulings as an excuse to persecute known Shiites for fiscal, as opposed to ideological, reasons such as banditry and tax evasion.

After the mid-sixteenth century, Ottoman imperial documents and chronicles saw a significant increase in the mention of *Kızılbaş*, and also the emergence of a clear distinction between *Kızılbaş*-born and converted *Kızılbaş* subjects of the empire. Istanbul paid extra attention to those who were receptive to the ongoing propaganda campaign, as it perceived the dissemination of pro-Safavid religio-political ideology as a threat to its geopolitical and religious legitimacy. Specific actions that challenged Istanbul's authority, such as organising rebellions with direct (and sometimes indirect) Safavid involvement; sending alms to the Safavid shahs; refusing to fight against the Safavids under the Ottoman banner; and/or migrating to the Safavid Empire were their primary focus and the capital devoted considerable attention to finding and punishing those '*Kızılbaş*', as well as agents of the propaganda, including Safavid disciples (called *halife*s), soldiers, and in some cases merchants. As political and religious loyalties were viewed as being closely linked in this period, 'turning *Kızılbaş*' or 'turning Sunni' more often than not meant publicly switching allegiance from the Ottoman sultan to the Safavid sheikh/shah or vice versa.[47] In this context, phrases such as *Kızılbaşa dönmek* or *Kızılbaş olmak* (*Kızılbaş şodan*) (to turn *Kızılbaş*) were used to emphasise that a subject was a convert.

Furthermore, Ottoman official sources repeatedly emphasised the significance of owning, circulating and wearing the *kızıl tac* as the primary identity marker and conversion tool for Safavid sympathisers in Anatolia. A specific order sent to Baghdad, for instance, instructs the governor to thoroughly investigate the claims that a certain Mehmed, a resident of Baghdad, 'donned the *tac*'.[48] Another order sent to the governor of Şehrizor (Kirkuk) mentions the commander of a frontier fortress, Hasan, to whom the fortress was given on condition of giving up his *kızıl tac* (i.e., loyalty to the Safavid shah). The order, after making a comparison with a certain Iskender, who – unlike Hasan – sent his *tac* to Istanbul to keep his *sanjak* (or district), accuses Hasan of not being reliable and directs the governor not to trust him again, to remove him from his official position and to confiscate the *tac*.[49]

The Ottoman central and provincial authorities often utilised monetary measures either to prevent individuals and groups from 'becoming *Kızılbaş*' or to punish those who 'became *Kızılbaş*'. In an imperial order from 1574, for instance, the governor of Diyarbekir was instructed to honour Shaykh Ebulhayr Salif Efendi with 10 *akçe*s (silver coins) for not becoming *Kızılbaş* (*Kızılbaş mezhebine girmeyib*).[50] In a similar vein, an official order from 1632 ordered the governor of Mosul to sell, without an auction, the property of a certain Mehmed who had turned *Kızılbaş*.[51] At the same time, the Ottoman central authority remained highly sceptical of tribes and large groups of people in the border regions who returned to the Ottoman realm (*tekrar avdet eyleyen*) after previously becoming *Kızılbaş* and migrating to Safavid territory.

In addition to imperial documents and court chronicles, the corpus of popular literature also emphasised the alleged danger of the *Kızılbaş* due to their relationship to the Safavid court. For instance, Me'āli, a poet from the long era of Suleyman (r. 1520–66), known for producing poetry written in easily accessible language, as opposed to the elevated language of the court, continuously bashed the *Kızılbaş* and the necessity for their execution.[52]

To sum up, in many cases during this period, Istanbul justified oppression and persecution of, and even 'inquisition' against, the '*Kızılbaş*' (both Ottoman and non-Ottoman) with the direct attribution of the meaning 'the heretic follower of the Safavid Shah'. However, more often than not, non-confessional issues were the ones primarily at stake.

The Kızılbaş *as 'Peaceful Subjects of the Empire'*

Various scholars have argued that throughout the early modern period, the Ottoman central authority constructed a unique set of policies centred on the practice of persecution towards its *Kızılbaş* population. Based on the capital's 'uncompromising' religious and political stand, they further claimed, 'mass executions and mass deportations were standard Ottoman practices in the treatment of the *Kızılbaş*'.[53] However, a more careful reading of the full range of sources suggests that even though Istanbul from time to time pursued policies targeting the *Kızılbaş* population en masse (such as during Selim I's reign), not every *Kızılbaş* mentioned in

Ottoman sources was 'a rebellious heretic subject' whose utmost loyalty was to the Safavid shahs, and not every Ottoman policy engaging with the *Kızılbaş* was centred around the practice of persecution.

In fact, a large portion of those labelled as *Kızılbaş* in the Ottoman official and semi-official sources were subjects of the empire from Anatolia, as well as the Balkans, Greater Syria and Iraq, with no clear connection to the Safavid shah and/or court. Many of these *Kızılbaş* subjects forged close connections with both the central and local Ottoman administrative agencies as 'loyal' subjects of the empire and were rewarded with money, titles and/or land in return. Furthermore, in many criminal cases and various other situations, the *Kızılbaş* individuals or groups mentioned were either ordered to be 'left alone' upon verification of their fiscal and political loyalty to Istanbul, or the term *Kızılbaş* was a simple identification detached from insinuations of any possible political sympathy for the enemy, or any manifestation of overt heresy. In other words, while religion in many cases played a significant role in determining the nature of the relationship between the ruler (i.e., the Ottoman capital) and the ruled (i.e., the *Kızılbaş*), the empire's geopolitical and fiscal legitimacy – meaning its ability to collect taxes and recruit soldiers, as well as its day-to-day concerns about safety and security – were often the primary concern dictating policy, rather than the confessional identities of individual subjects.

To begin with, many Ottoman sources attached additional adjectives to the term *Kızılbaş* to differentiate between the so-called 'peaceful' and 'heretic' ones. Among various combinations, *Kızılbaş-ı evbāş* (wicked), *Kızılbaş-ı bed ma'āş* (unworthy), *Kızılbaş-ı bi-nemāz* (non-observer of daily prayers), *Kızılbaş-ı bi-dīn* (disbeliever), *Kızılbaş-ı hannās* (troublemaker), *Kızılbaş-ı şum* (ominous) were frequently used descriptors of individuals and communities. With these types of categorisation, the Ottoman central and provincial authorities often aimed to separate the tax-paying, land-cultivating and battle-ready *Kızılbaş* from the tax-evading and migrating *Kızılbaş*, which proved to be more crucial for the empire.[54] In other words, when relations with the Safavids were rough or when the Ottoman *Kızılbaş* subjects wished to show their spiritual devotion to the Safavid shahs by sending financial support to the centre of the order at Ardabil or to the capital of the state, or by moving to Safavid Iran, the Ottoman central authority deemed them an economic and geopolitical threat to its stability, and suppressed them more forcefully than other *Kızılbaş* subjects who did not engage in similar actions.

On the other hand, opportunities for advancement, albeit limited, were also given to specific members of the *Kızılbaş*, as various individuals and groups received imperial favours, lands and titles. For instance, several

Kızılbaş subjects were given timar *tevcihi* (preference for a timar) in the sixteenth century, particularly right after the Amasya peace treaty was signed between the two empires.[55] A *mühimme* order, in a similar vein, asked Cafer Pasha, the *beylerbeyi* of Anatolia, to give *zeamet ve* timar in the frontier region (*serhad*) to a group of *Kızılbaş* who had migrated to 'this side' from Tabriz after the Treaty of Constantinople was signed in 1590.[56] Furthermore, several imperial orders banned local authorities from granting *dirlik*s to the *Kızılbaş*, which indirectly shows that they were granted previously.[57] It is also known that Celal (d. 1518), whose name was later applied to the Celali Rebellions of the 1590s and early 1600s, was a *Kızılbaş* timar-holder from the region of Amasya-Tokat.[58] In this environment, Ottoman fiscal reports from various provinces of the empire mention certain *Kızılbaş* individuals and/or families as *mukāta'a* holders, such as a tax farmer from Jubayl, 'Isma'il Hamada the *Kızılbaş*'.[59] These examples show Istanbul's diverse approach towards its *Kızılbaş* subjects, which is reflected through its language and decision-making processes.[60]

In other cases, official orders sent to the provinces to deal with the '*Kızılbaş* threat' included an exit clause, instructing local authorities to 'leave alone' (*kendi haline/halinde*) the *Kızılbaş* individual or group if allegations of collaborating with the Safavids proved to be baseless. For instance, a series of orders from 1558–60 mention two *Kızılbaş* individuals, Hakkı and Sohrab, from the town of Kırşehir in central Anatolia, who were accused of being in contact with the Safavids. Istanbul first ordered the Bey of Kırşehir to confiscate their property but then suddenly told him to stop the process, because evidence had emerged that the allegations were false.[61] Similar orders were also sent to other regions of the empire, including the Balkan provinces, directing governors or other local authorities to differentiate between 'peaceful' *Kızılbaş* or *ṣalāh üzere olanlar*, and hostile *Kızılbaş* or *hilāf-ı şer olanlar* (literally, 'unlawful ones'), and *Yukarı Cānib ile ittihād edenler* (those who were allied with the Yukari Canib, meaning the 'upper side', i.e., the mountainous Safavid territory), before implementing any punitive actions.[62] While the first group was either left alone or exiled, the second group faced harsher policies, including long terms in prison and execution.[63]

Nonetheless, the relatively pluralistic approach taken by the Ottoman state towards its *Kızılbaş* subjects outlined here should not be seen as either an example of 'Ottoman tolerance' or the 'exceptions to' or 'aberrations in' the tense relationship between Istanbul and its *Kızılbaş* subjects. They are in fact examples of the imperial centre's complex policymaking procedures to manoeuvre around the issues of political, fiscal and religious legitimacy. In other words, the Ottoman authorities' willingness to overlook someone's non-Sunni confessional identity was at times tied to their political and fiscal concerns and, in many cases, various categorisations were applied to differentiate between the 'peaceful' and 'hostile' *Kızılbaş*. The oscillation of the Ottoman central authority between the two ends of the spectrum (i.e., persecution and accommodation) is easily detectable in imperial registries and edicts, which were closely associated with the day-to-day problems and practices of the empire, rather than a broad ideological and sectarian rhetoric that dominated religious rulings, official court accounts and/or polemical literature.

The Kızılbaş *as the 'Enemy in the East'*

The third and last group labelled as *Kızılbaş*, according to various Ottoman sources, was the Safavid state and its subjects in general, regardless of their religious identity. Although the Shiitisation of the Safaviyya order dates back to the early fifteenth century, and Shah Ismail declared Shiism as the official religion of the state in 1501, Safavid Iran's population remained majority Sunni up until the late sixteenth century. Despite the complexity associated with the term *Kızılbaş*, often-cited academic studies[64] have failed to analyse the context of imperial orders calling for *Kızılbaş* to be located, exiled, punished and/or executed; instead, they emphasise the use of the term in these sources while assuming that every *Kızılbaş* mentioned in these sources was a Shiite Ottoman subject. In fact, Ottoman *mühimme*s, *fermān*s, fatwas and *sicil*s, as well as chronicles and poetry, often use the term *Kızılbaş* for the Safavid state; this would include its leaders, subjects, soldiers and merchants, often in a way that is difficult to determine without a proper analysis of the context.[65] This approach has also reinforced the idea of continual persecution of the Anatolian *Kızılbaş* by the Ottoman central and local authorities, based on the assumption that the executed or prisoned *Kızılbaş* was an Ottoman subject, even though in many cases he or she was the subject of the rival Safavid Empire.

In addition to official state records, literary accounts and court chronicles used the term '*Kızılbaş*' or *sürh-ser* (red head in Persian) in a similar fashion. For instance, Taşlıcalı Yahya Bey (d. 1582)'s *kaside*s (eulogies), which he presented to Suleyman in 1548 at the time of his campaign in Safavid Iran and Iraq, refers to the Safavid state and court as *sürh-ser*.[66] Selim I (r. 1512–20), who wrote his poetry in Persian, also used the Persian version of the term *Kızılbaş*.[67]

Conclusion: Erosion of Kızılbaş Influence at the Safavid Court and the Subsequent Decrease of the Term Kızılbaş in Ottoman Sources

The Safavids' gradual evolution from a loose interpretation of Shiism towards a conservative version of Imamism was completed by the mid-seventeenth century. One of the major dynamics affecting this transformation was the decreasing influence of the *Kızılbaş* tribal emirs at the Safavid court. As this gradual decline extended to their political relevance, conversion to and from *Kızılbaş* Islam lost its political significance for both the Ottoman and Safavid central authorities, specifically after the 1630s. This transformation at the Safavid court led to the stabilisation of the Safavid Empire under Shah Abbas (r. 1588–1629), on the one hand, and the cessation of the pivotal role of the *Kızılbaş*, on the other. Consequently, the Anatolian *Kızılbaş* ceased to play a significant role as a buffer between the two empires, and Safavid and Ottoman propaganda activities in central and southeastern Anatolia decreased significantly.[68] Following the Treaty of Zuhab (or Kasr-ı Şirin) in 1639, which not only ended the intermittent conflicts of more than 150 years between the two sides but also drew the borders between the two states for centuries to come,[69] the term *Kızılbaş* appeared considerably less in Ottoman sources and lost its multifarious meanings once again, this time becoming a pejorative term mainly referring to the Turkish- (and in some cases Kurdish-)speaking Shiites of Anatolia who transitioned into a closed and isolated mystical movement in 'the sea of Ottoman Sunnism'.[70] On the other hand, authorities in the capital occasionally invoked the religious rulings of the sixteenth century castigating (and in some cases calling for the execution of) the Syrian and Iraqi Shiites as '*Kızılbaş* heretics' in response to non-political and religious offences such as tax evasion, robbery and inter-tribal conflicts, even though both the central and local authorities were well aware of the fact that these '*Kızılbaş*' were not in any way connected with the Anatolian *Kızılbaş* or the Safavid court.[71] Lastly, in a few sources from the eighteenth century, Ottoman authors used the term *Kızılbaş* to refer to the Safavid court and its subjects.[72]

This chapter is an effort to demonstrate the complex relationship between not only the Ottomans and Safavids but, more importantly, between the Ottoman Empire and its *Kızılbaş* subjects, in an attempt to better define the contexts in which the term *Kızılbaş* is used with its multifarious meanings and connotations by political and religious authorities. As Vefa Erginbaş has noted, 'Ottoman Sunnism [in the early modern period] was far from monolithic',[73] and, therefore, despite the dominance of punitive actions in the Ottoman central authorities' interaction with their *Kızılbaş* subjects, complex relationships among the major actors of the region (i.e., the Ottoman and Safavids courts, along with the *Kızılbaş* population in between), as well as the regional and political diversity within the *Kızılbaş* population itself, led to wildly varying state policies which could also include acceptance and accommodation. Within this complex arrangement, the term *Kızılbaş* carried more than one singular implication and each connotation, regardless of a person's confessional identity and/or connection with the Safavid court, was contingent upon central and local administrative realities, the geographical location of certain individuals and groups, and/or the genre of a specific source targeting different audiences for different purposes.

Notes

* I would like to mention Shahzad Bashir's well-articulated and thought-provoking article, 'Origins and Rhetorical Evolution of the Term *Kızılbaş* in Persianate Literature', *Journal of the Economic and Social History of the Orient* 57 (2014): 364–91, which inspired me to question the origins and the various meanings of the term '*Kızılbaş*' within the context of early modern Ottoman sources. I am also grateful for the meticulous critiques, comments and questions offered by Guy Burak, Vefa Erginbaş, John Curry and Beau J. Brammer and the anonymous reviewers.

1. According to Ross Anonymous, one night Ali b. Abu Talib (d. 662), the first imam of Shiites, appeared in Haydar's dream and said to him, 'Oh my son, the time is now at hand when my child from among your descendants will sweep infidelity from the face of the earth. It now behooves you to fashion a cap for the Sufis and your disciples, and you must make it of scarlet cloth.' Ross, 'The Early Years' pp. 254–5. Besides this gross fabrication, the origin of the red headdress is still a matter of debate for scholars. For further details on the origins of the *kızıl taj/tac*, see Babayan, *Mystics, Monarchs, and Messiahs*; Baltacıoğlu-Brammer, 'Safavid Conversion Propaganda'.

2. The Italian traveller Giovanni Tommaso Minadoi (d. 1615) reports, '… afterwards the Persians were called Cheselbas [*Kızılbaş*] because of a certain red mark which they carried on their heads, by an ordinance that was instituted for them by Arduelle [Ardabil], who was esteemed a very holy man, which name was confirmed afterwards in the succession of Isma'il'. Minadoi, *The History of the Warres*, p. 45.

3. Khunji uses the term *Kızıl Kulah* (red hat) and mentions the act of wearing it in a sharp binary framework in which he highlights the suddenness of the transformation of the order from a Sunni – and therefore good – past to a Shiite – and therefore evil – present: 'The next day in the morning, the blue-wearing Sufi [Sheikh Haydar] put the **red hat (*kulāh*)** on his head and opened up his hand to the exercise of the sword from horizon to horizon.' Fażlallāh

One Word, Many Implications

b. Rūzbihān Khunjī-Iṣfahānī, *Tarīkh-i 'ālam-ārā-yi Amīnī*, 251, 297, cited in Shahzad Bashir, 373 (emphasis mine). In a similar vein, a previously unknown colophon dating 1488, mentions the red-hat wearing Sufis, again in highly negative way while describing the enemies of the Christians: '... The great Sufi of the city Ardabil gathered by his letters all his Sufis from the whole earth. For it was their statues and custom that every year the **red-hat** Sufis were hurrying to his call from every land, and they were taking up arms for him with their own wages. And instead of receiving anything from him, they themselves were giving to him much gold and silver, and in all battles wherever he went they were willingly fighting and dying in front of him. At this I too marveled and I was astonished at such fleeting mindless simplicity, that those who had wandered from truthfulness were calling this man, the deceiving sodomite, a great prophet, and they were praising his name with miracles, that with dry feet he passes over rivers, and with his axe made of felt he cuts stone, iron and everything.' Thomas A. Carlson, 'Safavids Before Empire'. Shahzad Bashir's successful examination of the Persinate literature shows that the term *Kızılbaş* acquired its symbolic meaning with a direct connection with the inventor of the headpiece, Shaykh Haydar, or the founder of the Safavid Empire, Shah Ismail, only gradually in the seventeenth century. Bashir, 'Origins and Rhetorical Evolution of the Term *Kızılbaş*', p. 364.
4. The main periods of war between the Ottoman and Safavid empires were 1532–55, 1578–90 and 1623–39, and the main peace agreements signed were the Amasya Peace Treaty (1555), Istanbul (Constantinople) Peace Treaty (1590) and Kasr-ı Şirin (Zuhab) Peace Treaty (1639).
5. For instance, Abdulbaki Gölpınarlı stated that, '... her isteyen bu tarikate [Bektaşilik] girebilir ise de Kızılbaşlığa giremez. Kızılbaş, erkek olsun kadın olsun, mutlaka Kızılbaş soyundan gelir'. *Kızılbaş*, p. 789.
6. For an example, see Saray, *Türk – İran*, p. 24.
7. Erginbaş, 'Problematizing Ottoman Sunnism', pp. 614–46.
8. Winter, *Shiites of Lebanon*. For further revisionist discussions in the literature, see Krstić, *Contested Conversions*; Terzioğlu, 'How to Conceptualize Ottoman Sunnitization', pp. 301–38; Karakaya-Stump, 'The Wafā'iyya', 279–300; Karakaya-Stump, 'Documents and Buyruk', pp. 273–86; Yıldırım, 'Sunni Orthodoxy vs. Shi'ite Heterodoxy?', pp. 287–308; Stewart, 'The Ottoman Execution', pp. 289–347.
9. For emblematic cases of this approach, see Imber, 'Persecution of Ottoman Shiites', pp. 245–73; Zarinebaf-Shahr, 'Kızılbaş "Heresy"', pp. 1–15.
10. Burak, *The Second Formation of Islamic Law*.
11. Dressler, 'Inventing Orthodoxy', pp. 151–73.
12. See Baltacıoğlu-Brammer, 'Safavid Conversion Propaganda', chs 2, 3. Also, as opposed to the long-held dichotomies of orthodox versus heterodox and Sunni versus Shiite, the period predating the Ottoman–Safavid conflict witnessed an amalgamation of complex religiosities that incorporated various versions of 'confessional ambiguity' based on specific geopolitical, histori-

cal and social contexts. For a well-articulated discussion on this topic, see Yıldırım, 'Sunni Orthodoxy vs. Shi'ite Heterodoxy?' Yıldırım further shows that among many inhabitants of medieval Anatolia, the term 'Sunni' actually meant someone with a profound love and admiration for the Prophet's family, rather than having anti-Shiite tendencies; Yıldırım, 'Shiitization of the Futuwwa Tradition', p. 60.

13. Arjomand, *The Shadow of God*, p. 78.
14. While the reason for the Ottomans' payments to the Safaviyya order is unknown, we can speculate that the sultan's affinity for the order, or his desire to patronise a newly emerged religio-political movement was the main motivation. Anatolia was not yet under full Ottoman control when Junayd was the leader of the order, and it is probable that the Ottomans saw the Safaviyya order as a buffer against the kingdom of Trabzon, the Mamluks, the Karamanids and the Isfendiyaroğulları, among others.
15. For instance, in his famous work *Müzekki'n-nüfûs*, Eşrefoğlu Rûmî (d. 1469), the founder of the Eşrefiye branch of the Kadiri Sufi order in Anatolia, on multiple occasions referred to Shaykh Safi's sayings and counted him among the greatest names in Sufism. Eşrefoğlu Rûmî, *Müzekki'n-nüfûs*, pp. 179, 303, 382, 478. Even in the following centuries, pre-Junayd leaders of the Safaviyya order were considered as revered religious figures. Scherberger, 'The Confrontation', p. 51.
16. Neşri, *Kitāb-ı Cihan-nümā*.
17. *Aşıkpaşazade Tarihi*, p. 332.
18. Ibid.
19. For further discussions on Aşıkpaşazade's biography and the speculation on the year of his death, see Atsız, *Osmanlı Tarihleri I*; Babinger, *Osmanlı Tarih Yazarları*; İnalcık, 'How to Read', pp. 139–56.
20. Şahin and Emecen, *II. Bayezid Dönemine*, Order Nos 27, 71, 111, 281, 453, 454.
21. For instance, Lūtfi Paşa in his *Tevarih-i Ali Osman* narrated that when Bayezid II left his throne to his son, he uttered '*Kızılbaştan ehl-i İslamın intikāmını alıveresin*'. However, one should not forget the fact that Lūtfi Paşa wrote his account in the 1550s, way after the direct connection between the 'heretic subjects of the empire' and the term *Kızılbaş* was established. Tansel, *Yavuz Sultan Selim*, p. 31, fn. 40.
22. Topkapı Palace Archive, Doc. No. 3192, cited in Tansel, *Yavuz Sultan Selim*, pp. 20–2.
23. Ibid., pp. 27–8.
24. For a well-rounded discussion on the use of fatwa and its role at the creation of an Ottoman legal invention (*tajdīd-i īmān*) in the sixteenth century, see Burak, 'Faith, Law and Empire', pp. 1–23.
25. Tansel, *Yavuz Sultan Selim*, p. 35 (added emphasis), translated by Scherberger, 'The Confrontation', pp. 54–5. While Tansel noted that the document was written during the *Şahkulu* Rebellion (1510–11), Atçıl argues that the content

of the document indicates a later period, probably right before the Battle of Chaldiran and after the military camp of Fil Çayırı in 1514. Atçıl, 'The Safavid Threat', pp. 298–301.
26. Kemalpaşazade, *Tevārih-i Ali Osman*, IX. Defter, No. 2447, verses 123b–125b, cited in Dalkıran, 'İran Safavi Devletini', p. 78 (added emphasis).
27. Alleged gullibility or vulnerability of the Ottoman *Kızılbaş* was insinuated in numerous other Ottoman sources, as well. For instrance, a *tahrir* registry from 1515 mentions how the locals in Trabzon were obeying the Safavids out of necessity (*zaruri*). BOA TD, No. 52, cited in Sadullah Gülten, 'Some Considerations on Usage of the Word Alawite in the Ottoman State', p. 35.
28. These territories include, among others, Erzincan and Azerbaijan. Uğur, *The Reign of Sultan Selim*, pp. 101–4; Atçıl, 'The Safavid Threat', p. 302.
29. One should not forget that while the Safavid shahs were Shiites, the Shiitisation of Iran was not completed up until the end of the sixteenth century.
30. Dalsar, *Türk Sanayi ve Ticaret*, pp. 166–236.
31. For a discussion on the nature and the limits of Ottoman pragmatism, see Dağlı, 'The Limits of Ottoman Pragmatism', pp. 194–213.
32. For further details on pro-Safavid propaganda in early Ottoman realm, see Baltacıoğlu-Brammer, 'Safavid Conversion Propaganda'.
33. '... ömrinde tīmār yimeyen, diyārinda kimse kendüye ādem dimeyen bī-kārlar tümen begleri olub, hadden ziyāde i'tibār buldılar ... Yurdun terk idüb, çiftin çubuğun tāġıtdı, evin ocaġın yıkdı, yakdı ḫarāb itdi. 'Anda varan begler olurmuş' diyü ẕikr olan ṭā'ife-i ḫalife ḳalanları daḫi kemān-ı intikām kurmuşlardı'. *Tevārih-i Al-i Osman, Defter VIII*, published by Uğur in his *The Reign of Sultan Selim*, p. 43. Kemalpaşazade further adds that '... Sonra, Terākime'nün devri āhir oldu; mülkün bedeninde Kızılbaş zahir oldu ... elin uzatmaduk yir komadı', ibid., p. 33.
34. Minorsky, 'Shaykh Bali-Efendi', pp. 441–8.
35. 'Now, my son ... the requirement ... is that it is necessary to defeat by the sword and to destroy by force (*qahr*) that tribe [the *Kızılbaş*], its great and its small (*ulusuni kiçkisini*), its property and women, with the exception of the children (*sibyan*). There is no other way, for it is impossible to reform (*ıslāh*) this tribe by kindness and mercy.' Cited in ibid., p. 445.
36. Atçıl, 'The Safavid Threat', pp. 298–300; Tansel, *Yavuz Sultan Selim*, pp. 364–9.
37. Süleymaniye Manuscript Library, Özel Collection, Doc. No. 626.
38. Ibid. I would like to thank Ahmet Yusuf Yüksek, who translated this specific *fatwa* for a graduate seminar assignment. The oft-cited version of the fatwa cited in Düzdağ's *Şeyhülislam Ebussuud Efendi Fetvaları*, has problematic transliterations from the original text to Turkish.
39. 'Ammā şehirlerde ve köylerde kendi ḥālinde ṣalāḥ üzre olub bunlar 'ıḳābından ve ef'ālinden tenezzüh üzerine olub ẓāhir ḥālleri dahi ṣıdḳlarına delālet eyleyen kimesneleriñ kendüleri ẓāhir olmayınca üzerlerine bunlarıñ

ahkamı ve 'uḳūbātı icrā olınmaz ve bu ṭā'ifeniñ ḳitāli sā'ir kefere ile ḳitālden ehemdir.' Ibid., 2v.

40. Stefan Winter cogently documents how a single fatwa issued in the mid-sixteenth century was invoked in the following decades for various conflicts between Shiite tribes of greater Syria historically called *Kızılbaş* even though their connections with the Safavid Empire was more ephemeral than steady like the Anatolian *Kızılbaş*. Winter, 'The *Kızılbaş* of Syria', pp. 171–83.
41. MD, vol. 33, No. 413 (8 Zilkade 985/16 January 1578).
42. For example, the Jews of Safed were ordered to relocate to Cyprus at the same time, but the decision was revoked after the governor of Safed complained. Heyd, *Ottoman Documents on Palestine*, pp. 167–8.
43. Winter, *The Shiites of Lebanon*, pp. 16–17.
44. An account from 1570, in which Istanbul asks the governor of Baghdad to find those *Kızılbaş* who were allegedly sending money to Yukarı Canib (i.e., Safavid Iran) as alms, presents a good example. In it, the Ottoman central authority also asks the governor to inquire about the nature of the communication between its *Kızılbaş* subjects and the Safavid *Kızılbaş* who came to the Ottoman realm to collect arms. Baltacıoğlu-Brammer, 'The Formation of *Kızılbaş* Communities', p. 37.
45. Baltacıoğlu-Brammer, 'Safavid Conversion Propaganda'.
46. Süleymaniye Manuscript Library, Özel Collection, No. 626.
47. An official decree from 1519, for instance, lists the names of *Kızılbaş* Ottomans who served in the shah's army in his campaign to Georgia. Topkapı Palace Archive, D. 5720 (926/1519), cited in Yıldırım, 'Turcomans between Two Empires', pp. 560–2.
48. MD, vol. 9, No. 230 (22 Şaban 977/29 January 1570).
49. MD, vol. 35, No. 816 (26 Şaban 986/28 October 1578).
50. MD, vol. 25, No. 1627 (17 Sefer 982/7 June 1574).
51. BOA, İbnülemin Tasnifi Maliye, File No. 11, Document No. 952 (1042/1632).
52. Gör Kızılbaşun halini / Zulme uzatdı elini / Tutmasun Osman ilini / Yetiş Gazi Hünkar yetiş … Ey Me'ālī aceb haldür / Kızılbaşun işi aldür / Şübhesüz kanı helaldür / Yetiş Gazi Hünkar yetiş. Ambros, *Candid Penstrokes*, p. 189.
53. Abu Husayn, 'The Shiites in Lebanon', pp. 112–14.
54. MD, vol. 14, No. 311 (14 Safer 978/18 July 1570); MD, vol. 14, No. 488 (12 Ramazan 978/7 February 1571); MD, vol. 58, No. 206 (17 Cemaziyelevvel 993/17 May 1585). For a similar situation, see MD, vol. 62, No. 27 (2 Sefer 995/11 January 1587).
55. For an example, see MD, vol. 2, No. 1841 (24 Safer 964/26 December 1556).
56. MD, vol. 67, No. 180 (21 Rebiülevvel 999/21 January 1591). With the Treaty of Constantinople, the Safavids recognised Ottoman sovereignty in most of the southern Caucasus (including Georgia, Dagestan and Azerbaijan). One of the most important articles of the treaty, however, was about preventing migration between the two empires. According to the treaty, each side was obliged to stop its subjects' migration to the neighbouring state. Moreover,

the Safavids agreed to cease official cursing of the first three caliphs, as well as the persecution of Sunnis in the Safavid realm. In return, the Ottomans agreed not to attack any *Kızılbaş* territory in either the Safavid or Ottoman domains. Kütükoğlu, *Osmanlı-Iran*, pp. 195–6.

57. For an example, see MD, vol. 60, No. 130 (993/1585).
58. Uzunçarşılı, *Osmanlı Tarihi*, pp. 283–4.
59. Winter, 'The *Kızılbaş* of Syria', pp. 176–8.
60. Even when the Ottomans and Safavids were at war, the Ottoman authorities dealt with 'trouble-making' *Kızılbaş* individuals in multi-faceted ways, executing those identified as agents (*halife*) of the Safavids or as converts, but subjecting others to surveillance, banishment and a variety of lesser forms of punishment. For further examples, see MD, vol. 30, No. 92 (28 Muharrem 985/17 April 1577) and MD, vol. 30, No. 488 (11 Ramazan 985/22 November 1577): 'Bozok beyi Çerkes beye ... Kızılbaşlıkla müttehem olan kimesneler ... şer ile teftiş olunup sābit olursa i'dām edilüp ... şer ile sābit olmayup lakin müttehem olduklarına ḳanā'at gelürse Kıbrıs'a sürülmeleri ...'
61. MD, vol. 3, No. 1295 (966–8/1558–60).
62. MD, vol. 3, No. 172 (10 Muharrem 967/12 October 1559), also cited in Savaş, *XVI. Asırda Anadolu'da Alevilik*, p. 183. Savaş, however, neglects the conclusion of the order, which clearly mentions a distinction between the two groups of *Kızılbaş* (*Işık ahalisi* in this particular order); instead, he presents this order as another example of straightforward Ottoman brutality against *Kızılbaş* subjects.
63. MD, vol. 29, Nos 488 and 489 (14 Zilkade 989/11 December 1581) and Nos 490, 491 and 500 (14 Zilhicce 989/9 January 1582); MD, vol. 31, No. 66 (28 Ramazan 985/8 December 1577). These orders, which were sent to the district governors of Dulkadir, Rum, Bozok and Baghdad, specifically ask local officials to find other excuses to carry out the punitive actions against those whose relationships with the Safavids were proven.
64. Imber, 'The Persecution of Ottoman Shiites'; Şener and Hezarfen, *Osmanlı Arşivinde*; Öz, *Alevilik ile İlgili Osmanlı Belgeleri*.
65. MD, vol. 1, Nos 70, 86 and 409 (961–2/1553–4); MD, vol. 10, No. 279 (979/1571); MD, vol. 12, Nos 822, 832 and 833; MD, vol. 63, No. 52 (23 Sefer 996/22 January 1588); BOA, Hatt-ı Hümayun, File No. 1654, Document No. 4 (1014/1605); BOA, Hatt-ı Hümayun, File No. 1446, Document No. 21 (1015/1606). MD, vol. 1, Nos 70, 86 and 409 (961–2/1553–4); MD, vol. 10, No. 279 (979/1571); MD, vol. 12, Nos 822, 832 and 833; MD, vol. 63, No. 52 (23 Sefer 996/22 January 1588); BOA, Hatt-ı Hümayun, File No. 1654, Document No. 4 (1014/1605); HHT, File No. 1446, Document No. 21 (1015/1606).
66. Çekelüm gün gibi sancağ ile şarka çeri / Kara toğrağa karalum kıralum *sürhseri* / İnmesün mülhid ile Rafizinin başından / Gürz ile tigumuzun zamme ile fethaları / Keselüm aslı ile şah-ı vücudunu hema / Uralum cümle teberrayiye tig u teberi. Çavuşoğlu, *Yahya Bey Divanı*, p. 41.

Ottoman Sunnism

67. Leşker ez taht-ı Sitanbul sūy-ı İran tahtem / *Sürh-ser* ra garka-ı hun-ı melamet sahtem. Akçay, 'Bir Propaganda Aracı', p. 204.
68. For further details, see Babayan, *Mystics, Monarchs, and Messiahs*; Babayan, 'The Safavid Synthesis', pp. 135–61; Abisaab, *Converting Persia*. Babayan argues that the tension between the spiritual landscape of Kızılbaş Islam and the newly adopted imperial religion, Imami Shiism, intensified in the seventeenth century, even though it had existed from the very beginning of Safavid rule. With the gradual establishment of Twelver Shiite dogma at the Safavid court, Kızılbaş belief became increasingly marginalised and was finally condemned as heresy. While Safavid conversion efforts continued in Anatolia in the following decades, imperial orders after the 1630s do not refer to them with the same frequency. Either the number of *halife*s sent to Anatolia by the Safavid central authority declined or the Ottoman central authority began to pay less attention to them.
69. Rudi Matthee cogently argues that the Treaty of Zuhab, signed in 1639, ended a century and a half of intermittent Safavid–Ottoman hostility and revitalised the Anatolian overland trade route, which was no longer threatened by warfare and commercial boycotts. Moreover, improving maritime contacts between the two empires, as well as the abolition of restrictions on travel and trade across Ottoman borders caused the *Kızılbaş* emirs of the Safavid court to lose leverage. Matthee, *The Politics of Trade*, pp. 75–85.
70. Dressler, 'Inventing Orthodoxy', pp. 151–73. On the other hand, a few sources show Safavid conversion activities continuing after the 1630s. In one document, Çeşmi Efendi, the qadi, or judge, of Constantinople in the late 1620s and the *kadıasker*, or supreme judge, of Anadolu for Sultan Murad IV (r. 1623–40), reports some *mülahide*, or heretics, living in Constantinople. While Çeşmi Efendi does not mention the word Safavid or *Kızılbaş* in his report, it is clear whom he means: 'When they were asked about their *mürşid* [spiritual guide], they all said Shah Abbas.' Moreover, Çeşmi Efendi, after mentioning that these 'heretics' recite the *mani*s, or couplets, of Shah Ismail Hatayi in their secret gatherings, ends his short report with prayers for their extermination. Minorsky, 'Shaykh Bali-Efendi', pp. 448–50.
71. Winter, 'The *Kızılbaş* of Syria', p. 181.
72. For an example, see the Ottoman chronicler Şemdanizade Süleyman Efendi (d. 1779)'s *Mür'i't-Tevarih* and his description of the events of 1730–5, which marked a military conflict between the Ottomans and Nader Shah (d. 1747), who brought an end to the Safavids when he emerged as the first ruler of the Afsharid Dynasty in Iran (r. 1736–96). Şem'dani-zade, *Mür'i't-Tevarih*.
73. Erginbaş, 'Problematizing Ottoman Sunnism,' p. 620.

4

Reappraising Ottoman Religiosity in the Last Decades of the Sixteenth Century: Mustafa Darir's *Siret* and its Alid Content

Vefa Erginbaş

Introduction

The past decade has witnessed a proliferation of studies on Ottoman religiosity.[1] These studies locate Ottoman religious culture in its domestic and international contexts and argue that the Ottoman state followed a path similar to its Habsburg and Safavid rivals in drawing confessional boundaries.[2] In this milieu of 'confessionalisation', the Ottomans, who traditionally adhered to the Sunni branch of Islam, solidified their Sunni identity vis-à-vis its political rivals. On the other hand, within the empire, through its close watch, deterrence and sometimes outright destruction of 'unorthodox/heretical' individuals and groups,[3] the Ottoman state apparatus became almost militantly Sunni from the early sixteenth century onward. The sixteenth century has therefore been identified as a watershed moment in this Sunnification campaign, as the Ottoman state had gone to extremes to deal with Safavid sympathisers in Anatolia by massacring them wherever they were found. Certain prominent members of the Ottoman ulema also participated in this effort by denouncing various sects and groups and legitimising their destruction with reference to Islamic law.[4] Moreover, in the seventeenth century, this trend of Sunnitisation gained new steam with the birth of populist and puritan movements, such as the *Kadızadelis*. This growing emphasis on uniformity and conformity led to the policing of public behaviour, building new mosques to demonstrate pious acts of patronage and patrolling the prayer attendance.[5] Furthermore, recent studies have examined Islamic catechisms that discuss proper religious behaviour, which were meant to educate the lay public, and had become widespread thanks to the efforts that aimed towards a popularisation of a 'Sunna-minded orthodoxy'.[6]

In contrast to this trend, in his final *magnum opus*, the late Shahab

Ottoman Sunnism

Ahmed presents a refreshing conceptualisation of Islam. To explain 'diversity in the unity' of Muslims, he introduces a concept he calls 'coherent contradiction'. Even though what he defined as the 'legal-supremacist' interpretation dominates the definitions and trajectory of religion, Islam, as Muslims experience it, has historically been much more complex than this conservative reading would us have believe. Throughout their history, Muslims produced a vibrant accompanying discourse alongside the legal and juristic texts, which had at times been at odds with the legalist one. Although we all tend to associate Islam with the law and various restrictions and prescriptions, Islam in its 'historical and human' form encompassed all these seemingly contradictory discourses.[7] I believe Ahmed's invigorating approach could help us understand Ottoman religiosity (or Sunnism). In the Ottoman case, an emphasis on the prescription of texts – shall we call it orthodoxy? – and how it was carried out by the state and various actors (such as the Ottoman *şeyhülislam* or *Kadızadeli* preachers) leave us with the impression that the one and only true Islam is the construction of Islam represented and propagated by the jurists and like-minded scholars. This increasing emphasis on Sunnification at the state and ulema level leaves us with little distinction with regard to what being a Sunni really meant in the broader Ottoman social context. A good analogy here would be associating modern Turkish Islam with what the Directorate of Religious Affairs (*Diyanet İşleri*) say or do, while ignoring the versions of Islam understood, represented and disseminated by the Sufi orders (*tarikat*) or religious communities (*cemaat*) and associated religious culture.[8]

A little-recognised fact about Sunnism, at least as the Ottomans had experienced it, was the strong *ahl-al-baytist* bent it incorporated. *Ahl-al-baytism* is defined as reverence among Sunnis towards the family of Muhammad and his descendants, including the Twelve Imams.[9] Traditionally, the most dominant form of Shiism is the Twelver version, in which the Twelve Imams are considered infallible and have absolute authority. They are the undisputed leaders of the Muslim community, and it is incumbent upon Muslims to obey them. Among the Sunnis, the fourth caliph Ali, and his sons Hasan and Husayn, along with his wife Fatima, are revered as the family of the Prophet, or *ahl-al-bayt*. Even though Sunnis could revere Ali and his descendants to an equal or even superior degree than Shiites, *ahl-al-baytism* is different than being openly Shiite. The *ahl-al-baytist* individual would continue to revere the first three caliphs, and would not necessarily accept various notions tied to the Shiite version of the imamate. Revering Ali has been integral to Sunni Islam as Ali was the legitimately recognised as fourth caliph, however, with the impact of cross-sectarian fertilisation in the Islamic world that came after the Mongol invasions[10] and the increasing role of Alid Sufism, *ahl-al-baytism* made great strides in Sunni communities. This tradition, which openly venerates *ahl al-bayt*, first manifested itself in the *futuwwah*[11] networks and various Sufi groups.[12] The early Ottoman Empire had also been influenced by this fertilisation, as we know very well how confessionally ambiguous the early Ottomans were.[13] Rıza Yıldırım has demonstrated more than once how in fourteenth- and fifteenth-century Anatolia, Sunnism carried heavy *ahl-al-baytist* notions; in fact, he argued that the very term 'Sunni' meant someone who was a follower of *ahl-al-bayt* in some of the sources from the fourteenth century.[14]

In this chapter, I will examine in detail what is arguably the most famous Turkish-language biography of the Prophet Muhammad ever circulated in the Ottoman Empire, with an emphasis on its sources, main themes and the role of Ali b. Abu Talib in it. This work is Mustafa Darir's[15] *Siretü'n-Nebī*, which is also known as *Tercümetü'z Żarir*.[16] Darir's work is one of the most significant cultural productions of the fourteenth century, and probably the earliest account of the Prophet Muhammad's life and the rise of Islam in Turkish. Darir's work has been studied either as an example of fourteenth-century Turkish literature,[17] or with reference to its illuminated version, commissioned by Sultan Murad III (r. 1574–95) and supplied with 814 miniatures.[18] Studies dealing with its importance as an archetype of medieval Turkish literature emphasise Darir's mastery of the Ottoman Turkish language and the work's usefulness for philological study. However, the majority of these studies of Darir's *Siret* concentrate on Murad III's sixteenth-century manuscript, whose study usually falls to the lot of art historians, who treat it as an artistic masterpiece demonstrating Ottoman refinement of the art of miniatures.[19] Neither the philological nor the art historical approach scrutinise the content of Darir's *Siret*.[20] However, a content-based analysis of the *Siret* offers us an opportunity to see what circulated in the Ottoman Empire about the life of Islam's founding Prophetic figure, along with his major companions and successors – and especially Ali b. Abu Talib. A critical analysis of the content of the work can thus demonstrate how Alid narratives influenced religious and cultural production in the Ottoman Empire, and how these narratives were received and reproduced in the Ottoman Sunni context. Even though this work was composed in the fourteenth century, this chapter situates it within its late sixteenth-century context because of its dissemination and popularisation during that time.

A Rumi in the Mamluk Palace

Mustafa Darir was neither an Ottoman nor a Mamluk subject, but his work played significant roles in the intellectual circles of both of these empires. While he does not specify his date of birth or ethno-regional origin directly in his works, one of the titles he uses suggests that he was somehow linked to the city of Erzurum, and was born in or near this town at the turn of the fourteenth century.[21] A close study of his language and vocabulary also suggests that he indeed grew up in eastern Anatolia. At the beginning of his *Siret*, he provides some information on his life immediately before he started compiling his work. In 779/1377, he recorded that he came to Egypt and joined the conversational circles of the Mamluk sultan al-Mansur Ali (r. 1377–81).[22] Mustafa was blind – hence, his nickname 'Ḍarīr' (ضریر)) – and he asserts at the beginning of his work that despite his blindness, his memory is sharp, his style is sweet and eloquent, his poetry is beautiful, and his prose is candid. He also claims that although his education is limited, his mind is flawless (*muḥkem*).[23] In the presence of the sultan, he told the stories of the Prophet Muhammad and his companions every night, and these conversations continued for five years.[24] Even though Arabic was the language of learning and instruction for educated Mamluks, they used Turkish in a secondary fashion for the edification and amusement of the Mamluk cadres.[25] When these gatherings came to an end, al-Mansur Ali urged him to write a biography of the Prophet Muhammad, as his style had impressed the sultan.

While he was in the Mamluk palace, he became acquainted with the mufti (jurisconsult), Akmal al-Din Muhammad b. Muhammad Mahmud al-Babirti (also known as al-Babarti or al-Bayburti).[26] Al- Babirti was one of the leading intellectuals of the Islamic world in the fourteenth century. Many early Ottoman intellectuals, including Ahmedi, the earliest author who composed a history of the Ottoman dynasty, studied with him when he was in Cairo.[27] His place of origin, Bayburt, a small town in the eastern Black Sea region, located a mere 90 miles northwest of Erzurum, suggests that the chief mufti was also a *Rūmī* or Anatolian. Darir may even have been accepted into the sultan's circle on the shaykh's recommendation. The ethno-regional alliance between the shaykh and Darir seems evident. Their bond also explains how Darir entered the inner circle of al-Mansur Ali and became one of his boon companions. Unfortunately for Darir, his patron's fate would go awry when he was dethroned by the Circassian Mamluks, led by Barquq (r. 1382–9, 1390–9), who became sultan in 784/1382. Darir's fate, which was certainly bound to that of his ally, Akmal al-Din, also seems to have taken a turn for the worse after Barquq was enthroned. The new sultan, at least at the beginning of his reign, did not favour the shaykh. In the same year, Darir moved to Anatolia and settled in the state of Karaman, one of the most powerful rivals of the Ottomans in the fourteenth century, and he wrote most of his works during his stay in the Karamanid emirate. He resided there until 1392, when he moved to Aleppo and became a client of Melik Çolpan, the Mamluk governor (*nā'ib*) of Aleppo, about whom we do not possess much information. Although Darir spent most of his time in Anatolia while he was writing his *Siret*, he ironically ended up presenting his work to Sultan Barquq. Indeed, the very first miniature in the sixteenth-century manuscript shows Mustafa Darir presenting his work to him.[28]

Mustafa Darir, as well as the fifteenth-century chroniclers Ahmedi and Enveri, are good examples of the intellectuals of the post-Saljukid Anatolian principalities (*beylik*). These intellectuals, who were mostly poets, freelanced their way through various principalities and sought their fortunes from different local dynasts. They presented their works to some of these leaders in the hope of earning a good living or reputation. In case they could not find what they were hoping for, they switched their alliances and became companions and clients of others.

One of the titles Darir used, 'el-Mevlevi', suggests that he joined the *Mevlevi* order at some point in his life. The Sufi order inspired by Mawlana Jalal al-Din Rumi (1207–73) had become one of the strongest and most prominent Sufi orders in Anatolia in the century following the death of Rumi, largely as a result of the efforts of Rumi's son Sultan Veled (d. 1312). Darir also uses many couplets from Rumi's *Mesnevi* in his *Siret*, showing his mastery of Rumi's work.

When he was working on the idea of writing his *Siret*, Darir consulted the aforementioned Akmal al-Dīn as to which of the earliest accounts of the Prophet's life to choose as the backbone of his *Siret*. The shaykh recommended that he choose Abu Hasan al-Bakri's *Sirāt* instead of Ibn Ishaq's (704–67) well-known account, as redacted by Ibn Hisham (d. 834). The shaykh argued that the *Sirāt* of Ibn Ishaq as redacted by Ibn Hisham was the work of a Qur'an commentator and included jargon that was difficult for uneducated people to understand. Al-Bakri's account, in contrast, was based on one source, and easier for the common people to comprehend.[29]

That being said, Mustafa Darir's work is actually a synthesis of Ibn Ishaq and al-Bakri's *Sirāt* works. However, he uses Ibn Ishaq somewhat sporadically throughout the work, and it is really al-Bakri's work that permeates the majority of his narrative. Thus, one could safely argue that Mustafa Darir's *Siret* is mostly a translation and re-telling of al-Bakri's work. It is therefore imperative to establish al-Bakri's identity and his influence in order to appraise Mustafa Darir's work accurately.

Al-Bakri: A Shiite Link?

Al-Bakri is one of the most intriguing personas of the medieval period, although his identity is shrouded in mystery and his very existence is debatable. His *Sirāṭ* was popular among the public but frequently condemned by the medieval giants of Islamic scholarship, including Ibn Kathir (1301–73), Ibn Hajar al-Asqalani (1372–1448) and others.[30] Even the exact title of his *Sirāṭ* is not clear, and no fully extant copy of it has been found to date. Surviving versions, which only includes the history of Muhammadan light and anecdotes from the life of Muhammad such as his marriage to Khadija, are known as *al-Anwār wa'l Misbah*,[31] and most copies of it date only from the seventeenth or eighteenth century.[32] Franz Rosenthal argues that al-Bakri did exist, even though medieval biographers consistently failed to mention him or his works.[33] Boaz Shoshan, in his study of popular culture in medieval Cairo, asserts that the elaborate titles of al-Bakri's works are products of later imaginations. He argues that al-Bakri belonged to the pre-*Sirāṭ* writers of the genre of *qiṣaṣ al-anbiyā*, or stories of the prophets, who might have influenced later and more professional *Sirāṭ* writers such as Ibn Ishaq (704–67), al-Waqidi (748–822) and Ibn Sa'd (784–845). These storytellers, he believes, played an important role in the dissemination of Islam and of the Prophet Muhammad's religious persona among rank-and-file Muslims.[34] Regardless, when Darir wrote his Turkish *Siret*, he definitely used a copy of al-Bakri's work; thus, al-Bakri, whether real or imaginary, was definitively known to Muslim intellectuals by the fourteenth century. It is true that Muslim biographers did not mention him until the thirteenth century when (mostly negative) references to him began to appear; it is thus possible that he lived at that time.[35]

A content analysis of Darir's *Siret*, which is not an exact translation of al-Bakri's *Sirāṭ* but a synthesis of his work with that of Ibn Ishaq,[36] suggests that al-Bakri's account is permeated with fabulous tales and fables, although there are parts that may be true that are shared across other *Sirāṭ* writers. A case in point is an account of one of the miracles that the Prophet Muhammad allegedly performed when he was a child. In this miracle, the Prophet saves his followers from persecution by an enemy by splitting a river so that the enemy could not cross in pursuit. This account appears in Darir's *Siret*, but not in that of Ibn Ishaq.[37] This story is clearly influenced by the Old Testament (and the Qur'anic) story of Moses parting the Red Sea. This, and many other stories included between al-Bakri's and

Darir's *Siret*, may have been fabricated at a later date to establish the signs of prophetic mission through various key tropes by showing Muhammad performing miracles even before he began receiving revelations.[38]

Both al-Bakri and Darir depict Jews as perennially attempting, often with demonic assistance, to destroy Muhammad's primordial light (*nūr-u Muhammedī*), which is supposed to have been transmitted from Adam to Muhammad over the course of many generations. Satan works with the Jewish elders to first prevent Hashim from getting married to Salma, and once the marriage is consummated, getting rid of their son Abdulmuttalib, who was Muhammad's grandfather. In contrast to the Jews, both authors depict the Christians in a somewhat more positive light. In one of the dreams, the Roman emperor sees, before the birth of Muhammad, an old and wise priest directing him to embrace the coming religion of Muhammad, which he believes will annul an already corrupted Christianity. The emperor at first refuses to accept this proposition, but he saw that the priest died before he could punish him and took this as a sign from God to convert to this religion prior to its emergence. Al-Bakri took a harsh stance towards the Jews, but a somewhat lenient approach towards the Christians. His approach must be related to the sectarian milieu from which he was writing. In this milieu, each religion competes to prove in a polemical sense the other's falseness and invalidity.[39]

For the purposes of this study, another aspect of al-Bakri and his *Sirāt* is important. In a few biographical accounts, along with Darir's *Siret*, al-Bakri is called *al-wā'idh al-Basrī*, 'the Basran preacher'. Basra was a town of mixed religio-political opinions; the Basrans sided with Ali b. Abu Talib in the Battle of Siffin in 657, in which Ali fought against Muawiya. In the eighth century CE, the rationalist Mu'tazilite theological school, to which Shiites eventually came to be incorporated, was developed in Basra by Wasil b. Ata, as was the mystical tradition of Hasan al-Basri.[40] Even though it is difficult to prove with certainty that al-Bakri was a Shiite, he was most definitely influenced by the Shiite notions and this, along with his fabrications, could explain the enmity of Sunni scholars of the medieval period towards him. Even though the surviving parts of al-Bakri's *Sirāt* lack explicit Shiite content, such as the vilification of the first three caliphs and various notions of the imamate, one should locate al-Bakri within the broader framework of confessional ambiguity that developed in the Islamic world right after the Mongol invasions. This confessional ambiguity was characterised by *tashayyu' hasan*, or a moderate inclination towards Shiism among the Sunnis of the medieval age. It seems that al-Bakri did capitalise on that sentiment in his various works and became possibly the most overt example of such cross-sectarian fertilisation.[41]

Primordial Light of Muhammad: Another Shiite Connection?

An additional reason for the popularity of al-Bakri's *Sirāṭ* among Shiite intellectuals, according to Shoshan, may have been its connection to the concept of a primordial *nūr-u Muhammadī*, or 'light of Muhammad',[42] a concept developed by the sixth Shiite imam, Jafar al-Sadiq (702–65). The concept of Muhammadan light seems to be based on a hadith in which Muhammad is said to report that when Adam was in between water and mud, or body and spirit in another version, his (Muhammad's) light was created. Even though Muhammad did not specify what he meant by this term, later authors developed a long list of genealogy that attempted to prove that the light of Muhammad was transmitted from one ancestor of Muhammad to another in a continuous fashion. In her study on devotional piety in Sunni Islam, Marion Holmes Katz argues that one of the two independent narratives regarding the primordial light of Muhammad was actually first seen in works composed in the tenth century. These narratives go back to Ka'ab b. Ahbar and Wahb b. Munabbih, the Jewish scholars of the Torah who lived during the era of the first caliphs after Muhammad's death; Ka'ab converted to Islam during the caliphate of Umar, while Wahb was born in Uthman's time.[43] Since the Genesis story in the Torah begins with God saying 'let there be light, and there was light' (Genesis 1:3), it may not be unreasonable to assume that the scholars of the Torah, who converted to Islam, first introduced this concept into Islamic scholarship. In this way, they sought to find ways to marry the teachings of the Torah with those of the Qur'an and Muhammad. Even though the history of the concept of the primordial light of Muhammad has been a convoluted one, it seems that the Shiites introduced this concept first, and they were also the ones who wrote most about it, although some Sunnis subsequently adopted it as well.[44] The most authoritative biography of Muhammad, Ibn Ishaq's *Sirāt*, includes the concept of Muhammadan light. However, medieval Sunni scholars such as al-Ghazzali and Ibn Taymiyya actually found it absurd to believe that Muhammad was created before his parents. Al-Ghazali argued that what was meant by this hadith was that God preconceived the creation of Muhammad at the beginning of the creation, just like an architect preconceives his building before he builds it.[45]

Ali b. Abu Talib: 'Lion of God' and 'Sword of Islam'

Another element with an appeal to Shiites would have been the dominant role of Ali b. Abu Talib in the narratives attributed to al-Bakri.[46] One of these works is about the *ghazawāt* of Ali b. Abu Talib against the king of the Huddam region in Yemen in 631. Muhammad dispatched Ali to Yemen to invite the Banu Nakha to Islam, and he gave him specific instructions to follow. This episode is narrated in al-Tabari's famous history[47] and mentioned in one hadith in Sahih al-Bukhari. This book of *ghazawāt* must be a legendary work on various heroic acts of Ali mainly inspired by Shiite folk narratives.

Even a cursory look at Darir's *Siret* demonstrates that both Ali and his father played an important role in the narrative. In one instance, a soothsayer named Satih summons Abdullah, the father of Muhammad, and Abu Talib, the father of Ali. He predicts that each of them will have a son; one would be a prophet, the other would be his deputy; one would bring a new law, the other would fulfil that law.[48] In a similar episode, a Christian priest foretells not only the coming of the Prophet Muhammad but also that of Ali.[49] These stories and many similar ones that Darir included in his *Siret* can be traced to the missing parts of al-Bakri's lost work.[50]

Many miracles surround Ali's birth just as they do Muhammad's. Ali's mother, who Darir identifies as 'Fatima' in his *Siret*, was unable to conceive children. This was because she was sacrificing gifts to Lat and Uzza, the Meccan deities. Muhammad warned her, and asked her to sacrifice to Allah instead, which she did. Afterwards, she saw a dream in which a sword turned into a beautiful face and then into a lion, which apparently represented her unborn son, Ali. Darir then intervened in the story with a poem about Ali, in which he stated that Ali's features were beyond description, and that his sword would serve as the banner of Muhammad's prophecy.[51] Four months into the pregnancy of Ali's mother, Muhammad visited her and asked her to give the child to him so that he could raise him. During her pregnancy, whenever she knelt to prostrate for the Meccan deities, the baby in her womb would not let her do that. When her pregnancy was over, Ali was born effortlessly and bloodlessly in the Kaba right next to the legendary Black Stone (*Hacer'ül Esved*).[52] Right after the baby was born, he was already prostrating. Not only was his birth miraculous but so was his conversion. Ali converted to Islam when he was eight years old, and completely of his own volition, so he would never be a polytheist.[53] Muhammad then raised Ali, as Ibn Ishaq also mentioned. When it was time for Ali to get married, he got Fatima as his bride, who had apparently rejected the best of the Meccans until she was married to Ali through divine guidance. Many miracles can be observed in Ali and Fatima's marriage, which is depicted by Darir (again with reference to al-Bakri) as a divine match like no other.[54]

Surely, Darir's work does include some anecdotes about the first three caliphs after Muhammad. However, none of the episodes about the other three caliphs include supernatural aspects or miracles. The narratives about Ali, on the other hand, are flooded with various miracles, and extraordinary things either happened to him or were shown by him. Even though Darir's work lacks the explicit Shiite content one would see in a similar work written around the same time by the Shiites, this special treatment of Ali, which one cannot see for the other caliphs, is a clear testament to the strong *ahl-al-baytism* in the work. Darir tells us that loving Ali is a near-obligatory thing to do for all Muslims because he is the imam of the believers and loving him would bring happiness in this and the next world. In the following poem, he attests that after Muhammad, Ali is the most superior among all the other creatures.[55] Many other poems glorify Ali as the ultimate heir to Muhammad.

Ali is not only a courageous hero who always protects Muhammad, but he is also an extremely smart one as the following illustrates: in one episode, Ali shrewdly displayed how the notables of Mecca lied to bring Muhammad and Ali into disrepute. Ali solved the puzzle by sending each of them out of the room and inviting them one by one and asking about the details to each of them in turn. Obviously, they could not effectively corroborate each other thereafter. They ended up being seen as disreputable thanks to the sheer genius of Ali.[56] After Muhammad's emigration to Medina, Muhammad sends Ali to Mecca to bring back his family, and the leaders of the Meccan opposition attempt many tricks to kill Ali, but in each of them Ali was able to beat them at their own game with his intelligence and bravery. In the end, he even defeats Satan, hiding in an idol, with a few verses from the Qur'an.[57] When the Meccans continue to pressure him and attack him with three hundred men, Ali gets the better of all of them.[58]

Ali as the Ghazi: Sirat in the Fashion of **Ghazawāt**

Another remarkable feature of Darir's *Siret* is the various *ghaza* narratives that he incorporates into Muhammad's biography. In the majority of these narratives, Ali emerges as the main protagonist. These sections remind one of similar *gazavātnāme* and *danişmendnāme* works, which became popular first during the Seljuq period and then during the first two centuries of Ottoman rule. If one remembers that Darir's *Siret* was principally a product of the late fourteenth century, it should not be surprising. His choice of Ali as the main ghazi figure should perhaps not be surprising because Ali is known to *Sirat* writers not only as Muhammad's chief aide, but also as someone famous for genuine military skills. Ali, in Darir's *Siret*, however, is a lot more imaginary hero than the picture that mainstream *Sirat* writers depict him as being. For example, on one occasion in Darir's *Siret*, he slays a gigantic serpent,[59] in another, he saves Muhammad's companions by slaying a lion and moving an unmovable stone obstructing their way.[60] In another of his expeditions, along with his few friends, he fights with a thousand men in an epic battle that lasts all night; a battle that is reminiscent Digenes Akritas, or the *Siret Dhu'l-Himma* epic cycle of the Arab–Byzantine–Turkish frontier zones.[61] In the end, he not only captures the fortress but also returns with enormous amounts of booty and slaves.[62] In an Achilles-like fashion, he defeats each and every enemy that he faces. Just like in other *ghaza* narratives, each of these *ghaza* expeditions is also about conversion. Ali repeatedly asks his opponents to convert to Islam, and upon their refusal, he either kills or enslaves them. Sometimes, they miraculously convert to Islam just by seeing Ali's face. Other *ghaza* stories include various adventures of *ghazi*s plundering newly conquered areas and seeking conversion. None other than the Angel Gabriel brings the good news of Ali to Muhammad after his conquests.[63] Some of Ali's battles, such as the one against Amr b. Abu Wu'ud, are also reported by mainstream *Sirāṭ* writers such as Ibn Ishaq, however, many others mentioned in Darir's *Siret*, that he mostly attributes to al-Bakri, seem to be the products of imagination.

What has been described above actually fits neatly into what Hagen calls the 'heroic age' of Turkish literature, and carries almost all of the characteristics of the productions of that age. In this time frame, which began in the fourteenth century and peaked in the fifteenth century, a good number of heroic (or epic?) narratives were written in Turkish. These narratives were meant to deliver an image of the past (i.e., in the form of a collective memory of a nomadic and freelance lifestyle) that would also be relevant and meaningful for the present. As Hagen puts it:

> Violent confrontation with an eternal enemy is at the heart of these heroic narratives – there is no end to raging battles, mortal combat, chopped-off heads, and spilt blood in these tales. The conflict with this enemy tends to be primeval, it does not seem to have an origin or a cause, and, despite the victories gained by the hero, it does not fundamentally change. When the hero ultimately dies – often in combat or otherwise at the hand of the enemy – the primeval confrontation is reverted to its previous stage. It is an important characteristic of these pseudo-historical epics, as we may call them, that they should cover the entire life span of the hero. However, between legends of childhood, and the exemplary death of the hero, the episodes are arranged in sessions, or cycles, which often do not have a chronological order, and can be expanded as the reciters or popular imagination see fit.
>
> The confrontation makes the hero's superiority, his heroism manifest.

> Throughout our range of texts, heroism is inherent in a person, announced at or before his birth; it is not acquired, and does not change over time. As we shall see heroism can manifest itself in many different ways, but the lack of fear and the confrontation with a technically or numerically superior adversary, be it an army, a dragon, or another hero, and victory by transcending the natural boundaries of human capability, are central. On the other hand, it seems to be of secondary importance if his superiority originates from his faith and just cause, his intelligence, a God-given supernatural strength, or any combination thereof. Heroism is, finally, a matter of the individual. Epics don't know collectivities as agents, every new turn of the plot is motivated by individuals (including some supernatural ones). Their good or evil character decides the course of events.[64]

According to Hagen, this heroic age came to an end when these popular narratives were set down in writing at the beginning of the sixteenth century. If this heroic age came to an end at the beginning of the sixteenth century, then, the choice of Darir's *Siret* by Murad III towards the end of the sixteenth century should not be about its tone that reflects the tensions of a frontier principality.

Reappraising Ottoman Religiosity at the End of the Sixteenth Century

As it is clear from the above account, Mustafa Darir's *Siret*, if not a form of openly Shiite propaganda, was still the work of someone who was inspired by Shiism. It is true, as Hagen argues, that Darir's *Siret* and similar works are representatives of a 'sacred trope' and they should be interpreted in the milieu in which they were written. However, we are concerned here not with the fourteenth century, when it was first recorded, but rather the sixteenth century, when it was popularised. I argue that the popularisation of this work at the end of the century is not aimed at preserving nostalgia about a nomadic past. The Ottoman intellectuals of this century were already producing sophisticated historical narratives devoid of heroic or epic characters or events. One could argue that they were even deliberately abstaining from those forms to create more urbane pieces. Mustafa Ali and Hoca Sadeddin's histories are testaments to that effect. Therefore, the popularisation of this work by Murad III is an anomaly in an age in which more sophisticated forms of literature, as well as more mainstream religious narratives, were coming to be increasingly valorised. I contend that it has a good deal to do with its specifically Alid content.

Ali figures in the narrative as a hero with supernatural qualities on a par with Muhammad. It is in the explicitly Shiite works that one usually finds similar stories. These stories depict Ali as a supernatural hero with an almost divine nature. While Darir mentions the other three caliphs with respect, Ali is the only one who appears to be sent by Muhammad on various military expeditions, and whose qualities were enumerated by none other than the Prophet himself. Darir's work, besides its clear references to Ibn Ishaq, was a recap of al-Bakri's now-lost *Sirāṭ*. This leaves us with the question of why, and how, a *Sirāṭ* of the Prophet Muhammad written by someone inspired by Shiite ideas and themes came to be adopted by the Ottoman Sultan Murad III and popularised in the centuries that followed. It is certainly true that Darir was not as concerned as a sixteenth-century Ottoman jurist might have been with the Shiite tendencies of a particular author; and obviously, al-Bakri's account is not simply Shiite propaganda since it speaks respectfully of the first three caliphs. Nevertheless, he depicts Abu Bakr merely as a companion and friend of Muhammad, whereas he depicts Ali almost like a virtual saint, in line with Shiite narratives. Still, why did Murad III, supposedly a strict Sunni, during whose term the Ottomans fought with the Safavids for a decade and a half, (1575–90) champion a work inspired by the account of al-Bakri, who could be argued as having Shiite sympathies?

Darir's account was written in simple Turkish and was intended to entertain with its mixture of poetry and prose, so Murad III may have had the goal of entertaining and educating his sons with this expensive project.[65] But it is likely that there would be additional reasons that went beyond this simple one in explaining his commissioning of the work. It is hard to pass definitive judgements on Murad III because of his seemingly contradictory actions, which, according to Mustafa Ali, emanated from his personality.[66] However, it should attract our attention that Murad III was a strong follower of a Sufi master, Şüca Dede,[67] who belonged to the *Şabaniyye*, a branch of the *Halveti* Sufi order. and John Curry successfully displays the complexity of this relationship, which cannot be boiled down to simple assertions. Even though the Sufi orders are adept at incorporating both Sunni and Shiite lineages and important religious personas in their *silsile*s, as it is also shown by John Curry on the *Halvetiyye* order,[68] the majority of Sufi orders trace their lineage back to Ali b. Abu Talib. Alid loyalty has been a prominent feature of Sufism since at least the thirteenth century, though of course this loyalty is not equivalent to them being all Shiite orders. Murad's dream accounts suggest that he may have had delusions of being a Mahdi-like figure. In a few dreams that he sought to have interpreted by his Sufi mentor Şüca Dede, Murad saw himself as being trans-humanised (*ḥulūl*) to Ali. Özgen Felek suggests that Murad aimed to claim governance over both Sunnis and Shiites by turning first into the Prophet Muhammad, and then to Ali, and then by referencing himself as the twelfth sultan of the Ottomans, akin to the twelfth Imam.[69] Ottoman–Safavid conflict did indeed force both states to clarify their religious standing mainly as a reaction to each other's policies, especially during the reigns of Ismail I and Selim I, and in the Ottoman case due to the encouragement of the growing Sunni ulema. However, political domination was at stake in this conflict rather than religious zealotry. Some of Murad's views on Islamic esotericism, like the one about his *hulūl* to Ali, would have been called 'heretical' had they been uttered by someone else. Mustafa Ali, who was of course the least sympathetic to Murad among his contemporaries, calls Murad III's mentor Şüca a heretic and accuses him of 'violating the unity of God (*tevhid*)', in this case by putting himself in place of God.

Other evidence that demonstrates strong Alid loyalty in Murad III is a poem he wrote right before he went on one campaign. In this poem, Murad evoked the martyrs in Karbala, and asked for God's help for the sake of those martyrs. Further research would be required to determine if this kind of evocation was common among Ottoman sultans, but in Murad III's case it shows his strong devotion the *ahl-al-bayt*. Consequently, it did not seem so problematic to Murad to sponsor and popularise Darir's *Siret*, a work with clear Shiite overtones. Since Darir's work lacked explicit Shiite content, it must have been even more convenient for Murad to do so.

Darir's *Siret* and its popularisation at the end of the sixteenth century is a clear testament to the strong *ahl-al-baytism* that was prevalent in the Ottoman Empire. The Ottomans are often depicted as Sunni zealots; however, this blanket view blinds us from seeing what this Sunnism really entailed. Moderate inclination towards Shiism made great strides in the Islamic world beginning in the thirteenth century. *Ahl-al-baytist* notions, and even extreme Shiite views and interpretations, which were already prevalent in fourteenth- and fifteenth-century Ottoman domains, continued to exercise influence in the sixteenth century not only on the people at large but even on the sultans. Even though they made every effort to be seen as officially Sunni, the Ottomans demonstrated a continuing connection with this influence, while in Safavid Iran this form of religious eclecticism paved the way for the official adoption of Shiism.[70] Darir's *Siret*, among many other works, shows that *ahl-al-baytism* continued to be a major cultural and religious force towards the end of the sixteenth century.

Notes

1. Burak, *The Second Formation of Islamic Law*; Burak, 'Faith, Law and Empire', pp. 1–23; Terzioğlu, 'How to Conceptualize Ottoman Sunnitization', pp. 301–38; Dressler, 'Inventing Orthodoxy', pp. 151–73; al-Tikriti, 'Kalam in the Service of State,' pp. 131–49.
2. See Krstić, 'Illuminated by the Light,' pp. 35–63; Krstić, *Contested Conversions*; Pfeiffer, 'Confessional Polarization', pp. 15–55.
3. Imber, 'The Persecution of Ottoman Shiites', pp. 245–73; Ocak, *Osmanlı Toplumunda Zındıklar ve Mülhidler*, pp. 348–54; Zarinebaf-Shahr, 'Kızılbaş "Heresy"', pp. 1–15.
4. Öçal, *Kemal Paşazade'nin Felsefi*, pp. 375–415; Düzdağ, *Şeyhülislam Ebussuud Efendi*. In a recent article, Atçıl challenges the view that all the jurists in the sixteenth century were merely serving government interests in their rulings against the Kızılbaş and the Safavids; he argues that, for example, Ebusssuud relied heavily on previous juristic authority rather than political impulses. Atçıl, 'The Safavid Threat', pp. 295–314.
5. Based on architectural and textual evidence, Necipoğlu presents a strong case for this in *The Age of Sinan*, pp. 27–71.
6. Terzioğlu, 'Where İlm-i Ḥāl Meets Catechism', pp. 79–114; Krstić, 'From *Shahāda* to '*Aqīda*', pp. 296–314; Krstić, 'State and Religion, "Sunnitization"'.
7. See Ahmed, *What is Islam?* For an analysis of the book, see my review of the book in the *Journal of Ottoman and Turkish Studies Association*.
8. James Grehan in his *Twilight of the Saints* demonstrates that much of seventeenth to nineteenth-century activity and praxis in the Arab provinces of the Ottoman Empire had stronger roots in popular rituals and festivals than anything sanctioned by the scholarly elite.
9. I owe this term to McChesney, *Waqf in Central Asia*, pp. 33–4, 268–9.
10. For this phenomenon, which is also called 'confessional ambiguity', see Woods, *The Aqquyunlu*, pp. 4–5; Amoretti, 'Religion in the Timurid and Safavid Periods,' pp. 610–55. Judith Pfeiffer argues that this confessional ambiguity cannot be generalised to each and every area of the Islamicate world. She argues that the Shiites under the Ilkhanate actually used the coming of the Mongols to further solidify their positions and confessional standing. Pfeiffer, 'Confessional Ambiguity', pp. 129–68; Morimoto, 'How to Behave toward *Sayyid*s and *Sharif*s', p. 17.
11. Ali b. Abu Talib is indeed the spiritual leader of the *futuwwah*. He is the ideal youth, 'fatā'. Various *Fütüvvetname*s carry a very strong Shiite influence. See Breebaart and Chakrabarti, 'The Fütüvvet-nāme-i kebīr', pp. 203–15; Loewen, 'Proper Conduct (Adab) is Everything', pp. 543–70; also see Yıldırım, 'Shiitization of the Futuwwa Tradition'.
12. More than forty years ago, B. G. Martin argued that if *Halvetiye* was not forced to adopt a Sunni attitude by the Ottoman ulama, they could have easily ended up being a Shiite *tariqa* given their early attachment to Shiism.

Martin, 'A Short History', p. 284; in a recent appraisal of the Halveti order in the Ottoman Empire, John Curry opposes Martin's argument: 'In the end, the inclusion of the six imams of the Shi'ite tradition in the constructed identity of the Halveti silsile need not be taken as decisive proof of crypto-Shi'ism.' Curry, *The Transformation of Muslim Mystical Thought*, p. 25. For an excellent treatment of the relationship between Shiism and Sufism, see Nasr, 'Shi'ism and Sufism'.
13. Kafadar, *Between Two Worlds*, p. 76.
14. Yıldırım, 'Beylikler Dünyasında Kerbela', pp. 344–72; Yıldırım, 'Anadolu'da İslāmiyet: Gaziler Çağında', pp. 93–124.
15. His full name was Mustafa b. Yusuf b. Ömer el-Mevlevi el-Erzen el-Rumi.
16. Manuscripts of this work are housed in various libraries throughout the world. Mustafa Erkan mentions fifty-two copies of the various volumes and miniatures of the work. For a comprehensive list of these manuscripts and their locations, see Erkan, 'Siretü'n Nebi (Tercümetü'ż Żarir)', XXII–LIV. In this study, I utilised Topkapı Palace Library MS Koğuşlar 1001, as transcribed by Mustafa Erkan in his dissertation, and the six-volume modern Turkish rendition by Gürtunca, *Siyer-i Nebi*. One could also benefit from the textual history discussion by Gottfried Hagen, in which he introduced and expanded upon the manuscripts of Darir's work kept in German libraries. Hagen argued for the possibility of many versions of the work composed by Darir. Hagen is also the only author who engaged in a closer reading of the contents of the work, see Hagen, 'Some Considerations', pp. 323–37.
17. Mustafa Erkan's doctoral thesis ('Siretü'n Nebi (Tercümetü'ż Żarir)'), and many other theses produced in Turkish universities are good examples of literary studies of Darir's work.
18. Good examples of pictorial reading of Darir's *Siret* are Fisher, 'The Pictorial Cycle'; Fisher, 'A Reconstruction of the Pictorial', pp. 75–94; Tanındı, *Siyer-i Nebi*.
19. See note 18, above.
20. Partial references to its content can be found in Hagen, 'Some Considerations'.
21. For Darir's biography, see Erkan, 'Darir', pp. 498–9.
22. The page numbers refer to the first volume of the Topkapı Palace Library manuscript (MS Koğuşlar 1001), which is transcribed and presented with a glossary and index by Erkan. Darir, *Siret*, 5b.
23. Darir, *Siret*, 6b.
24. Darir, *Siret*, 6b.
25. Flemming, 'Literary Activities in Mamluk Halls', p. 251.
26. For Babirti, see Aytekin, 'Bābertī, pp. 377–8.
27. Lewis, 'Ahmadi, ' pp. 299–300.
28. For a complete list of the miniatures in various volumes of Darir's *Siret*, see the end of Tanındı, *Siyer-i Nebi* (no page number).
29. Darir, *Siret*, 7a.
30. Shoshan, *Popular Culture in Medieval Cairo*, p. 23.

31. Abi al-Hasan bin 'Abdullah al-Bakri, *Al-Anwār fī mawlid*; al-Bakri, *Al-Anwār wa-maṣbāḥ*.
32. Rosenthal, 'Al-Bakri', pp. 964–5.
33. Shoshan, *Popular Culture in Medieval Cairo*, p. 36.
34. Ibid., p. 37.
35. The sources of al-Bakri's *Sirāṭ* further complicate his identity largely because he relied on two controversial figures of hadith literature: Ka'b al-Akhbar and Wahb b. Munabbih. Ka'b al-Akhbar was a former rabbi who converted to Islam during the caliphate of 'Umar. He was accused of attempting to incorporate Jewish elements into Islamic tradition. Wahb b. Munabbih was born during the reign of Caliph 'Uthmān (644–56) and was also well read in Jewish tradition, which he specifically attempted to incorporate into Qur'anic exegesis even though he was not a Jew himself. Although they reported hadith from reliable sources, and were mostly considered trustworthy by Islamic scholars, these two figures were considered suspect by Sunni and Shiite authorities alike in some cases. Since al-Bakri's account is not extant today, it is hard to establish in which instances he used them. For Ka'b al-Ahbar, see Schmitz, 'Ka'b al-Ahbar', pp. 316–17; Kandemir, 'Ka'b el-Ahbar', pp. 1–3. Tabari mentions him in regard to his famous prediction for Caliph 'Umar's death, *The History of al-Tabari*, vol. 14, pp. 90–2. For Wahb b. Munabbih, see Khoury, 'Wahb b. Munabbih', pp. 34–6. Demir and Özafşar, 'Vehb bin Münebbih', pp. 608–10.
36. Ibn Ishaq, *Sirāṭ Rasūl Allāh*.
37. Darir, *Siret*, 193b.
38. See Rubin, *The Eye of the Beholder*.
39. Examples of similar situations can be found in other parts of the text. The figure known as 'Abu Jahl' to Muslim authors was one of the leaders of the Meccan opposition to Muhammad. He belonged to the same tribe as Muhammad, and opposed his mission from early on. He was killed in the Battle of Badr, in which the Meccans fought against the Muslim forces in 625 CE. The claim that Abu Jahl opposed Muhammad from his birth implied that Muhammad knew that he was going to become a prophet, which is information that is not included in the more mainstream *Sirāṭ*s. The additions of a sectarian nature, as well as the presentation of polytheist figures like Abu Jahl as Muhammad's enemy from before Muhammad's birth, suggest the later and mostly fabricated nature of al-Bakri's account.
40. Pellat, 'al-Baṣra'.
41. See the following works for references to such confessional ambiguity: Morimoto, 'How to Behave toward *Sayyid*s and *Sharif*'s'; Woods, *The Aqquyunlu*; Amoretti, 'Religion in the Timurid and Safavid Periods,' pp. 610–55; McChesney, *Waqf in Central Asia*. It seems that not only in the medieval but also pre-modern period, al-Bakri's work was used by Shiites as an inspirational source. Shoshan observes that the famous seventeenth-century Twelver Shiite scholar Muhammad Baqir al-Majlisi (1616–98) used

al-Bakri's account extensively, even suggesting that it be read during celebrations of the Prophet's birthday (*mawlid*). Even though al-Majlisi confused al-Bakri with a sixteenth-century scholar of the same name, the work that he recommended to the Shiite ulema is al-Bakri's *Sirāṭ*.

42. For this phenomenon, see Uri Rubin's seminal article on the subject, 'Pre-existence and Light', pp. 62–119. A more concise version by the same author can be found in 'Nur Muhammadi', p. 125. For a more recent and extensive treatment of the primordial light of Muhammad, see Katz, *The Birth of the Prophet*, pp. 12–29.
43. Katz, *The Birth of the Prophet*, pp. 16–24.
44. Ibid., p. 13.
45. Ibid., p. 14.
46. Shoshan, *Popular Culture in Medieval Cairo*, p. 38. For a fairly comprehensive list of these works, which are in various fragments, see ibid., endnote 13, pp. 97–9. Per Shoshan summaries of some of these works can be found in Paret, *Die Legendare Maghazi-Literatur*.
47. Al-Tabari, *The History of al-Tabari*, vol. 9, p. 89.
48. Darir, *Siret*, 67a. About Satih, see, Katz, *The Birth of the Prophet*, pp. 39–41; Ibn Ishaq, *Sīrāṭ Rasūl Allāh*, p. 4.
49. Darir, *Siret*, 205a.
50. Ibn Ishaq mentions only one such incident, and it is related not to Ali but to Muhammad: 'Yahya b. 'Abbad b. 'Abdullah b. al-Zubayr told me that his father told him that there was a man of Lihb who was a seer. Whenever he came to Mecca the Quraysh used to bring their boys to him so that he could look at them and tell their fortunes. So Abū Tālib brought him [Muhammad] along with the others when he was still a boy. The seer looked at him and then something claimed his attention. That disposed of he cried, "Bring me that boy." When Abū Tālib saw his eagerness he hid from him and the seer began to say, "Woe to you, bring me that boy I saw just now, for by Allāh he has a great future." But Abū Tālib went away.' Ibn Ishaq, *Sīrāṭ Rasūl Allāh*, p. 79.
51. Darir (Gürtunca ed.), vol. 1, pp. 568–9.
52. When they were looking for a name for the baby boy, his mother suggested Abu Turab (the father of the dirt) because he was born into the soil all by himself. This incident shows how much al-Bakri's and thus Darir's work altered the original narratives about Muhammad and Ali. In reality, Ali would be named Abu Turab by Muhammad only later, when he was sleeping in the mosque and her face was dirtied by the soil, not when he was born.
53. Dairir (Gürtunca ed.), vol. 1, pp. 626–7.
54. Ibid., vol. 2, pp. 570–600.
55. Ibid., vol. 1, pp. 566–7.
56. Ibid., vol. 2, pp. 491–7.
57. Ibid., vol. 2, pp. 488–501.
58. Ibid., vol. 2, pp. 501–5.
59. Oya Pancaroğlu traces the history of the dragon-slaying saint back to early

Christian narratives about saints. In twelfth-century Anatolia, it seems that similar narratives were adopted by Muslims, as they are reflected in various visual artefacts, as well as epics. Pancaroğlu, 'The Itinerant Dragon-Slayer', pp. 151–64. Also see Ocak, *Kültür Tarihi Kaynağı Olarak*.
60. Darir (Gürtunca ed.), vol. 3, pp. 366–9.
61. Yorgos Dedes.
62. Darir (Gürtunca ed.), vol. 3, p. 371.
63. Ibid., vol. 3, p. 388.
64. Hagen, 'Heroes and Saints', pp. 351–2.
65. The illuminated sixteenth-century manuscript, prepared in the royal workshops, cost more than 300,000 piasters, a remarkable sum for a book. The project itself clearly was meant to boost Murad's image as a patron of the arts and sponsor of religious literature.
66. For Mustafa Ali's treatment of Murad III's reign, see Fleischer, *Bureaucrat and Intellectual*, pp. 293–307. For a short though outdated biography of Murad III, see De Groot, 'Murad III', pp. 595–7.
67. Mustafa Ali's biography of him provides a contemporary account of his life: he recounts that he was originally drawn from an Albanian child-levy (*acemi oğlanı*), who worked as a gardener in notable people's houses. Upon his correct interpretation of Murad's dream that he would ascend the throne shortly, he became Murad's closest companion and Sufi master. Ali accused Şüca of being of lowly origin, greedy and guilty of illicit sexuality, among other accusations. He also implicitly accused Murad of blindly obeying him despite these faults. See Çerçi, *Mustafa Ali'nin Künhü'l Ahbar'ında*, pp. 245–9. John Curry's 2012 study stands as the most significant scholarly assessment of the relationship between Şüca and Murad III: Curry, 'The Meeting of the Two Sultans', pp. 223–43. See also Curry, *Transformation of Muslim Mystical Thought*, pp. 76–7.
68. Curry, *Transformation of Muslim Mystical Thought*, pp. 24–8.
69. Felek, '(Re)creating Image and Identity', p. 264.
70. Arjomand, 'Religious Extremism', pp. 29–32.

5

Confessionalisation or a Quest for Order? A Comparative Look at Religion and State in the Seventeenth-century Ottoman, Russian and Habsburg Empires

Yasir Yılmaz

From the beginning of the seventeenth century up to the 1680s, there were simultaneous disputes and collaboration between the courts of the Ottoman Empire, Russian tsardom and the Habsburg Monarchy on the one hand, and pietistic preachers, religious officials and patriarchs, on the other. At the centre of their struggles, there was seemingly a competition for influence over subjects about the correct forms of religious practice. In due course, all three contests over allegedly religious issues evolved into a struggle over wealth and power. In Istanbul and Moscow during the first half of the seventeenth century, pietistic Muslim and Orthodox Christian elements, *Kadızadeli*s and a group of reformist patriarchs, respectively, aimed to eradicate religious rites and rituals that they deemed heretical and pressured their courts to issue decrees regarding what was considered true Islamic or Orthodox Christian practice. There were parallels as well as discrepancies between the professed motives and actual intentions of these two religious groups and the essential qualities of the interplay between their most prominent figures and the ruling monarchs and courtiers. Yet the most significant commonality of the interaction between the *Kadızadeli*s and the Russian Orthodox patriarchs, on one side, and the Ottoman and Romanov courts, on the other, was that the outwardly spiritual struggle – and occasional cooperation – between them gradually transformed into a contest for dictating the rules of the land. Certainly, the imperial courts in Istanbul and Moscow and the clerical leaders in those capitals had symbiotic lives in one form or another until the reform movements of the nineteenth century. But the seemingly spiritual disputes between pietists and central courts contained significant non-religious ambitions. By the end of the seventeenth century, these developments would result in state hegemony over religion in Russia, whereas in the Ottoman Empire basic features of the coadjuvant relationship between religion and political power would not alter.

Confessionalisation or a Quest for Order?

In the Habsburg Monarchy, the nature of the challenge was essentially similar: an ostensibly spiritual struggle between the Catholic Habsburgs and Protestant princes across the Holy Roman Empire turned into open conflict in the Thirty Years War (1618–48). After 1648, the Habsburgs focused on their own domains and instrumentalised baroque art while reviving medieval forms of pietism to enhance their Catholicisation efforts. When compared with the Ottoman and Russian cases, the difference lay in the direct involvement of devout Habsburg emperors who carried the torch of proselytisation themselves: Ferdinand II, first as the archduke in Inner Austria (1595–1619), and then as emperor (1619–37), rose to prominence as a militant champion of the Catholic cause. The rule of Ferdinand III (1637–57) was, in general, more balanced due to the successes of Protestant forces in the final years of the Thirty Years War. But Leopold I (1658–1705) expanded and solidified Ferdinand II's achievements with a renewed pietism. The well-documented zealotry of ruling monarchs added an undisputable genuineness to the religious efforts of the Habsburgs. In its final stage, however, just as in the Ottoman and Russian cases, if the fierce rivalry between the Roman Catholic Habsburgs and Protestants was, on the surface, about spiritual matters, underneath it was a struggle for authority, power and wealth.

The following comparative analysis of the above three cases is undertaken in the spirit of a proposal by the Russianist Robert O. Crummey who noted that 'instead of cosmic exercises in historical comparisons', as done by sociologists, historians are 'by instinct and training better suited to a more modest, but no less challenging task, namely, the study of specific features of the institutional and social structure of two or more societies in order to determine how they are the same and in what ways they differ'. In a similar vein, the following analysis addresses the popular trend among Ottomanists to comparatively analyse the early modern Ottoman Empire within the framework of an assumed Mediterranean age of confessionalisation, which clearly goes against Crummey's astute observation.[1]

This study by no means rejects comparative methodology, which inspires new perspectives in historical research and helps us to understand how and why Ottoman, Russian and Habsburg states developed different strategies against characteristically comparable challenges throughout their existence. From an Ottoman historical point of view, our existing knowledge of the Ottoman world illustrates the existence of sophisticated links between the Ottoman world and Europe that transcended political and cultural borders; knowledge, individuals and goods have travelled with ease from one domain to the other in both directions. Only a comparative approach can help us understand that entangled history. What

I am questioning, through the following juxtaposition of three different seventeenth-century cases of state–religion interplay, is, first, the growing tendency in the field of Ottoman studies to research and write the empire's history as if it makes sense only within the broader context of European history and historiography. This attitude marginalises Ottoman history at the periphery of an external historiographical tradition. Second, I think that we should always consider the basic fact that parallels between histories of contemporaneous or neighbouring empires may not always be an indication of omnipresent factors propelling the histories of those empires in the same direction, which we can then collectively squeeze into one paradigm. In the seemingly religious disagreements about what constituted correct forms of religion, the primary concern of the Ottoman, Russian and Habsburg courts were the longevity of their empires and the preservation of order. Such matters do not and did not become a government's priority as a result of extraneous impetus or inspiration; throughout history, they have been inherent goals of any polity, embedded in and feeding into every initiative.

The Case of the Ottoman Empire

*Kadızadeli*s (lit. the followers of *Kadızade*) were a group of preachers named after Kadızade Mehmed Efendi (d. 1635).[2] The *Kadızadeli* movement, despite its far-reaching impact in the Ottoman capital, never amounted to an independent school of thought, nor did it gain an institutional character. The term '*Kadızadeli*s' is used to refer to those scholars and judges who held a certain interpretation of Islamic matters during the reigns of Murad IV (1623–40), Ibrahim (1640–8) and Mehmed IV (1648–87). During the seventeenth century, the *Kadızadeli*s exerted influence on Istanbul's population in three subsequent waves under the charismatic leadership of three preachers: Kadızade Mehmed himself, Üstüvani Mehmed from Damascus (d. 1661) and Mehmed b. Bistam of Van (known as 'Vani' Mehmed; d. 1685).

The rise of the *Kadızadeli*s took place within a specific historical context. Ottoman historians frequently reiterate that the late sixteenth and early seventeenth centuries of the empire were marked by social and political turmoil accompanied by institutional reform.[3] The protracted wars at the turn of the seventeenth century depleted the treasury and set the stage for social change and transformation. The inefficiency of the *sipāhi* cavalry in the wars against the Safavids (1578–90, 1603–18) and the Habsburgs (1593–1606) forced the Ottoman state to form new corps and recruit *levend*s (landless vagrant peasants of Anatolia) as mercenaries equipped with firearms. When not in service, these *levends* were mostly uncontrolled and soon began to terrorise the countryside. In response, the central government deployed newly recruited (and non-*devşirme* originated) Janissary corps in provinces for the protection of subjects against the *levends*. The process had two major consequences: first, in major Anatolian towns, the Janissary population increased and this eventually led to the urbanisation or 'civilisation' of the Janissaries who neglected their military duties and participated in local socio-economic life. This phenomenon has more recently attracted the interest of Ottomanists and is yet to be fully comprehended. The second impact of this change was in the capital and it was much more significant: selected Janissary officers served inside the palace as sultan's household troops and many of them held high offices.[4] In 1622, the 'Janissary junta' in the capital organised a coup which ended with the execution of Osman II.[5] Until 1656, the Janissaries would remain as the most influential clique in courtly politics.[6]

At a time of such social and political instability perpetuated by the lack of authoritative statesmen, the 'populism'[7] of *Kadızadeli* preachers and the influence they enjoyed on the population of Istanbul likely seemed a useful instrument to the court, which could exploit the preachers' charisma in the eyes of the population as an intermediary to reaffirm its control over the masses. Murad IV appears to have been the first sultan to employ *Kadızadeli*s for that purpose. The first nine years of Murad IV's reign appears to have been under the control of Murad's mother Kösem Sultan (1590–1651).[8] Nonetheless, *sipāhi* despots had become the actual disposers of state affairs. In the Ottoman land tenure system, the *sipāhi*s possessed privileges over tax collection across the empire and they had started to abuse those privileges by the first half of the seventeenth century. As their population increased unnecessarily, they also took over duties that did not belong to them, such as collecting tax from sultanic estates. In an effort to suppress *sipāhi* power, Murad issued a *fermān* (imperial decree) in spring 1632 and annulled the privileges of the *sipāhi*s in tax affairs. Upon hearing of the decree, the *sipāhi*s gathered in Hippodrome square by the Sultan Ahmed (Blue) Mosque. Murad IV reacted by gathering an *ayak divanı*, an emergency session of the imperial council with the ability to talk to the sultan directly and attended by all high-ranking statesmen and dignitaries as well as any plaintiff. The sultan's goal was to receive the support of all administrative and religious representatives. He openly criticised *sipāhi* leaders who were present at the meeting, and, in the end, he took written allegiance of the members of the *askerī* (Janissaries, statesmen and administrators), *kapıkulları* (sultan's household troops) and the ulema (scholars). Murad IV placed himself again at the head of the decision-making mechanism and restored the court's authority.[9] An important figure who was present at the emergency session was Kadızade Mehmed, who had been appointed a year earlier as the preacher at the Hagia Sophia, the imperial mosque situated next to the sultan's palace. He was a popular figure in the capital. Clearly, Murad IV, who wanted to secure support from all segments of Ottoman society, wanted to further elevate his public standing by having Kadızade Mehmed next to him. Thus, the sultan took advantage of the preacher's charismatic influence, leading to the establishment of a mutually beneficial relationship between the court and the followers of Kadızade.[10]

What were the origins of this group that enjoyed such close relations with the Ottoman sultan? The ideas promoted by the *Kadızadelis* had been expressed by other Muslim scholars before the seventeenth century, most recently in the Ottoman Empire by Birgivi Mehmed Efendi (d. 1573). Birgivi was born in Balıkesir; he later moved to Istanbul where he pursued a scholarly career before becoming a teacher in a small village in western Anatolia. Birgivi had rejected even the slightest innovation in religious matters. He argued, for instance, that it was by no means permissible to teach the Qur'an for money or to receive payment for any act of worship. Birgivi also harshly criticised the establishment of monetary foundations or endowments of cash to these foundations. He disagreed about this matter, for instance, with Ebussuud Efendi, the influential grand mufti (*şeyhülislam*) of Süleyman the Lawgiver (1520–66).[11] Birgivi's disapproval of such administrative and social practices did not make the impact he would have desired in his own lifetime. Yet, from the early decades of the seventeenth century, his ideas grew to span a wide group of orthodox preachers in the capital, and by the mid-seventeenth century, these orthodox preachers had established close relations with courtiers.

Kadızade Mehmed Efendi was the first among these preachers to establish such close connections with the court. Kadızade Mehmed was a fellow townsman of Birgivi; he was educated in Balıkesir by the learned disciples of the latter. By the time Kadızade Mehmed moved to Istanbul he was already a follower of Birgivi's ideas. Having decisively established his career as a religious instructor in the capital, he was promoted in 1631 – most likely under the auspices of Sultan Murad IV – as a preacher in the Hagia Sophia. Kadızade Mehmed and his disciples argued that the Islamic community had strayed from the path of the Prophet.[12] Inspired most recently by Birgivi, Kadızade and preachers following his ideas in the capital especially vindicated what they saw as innovation in religion (*bid'a*). Anything that was not mentioned in the Qur'an was an innovation for them: blessing another by saying 'God be pleased with him', chanting the Qur'an and the call to prayer with a musical tone, or the anniversary of the conception of Muhammad were all condemned by *Kadızadeli*s. These criticisms also translated into uncompromising attacks on Sufi mystics who danced, whirled and played music while focusing on inner dimensions of spirituality.[13] The *Kadızadeli*s' hard-line dismissal of Sufi mysticism was essentially a passionate re-emergence of a discord in Islamic history between 'holy law-defined orthodoxy and the methods and claims of Islamic mysticism'.[14] *Kadızadeli*s condemned singing, chanting, musical accompaniment, dancing, whirling and similar rhythmic movements, all practices often attributed to Sufis.[15] Allegedly, the ban on coffeehouses, taverns, tobacco and wine during the reign of Murad IV was partially or completely inspired by Kadızade Mehmed.[16]

*Kadızadeli*s and the Ottoman court became even closer during the life of another pietist preacher, Üstüvani Mehmed Efendi, whose rise to prominence among the population of the capital, as well as the courtiers, marked the second stage of the *Kadızadeli* campaign.[17] Üstüvani's first appointment in the capital was to the Hagia Sophia, where imperial courtiers, teachers and students of the boarding school inside the palace (*Enderūn*) and other servants working there were regular attendees at daily prayers. Through the mediation of these circles, Üstüvani gained a reputation in the court. Eventually, he cultivated such intimacy with Mehmed IV that ultimately he became the sultan's personal preacher in the Privy Chamber (*has oda*), gaining an unofficial status as *padişah şeyhi*, or the shaykh of the sultan.[18] In later years, Üstüvani also began to preach at other highly revered mosques in the capital, including the Sultan Ahmed and Fatih mosques. Once links to the highest echelons of the court were established, Üstüvani and his followers began to seek official approval of their ideas by the *şeyhülislam*. At least one Sufi lodge was shut down in the capital due to the efforts of *Kadızadeli*s, encouraging them to increase their pressure on the court – especially on the person of the grand mufti – for a general ban on Sufi activities as well as all religious practices that *Kadızadeli*s looked upon as innovation. After much effort to persuade the court, Üstüvani and the *Kadızadeli*s managed to have the sultan order a meeting among scholars to discuss the ideas of Birgivi Mehmed, whose adherence to Islamic orthodoxy had informed the *Kadızadeli* movement from the beginning. Although an imperial order eventually forbade criticism of Birgivi and condemned Sufi denominations, the appointment of Köprülü Mehmed Paşa (1656–61) to the grand vizierate marked the end of Üstüvani's halcyon days. Köprülü Mehmed Paşa was not an advocate of the Sufis, nor did he enjoy – as an old and stubborn loner – the support of any group or faction in the capital or inside the court. To the new grand vizier, the involvement of the *Kadızadeli*s in the capital-wide unrest in 1656 was a display of militancy that threatened the stability of the government. An extremely precarious political conjuncture in Istanbul forced the grand vizier to take firm precautions against the *Kadızadeli*s along with rebels in the capital. As armed *Kadızadeli* supporters marched towards the Fatih mosque, Köprülü had Üstüvani and his leading abettors banished to Cyprus.[19]

The relationship between the *Kadızadeli*s and the Ottoman court took a new turn with Köprülü Mehmed Paşa's death and the transfer of the sultan's seal to Köprülü's son, Fazıl Ahmed Paşa (1661–76). In September 1659, Ahmed Paşa was appointed the governor of Erzurum province. In Erzurum, he met Vani Mehmed, who was a resident scholar and preacher in the town, as well as a keen exponent of *Kadızadeli* ideas. Ahmed Paşa had spent his early years among men of letters – hence, the appellation '*Fāzıl*' (virtuous) – and he soon became an admirer of Vani Mehmed. Upon his appointment as grand vizier in November 1661, Fazıl Ahmed took Vani with him to Istanbul. Soon, like his *Kadızadeli* predecessors, Vani Mehmed gained the confidence of the sultan. As with previous *Kadızadeli* preachers, Vani Mehmed targeted Sufi practices, their hospices and followers. The bans on wine and tobacco were renewed and expanded. Vani even rejected long-standing Ottoman traditions such as communal prayers at times of plague and campaigns against Christian powers, eventually imposing his will on the latter issue against the grand mufti of the time. Vani Mehmed's close relations with Mehmed IV and Fazıl Ahmed Paşa marked the height of *Kadızadeli* influence, which lasted until the notorious Ottoman defeat before the walls of Vienna in 1683. Before the Vienna campaign, Grand Vizier Kara Mustafa Paşa had Vani Mehmed and a number of other preachers give sermons about the necessity and rightfulness of a campaign against Austria. Vani Mehmed personally participated in the Vienna campaign as the military chaplain and roamed through Ottoman trenches during the siege to lift soldiers' spirits.[20] At the end of the disastrous defeat on 12 September 1683, Vani faced the same denouement as Üstüvani Mehmed with banishment from the capital. He died in Bursa in 1685.[21]

Many other reasons justify questioning the actual scope of *Kadızadeli* influence on the processes of decision-making within the court. Although seventeenth-century Ottoman chroniclers argued that there existed a mutually beneficial relationship between *Kadızadeli* preachers, on the one hand, and the sultan, statesmen and courtiers, on the other, one cannot be certain that the statesmen and sultans had internalised *Kadızadeli* ideas. The fact that the *Kadızadeli* preachers inspired the closure of coffeehouses or the prohibition of tobacco does not directly suggest that statesmen were incorporating *Kadızadeli* ideas into all aspects of administrative affairs. Given that the movement's sphere of influence in the courtly processes of decision-making expanded only when charismatic preachers represented them is significant in that regard. The movement lost ground before the end of the seventeenth century. It is true that the *Kadızadeli* preachers instigated social turmoil. Yet whatever uproar they abetted was largely restricted to the capital; there are only a few existing records about *Kadızadeli*-inspired incidents, social unrest or violence outside Istanbul.[22] The evidence showing direct *Kadızadeli* influence on the actual decision-making mechanisms are likewise few and far between. *Kadızadeli* preachers were neither appointed as grand mufti nor served as *kadı*s (judge). These positions were usually occupied by the scholars who were trained in the capital and held professorial positions, whereas *Kadızadeli*s usually competed for preacher positions in mosques. Their provincial origins made *Kadızadeli*s in essence *ecnebī*s (outsiders/strangers), while the Sufi hospices in Istanbul, which had produced many grand muftis and qadis, had been founded a long time ago and operated under the protection of the Ottoman dynasty. In essence, the aggressive discourse of *Kadızadeli* preachers against widely practised rituals by Sufis and the public was also levelled at the court. *Kadızadeli*s harshly criticised the extravagance of courtiers and lavish assemblies among dignitaries. It should have been much easier for the masses to identify themselves with the ideas of spirited, dissident preachers to whom they could listen on a daily basis at major mosques than a commitment to the ideals of a dynasty and court lacking charismatic leadership. So how did *Kadızadeli*s manage to receive protection directly from sultans and grand viziers despite this dynamic? Given the flow of events, one realises that the Ottoman court did not principally advocate the ideas of the *Kadızadeli*s. The two parties developed a mutually beneficial relationship, the impact of which depended on the personalities of sultans and courtiers, on the one hand, and preachers, on the other. For the preachers, physical proximity to sultans and grand viziers was a means of exercising social influence; for the Ottoman court, the preachers were a middle ground to reach and control the crisis-afflicted masses in the absence of skilled leadership. Therefore, Köprülü Mehmed Paşa, who filled that administrative vacuum, was able to repress and exile prominent *Kadızadeli*s, because he lacked such concerns. In short, until the mid-seventeenth century, the *Kadızadeli*s functioned as a medium of social control and discipline in the capital; sultans and courtiers probably never articulated such a goal, but they clearly appreciated the influence *Kadızadeli*s enjoyed in the capital. When evaluated from such a perspective, the close relations between the *Kadızadeli* preachers and the

Russian Tsardom

During the decades in which the *Kadızadeli*s took advantage of social unrest to exert a limited influence in the Ottoman capital, there took place a fierce competition over who would rule the tsardom. According to the Russian tradition, keeping the tsar righteous was an obligation laid upon the people, inspired by the Christian ideas of compassion and righteous advice to rulers. Among the people, the clergy's responsibility was greatest. As a rule, the tsars, even the most authoritarian ones, respected this tradition. At the Council of a Hundred Chapters (*Stoglav*) in 1551, a meeting that solidified an alliance between the tsar and the church, Ivan IV asked the present members of the church hierarchy to speak out and assist him in unanimity.[23] In return for the guidance of the clergy, the tsars had a duty to protect the Christian faith and the Orthodox Church, as stated at Ivan IV's coronation by Makarii (Macarius), who had been the Metropolitan of Moscow since 1542. Yet the relationship between the tsars and the institution of the Church was not always as straightforward and harmonious as Ivan IV's later rule suggested.[24] Over the course of the late sixteenth and seventeenth centuries, the spiritual authority of the Russian Orthodox Church increasingly evolved into a quest for power and privileges outside the religious sphere, under the direction of ambitious patriarchs.

An important watershed in the eventual rise of patriarchs as a major power-house in Russian politics in the early seventeenth century was the establishment of the autocephalous Russian Patriarchate in 1589 during Boris Godunov's regency.[25] As the prime secular figure behind the establishment, Godunov set the pattern of the prospective partnership between future tsars and patriarchs. Godunov and his conciliar ambassadorial secretary A. Ia. Shchelkalov were the main negotiators with Patriarch Jeremiah of Constantinople, who had come to Russia to discuss the foundation of the patriarchate, and eventually agreed to the proposal under pressure. Boris Godunov's supporter Metropolitan Iov (1589–1606) became the first patriarch of the newly founded church. From that moment of rapprochement between the tsar and the church, the two entities increasingly depended upon each other. Godunov received the support of the clergy in his election in 1598 as the 'Tsar of All Russia' and relied on the clergy thereafter for the further legitimisation of his rule.[26] The so-called Time of Troubles (1603–13) that began with the appearance of the First False Dmitrii in Poland and continued with challenges to the crown by a series of impostors (who claimed to be the rightful heirs to the throne through lineage to the Riurikid dynasty that had died out in 1598) would have deep influence on the later history of the Muscovite Church. In the absence of a tsar, the patriarchs would be looked upon as unifying figures for the faithful masses. In the aftermath of the Time of Troubles, the Russian patriarchs maintained that status. Benefiting from this image, the leading seventeenth-century patriarchs, including Germogen (Hermogen, 1606–12), Filaret (1619–34), Nikon (1652–58 or 66) and Ioakim (1674–90), used their authority to restore the control of the Orthodox Church over the highly varied religious practices and understandings across the Russian landscape. More importantly, they also strived to maximise the radius of their influence in the political sphere. These efforts eventually brought the church into open conflict with the Russian court, and the confrontation would have significant consequences by the end of the century.[27]

Part of Patriarch Germogen's significance in seventeenth-century Russian history is in his spiritual and military leadership against the Polish occupation during the Time of Troubles. That the patriarch, a man of God, called the people to refuse and resist the crowning of a non-Orthodox ruler in Moscow 'by arms and also by faith' spurred a contemporary writer to discuss the morality of Germogen's involvement in the bloodshed. Such discussion in the early 1600s about the moral implications of a patriarch's actions was, in its own right, a precedent for further debates and reform initiatives by Orthodox clergy later in the century.[28] Germogen's bold manner and assertive guidance set an example for his successors, and Patriarch Filaret took Germogen's legacy even further. Filaret, a 'fully developed political figure to the historian', and formerly known as Fedor Nikitich Romanov, was the father of the first Romanov tsar, Mikhail Feodorovich (r. 1613–45).[29] Filaret was most likely the strongest candidate for the throne in 1613, but he was in Polish captivity at the time of the Assembly of the Land (*zemskii sobor*) that had elected his son Mikhail as tsar. Also, Filaret was previously tonsured against his will by order of Boris Godunov. According to the Eastern Orthodox tradition, once a person was tonsured and entered the ranks of the clergy, he could not occupy a secular office, even when he was formerly a courtier and politician as Filaret had been. Therefore, when he returned from Polish captivity in 1619, he occupied the seat of the patriarch, which had remained vacant for seven years after Germogen's death in 1612. Thereafter, Filaret and Mikhail, as father and son heading up the state and church alike, ruled Russia together 'for the first and last time in Russian history'.[30] Filaret was very influential in both spiritual and secular matters. He often acted like a de facto ruler and made decisions himself on issues, including even the reorganisation of the military. In a sense, he had his own autonomy within Russia. In the words of historian Robert Crummey, Filaret 'virtually made himself ruler of a separate principality within the realm, a precedent that the more ambitious of his successors eagerly followed'.

Yet in the post-Filaret seventeenth century, the impact of the church across the vast Russian geography would be limited. The huge distances translated into very large dioceses where parish priests and bishops were separated from each other. In order to overcome this problem in the second half of the seventeenth century, the patriarchs and priests in Russia sought ways for more effective communication with the people. The success of this policy would be mixed, however, as monasteries continued to enjoy more influence in a great portion of the periphery that remained outside the reach of central authorities. Only by the end of the seventeenth century would the trends come to favour the central authorities, but this did not occur before major developments came to transform the entire nature of church–state relations in Russia.

Filaret and his successors wanted to overcome the lack of coherence and consistency in the Russian religious landscape. Filaret's term in office concluded without any major flashpoints, but he had introduced new ideas. For example, he ruled that the ritual of baptism required triple immersion, instead of simply pouring water over the head.[31] These initiatives to reform Russian rites and rituals were essentially a product of the search for order. Mainstream Russian historiography maintains the view that with the crowning of Tsar Alexei Mikhailovich (r. 1645–76), reformers who were dissatisfied with the extensive variations in religious practices found a patron who supported them and their efforts to purify the Orthodox Church from popular forms of worship.

This quest for tsarist endorsement had remarkable parallels with the *Kadızadelis*' efforts to receive sultanic approval in the Ottoman Empire. More remarkable, however, was the overlap between the ideas of the *Kadızadelis* and a group of learned Russian churchmen who came to be known as the Zealots of Piety, and who played a key role at the beginning of the reform initiatives in the 1640s. The Zealots were against many popular practices in the Orthodox Church. They strongly disapproved of drinking and the use of tobacco by priests and deacons, along with all sorts of moral offences, folk beliefs and pagan practices. They rejected *mnogoglasie*, which was 'the practice of chanting up to "five or six" different parts of the service simultaneously' which was devised to shorten the duration of worship'.[32] They advocated a strict programme of reform to standardise the liturgy, which they thought was the key to revitalising the parish life. These spiritually-oriented goals, however, were not completely satisfying for one group of the Zealots, and it was here that the divergence between the *Kadızadeli*s and the ambitions of Russian reformists began. Tsar Alexei, his two close associates F. M. Rtishchev and Stefan Vonifat'ev, and Nikon, the Metropolitan of Novgorod and the future patriarch, wished to make the Russian Orthodox Church the highest authority in Eastern Christianity.[33] Aiming to realise both goals, the tsar began to issue a number of decrees in 1648 to officially initiate the reform movement. In 1649, as part of the *Ulozhenie* law code issued in that year, Tsar Alexei also founded the Monastery Chancellery (the predecessor of the Synod that would be established in 1721 by Peter the Great) and took a pivotal step towards the supremacy of the state over the Orthodox Church.[34]

Yet the reforms also marked the origins of what went into the history books as *raskol*, the Russian schism. The schism was a direct product of the increasingly imposed methods of reforms that Nikon implemented as patriarch after his appointment in 1652. Before assuming that position, Nikon stipulated that the tsar 'obey him in spiritual affairs and that he should have the same power and authority as his tsarist majesty's grandfather – Filaret Nikitich'.[35] The new patriarch was an ambitious reformer, but his ambitions were not limited to purging what he deemed to be folk religion and pagan practices from Russian spirituality. Following the footsteps of Filaret, he expanded the landholdings of the church, and he also worked to increase his personal power. He even aimed to place himself over the tsar in the ceremonial hierarchy. His foundational conviction was that the church leaders – not the tsar and secular elites – were the ultimate guardians of Russian spirituality.[36] Nikonian reforms disturbed many Russians, due to the patriarch's idea that the best way of revitalising the Russian Orthodoxy was to establish close relations with the ecumenical Eastern Orthodoxy and Greek Church. Moreover, he regarded the Greek Orthodox liturgy as more authentic than its Russian counterpart. In 1655, at a church council, he declared that he was a Greek in his convictions and faith. On one occasion, he even put on a Greek monastic cap before a congregation. Moreover, Nikon had Jesuit-trained advisers from Ukraine and White Russia. Eventually, his reforms also rejected many rulings of the Stoglav Church Council in 1551.

The historian Vasily Kliuchevskii argued that Nikon's domineering methods in implementing reforms without preparing public opinion were designed to awe people and assert ecclesiastical authority, rather than being a product of genuine hatred against old rites.[37] But whatever

Nikon's true intentions were, his ideas denied the ecumenical centrality of Russian Orthodoxy and deeply disturbed the defenders of the old rites, who raised their voice against the eradication of the distinctive qualities of Russian Orthodoxy. Among these groups were dissidents led by Avvakum Petrovich and Ivan Neronov (two former associates of Nikon alienated by his ambitions as patriarch), who strongly defended local and traditional practices. Eighteenth-century Russian writers retrospectively called them 'Old Believers'.[38] The Old Believers wanted to preserve and restore pre-Nikonian Muscovite piety because they firmly believed that the rites and rituals from earlier centuries were the true forms of Orthodoxy.

Initially, Nikon eliminated individual and relatively minor resistance to his reforms through excommunication. Printing offices and other governmental sources were put to his use to spread the reforms. However, in 1658, an abrupt disagreement grew between the tsar and the patriarch. Nikon did not abdicate from his position, but he left his duties and went into self-imposed exile. In the light of Nikon's *Refutation*, where the patriarch boldly stressed that his spiritual power was superior to the secular servants of the state, the nature of the tension was clear: it was a battle between the church and the court about who ruled Russia.[39] Tsar Alexis' dissatisfaction with Nikon's ambitions and his desire to subjugate the church to the state was analogous to the general trends in contemporary Europe. Monarchs of all ranks in the seventeenth century were taking steps to employ churches to establish and maintain political cohesion and social order. Spirituality was still omnipresent, but churches were gradually becoming instruments of states. Eventually, in late 1666, a council stripped Nikon of his title.

The ecumenical councils of 1666–7 were defining moments in the history of the state and church relations in Russian tsardom. These councils declared that the reformed liturgy comprised the only legitimate forms of rites and rituals and condemned traditional practices. In that sense, Nikon did not completely fail in his endeavour to refine the Russian liturgy. Where he failed was in his ambition to place the seat of the patriarch above the crown of the tsar in the administrative hierarchy. In the aftermath of the councils of 1666–7, the tsar and court became the ultimate arbiter of state affairs. According to Kliuchevskii, the eventual triumph of the state over church removed a great obstacle to western influence in Russia.[40] The councils continued to instigate widespread resistance and unrest led by the Old Believers, but any non-conformist individual or group knew thereafter that their resistance to reform was not simply a spiritual matter; they were opposing the authority of the central government. There have been scholars who underlined that the Russian Orthodox Church became a mere 'handmaiden of state', but many historians of Russian tsardom agree that from 1666–7, the superiority of tsars above patriarchs became doctrine in Russian state tradition.[41]

Habsburg Monarchy

According to a legend, the Polish Jesuit saint Stanislaus Kostka (1550–68) could not find a Catholic priest in Vienna where he had travelled to study in 1564. Although there is disagreement about the Catholic population of Vienna at the time, the majority of the population in the city were Protestants.[42] This situation would begin to alter by the 1570s, but a true transformation in the Habsburg capital and across the rest of the Monarchy would begin with the Battle of White Mountain in 1620. When compared with the Ottoman and Russian cases, what made the religious transformation of the Habsburg lands distinct during the next one and a half centuries would be the personal commitment of pious Habsburg monarchs to the Catholic cause and the Catholicisation of their hereditary lands. One may indeed speak with relative precision about the unmediated intervention of Habsburg rulers in the religious disputes of their times. Among the three empires examined here, the early modern Habsburg Monarchy represents the best-documented case of genuine dynastic adherence to faith and religious acts of piety. For historians, therefore, it is much easier to trace the concrete marks of an officially endorsed popular piety across the former monarchical lands. Habsburgs sincerely believed that their religious acts would lead to political and military success by way of 'influencing the grace of God'.[43] The Viennese court directly orchestrated a great variety of Catholic worship in the forms of processions, pilgrimages, construction of churches and statues, ornamentation of altars, name-giving, minting of coins and many other means possible, perceptively encapsulated as '*pietas Austriaca*' by Anna Coreth.[44]

The Protestant Reformation was born in the Holy Roman Empire under the Catholic Habsburg crown as a reaction to what Luther, Calvin and other reformist preachers summarily defined as the spiritual decadence of the Roman Catholic Church. From the emergence of Protestantism in the early sixteenth century, adherence to Protestant doctrines and ideals also became a political weapon for many princes in the Holy Roman Empire against the ambitions of Habsburg emperors. Beyond spiritual concerns, for princes, demanding Protestant privileges from emperors was an effective instrument of political bargaining and a means of reminding the Habsburgs that the imperial lands they ruled were elective, not hereditary. Habsburg emperors could not simply press these princes to convert, because the monarchical centre in Vienna practically lived hand-to-mouth in continuous need of financial support from German princes. During the earliest decades of the Protestant Reformation, Charles V (1519–56) and his relatively more accommodationist successors Ferdinand I (1558–64) and Maximilian II (1564–76) preferred to maintain this precarious balance. The signing of the Augsburg settlement in 1555 was a product of this rather lenient set of accommodations required by the House of Habsburg.[45]

But by the seventeenth century, not every Habsburg monarch was wise enough to appreciate the fragility of this delicate balance. Following the footsteps of their predecessors, Rudolf II (1576–1612) and Matthias (1612–19) sought for ways to reconcile with the Protestants, but with the beginning of the reign of Ferdinand II (1619–37), the future generation of Habsburg monarchs adopted a new approach to the matter. Ferdinand's days in Austria as a young archduke gave clear-cut signs about how he would struggle as emperor to dismantle Protestantism. As a graduate of Ingolstadt University, a Jesuit school, young Ferdinand was deeply influenced by the ideals of the Jesuit society. His closest advisers during his career, Bartholomew Viller and William Lamormaini, were Jesuits deeply immersed in high politics. Under their supervision Archduke Ferdinand declared himself the absolute authority over the Catholic Church in Inner Austria and closed Protestant schools, ordering Protestant preachers and teachers to leave his estates.[46] In the Regensburg Diet of 1608, Ferdinand was the principal commissioner on behalf of Emperor Rudolf II. The diet eventually failed to eliminate the growing disputes between the Protestants and Catholics. The pope, however, recognised Ferdinand's efforts on behalf of the Catholic cause at the diet. In a letter to the pope, the archduke declared that 'he would risk his state, his blood, and his life rather than permit that the Catholic faith or the Church suffer the least damage'.[47] Ferdinand's militancy would not be enough to stop the formation of the Protestant Union in the aftermath of the diet, but he demonstrated his commitment by joining the Catholic Union that was formed in 1609. The same year, Emperor Rudolf signed the Letter of Majesty that granted religious rights to the Bohemian Protestants to soothe the increasing tension between the Catholics and Protestants, but the developments were only the beginning of a major dissolution in the monarchy that would lead to a forceful attempt by the government in Vienna to impose Catholicism across the monarchy.

Emperor Matthias, too, confirmed the Letter of Majesty, but the emperor's cousin Ferdinand was not eager to do so when Matthias named him as his successor to the throne on his death in 1619. Instead of electing Ferdinand as the next emperor, Bohemian Protestants took this opportunity to unite against the militancy of the emperor-elect. The Bohemians constituted a Protestant assembly and offered the Bohemian crown to Frederick V of Palatinate in the aftermath of the well-known defenestrations at Prague Castle. In the meantime, the Hungarian prince Gabor Bethlen entered Royal Hungary. For a moment, the Habsburgs seemed to have lost their hereditary lands and political leverage in Central Europe against the backdrop of a purportedly religious strife, but the Catholic victory against the Protestant army at the Battle of White Mountain on 8 November 1620, decisively changed the flow of events. Frederick, who went into the annals of history as the Winter King, escaped to the Netherlands, leaving the scene to the new emperor who embarked on an ambitious mission to re-Catholicise Bohemia.

The carefully calculated punishments of twenty-seven prisoners in the Old Town Square in Prague on 21 June 1621, became 'the most celebrated executions in Czech history'.[48] Yet Ferdinand did not stop there. He firmly believed that his primary obligation as the shepherd of his people was to preserve and maintain the Catholic faith of his country and subjects. He was a pious Catholic, but he was also motivated by the contemporary idea that 'unity of religion was essential to civil peace and that heresy was the chief stimulus to rebellion'. The emperor's Jesuit confessor William Lamormaini also played a significant role during Ferdinand's reign. Lamormaini was a man who firmly believed that 'innumerable thousands of souls and all the progress of the Catholic religion in Germany' depended on the 'perfection and zeal' of the emperor. He was not only a committed missionary; he saw a providential hand, a prophetic vocation in everything he and his master undertook. Lamormaini pledged to help the emperor cultivate a Christian life 'to the highest point attainable'. In praise of the emperor, Lamormaini noted that the emperor 'often asserted both in writing and orally that he would give up his provinces and kingdoms more readily and more gladly than knowingly neglect an opportunity to extend the faith; that he would rather live on bread and water alone equipped only with a staff, beg his bread from door to door, be cut to pieces and torn apart for nothing rather than suffer any longer the harm done to God and the Church by the heretic in the territories under his rule'.[49] Together, the ultimate goal of the emperor and his counsellor was to restore Catholicism in the kingdom of Bohemia, Hungary and the rest of the monarchy, as well as in the empire.[50]

A true Jesuit, Lamormaini emphasised the importance of gradual conversion through education and persuasion. His emphasis on such rather rational methods was another unique aspect of the religious struggles in the Habsburg domains when compared with the Ottoman and Russian territories. Lamormaini argued that 'the broader Catholic project in

Bohemia was in large part dependent on efforts to regulate the schools and universities'. After the Battle of White Mountain, the Jesuits received the keys of Charles University for its reorganisation, though not without objections from Dominicans, Franciscans and Capuchins.[51] In the meantime, Lamormaini did not hesitate to suggest a forceful programme for the restoration of Catholicism. In 1628, Ferdinand issued the Edict of Restitution that ordered the return of all Catholic territory seized by the Protestants since 1552. Accordingly, nearly five hundred territorial ecclesiastical foundations, including monasteries, convents and churches, some of which were closely associated with the areas in which they were located, would be seized by the Catholic Church. The edict decreed that imperial commissioners would travel the land and investigate the claims of the despoiled about the lands taken from them. Ferdinand's courtiers were not very enthusiastic about the decree, except Lamormaini, who called it 'a deed truly worthy of this emperor'.[52] However, the Edict of Restitution was short-lived. Most German princes, France and, more consequentially, the Swedish King Gustavus Adolphus (1611–32) were utterly disturbed by the possibility of this disproportionate growth in Habsburg power. As a reaction to the edict and its objective of purging Protestants from Germany and northern Europe, the soldier-king Adolphus landed with his forces on the Baltic shore and advanced south to defeat the Catholic forces. He won a major victory in September 1631 and controlled much of central and southern Germany by spring. Yet what Adolphus earned on behalf of Protestants with a swift and unpredicted victory was lost a year later in the same fashion when the king died from wounds he received at the Battle of Lützen in November 1632, leaving the Swedes and Protestants without a leader. The Peace of Prague in 1635 provided many concessions – contrary to Lamormaini's pleas – to the Protestants on the Edict of Restitution, but the treaty's general impact on Ferdinand II's Counter-Reformation policies was relatively small.

Despite the seemingly religious nature of the struggle, the tide turned the other way, and showed yet again that religious agreement did not automatically translate into political harmony in international relations. Days before the Prague Treaty was concluded, Catholic France declared war on the Holy Roman Empire and the Spanish branch of the Habsburgs upon realising that the overall success of the Austrian branch of the Habsburg dynasty since the Battle of White Mountain was about to yield a Habsburg-dominated Europe. The French move, as intended, gave a new impetus to the Protestant cause. The militant emperor Ferdinand II did not live enough to see the long-term consequences; he died early in 1637. The new emperor Ferdinand III (r. 1637–57), described as a circumspect and wiser monarch than his predecessor, soon saw his hereditary lands and a large portion of Germany under Swedish and Transylvanian occupation, with Vienna coming under bombardment at one point. The only way out of this protracted chaos was to sue for peace. By the signing of Peace of Westphalia in 1648, the Catholics and Protestants returned to where they had begun: the principle of *cuius regio, eius religio* was reconfirmed by both parties roughly a century after it was first acknowledged by them.

The Westphalian treaty significantly reduced Vienna's influence in German affairs.[53] However, it also ushered in a new episode in the monarchy that culminated in the gradual cultural assimilation of the Habsburg dominions by the end of Leopold I's reign in 1705. This would be achieved during the reigns of Ferdinand III and Leopold I through the creation of a common culture characterised by pietistic Catholic elements. 'Visualization, interpretation, and enforcement of a well-defined and awe-inspiring sphere of sacredness' were the instruments of Baroque Catholicism during this bold episode of *pietas Austriaca*.[54] Members of the Habsburg dynasty and courtiers performed various acts of piety and sincerely believed in the efficacy of their actions. There were three popular forms of displaying and communicating dynastic piety to the public. The first was the veneration of the Eucharist in the presence of the Habsburg emperor who always stood in clear modesty, indicating the insignificance of the monarch in comparison with the heavenly lord. The second was the faith in the cross of Christ. From Charles V in the sixteenth century to Maria Theresa two hundred years later, Habsburg monarchs greatly revered the cross and made the crucifix a common theme in religious and public rituals, demonstrating an earnest belief in its protection. Regardless of whether the enemy on the battlefield was Protestant or Muslim, the cross, a sign of victory, was always present in the Habsburg army in the hands of monks and on the uniforms and armour of troops. The third was Marian Piety; to the Habsburg family, Mary was the supreme commander and patron, the empress and queen. Along with the crucifix, statues of Mary were erected across the monarch's domains to seek her care and patronage in all worldly affairs.[55]

In short, in everything they did, the Habsburg monarchs were firmly convinced that their dynasty had a God-given mission to communicate a distinctly Catholic piety to the public in all conceivable forms, including art, architecture, literature, public acts and popular culture. There was certainly a quest for social order behind all these public acts, but the religious effervescence of the Habsburgs was at least equally remarkable. Secular and spiritual realms seemed to have merged much more strongly in the Habsburg Monarchy in this regard in comparison with the Ottoman Empire and Russian Tsardom.

Conclusion: Revisiting the Comparative Evaluation

Ottomanists have recently suggested various explanations for the transformations that took place in the seventeenth-century Ottoman Empire. Baki Tezcan has argued that the period from 1580 to 1703 was marked by a struggle between the traditional patrimonial monarchy and the expanding political nation.[56] The origins of that struggle, according to Sam White, derived from climatic pressures of the sixteenth century, while Oktay Özel highlights the pressures of demographic growth in the second and third quarters of the sixteenth century.[57] Cumulatively, these developments set the ground for the Celali Rebellions in the Ottoman Empire, roughly coinciding with the Time of Troubles in Russia. As a reaction to the ensuing quest for order during the first half of the seventeenth century, Ottoman intellectuals discussed in detail the concept of justice, and how public order should be restored.[58] We may assume that such debates were generally unknown to the masses, who heavily suffered the consequences of ongoing political, social and economic shifts. *Kadızadeli* preachers seem to have successfully conquered this destabilisation of Ottoman state and society, while the court preferred to cautiously offer limited patronage to the *Kadızadeli*s rather than fully capitulating to them, or repressing their radical religious rhetoric. In effect, this made the *Kadızadeli* preachers intermediaries between the court and its subjects, particularly in the imperial capital. Certainly, the Ottoman court was aware of this role played by the *Kadızadeli* preachers. The court neither strongly supported the *Kadızadeli*s nor openly confronted their ideas. For the Ottomans, obviously, the preservation of the order was more important than taking a narrowly-defined religious/ideological position.

A recent study by Karen Barkey and Rudi Batzel has insightfully analysed the Ottoman response to the seventeenth-century crisis in comparison with Russian Tsardom and the Habsburg Monarchy. Barkey and Batzel suggest that the discrepancies (and similarities) between the policies of the three states were an outcome of their distinct patterns of territorial expansion, the organisation of property, and the resulting varieties of relations between centre and periphery in each empire.[59] They argued that the Ottoman and Russian states were able to more actively reshape social hierarchies in their domains because their governments were more centralised, as expansion by conquest had minimised centrifugal tendencies. In the Ottoman Empire, a newly acquired land nominally became a sultanic territory, but the local landowners preserved their position, even when they were assimilated into Ottoman administrative mechanisms. Russian central authorities preferred to recruit new military elites for the administration of newly conquered regions, and gathered the former landowner boyars in Moscow. The relationship between the boyars and the Russian centre remained 'constructive rather than oppositional'.[60] In comparison, the Habsburg Monarchy had expanded via marriages and union which left provincial aristocratic structures intact, hindering the monarchical centre from intervening in existing social hierarchies and patterns of property ownership. Barkey and Batzel concluded that the ambitious counter-reformatory policies of Ferdinand II and other Habsburg monarchs essentially aimed to overcome such weak vertical integration of provincial aristocracy.

This useful analysis disregarded the disputes about orthodoxy and orthopraxy. Nor did it question in depth the mutual dependency of such disputes and material concerns. How should we interpret the relatively tolerant Ottoman attitude towards a group of non-conformist preachers during the seventeenth century? The easy-going manner of the Ottoman patrimonial centre towards the *Kadızadeli*s is just another facet of a very well-known aspect of Ottoman history, yet it is repeatedly ignored in recent formulations proposed by scholars to describe Ottoman early modernity. It is evident that the religious and doctrinal criticisms of the *Kadızadeli*s could easily make the members of the dynasty and courtiers a target of the masses who regularly listened to the preachers. The entire court, including reigning sultans, were practitioners, sponsors and participants in many rites and rituals that the *Kadızadeli*s attacked in vitriolic sermons at the biggest mosques of the capital. Contrary to the traditional assumption that religious orthodoxy intensified during the seventeenth century, one sees in the Ottoman court's treatment of *Kadızadeli*s signs of governmental and religious leniency that prioritised the preservation of order and deliberately avoided a strict commitment to a certain version of religion. The preservation of order and the longevity of the *devlet-i ebed müdded*, the eternal Ottoman state, was a greater concern for generations of Ottomans even when such concerns necessitated the coexistence – and sometimes even mediation – of religious unorthodoxies and the agents preaching them. The attitude of the Ottoman court towards *Kadızadeli*s thus suggests that the state did not strictly commit to a particular religious interpretation; instead, the Ottoman administrators manipulated and manoeuvred through emergent situations to protect the state as an institution and preserve the existing order.

The primacy of the state over all other individuals and corporate entities in Ottoman history is compellingly illustrated by Ottomanists. Abdurrahman Atçıl illustrates in his examination of the relationship between scholars and the Ottoman court during the first three centuries of Ottoman history that the Ottoman government ensured 'the loyalty and dedication' of scholars to the Ottoman enterprise by increasing their dependence. The result, Atçıl argues, was 'perhaps unprecedented in Islamic history': the emerging class of what he labelled *scholar-bureaucrats* were so attached to the court and government that they began to see 'the Ottoman enterprise as a blessing and dedicated themselves to its advancement [while] attempting to strengthen their own position in it'.[61] The early modern Ottoman court's readiness to recruit a sizeable number of Christian-European converts in its state service, a phenomenon recently explored by Tobias Graf, may also be evaluated from the same perspective.[62] Likewise, a large number of non-Muslims were employed as dragomans and go-betweens in various roles to facilitate negotiations with European courts.[63] Nathalie Rothman has noted that 'the ability of Ottoman statecraft to manage and contain a seemingly bewildering range of confessional groups was the source of both praise and awe', a trait that inherently defied confessional lines emerging in contemporary Europe.[64] Also remarkable is the rise of Greek Phanariots to ascendancy in the second half of the eighteenth century, in a process Christine Philliou describes as 'inadvertent integration', which lacked the deliberate and exclusive categorisations of European confessionalisation or Catherine the Great's Russia.[65] As such, the Phanariot ascendancy was just another indication of the Ottoman court's indifference to religious convictions for the sake of, first and foremost, longevity and also effective governance. One would have difficulty in finding in early modern Europe a city resembling Salonica, where there existed, according to a visitor as late as the mid-nineteenth century, 'a sort of fusion between the different peoples who inhabit the place and a happy rapprochement between the races which the nature of their beliefs and the diversity of their origins tends to separate'.[66] Historians always take such statements with a grain of salt. The Ottoman Empire was not a utopia; Sunni Islam was the dominant culture and the Ottoman court and Muslim subjects frequently infringed the rights of non-Muslims. There were also occasions where the court harshly repressed what it deemed to be Muslim heresies. Nevertheless, 'one can hardly overstate the internal diversity of the Ottoman Empire in almost every facet of life'.[67] The seventeenth-century Ottoman Empire was a multi-confessional state and as such the social setting of the empire lacked the strict confessional compartments that were becoming increasingly clear in the early modern Habsburg Monarchy. In the same period in Russia, as demonstrated in a seminal article by Peter B. Bowman, 'compared to European state-builders, the tsar was relatively free, largely without fear of political repercussions, to create institutions of his choosing and direct them to do as he wished'.[68] As a result, the Russian court suppressed unconventional religious forms with relative ease, including, for instance, the Muslims of the Volga-Ural region against whom Moscow's attitude would be 'generally restrictive and even antagonistic' at least until the reforms of Catherine II.[69] The Ottoman case was not a magical product of contingencies; it was a natural condition created by what we may call the Ottoman worldview which Douglas Howard alluded to at the beginning of his recent history of the empire.[70] The Ottoman multi-confessionalism, which made the early modern Ottoman Empire so different from contemporary Europe, did not survive the pressures of the modern era as the growing nationalist sentiments of Turks and other former Ottoman subjects together ruined whatever remained of the early modern multi-confessional empire.

In the specific cases of *Kadızadeli*s versus European confessionalisation there was another factor that certainly facilitated the Ottoman court's relative calmness. One of the key differences between the *Kadızadeli*s and their Russian and Habsburg contemporaries who concurrently defied established religious customs was that the *Kadızadeli*s were not landowners and they were not in possession of wealth. In the Ottoman Empire, the House of Osman was the sole distributor of land and material benefits. This was a theoretical ownership as the land was systematically allocated to subjects for cultivation, but the Ottoman dynasty maintained its position as the ultimate arbiter of land distribution, a privilege unchallenged in theory. In the Habsburg Monarchy, the status of church lands became a major issue of contention in the disputes between the dynastic centre and the seemingly religiously motivated opponents of central authority. Karin MacHardy has convincingly shown that the status of church lands was 'the most explosive conflict' in the confessional rivalries in the Habsburg realms at the turn of the seventeenth century. Spiritual convictions were real, yet the strife over resources was 'not a petty issue, nor was it a purely spiritual affair'.[71]

While the lack of a dispute over financial resources facilitated the rather flexible approach of the Ottoman court to the *Kadızadeli*s, the impact of the latter on Ottoman subjects fostered a mutual dependence between the two. Roy Mottahedeh notes in regard to early Islamic history that rulers often accepted the intervention of pious men in politics: 'they did so not only because they admired men of outstanding piety, but also because such men had a certain following'.[72] Several sultans and influential courtiers, in cognizance of the popularity of the preachers, established close connections with the most charismatic among the *Kadızadeli*s and made use of them as a means of appeasing public discontent against the court. One may assume that the *Kadızadeli* preachers were extremely pleased with the courtly affirmation they received, and fully exploited their privileged position to exert influence over the public. Naturally, their spiritual passion frequently blended into non-religious ambitions. As a group, the *Kadızadeli*s would lose their status soon after the fiasco in 1683, yet religious functionaries who held high offices in the empire, including the office of grand mufti, continued to interfere in politics. A remarkable example from the end of the seventeenth century was the Grand Mufti Feyzullah Efendi. His impact on decision-making was such that his modern biographer Michael Nizri writes that 'there had never been another case where the *şeyhülislam* had appropriated the tasks and the powers of the grand vizier to become the leading figure in the formation of imperial domestic and foreign policy'.[73] As Baki Tezcan correctly notes, Feyzullah's rise was just another moment when the Ottoman patriarchal centre searched for allies to reinforce the court's absolutism.[74] Feyzullah eventually paid the price for his ambitions with a most brutal death, another sign that any cooperation between the early modern Ottoman court and prominent religious figures, be they occupants of governmental posts or not, aimed to protect state and preserve order. No religious figure could gain ascendancy over the court. The intriguing part of this whole story is the absence, or non-emergence, of a secular formulation in Ottoman political thinking regarding the primacy of state and the legitimisation of order as in early modern Europe or Russia.

The merging of religious fervour with temptations of secular power was by no means an Ottoman specialty. Many patriarchs in contemporary Russia shared the religious aversion of the *Kadızadeli*s towards certain religious rites and rituals, albeit in an Orthodox Christian world, while exercising unique judicial powers due to their official position. Some of the patriarchs in the mid-seventeenth century exercised more power and influence than tsars in state affairs. Cloaked with spiritual authority and claiming that the restoration of true forms of orthopraxy was their ultimate goal, patriarchs competed with the Russian court over administrative power. Such ambitions could be pursued as a result of the significant roles patriarchs Germogen and Filaret fulfilled during and after the Time of Troubles, which gave future occupants of the seat a highly revered status in the eyes of the Russian people. Converting that legacy into considerable weight in politics was not a difficult task for ambitious and assertive individuals. Eventually, Nikon took those ambitions to a new level and aggressively introduced religious reforms, finding himself in a power duel with the tsar. In the end, Nikon lost the power struggle that followed with the tsar and his position, setting the scene for Peter the Great's (1682–1725) reforms which legally subordinated the seat of the patriarch to the crown. Even though Nikon's reformist ideas were confirmed by the court and, thereafter opposition to the reformed liturgy meant opposition to the state, the rise of secular power over the church in Russia would gradually take a western form as the culture of Baroque Europe seeped into the Russian court. Peter the Great 'would break the mould' and accelerate a process that culminated in the rise of secular power over the church.[75]

From the beginning of the Protestant Reformation, all forms of religious rebellion against the Catholic Church was inherently a political opposition levelled at the Habsburg dynasty, 'inseparably fused with material issues'.[76] During the sixteenth century and early seventeenth century, many German princes, Bohemians and Hungarians, camouflaged with an alternative religious discourse, fully exploited the geopolitical and financial fragility of the Catholic Habsburgs. The lenient approach of several Habsburg monarchs in the sixteenth century only helped the dissidence grow, until Ferdinand II decided to cope with the problem with a more direct and harsher strategy. By the mid-seventeenth century, the Habsburgs had lost their privileged status in Germany despite preserving the imperial crown. In the second half of the seventeenth century, a zealous piety governed all forms of public ceremonies and rituals in the monarchy. Vienna cooperated with nobles and clergy to rebuild a Catholic landscape. The *Pietas Austriaca* was real, but a generation of scholars have also shown that the arduous evangelisation policies went hand in hand with a desire to forge political unity and a well-knit society. Compared with the Ottoman and Russian cases, the Habsburg state in the eighteenth century would implement much more rational policies shaped by an increasingly scientific, and thus secular, methodology.

Avoiding Fallacies and Ideas for Future Comparative Research

The three seventeenth-century cases of dispute and contest between imperial governments and agents of religion took place in a pre-modern setting where there was a great deal of interdependence between the administrative, religious, military and economic spheres. In all three states, governmental ideals and military ambitions meshed with a genuine commitment to religious ideology, which invigorated troops on the battlefield while also soothing subjects at home. Without possession of cultivable and taxable land, however, neither could governments be run nor could armies be equipped and maintained. This was not a modern context, where each of these domains are strictly separated from one another and trusted to professionals working according to well-defined principles and regulations. Yet even modern institutions and structures often do not allow us to formulate concepts and paradigms that may reflect the true nature of phenomena without ambiguity. In the early modern Ottoman, Russian and Habsburg states there existed a remarkable interdependency between governments, armies, religious matters and financial issues. The notion that we may define the dynamics of this complex make-up is mistaken. For the modern historian, detaching a pre-modern historical actor who held a dominant role in one of these branches from actors attached to other branches is a challenge; in fact, such effort goes against the realities of the pre-modern world, and, therefore, frequently leads to anachronism. Moreover, the interplay between administration, spiritual concerns, territorial ambitions and land-based income unfolded in remarkably different ways across pre-modern Eurasia, with significant variations even within the territories of any single one of the three polities.[77] Imposing a single paradigm upon those variations for the sake of understanding and simplicity is very likely blurring a more complex reality. Therefore, going back to Robert Crummey's judicious remark mentioned at the beginning, historians – and publishers too – should resist the attractiveness of applying all-encompassing paradigms to early modern Ottoman (and Russian and Habsburg) histories.

The *Kadızadeli*s focused on religious doctrinal issues and identifying correct forms of worship based on their own perspectives. They did not articulate a clear-cut distinction between secular government and spiritual matters. As per Islamic tradition, there seems to have existed in Ottoman history a tacit acceptance that the two were inseparable, hence the absence of well-rounded definitions of secular and spiritual rule and leadership. Instead, the two are often subtly merged in theory and practice of *kanun* and sharia. In Russia, reformist patriarchs openly attempted to bring the state under spiritual rule. Nikon explicitly argued that the spiritual ruler was superior to the secular head of state. Nikon and other patriarchs were also heads of an institution that owned property; advocating the rights and privileges of the Orthodox Church also meant protecting ecclesiastical lands. In comparison, in the Ottoman Empire the *Kadızadeli*s and grand muftis such as Feyzullah Efendi seem to have been principally, if not singularly, concerned about their personal fortunes. Eventually in Russia, Peter the Great would make the patriarch a subordinate of the tsar and eliminate spiritual challenges to secular rule. Russianist Kliuchevskii may be pointing at a key reality when he argues that the eventual triumph of the state over church removed an obstacle in front of western influence in Russia. The impact, extent and meaning of Westernisation in Russian history has been a key matter of debate among historians of Russia to this day. In Ottoman historical frameworks, one has to be careful not to reproduce an orientalist narrative based on Islamic religious obscurantism, but if we apply Kliuchevskii's perspective to Ottoman history, the relative slowness of western influence in the Ottoman Empire (and elsewhere in the Islamic world) may indeed be due, first, to the lack of a binary articulation of spiritual and secular rule, and, second, to the state's uncontested hegemony over property, leaving no room even for a theoretical discussion about private property ownership at least until the reforms of the nineteenth century. Therefore, I propose that we stop searching for blanket terms such as 'confessionalisation' to link the histories of these three empires. Imposing a single paradigm to make sense of such fundamentally disparate features and characteristics of seemingly comparable events often come at a cost.

I fully agree with the author of a new review article about the current trends in Ottoman history: 'The overlaying of Europeanist themes and concepts upon sixteenth- and seventeenth-century Ottoman realities obscures as much as it illuminates …'[78] Rather than using Ottoman history as a laboratory of paradigms from outside the field, we should perhaps focus on conspicuous similarities (and contrasts) between the histories of the early modern Ottoman Empire, Russian Tsardom and the Habsburg Monarchy. Some of these parallels are obvious and have been studied comparatively, but whether they have been fully explored is questionable. Two most noteworthy similarities between the Ottoman Empire and Russian Tsardom are the relative security of the ruling dynasty's grip on power and the concentration of political power in central courts, though not necessarily always in the hands of an autocratic sultan or tsar, as often assumed in the broader literature. In the meantime, the Habsburg Monarchy survived during much of its history via continuous bargaining between rulers and subjects.[79] During the long seventeenth century, all three states suffered the consequences of what historians once called the 'age of crisis' due to popular rebellions, revolts, climatic fluctuations and major wars that swept through Eurasia and the wider world.[80] The Celali Rebellions in the Ottoman Empire, the recurrent Don Cossack revolts in Russian Tsardom, and the Thirty Years War in and beyond the Habsburg realms were only the most dramatic manifestations of a general crisis that shook th three polities during that century. Recently, as I have emphasised above, Ottomanists have also become enthusiastic about the links between religious debates and dissent in the early modern Ottoman Empire and the European age of confessionalisation. Several historians of the Ottoman Empire are now convinced that the letters exchanged in 1555 between Süleyman the Lawgiver (r. 1520–66) and the Safavid Shah Tahmasb (r. 1524–76), misleadingly referred as the Treaty of Amasya in the literature,[81] and the signing of the Peace of Augsburg in the same year was symptomatic of a Mediterranean age of confessionalisation.[82] The Stoglav Church Council that gathered in

1551 in Russia specifically to deal with the problem of heresy, however, did not lead historians of Russia to interpret Russian early modernity through the lens of confessionalisation, a concept that, I must underline yet again, has been thoroughly researched, discussed and criticised in the European historical framework.[83] Other scholars interested in structural comparisons have lately examined the concurrent transformation of the land grant systems and the evolution of state–society relations in all three polities.[84] Beyond these perspectives, entangled histories of the three empires in matters of geopolitics, nation-building and many aspects of borderlands continue to attract historians of all epochs, albeit with the post-1800 period taking the lion's share of the interest.[85]

In the meantime, one can point at other parallels for future analysis: that the zeniths of Ottoman and Russian power came after two episodes of major turmoil in their domains may tell us more about the dynamics of imperial expansion and resilience in the two pre-modern states. The Ottoman Interregnum (1402–13) preceded the conquest of Constantinople and the territorial expansion within the next one and a half centuries. Similarly, the Time of Troubles (1603–13) that ended with the installation of a Romanov tsar on the Russian throne marked the beginning of a two-century-long conquest of the steppes. Other remarkable parallels between the Ottoman and Russian states were the regulations on the tobacco trade and its consumption in the 1630s[86] and the use of religious ideology by all three early modern courts for the legitimisation of dynastic rule, though with great variations and modifications in each case. There are also many opportunities for structural comparisons between the Ottomans and Habsburgs. In their earlier times, subjects in both polities could directly appeal to the ruler. As both states grew territorially and institutionally, the physical distance between the rulers and subjects grew. With a hundred years' gap between, the reigns of Mehmed II (1444–6; 1451–81) in the Ottoman Empire and Ferdinand II (1556–64) and Maximillian II (1564–76) in the Habsburg Monarchy saw increasing difficulty in accessibility of the sovereign. Another similarity that may surprise some readers is that in a development identical to the increasing involvement of the Janissaries in economic life across the Ottoman Empire, a well-known story for Ottomanists, the imperial guards in Vienna created their own informal economy in the seventeenth century by learning crafts such as meat cutting, shoemaking and masonry, and even operating bathhouses.[87] A question worthy of analysis is why the former has always been linked with Ottoman decline, while the latter has not led to any declinists assumptions about the Habsburg monarchy.

In sum, even though proper venues of comparative research exist within

Confessionalisation or a Quest for Order?

the Ottoman Empire and European states in the early modern world, scholars and students of these policies must be careful in drawing overarching and encompassing parallels with no regard to their peculiar histories and historiographies.

Notes

1. I have elsewhere analysed the problems in direct application of the confessionalisation paradigm to Ottoman history: Yılmaz, 'Nebulous Ottomans vs. Good Old Habsburgs'. Kaya Şahin has also astutely discussed the problems in the application of the confessionalisation paradigm to Islamic history: Şahin, *Empire and Power*, pp. 208–9.
2. Literal translation of the word 'Kadızade' into English is 'son of qadi (judge)'.
3. İnalcık, 'Military and Fiscal Transformation'; Murphey, 'Continuity and Discontinuity'; Özel, 'The Reign of Violence'; White, *The Climate of Rebellion*.
4. İnalcık, 'Military and Fiscal Transformation', pp. 288–91.
5. İnalcık, *The Ottoman Empire*, p. 98.
6. A more recent analysis is in Aksan, 'Mobilization of Warrior Populations'.
7. İnalcık, *Devlet-i Aliyye*, vol. 2, p. 236.
8. A detailed survey of Murad IV's reign based on primary sources is in ibid., vol. 2, pp. 187–227.
9. Ibid., vol. 2, pp. 207–11.
10. Ibid., vol. 2, p. 236. Also see Sheikh, *Ottoman Puritanism*, p. 15.
11. For more information about Birgivi and his commentary on religious matters, see *TDV İslam Ansiklopedisi Online* (hereafter *TDV İAO*), s.v. 'Birgivi', available at: http://www.islamansiklopedisi.info/di a/pdf/c06/c060146.pdf, last accessed 10 September 2017; ,s.v. Birgewi', *Encyclopedia of Islam*, 2nd edn.
12. Zilfi, 'The *Kadızadeli*s'.
13. Baer, *Honoured by the Glory of Islam*, p. 66.
14. Zilfi, 'The *Kadızadeli*s', p. 251.
15. Mustapha Sheikh has recently noted that a binary approach to *Kadızadeli*s and Sufism is misleading. He argues that a hardline anti-Sufism would have prevented *Kadızadeli*s from rising in the hierarchy of preachers because Sufi ideas were deeply embedded in the traditions of Ottoman society and court, and many Sufis enjoyed personal closeness with ruling sultans. Sheikh, *Ottoman Puritanism*.
16. Zilfi, 'The *Kadızadeli*s', p. 254.
17. Öztürk, 'Islamic Orthodoxy', p. 215; Çavuşoğlu, 'The *Kadızadeli* Movement', p. 107. Both quoted in Sheikh, *Ottoman Puritanism*, p. 20.
18. *TDV İAO*, s.v. 'Üstüvani Mehmed Efendi', available at: http://www.islamansiklopedisi.info/ dia/pdf/c42/c420290.pdf, last accessed 10 September 2017; İnalcık, *Devlet-i Aliyye*, vol. 2, p. 238.

19. Zilfi, 'The *Kadızadeli*s', pp. 259–62. For a detailed survey of *Kadızadeli* influence on the Ottoman government and a list of matters discussed among *Kadızadeli* Mehmed and his Sufi opponent Abdülmecid Sivasi (d. 1639), see *TDV İAO*, s.v. 'Kadızadeliler', available at: http://www.islamansiklopedisi.info/ dia/pdf/c24/c240058.pdf, last accessed 10 September 2017.
20. *TDV İAO*, s.v. 'Vani Mehmed Efendi', available at: http://www.islamansiklopedisi.info/dia/ pdf/c28/c2 80262.pdf, last accessed 10 September 2017.
21. Zilfi, 'The *Kadızadeli*s', pp. 262–5.
22. Evliya Çelebi reported such an incident from Bitlis in eastern Anatolia where a disciple of a *Kadızadeli* preacher located in Tire in western Turkey intentionally damaged the miniatures inside a copy of Shah-name. Dankoff, *An Ottoman Mentality*, pp. 70–1.
23. Kollmann, *The Russian Empire*, p. 136.
24. Bogatyrev, 'Ivan IV (1533–1584)', pp. 246–9.
25. The Russian Church had enjoyed a degree of de facto independence since the rejection of the union with the Roman Church which Metropolitan Isidore had tried to introduce. When he fled, Bishop Iona was appointed Metropolitan of Moscow without consultation with Constantinople, making the Moscow Church de facto autocephalous. A brief discussion of the historical background is in Bremer, *Cross and Kremlin*, pp. 55–9.
26. Pavlov, 'Fedor Ivanovich', pp. 268–9.
27. Crummey, 'The Orthodox Church and the Schism', pp. 619–20.
28. Bushkovitch, *Religion and Society in Russia*, p. 133.
29. Ibid., p. 51.
30. Poe, 'The Central Government'.
31. As Catholics were also required to go through the same process, scholars have suggested in passing that such new practices may be interpreted in line with 'the hardening of confessional lines in Europe'. Bushkovitch, *Religion and Society in Russia*, p. 53; Crummey, 'The Orthodox Church and the Schism', p. 626.
32. The opposite of *mnogoglasie* was *edinoglasie*, the practice of singing in one voice only.
33. Kollmann, *The Russian Empire*, p. 256.
34. Hellie, 'The Expanding Role of the State in Russia'.
35. Lobachev, 'Patriarch Nikon's Rise to Power'.
36. Crummey, 'The Orthodox Church and the Schism', p. 630.
37. Kliuchevskii, *A Course in Russian History*, pp. 328–9.
38. Crummey, 'Past and Current Interpretations of Old Belief'; Michels, *At War with the Church*, pp. 13–18.
39. Quoted in Crummey, 'The Orthodox Church and the Schism', pp. 629–31.
40. Kliuchevskii, *A Course in Russian History*, p. 340.
41. Freeze, 'Handmaiden of the State?'; Bremer, *Cross and Kremlin*, pp. 19–20.
42. Vocelka, 'The Counter-Reformation and Popular Piety'.

Confessionalisation or a Quest for Order?

43. Ibid., p.128.
44. Coreth, *Pietas Austriaca*.
45. MacCulloch, *The Reformation*, pp. 428–30.
46. Bireley, *Ferdinand II*, p. 33.
47. Ibid., p. 57.
48. Louthan, *Converting Bohemia*, p. 22.
49. Bireley, *Religion and Politics*, p. 14.
50. Bireley, *Religion and Politics*, pp. 13, 20. During the Thirty Years War, Jesuit theologians were especially influential on decision-making processes and war policy in Vienna and Munich. They were not a monolithic group pursuing a single policy, but they militantly supported the Catholic cause. Bireley, *The Jesuits and the Thirty Years' War*.
51. Louthan, *Converting Bohemia*, pp. 84, 88–92.
52. Bireley, *Religion and Politics*, p. 78.
53. Ingrao, *The Habsburg Monarchy*, p. 49.
54. Winkelbauer, *Ständefreiheit und Fürstenmacht*, p. 186.
55. See relevant chapters in Coreth, *Pietas Austriaca*.
56. Tezcan also argued that the patrimonial monarchy would be replaced by a more inclusive bureaucracy after 1703. Tezcan, *The Second Ottoman Empire*.
57. White, *The Climate of Rebellion*; Özel, *The Collapse of Rural Order*.
58. A succinct analysis of these discussion is available in Darling, *A History of Social Justice and Political Power*, pp. 144–54.
59. Barkey and Batzell, 'Comparisons across Empires'.
60. Ibid., p. 238.
61. Atçıl, *Scholars and Sultans*, pp. 212–15.
62. Graf, *The Sultan's Renegades*.
63. Gürkan, 'Mediating Boundaries'.
64. Rothman, 'Dragomans and "Turkish Literature"'.
65. Philliou, 'Communities on the Verge'.
66. Mazower, *Salonica*, p. 65.
67. Toledano, 'Turkish Nationalism'.
68. Brown, 'How Muscovy Governed', p. 477.
69. Tuna, *Imperial Russia's Muslims*, p. 37.
70. See the introduction in Howard, *A History of the Ottoman Empire*.
71. MacHardy, *War, Religion and Court Patronage*, pp. 58, 69. The second chapter of this book is a compelling narrative of how confessional struggles within the Habsburg realms in the early seventeenth century were intertwined with material disputes.
72. Quoted in Baer, *Honoured by the Glory of Islam*, p. 68.
73. Nizri, *Ottoman High Politics*, p. 102.
74. Tezcan, *The Second Ottoman Empire*, p. 44.
75. Bushkovitch, *Peter the Great*, p. 48.
76. MacHardy, *War, Religion and Court Patronage*, p. 87.
77. Ágoston, 'A Flexible Empire'; Şahin, 'From Frontier Principality'.

78. Markiewicz, 'Europeanist Trends and Islamicate Trajectories'.
79. MacHardy, *War, Religion and Court Patronage*; Barkey and Batzell, 'Comparisons across Empires'.
80. Parker and Smith, *The General Crisis*; Parker, *Global Crisis*. The basic assumption of the proponents of the seventeenth-century crisis debate is that a 'general crisis' shook states and societies in throughout Eurasia. Recently in a forum in the *American Historical Review* scholars have re-evaluated the literature on this theme and discussed the relevance of the crisis concept today. See *American Historical Review* 113/4 (2008): 1029–99.
81. For the letter sent by the Ottoman sultan to the Safavid court, see Demirtaş, 'Celāl-Zāde Mustafa Çelebi', pp. 684–6. I would like to thank Tunç Şen for pointing out this detail on an online platform.
82. Krstić, *Contested Conversions*; Terzioğlu, 'Where 'İlm-i Ḥāl Meets Catechism'; al-Tikriti, 'Ibn-i Kemal's Confessionalism'.
83. Brüning, 'Confessionalization in the Slavia Orthodoxa'.
84. Ágoston, 'Military Transformation'; Barkey and Batzell, 'Comparisons across Empires'. A recent survey of Turkish and Ottoman studies in St. Petersburg and Moscow listed a number of comparative studies written from the Russian perspective which are not easily accessible to the majority of Ottomanists: Meyer and Zhukov, 'The Present State of Ottoman Studies'.
85. Some of the recent works in these fields are: Roshwald, *Ethnic Nationalism and the Fall of Empires*; Ingrao and Yılmaz, 'Ottoman vs. Habsburg'; Birdal, *The Holy Roman Empire and the Ottomans*; Reynolds, *Shattering Empires*; Marin, *Contested Frontiers in the Balkans*; Bartov and Weitz, *Shatterzone of Empires*; Frary and Kozelsky, *Russian–Ottoman Borderlands*; Meyer, *Turks across Empires*; Robarts, *Migration and Disease*; Vovchenko, *Containing Balkan Nationalism*. One should mention many articles and monographs by Virginia Aksan, Alfred Rieber and Dominic Lieven. There is also a project underway by Michael Portmann at the Austrian Academy of Sciences, Institute for Modern and Contemporary Historical Research, titled 'Between Sultan and Emperor'. The main themes of the project are 'the political culture and governance as well as the entangled imperial legacies in the Ottoman–Habsburg borderlands'. More information is available at: http://www.state-building-balkans.net/en, last accessed 14 August 2017. Germanophone literature on Habsburg and Ottoman history are primarily case studies of diplomatic contact and cultural exchange which fittingly avoid generalisations. Two examples are Kurz, *Das Osmanische Reich und die Habsburgermonarchie*; Strohmeyer and Spannenberger, *Frieden und Konfliktmanagement*.
86. Kermeli, 'The Tobacco Controversy'. Though this article did not deal with the Russian side of the tobacco ban, it examines a treatise against smoking that was written in the early eighteenth century by a Greek Orthodox Ottoman subject, Nikolaos Mavrokordatos.
87. Spielman, *The City and the Crown*, pp. 63–9

6

From the *Hamzaviyye* to the *Melāmiyye*: Transformation of an Order in Seventeenth-century Istanbul*

F. Betül Yavuz

In the conflict-ridden atmosphere of seventeenth-century Istanbul, a specific branch of the *Bayramiyye* Sufi order, which was known as either the *Hamzaviyye* or the *Idrisiyye* at the time, was able to take root among Istanbul's cultural and political elite.[1] The order, which during the eighteenth century came to be known as the *Melāmi* branch of the *Bayramiyye*,[2] transformed itself from what had been perceived as a low-class deviant Sufi movement into a spiritual brotherhood that ventured beyond the *tarikat* affiliation.[3] This interesting transformation has been noted by various studies, while the order's reassessment of its teachings as it moved from the rural to the urban geographically and from poetics to prose literarily has not been taken as a point of reference. These developments are underlined in the chapter, while the main concern is how the intellectuals of the order negotiated the limits of orthodoxy by developing new interpretative tools to represent their beliefs and traditions in Istanbul. This effort was a necessary part of forging a new image for the order, and it enabled them to be included within the Sunna-conscious Sufi networks in the following centuries.[4]

One of the critical steps in this process was the order's adoption of the concept of *melāmet*.[5] In one sense, this chapter is concerned with the questions of how the *Hamzavi*s came to be known as the *Melāmi*s, and how the concept was understood and explained to a seventeenth-century audience. In order to answer these questions, I focus on the life and writings of Sarı Abdullah (d. 1660)[6] and especially his *Semerātu'l-fu'ād fi'l-mebde' ve'l-me'ād* (*The Fruits of the Heart in the Beginning and the End*; henceforth *Semerāt*). This has been one of the central texts that informed the classical and modern scholarship regarding the order. I conduct a more nuanced and contextualised reading of this text, paying special attention to its aims, anxieties and appropriations as it presents the *Hamzaviyye* to the literate

Sufi audiences of Istanbul. I argue that the *Semerāt* was a work with a specific project, one that succeeded. I explore the circumstances of this success and place the text within a more detailed study of the social dynamics that influenced religious representations in seventeenth-century Istanbul.

To provide a background, this chapter first focuses on scholarly attempts to conceptualise the transformation and adaptation of non-conformist Sufi groups within the religious dynamics of the Ottoman realm. It then provides an overview of the social and political transformations of society in Istanbul during the seventeenth century as they pertain to the case of the *Hamzaviyye*. Following that, it turns to the figure of Sarı Abdullah, outlining his background as a Sufi, bureaucrat and intellectual of his time. In the final section, the focus is on the *Semerāt*, its topics and trajectory, and, finally, its treatment of the *melāmet* within broader Sufi thought and practice. The conclusion brings this all together to reflect on how the case of the *Hamzavi/Melāmi* penetration into the mechanisms of the state by the late seventeenth century puts into question top-down interpretations of the transformation of religious communities. Instead, change and transformation often took place first within the base, in a bottom-up fashion, and depended on the individual and communal desires to succeed and flourish in a new age that required new tools and strategies.

Discussions of Orthodoxy in the Ottoman Realm

The *Bayrāmi-Hamzavi* tradition was rooted in a particular worldview that had become quite widespread in the eastern lands of Islam under the Mongols and Timurids during the fourteenth and fifteenth centuries. Around this time, various movements that were marked by a particular mixture of Sufism and Shiism, messianic fervour, and various ideas inherited from what was considered *ghulāt*[7] in the heresiographical sources had become widespread.[8] While such ideas were intellectually pervasive, even contributing to the political images of the early modern emperors during the fifteenth and sixteenth centuries,[9] their manifestations in populist movements were seen as politically threatening.[10] By the seventeenth century, most of these movements had already been curbed and rehabilitated into Sufi brotherhoods that functioned well within the bounds of urban establishments and state mechanisms.

Scholars of Ottoman religious life have studied and described this process using various terms, including *institutionalisation* or *domestication*,[11] *Ottomanisation* or *urbanisation*[12] and *Sunnitisation* or *confessionalisation*[13] of non-conformist Sufi groups. In some ways, the transformation of the *Hamzaviyye* in seventeenth-century Istanbul can be seen as a process of domestication, urbanisation or Sunnitisation. In other ways, however, their story was quite unique. On the one hand, such adaptations are largely believed to have taken place in the first three centuries of Ottoman rule, during the 'state-building' period. The seventeenth century, therefore, is considered rather late for such activities to have occurred.[14] On the other hand, the *Hamzaviyye* did not become institutionalised in the sense that they built their activities around a Sufi convent or followed traditional Sufi rituals.[15] Instead, they slowly constructed an alternative mode of belonging to a spiritual community, one in which adherents enjoyed reading and discussing some of the fundamental texts of the Sufi theosophy. The *pīr*s (the heads of the order) continued to reside at their houses and accept visitors there rather than inhabiting Sufi lodges, and common Sufi practices of excessive worship and *zikr* (remembering and reciting the names of God in a certain manner) were hardly ever employed. Finally, and quite significantly, in contrast to their illiterate/vernacular beginnings, literacy and learning became a mark of the order's hold among the bureaucrats.

I believe that this late and unique process can be best understood as an incorporation into the cultured milieu of Sufism in Istanbul. This term can encompass what is sometimes referred to as Sunnitisation or confessionalisation without being complicated by the convoluted and ever-changing nature of Sunna or orthodoxy in any period of Islamic history. The process of defining orthodoxy always involved multi-faceted undercurrents and has always been affected by communal and intellectual dynamics.[16]

The **Hamzavis** *and their Unexpected Success in Istanbul*

Various sources and documentary evidence written around the beginning of the seventeenth century represent the *Hamzavis/Idrīsi*s as heretics.[17] Such a designation seems to have been quite widespread among the Sufi literati, who often associated the order with the *Ḥurūfī*s[18] and accused them of holding beliefs that were not compatible with the basic tenets of Islam. There were several reasons for this attitude. For instance, the genealogy of the order posed a problem. Their previous *pīr* (Bosnian Hamza Bali) had been executed in Istanbul under charges of heresy, and a few decades before that in 1539, another *pīr*, İsmail Maşuki, had shared the same fate.[19] Furthermore, the order's practices were seen as peculiar. The *pīr*s did not reside in convents, did not accept state control or endorsement, and kept their beliefs and rituals hidden from outsiders. Their meetings took place in secrecy in the basement of the market place and were attended mainly by trusted shop owners and artisans. It was said that followers even insisted on marrying among themselves in order to keep strangers away. Critics often saw followers as simple, illiterate folk who did not know any better.[20]

Up until the beginning of the seventeenth century, the *pīr*s of the order had dwelt mostly in small Anatolian and Balkan cities. The first *pīr* to reside in Istanbul until his death was İdris Muhtefi (the Hidden Idris, d. 1615),[21] a wealthy merchant who led a comfortable life in a central Istanbul neighbourhood under the alias Hacı Ali Bey. After his death, Hacı Kabayi (d. 1626)[22] and Beşir Ağa (ex. 1662)[23] were accepted as the heads of the order. While the former was a circumspect and careful leader who avoided any exposed activity, the latter openly admitted visitors to his residence. His activities continued for almost four decades until he was declared a heretic by the fatwa of the grand mufti, strangled and thrown into the sea.[24] The event, which seems to have occurred a few years after our author Sarı Abdullah's death, was considered to be catastrophic for the order by Sarı Abdullah's great-nephew, La'lizade, another historiographer of the order. La'lizade suggests that after this, the order never regained its previous levels of activity, and the *pīr*s became completely secretive.[25] This comment, however, should be taken with caution considering the fact that La'lizade was an open devotee and a very important figure in the court under the patronage of the grand vizier Şehid Ali Paşa (d. 1716), who was secretly head of the order at the time.

It seems that, despite the setback of the execution, the order's settlement in Istanbul proved to be a successful enterprise. In the early seventeenth century, the order produced scholarly figures who were recognised in Istanbul for their learning and sophistication. Figures like Lamekani Hüseyin (d. 1625),[26] Abdullah Bosnevi (d. 1644)[27] and Oğlan Şeyh İbrahim (d. 1655)[28] were all able to reap respect and adoration, despite the fact that their ties to the *Hamzaviyye* were not entirely secret. In the meantime, the *Hamzaviyye* continued to insinuate itself into the palace power networks. Although it is not clear exactly how these chains of loyalty worked, by the early eighteenth century the *Melāmi*s had become one of the most important nodes of power in the capital city, and association with them was one of the surest ways of climbing the intricate steps of a career in the palace.[29]

Although we lack detailed studies of the *Hamzavi* worldview during this period, several historians have underlined the transformation of the order and commented on its circumstances. For instance, Colin Imber has remarked that:

> There are indications that, by the time of Beşir Ağa, the order had largely changed, or were changing their character to become an orthodox *tarīka* ... The report that the vizier Ferhad Paşa (d. 1595) became a disciple of Hüseyin

Lamekani is perhaps significant; as members of the Ottoman ruling establishment began to join the sect, it would, by definition, become orthodox.[30]

Hamid Algar, who wrote on the *Hamzavi* activity in Bosnia as a Sufi deviation, also marked the curious development. Noting that by the early eighteenth century, the order had gained such respectability that we find even a *şeyhülislam*, Paşmakçızade Seyyid Ali (d. 1712), and a grand vizier, Şehid Ali Paşa, among its luminaries, Algar wondered if the change was due to a sophisticated and rigorous practice of taqiyah, or prudent dissimulation. He further commented:

> The renunciation of extremist doctrine, originally a matter of outward precaution, seems ultimately to have been interiorized. One consequence of this was a blurring in the memory of the actual teachings of Hamza Bali and his predecessors and immediate successors; this permitted him to be honored as 'a martyr of divine love' revered by Sufis of various allegiances.[31]

Derin Terzioğlu, in turn, suggested that 'during the seventeenth century, not all of those who were disenchanted with institutionalized Sufism switched sides to become *Kadızadelis*, some embraced an increasingly Sunnified *Melāmi*sm'.[32]

Although we may not fully elucidate the nature of the order's inner transformation at the time, we can underscore some developments that were happening in the wider society and from which the *Hamzavis–Melāmis* benefited. The specifics of the transformation, therefore, might be better evaluated in the light of a closer reading of society in Istanbul at the time.

Social Transformation in Seventeenth-century Istanbul

The seventeenth century was a time of political and economic transformation for the Ottoman state. Recent scholarship has abandoned the concept of 'decline', instead viewing the Ottoman seventeenth century as part of broader early modern developments, underlining some of the common elements that influenced other political entities around the same time.[33] Among the trends shared by early modern societies and polities, scholars have identified urbanisation, monetisation and the spread of literacy as having played significant roles in shaping new social constructions.[34]

One of the most important developments of the time was the emergence of moneyed city folk who were able to enjoy life as members of upper- and middle-income households.[35] The first *Hamzavi pīr* to settle in Istanbul, Idris Muhtefi, was a wealthy merchant and can be understood to have belonged to this class. It was also within the class of such gentlemen that he endeavoured to establish connections beyond his dedicated followers among the small shop owners in the marketplace.[36] He seems to have achieved this by turning his house into an alternative space for socialisation, a gathering place where a plethora of gentlemen from different social strata could enjoy poetry, satisfying conversation regarding the mysteries of the universe, and the trappings of refined society. The same kind of atmosphere seems to have been established by pseudo-*Hamzavi* shaykhs who operated in various convents belonging to well-received Sufi orders.[37] Through these efforts, they were able to establish footholds within a network that included palace workers, statesmen, poets and cavalrymen.

The seventeenth century was also a time of increased literary activity for the Ottoman public. Scholars have noted a significant surge in personal writings, as well as religious and didactic works.[38] The *Hamzavi* community also reflected this general trend as its main medium of self-expression shifted from vernacular poetry to prosaic works that explained their ways of life and practice.[39] In this sense, it might be described as a period when the order transitioned from the oral/poetic tradition to a written/prosaic one. Vernacular, fiery and highly polarised sentiment that signified its poetical works, which functioned as the main vehicle of expression for the order's *pīr*s in the sixteenth century, seems to have mellowed, becoming more amiable and compliant as it was expressed in prose by the order's intellectuals. As we shall see, this observation might also be applied to the concept of *melāmet* as it was expressed in the poetic works of İsmail Maşuki and Sarban Ahmed as opposed to the later writings of Sarı Abdullah.

In fact, Sarı Abdullah's life story is a gateway to understanding how he managed to maintain his dedication to the *Hamzaviyye* while pursuing a career within palace circles. While his specific circumstances cannot account for all the variety of ways people belonged to the *Hamzaviyye* at the time, Sarı Abdullah is one of the few elite personalities whose relationship with the order is described in detail in the classical sources, and he represents a critical opportunity to evaluate the transformation of the *Hamzaviyye* in this era.

Sarı Abdullah and his Ṣemerāt

At a time when family ties were lifelines for building careers in the capital city, Sarı Abdullah was born into a well-established family. His father was a scion of one of the North African princely houses and had settled in Istanbul as a young man. Abdullah's mother's family, on the other hand, had critical political ties to the palace, which determined his prospects.

From the Hamzaviyye *to the* Melāmiyye

His mother was the daughter of Mehmed Paşa (d. 1589), who had been a commander in chief (*beylerbeyi*) and a close counsellor of Murad III (r. 1574–95). Mehmed Paşa and his brother, *Damat* or *Maraşlı* (or mistakenly in some sources, *Kayserili*) Halil Paşa (d. 1629), were both raised in the palace school (*enderūn*) and held important military and governmental positions. Halil Paşa served as a successful chief commander of the navy (*kaptan-ı derya*) multiple times and was also granted the office of the grand vizier for short intervals. This experienced statesman would play an essential role in Sarı Abdullah's upbringing since his father and grandfather had both died when Abdullah was a small child.

As a young man, Abdullah served as Halil Paşa's private secretary (*tezkireci*), accompanying his patron in the Persian campaign in 1618. He eventually received higher posts in the central government, even serving briefly, twice, as the chief of scribes (*reīsü'l-küttāb*). His bureaucratic engagements continued until he retired from public life in 1655. He was also known as a man of letters, a proficient calligraphist and a talented cultivator of flowers, especially tulips.[40] Also, he was a respected figure in the cultured Sufi milieu of the time. He attended the Celveti Shaykh Hudai's (d. 1629) convent from a young age, and in his adult life he developed close relationships with the *Mevlevi* circles. He was known as a commentator of Jalāl al-Dīn Rūmī's (d. 1273) *Mesnevi* and was admired for his proficiency in Persian and Arabic literature of classical Sufism.[41]

Although he was deeply involved with various mystical brotherhoods, Sarı Abdullah saw himself as a *Bayrami-Hamzavi* and a devotee of Idris Muhtefi. It was his adoptive father, Hüseyin Ağa, who took him to the Kırkçesme marketplace when he was quite young and introduced him to Idris' followers who were shop owners and artisans in this area. Abdullah was initiated into the order through a ceremony that affected him profoundly.[42] A close relationship with the *pīr* of the time, Idris Muhtefi, seems to have been impossible, but as far as we understand, he met the *pīr* at least once after a communal Friday prayer at the Ayasofya Mosque.[43] After Idris' death, Abdullah became a follower of his successor, Hacı Kabayi. The latter, however, did not typically meet with followers and Sarı Abdullah had to spend time away from Istanbul accompanying his great-uncle on a military campaign. In fact, he became aware of Kabayi's death under unusual circumstances.[44] After his arrival in Istanbul, his acquaintances from the order refused to tell him who the current *pīr* was. After an interim period of confusion, Abdullah became acquainted with Beşir Ağa and visited him often.[45]

The *Şemerāt* was one of Sarı Abdullah's earliest writings. It was widely read and eventually appeared in print as well. Conceived as a Sufi manual, the *Şemerāt* tackles some of the most basic aspects of Sufi teachings in five chapters and concluding remarks. The first chapter explains how the universe came to be from the overflowing love of God, and how the human being (Adam) is the best representation of this love, a quality that makes him the steward (*khalīfa*) of all other creatures. The second chapter explains the need to search for the real love (*ḥub-i aṣlī*) that surrounds the universe, to cleanse the heart, and find the perfect man of the time (*insān-ı kāmīl*). The third chapter details the various ways to follow the path (*sulūk*), and how the sudden and unexpected rapture (*cezbe*) of one disciple can be superior to the continuous hard work of another one. The fourth chapter focuses on the need to turn away from this world and adhere to the perfect guide (*mürşīd*) of the time. Finally, in the fifth chapter, Sarı Abdullah provides an overview of the *tarikat* genealogies in the Ottoman Empire, mostly dealing with the *Nakşbandīyye* and the *Halvetiyye*. He focuses on the *Halveti* genealogy in the most detail, eventually reaching the beginnings of the *Bayrami* genealogy and tracing the *Hamzavi*s from there. Given its pejorative nature, the title *Hamzaviyye* never appears in the book, and its namesake, Hamza Bali, is mentioned only briefly as a *pīr* who exhibited unbounded love and ecstasy but had to suffer due to the misunderstanding of his teachings. Sarı Abdullah is quite open about his loyalty to Idris Muhtefi, describing him as the perfect guide of the age.[46]

The Content of the Şemerāt *and its Adaptations*

Sarı Abdullah was deeply connected to the Sufi world of seventeenth-century Istanbul. He instinctively understood the aspirations and ideals of its practitioners and was deeply involved in its networks. He must have realised how the *Hamzaviyye* could become a valid part of it, and how bridges could be built in the midst of a rather hostile milieu. The *Şemerāt* includes instances where he works through some of the problematic characteristics of the *Hamzaviyye* and adapts them to the intellectual Sufi audiences of Istanbul. These adaptations, and the terminology in which they are conveyed, display how Sarı Abdullah envisaged the implicit *doxa* of the time and sought to locate the *Hamzavi* worldview within its boundaries. His choices provide us with fascinating insights into which beliefs were deemed acceptable at the time, and how different viewpoints about the divine and the nature of prophecy could be accommodated.

It is significant that Sarı Abdullah adheres to the particular characteristics of Sunnism that were held in his time in his efforts to reconstruct the Islamic past. He venerates the companions of the Prophet, and specifically the four caliphs and the ten companions who were awarded entry to heaven

From the Hamzaviyye *to the* Melāmiyye

(*'aşere-i mübeşşere*).⁴⁷ He also treats the Twelve Imams of the Alid lineage with great respect.⁴⁸ In addition, the *Şemerāt* describes the founders of the juristic schools (the imams Abu Hanifa, Shafi'i, Malik and Ibn Hanbal) in hagiographical terms, and particularly emphasises their friendly interactions with the imams of the Alid lineage. It does not mention any points of conflict that might have separated these figures in history, presenting all of them as individuals who deserve the utmost respect.

This harmonious portrayal of the Islamic past, however, was not necessarily a hallmark of sixteenth-century *Bayrami-Hamzavi* poetry. It is well attested that an extreme dedication to and love for Ali, the son-in-law of the Prophet, as the rightful inheritor of prophetic wisdom was a striking feature of that tradition.⁴⁹ This fervour for Ali appears in various sources, and the concept of the mystery of Ali (*sırr-ı Ali*), meaning the esoteric knowledge and responsibility that Ali entrusted to the saints, constitutes the most distinguishing aspect of the *Bayrami-Hamzavi* understanding of sainthood. The concept also appears quite often in the order's sixteenth-century written sources, particularly in 'Askeri's *Mir'ātül Işk*, which is otherwise a highly normative Sunni piece of writing.⁵⁰

Although the specific concept of the mystery of Ali does not appear in the *Şemerāt*, the idea behind it is articulated in a nuanced and acceptable manner. In the 'eyes of the beholders of the reality', Sarı Abdullah explains, 'Ali is the only successor of Muhammad' and 'all orders, in fact, derive from Ali'.⁵¹ He also deals carefully with the case of the *Nakşbandīyya*, the origins of which have traditionally been attributed to Abu Bakr. Although he first reports that the Prophet personally taught the silent remembrance of God (*dhikr-i khafi* – a trademark of the *Nakşbandī* practice) to Abu Bakr, he later exerts a great deal of effort explaining how this order should also be traced back to Ali.⁵²

Another significant adaptation relates to the messianic fervour within the *Bayrami-Hamzavi* tradition and the possible declarations regarding the beginning of a new age in which juristic law would be understood differently.⁵³ In general, by the seventeenth century, the urban *Hamzavi* intelligentsia had already abandoned these apocalyptic yearnings. However, the extraordinary loyalty and dedication to the saints (*awliyā*), which can be seen as a holdover from this tendency, is regularly invoked in the *Şemerāt*. The notion that there is bound to be one unique spiritual persona (*kutb*), who is the mirror of divinity in any given age is particularly significant in this regard. Such ideas, however, were not alien to the broader Sufi milieu of the time, and writings that were admired among the cultured Sufis of Istanbul, particularly those of Ibn 'Arabi (d. 1240), were known to have expressed similar ideas. Therefore, it was not seen as alarming when

Sarı Abdullah wrote the following without revealing any overt political agenda:

> even now, the time is not devoid of the esteemed person who is the rising [ḳāim] saint of the time, the inheritor of the legacy of the absolute and complete sainthood of Muhammad. This celebrated person who is the inheritor of the true perfection of the prophet is called the axis of the ages [ḳutb-u devrān], the greatest succour [gavs-i 'azām], and the unique one of the age [vāhīdu'z-zamān]. [Imam] Ali said: 'whoever dies without knowing the leader [imām] of his time, dies as someone from the time of ignorance'.[54]

The concept of *devr* posed an additional problem. For the *Hamzavi* community, *devr* encompassed a cyclical view of time in which the divine creative light emerged from the absolute entity, forming the universe by successively taking the shape of minerals, plants, animals and, finally, human beings. When a person achieved perfection (*kemāl*), the divine light was able to manifest itself fully within him and reunite with its point of origin.[55] The *Bayrami-Hamzavi* and the *Bektaşi-Alevi* tradition both produced various *devriye*s – poetry written to describe this circular voyage.[56] The tone of this poetry could go beyond a symbolic description of the inner transformation of the human being and bear markings of a transformation and evolution in the biological sense of the word. When this happened, the idea seemed to resonate with the heresiographical understanding of *tanāsukh*, the transmigration of souls. This association was furtively embraced by some seventeenth-century figures, and we can find positive attitudes towards *tanāsukh* expressed in sources from the time.[57] However, the sensitivity around this issue is apparent in a letter penned by *pīr* Beşir Ağa forbidding his followers from talking about *devr* in public.[58]

In the *Şemerāt*, the idea is discussed in cautious terms, taking reputable Sufi poetry and prose as a guide. Although the term *devr* does not actually appear in the text, there is a section on 'stages and stations in the creation of the human being' that seems to deal with this particular idea.[59] In this section, Sarı Abdullah explains that human beings are representatives of certain names of God, and that they gain this representation in connection with the long voyage of the elements that shape their embryo while they are in the uterus. The elements, in their most basic form, represent the names of God according to their capacity and they continually strive to reach their most perfect forms. Those that can achieve this state move on to a higher level of being, while those that cannot, return to their previous location. They continue on this voyage of construction and deconstruction until they fully realise their true potential in the construction of the perfect

From the Hamzaviyye *to the* Melāmiyye

human being (*insān-i kāmīl*).⁶⁰ Sarı Abdullah assures the reader that this is quite different from the idea of *tanāsukh*, and he provides examples from the Sufi literature denying such an association.⁶¹

The Concept of **Melāmet** *in the* **Şemerāt**

The term *melāmet* was understood in the *Bayrami-Hamzavi* heritage in a variety of ways, and a shift can be noted in its usage even before Sarı Abdullah's writings. In the sixteenth century, the concept appears in the poetry of the poet-*pīr*s who underline the necessity of forsaking social status and societal markings in order to be sincere followers of the path. Ismail Ma'şuki, for instance, declares, 'Leave behind the [good] name and the sign, wear the cloak of *melāmet* [reproach] / Many sultans are hidden behind this cloak of *melāmet*.'⁶² A similar attitude also appears in the poetry of Ahmed Sarban, who praises those who condemn his way of life in the fashion of a true *melāmetī*: 'Whoever condemns us from human kind / May God protect him from fear and danger / Whoever mentions our wrong-doing / Oh God, make his mouth sweeter than honey and sugar.'⁶³

Both of these poet-*pīr*s seem to celebrate and derive pleasure from society's reproach rather than resenting it. This is not surprising, since the term *melāmet* was one of the common metaphors of Turkish lyric poetry at the time and was employed not only as a useful rhyming antonym to safety (*selāmet*) that the lover had to abandon in order to be sincere in his love, but also in various phrases in the vernacular language, such as *melāmet olmak* (to receive reproach and not be bothered by it). Nevertheless, by cherishing the virtues of being a target of blame and reproach the term disrupted the basic social instinct to regard one's honour as the most valuable of possessions and to protect it at all costs.⁶⁴ In this sense, it was a proper reflection of the anti-privilege and reactive spirit of the order in the sixteenth century.

This temperament, however, cannot be found in the writings of dervish authors who belong to the same tradition. For instance, the *Mir'ātu'l Işk* (*The Mirror of Love*), penned after the execution of Ismail Maşuki in an effort to absolve Pir Ali Aksarayi (d. 1539) from his son's deviant ways, advises the true followers to stay away from blame-inducing behaviour.⁶⁵ For this, they need to obey the sharia and adhere to the proper conduct (*adab*) of the path. The same mind-set is also evident in the *Irşādnāme*, one of the few sources that were written before the *Şemerāt* in Istanbul. Followers are admonished to make sure that they do not become receivers of social stigma:

When it comes to those who do not follow the divine commands and abide by the prescribed conduct of the path and the sharia, they become tainted with malevolent and repugnant acts. They receive reproach [*melāmet*] from commoners, and because of them, the perfect guide and his path, as well as followers of other Sufi orders receive reproach and rebuke. Such people did wrong to themselves, to their *pīr*, to the path, and also to all people of the path. May God protect us from evil of this kind![66]

The term *melāmet*, nevertheless, signified other modes of behaviour as well. It was often associated with working manually to make a living in the marketplace rather than relying on the comforts of a convent, a mentality that can be noted early in the foundations of the *Bayramiyye*. Hamiduddin Aksarayi (d. 1408), who was the spiritual guide of Hacı Bayram Veli (d. 1430), and was the one who brought the *Halvetī*/Safavid tradition into Anatolia, is described as having disguised himself as a simple bread-seller in Bursa, where he became known as the *Somuncu Baba*, the bread-seller. His successor, Hacı Bayram, went on to establish a convent in Ankara, and after some initial disputes, preferred to get on well with the Ottoman state, relying on its financial contributions. His successor Akşemseddin (d. 1459) continued this practice but was challenged by Emir Dede (d. 1476), who became the founder of the *Bayrami-Hamzavi* branch. He was known by his occupation as a knife-maker (*al-Sikkīnī, Bıçakçı*), was very likely illiterate, and refused to settle into the ways of life in the convent. Indeed, in some ways, he signalled a return to the ways of life and socio-ethical position that had characterised the *Bayramiyye* before their institutionalisation.

Emir Dede's followers grounded their refusal to wear distinctive Sufi garments and reside in convents in an episode of confrontation between Emir Dede and Akşemseddin. Accordingly, Emir Dede, criticised and reproached by Akşemseddin for not following the rituals of the lodge, was desperate to explain his point of view and challenged the latter to a public demonstration of spiritual competence. When the time came to meet, Emir Dede stepped into a cooking fire and emerged unharmed. His *Bayrami* cloak and headdress had been burnt away, but his flesh and skin survived the fire unscathed. After this event, those who followed him did not wear Sufi garments and did not dwell in Sufi convents, underscoring the vanity of attributing too much importance to distinctive Sufi clothes, hierarchies and rituals.[67]

It is in connection with this incident that Sarı Abdullah uses the term *melāmet* to explain Emir Dede's choices and sensibilities. He explains that the order entered the realm of *melāmet* after this point, choosing to be among those who are protected by the veil of anonymity. They sought secrecy, not because of shameful behaviour or heretical belief, but because they needed to hide the extent of their spiritual accomplishments. God ordains that he chooses to veil his most precious devotees:

> After this Emir Dede did not accept the headwear and the cloak [*tāc u hırka*] having gone over to the way of the *melāmetī*. Even now, masters of this path and *pīr*s of this respected order continue to live under veils [*kıyāb*] included in the *melāmetī* community within the group: 'My friends [*evliyā*] are under my domes, nobody knows them but me.'[68]

He continues to explain that by refusing to wear distinctive garments, the followers of Emir Dede avoided pride and egoism and were able to conceal their true spiritual state from the eyes of outsiders. They maintained regular jobs at the market and sought closeness to God among the crowds of people. Since they did not occupy themselves with what others thought of them, slander and praise did not differ much in their eyes. They were embedded in ecstasy and divine love in their own private lives:

> These are the guides of the true path [*murşīdān-i ṭarīk-i Ḥak*], and their methods of the true way are through rapture [*cezbe*], directing the heart and love [*'işk*], and absorption [*istiğrāk*] in the manifestation of the oneness of the Essence. They have chosen *melāmet* and to be hidden under the veils, and have become clean of arrogance and presumption. They were concealed and free from the eyes of the outsiders. But in choosing *melāmet*, their intent was not to commit illicit acts. It was rather that they were inclined to occupy themselves with buying and selling, earning and making a living without a Sufi scarf [*şal*] and cloak [*hırka*]. [In this way,] the eyes of the people were not able to reach their imaginations, and their empty wishes could not find a way into their hearts. They blended in with the common folk on the outside, but their hearts were removed from everything but God, and their zeal [*himmet*] was unique among all. They practiced solitude with God among the masses [*halvet der encümen*] and regarded people's praise and rebuke as the same. They took off the cloth of fame and wore the white robes [*ihrām*] of reproach [*melāmet*]. Because they emptied [*tahliye*] their hearts on the steps of the beloved, they might be called *Halveti*s, and because their hearts are engraved with [*nakşband*] the love of God, it might be proper to call them *Nakşbandīyya*.[69]

In this regard, Sarı Abdullah connects the order with the *Halveti* and the *Nakşbandī* traditions, both of which were quite influential in Istanbul at the time. He continues to use the same language of adoration and respect as he further explains that the order might also be called the *Bayrami*s, since they have sacrificed their desires and aspirations in the way of God and stood in their white robes in self-denial like a person carrying out the rituals of the pilgrimage does.[70] Thus, he seems to indicate that it is not just their genealogy, but also their praxis and proper etiquette that tie them to these Sufi networks.

There are other ways in which Sarı Abdullah reclaims the controversial history of the order through the adaptation of the *melāmī* concept. In this sense, he employs the term *melāmet* to signify spiritual superiority and closeness to God, while at the same time having to suffer false accusations and insults. His comments regarding one of the early masters of Sufism, Zu'n-Nun al-Misri (d. 861) are interesting in showcasing his usage of the term:

> Zu'n-Nun al-Mısri was among the masters of *melāmet*. He was unique for his time in terms of [his knowledge of] the secrets of the unity of being, spiritual exercise, and self-mortification. Some Egyptians believed that this heavenly person was an infidel, and some remained suspicious and bewildered. It is astonishing that, even in our times, so many friends of God are not exempt from condemnation, hatred, and similar accusations.[71]

Sarı Abdullah also reminds the reader of the other Sufi masters who were executed in the past and underlines society's ignorance and cruelty in dealing with ideas that they do not comprehend. Those who are mentioned include, Hallaj (ex. 922),[72] 'Ayn al-Kudat Hamadani (ex. 1131),[73] Majd ad-Din Baghdadi (ex. 1219),[74] Şams Tebrizi (d. 1247)[75] and Nesimi (ex. c. 1417).[76] For him, these masters of the Sufi way had to suffer in their lifetime, because common people could not appreciate their points of view. In the same way, Sarı Abdullah asserts, the *Bayrami-Hamzavi*s suffered blame and reproach because society did not understand their way of thinking and living. He emphasises the need for compassion and understanding towards the wretched ones among the Sufis (*fukarā*) and maintains that negative assumptions harm society as a whole.[77]

Therefore, in the *Semerāt*, Sarı Abdullah not only manages to make his loyalties to the genealogy of the *Hamzaviyye* known, but he also depicts their non-standard form of devotion as something that is an integral part of an esteemed Sufi history. Further, his portrayal of the *melāmetī* in his *Semerāt* serves to accomplish several specific goals. First, his discussion of the concept abandons its former poetic/unruly/nomadic associations. It is no longer associated with a revolutionary and divergent spirit, but, rather, with a superior level of wisdom and knowledge that common people cannot comprehend. Second, by highlighting the concept's connection to participation in daily life as a commoner, Sarı Abdullah elaborates a more domesticated and urbanised perspective. In this new interpretation, the concept becomes suitable for the needs of the sophisticated city-dweller who is eager to be part of urban establishments. Third, he discusses the possibility that spiritual accomplishments do not always open the way to a more prominent life in this world. The *melāmetī* is superior in his understanding of God, and yet is denounced because common people are not capable of understanding them. A certain amount of secrecy, therefore, is essential to ensure a respectful standing in society. Therefore, Sarı Abdullah tames and urbanises the concept of *melāmet*, transforming its previous connection with the unruly and the perverse into a characteristic of the mysterious, humble and awe-inspiring follower of the *Bayrami* way.

Conclusion

Throughout the seventeenth century, as Anatolian and Balkan towns lost their previous importance in the genealogy of the order, *Bayrami-Hamzavi* activity became centred in Istanbul. Although their attempt to survive in the city was hampered by suspicion and persecution, these circumstances did not prevent *Hamzavi* intellectuals from exploring new relationships, concepts and opportunities in order to build reputation and prestige for themselves and their traditions.

Sarı Abdullah was one of these intellectuals. However, he was not overly influential at the time he wrote the *Şemerāt*. It is possible that there were multiple voices and opinions, and that the community was not devoid of inner conflict. It is likely that some saw Sarı Abdullah as a nuisance, as a man who talked and wrote much while understanding little.[78] Sarı Abdullah had to negotiate on various fronts not only within Ottoman society in general, but also within the small and intricate community of the *Hamzavi*s.

Sarı Abdullah's rehabilitative approach – harmonising the *Hamzavi* tradition with the religious culture of Istanbul – however, proved to be quite convenient for subsequent generations of educated and urbanised members of a historically marginalised community. In their efforts to gain a foothold in the capital city and acculturate themselves into its power networks, they relied on Sarı Abdullah's vision, employed it in effective ways and even developed it further. The stream of scholarship that flowed from the ranks of the order after this time frequently relied on his writings and conceptualisations to situate the order within the larger Sufi tradition. The effort to succeed and prosper in contemporary Ottoman society had an impact not only on the *Hamzavi* community itself but perhaps more interestingly, on the culture of the Ottoman court, as their way of life infused into its structures and decision-making mechanisms as followers of the order became more dominant within it.

Ottoman Sunnism

Notes

* An earlier version of this chapter was presented at the 31st Middle East History and Theory Conference, University of Chicago, 6–7 May 2016. I would like to thank Cornell Fleischer and Daria Kovaleva for their comments. I am also thankful to John J. Curry for his comments.

1. In the first decades of the seventeenth century, Istanbulites would have known the order either as *Idrisi*s, referring to the *pīr* of that era, Idris Muhtefi (d. 1615), or as *Hamzavi*s, referring to the Bosnian Shaykh Hamza Bali who was executed on charges of heresy in 1572. The title *Bayrami-Melāmiyye* became common in the eighteenth century and its use for the era before that should be considered anachronistic. Some of the most important Turkish studies on the order include: Gölpınarlı, *Melamilik ve Melamiler*; Ocak, *Osmanlı Toplumunda Zındıklar ve Mülhidler* , pp. 251–313; Ocak, 'Kanuni Sultan Süleyman Devrinde'; Ocak, 'XVI–XVII. Yüzyıllarda Bayrami Melamileri'; Işın, 'Melamilik'; Işın 'Melamiyye (Ikinci devre Melamileri, Bayramiler)'. A short evaluation of the order can be found in Imber, 'Malamatiyya, in Ottoman Lands'. Also significant are the following studies: Holbrook, 'The Melami Supra-Order'; Holbrook, 'The Melami Supra-Order. Part Two'; Clayer et al., *Melamis-Bayramis*; Yavuz, 'The Making of a Sufi Order'.

2. Some of the eighteenth-century sources that use this designation include: La'lizade, *Ṭārīḳāt-i 'Aliyye-i Bayrāmiyye*; Üsküdarlı Haşim Baba (d. 1782), 'Esrāru'l-Ilāhiyyūn ve Etvāru'l-Melāmiyyūn' (can be found in Latinised form in Tek, *Melamet Risaleleri*, pp. 391–400); Müstakimzade Süleyman Sa'deddin (d. 1202/1788), 'Risale-i Melamiyye-i Bayramiyye' (Latinised form of this text can be found in Tek, 'Müstakimzade Süleyman Sadeddin', pp. 58–138).

3. Holbrook uses the term 'supra-order' to explain that they were considered a group that comprised those who completed whatever course of progress was offered elsewhere. Holbrook, 'Melami Supra-Order. Part Two', p. 16.

4. By the twentieth century, the order had come to be seen as the second phase of a three-wave Melami movement. See Haririzade Kemaleddin (d.1882), *Tibyān Vasāilu'l-Haḳāiḳ fī Bayān Salāsilu'l-Ṭarāiḳ*, vol. 3, No. 142, 140a–143b. This three-tiered understanding of the Melami movement can be also found in Vicdani, *Tomar-i Ṭuruk-u Aliyye* and Gölpınarlı, *Melamilik ve Melamiler*.

5. The concept of *melāmet* originates from the Arabic root *l.w.m.* indicating blame and reproach. Therefore, *melāmetī/melāmī* signifies the person who calls reproach upon him- or herself. In the third century of Islam, the term came to signify a group of people in Khurasan with a specific set of morals. The foundation of this movement has been attributed to Hamdun al-Kassar (d. 884), Abu Hafs al-Ḥaddad (d. 873) and Abu 'Uthman al-Hiri (d. 910). Recent publications on the *Melāmetiyye* agree on the intrinsic inward-looking piety of the original movement. It later became included under the rubric of

136

From the Hamzaviyye *to the* Melāmiyye

Sufism, which was originally based in Baghdad. *Melāmetī* fathers regarded all outward appearances of piety or religiosity, including good deeds, as ostentation. Therefore, the *melāmetī* made a point of renouncing any deed that would attract positive attention from the public and gain him a good title. He also made a point of renouncing special clothing that indicated spiritual attainment and chose to make a living relying on simple daily jobs at the market rather than living in seclusion. For more information, see Algar, 'Malamatiyya'; Chabbi, 'Remarques sur le développement', pp. 32–4, 53–7; Karamustafa, *Sufism: the Formative Period*, pp. 48–51, 161–5; Schimmel, *Mystical Dimensions of Islam*, pp. 86–8; Sviri, 'Ḥakim Tirmidhi'.

6. On Sarı Abdullah, see Huart and Burrill, 'Ṣarı 'Abd Allah Efendi'; Azamat, 'Sarı Abdullah Efendi'; Gölpınarlı, *Melamilik ve Melamiler*, pp. 137–42.
7. *Ghulāt* often rendered into English as 'extremists' was a term of disapproval for individuals accused of exaggeration (*ghuluww*) in religion. In practice, the term has covered all early speculative Shiites except those later accepted by the Twelver tradition (Hodgson, 'Ghulat').
8. For more information on this period, see Hodgson, *The Venture of Islam*, vol. 2, pp. 493–500; Babayan, *Mystics, Monarchs, and Messiahs*; Amoretti, 'Religion in the Timurid and the Safavid Periods'; Mazzaoui, *The Origins of the Safawids*; Bashir, 'Between Mysticism and Messianism', pp. 8–74; Bashir, *Messianic Hopes Mystical Visions*; Schimmel, 'The Ornament of Saints'.
9. Matthew Melvin-Khouski's recent publications are invaluable for their insight into the intellectual and political outreaches of this development. See Melvin-Khouski, 'Ibn Turka'. Cornell Fleischer's studies underline similar tendencies as they pertain to the imperial image of Süleyman I. See especially Fleischer, 'Ancient Wisdom and New Sciences'. For an evaluation of a cognate trend in the Mughal Empire, see Moin, *The Millennial Sovereign*.
10. The designation *anti-imperial* is used by Melvin-Khouski to characterise Şeyh Bedreddin's (ex. 1420) rebellion against the Ottomans, see Melvin-Khouski, 'Ibn Turka'. Also see Hodgson's characterisation of similar movements as *anti-privilege, anti-conventional* and *chiliastic* in *The Venture of Islam*, vol. 2, pp. 494–500.
11. For Ahmet Karamustafa's usage of the term, see 'Origins of Anatolian Sufism'.
12. For an insightful study of the Halveti urbanisation in the fifteenth century, see Karataş, 'The Ottomanization of the Halveti Sufi Order'. Also see these important studies for additional insight into Sufi traditions in Ottoman local settings: Le Gall, *A Culture of Sufism*; Curry, *The Transformation of Muslim Mystical Thought*; Emre, 'Crafting Piety for Success'.
13. Tijana Krstić suggested the use of the term as a framework for studying the connected histories of the Ottoman Empire and its European and Safavid neighbours and rivals. For her, 'the age of confessionalization and empire building' covers the period between the attainment of Istanbul with its imperial legacy, and the collapse of the *Kadızadeli* movement in the aftermath of the

Ottoman Sunnism

failure of the second siege of Vienna (1450s–1690s). See Krstić, 'Illuminated by the Light'; Krstić, *Contested Conversions*. Derin Terzioğlu often uses the term interchangeably with Sunnitisation. See Terzioğlu, 'Sufis in the Age of State-building'; Terzioğlu, 'How to Conceptualize Ottoman Sunnitization'. For the conceptualisation of confessional Europe, see Schilling, 'Confessional Europe'; Schilling, 'Confessionalization'.

14. Religious life in seventeenth-century Istanbul has largely been studied along the lines of the emergence of the puritanical *Kadızadeli*s and their call for moralistic reform. Some of the defining scholarship includes, Zilfi, *Politics of Piety*; Zilfi, 'The *Kadızadeli*s'; Öztürk, 'Islamic Orthodoxy'.

15. Convents belonging to the order appeared in Istanbul, and some even followed traditional Sufi practice. These convents included *Helvai tekkesi* in the Bayezid district and *Saçlı Emir Tekkesi* in the Kasımpaşa district. These places, however, were not seen as the main centres for the order's activities. The main figure, the *pīr*, did not live in a convent, but met with people at his own residence.

16. Alexander Knysh suggests the term *spontaneous orthodoxy* in his article '"Orthodoxy" and "Heresy" in Medieval Islam'; for a review of scholarly discussions around the issue, see Langer and Simon, 'The Dynamics of Orthodoxy and Heterodoxy'. The social dimensions of orthodoxy are discussed in El Shamsy, 'The Social Construction of Orthodoxy'; another insightful study is Calder, 'The Limits of Islamic Orthodoxy'.

17. We are able to trace the antagonistic view towards the *Hamzavi*s through various fragmentary writings. These include Mehmed Amiki's *Eyyuhe'l-Veled*, written in 1614 (Süleymaniye Library, Halet Efendi 764; studied in Gölpınarlı, *Melamilik ve Melamiler*, pp. 75–6); similar examples of fragmentary writings are discussed in Algar, '*Hamzaviye*', pp. 251–2. Derin Terzioğlu's recent studies on the seventeenth-century *ilmihal*s also indicate the negative view against the *Hamzavi*s, see Terzioğlu, 'Where 'Ilm-i Ḥāl Meets Catechism', p. 91. Abdulmecid Sivasi, a well-known Halveti figure of the time, was also highly critical of the *Hamzavi*s. Sivasi's comments in his *Durar-i Akāid* include, 'Those who believe in the firm texts of the doctrine of the *ehl-i sunnat* already know that *Hamzavi*s, İdrisis, and Ḥurūfis, all of them are unbelievers [*kāfir*].' Based on Kılıç, 'Ebu'l-Hayr Abdulmecid b. Muharrem es-Sivasi'.

18. The *Ḥurūfiyya* was a mystico-messianic movement founded by Fazlallah Ḥurūfi (ex. 1394). The Timurids as well as the Ottomans deemed their teachings and political discontent dangerous. Studies on the *Ḥurūfiyya* include: Browne, 'Some Notes on the Literature and Doctrine of the Hurufi Sect'; Browne, 'Further Notes on the Literature of the Ḥurūfis'; Gölpınarlı, *Hurufîlik Metinleri Kataloğu*; Algar, 'The Hurufi Influence on Bektashism'; Norris, 'The Hurufi Legacy of Fadlullah of Astarabad'; Bashir, *Fazlullah Astarabadi and the Hurufis*; Bashir, 'Enshrining Divinity'; Mir-Kasimov, *Words of Power*.

From the Hamzaviyye to the Melāmiyye

19. Some classical sources suggest that this incident took place in 1561, but I follow the dates that appear in the official documents and Muniri's *Silsilet'u-l Muḳarrabin*. For further information on Hamza Bali and his followers in Bosnia, see Algar, '*Hamzavīye*'; Ocak, *Osmanlı Toplumunda Mülhidler ve Zındıklar*, pp. 363–77; Telci, 'Hamza Bali ve Hamzavīlere Dair'.
20. These comments are found in the various treatises mentioned above, especially in Sivasi's *Durar-i 'Aḳāid*.
21. For more information, see Azamat, 'Idris-i Muhtefi'; Işın 'Idris-i Muhtefi'; Gölpınarlı, *Melamilik ve Melamiler*, pp. 123–8; Ocak, *Osmanlı Toplumunda Zındıklar ve Mülhidler*, pp. 310–13. The chronicler Atayi reports that Şeyh Ali Idris was from a virtuous family in Tırhala and was raised by his fraternal uncle who was a tailor working for Rüstem Paşa (Kanuni's grand vizier, d. 1561). He also reports that Ali visited the Bayramī pīr Hüsameddin Ankaravi (d. 1557) together with his uncle, when they were part of the military expedition against Iran in 955/1548–9. Şeyh Hüsameddin accepted him into his service and gave him the name *Idris* due to his training as a tailor just like the Prophet Idris (biblical Enoch). After Ankaravi's death (which occurred in 1556 according to Atayi), Idris settled in Istanbul and acted as his successor for sixty years. Atayi seems to have favoured Idris against the attacks of Sivasi. Atayi, *Ḥadaik*, pp. 602–3.
22. He was of Gregorian origin, a freed slave of Ibrahim Çavuş, who was a *Hamzavi*. Ḳabayi was his epithet, pointing to his profession as a salesperson of *ḳaba* (a piece of clothing worn over the shirt like a robe). He continued in this profession during the years he was recognised as the head of the order. (Gölpınarlı, *Melamilik ve Melamiler*, p. 156; La'lizade, *Ṭārīḳāt-i 'Aliyye-i Bayrāmiyye*, p. 50).
23. According to Müstakimzade, Beşir Ağa was originally from Albania, and had come to Istanbul as a young man having been recruited among *Bostancı*s, a military class that was responsible for taking care of the palaces in Istanbul. As a young man, he came to know a barber who was one of the guides (*rehber*) of Idris. When Idris died, Beşir Ağa retired from his job and dedicated himself to the new *pīr* Ḳabayi's service. He became Ḳabayi's closest companion, and after his death was accepted as the head of the order.
24. Beşir Ağa was an old man over the age of ninety at the time. Forty of his followers who protested the execution shared the same fate in the following days. According to La'lizade, the grand mufti, Sun'izade Seyyid Mehmet Emin Efendi (d. 1076/1665) worked in collaboration with the grand vizier, Köprülü Fazıl Ahmet Pasha (r. 1661–76) for the execution, and the two acted without the knowledge of Sultan Mehmed IV (r. 1648–87) who was away from Istanbul on an expedition (La'lizade, *Ṭārīḳāt-i 'Aliyye-i Bayrāmiyye*, pp. 54–5). It is also that possible Vani Efendi (d. 1096/1685), who was known for his strict anti-Sufi stance and his closeness to the sultan, played a role in the execution. According to Baer, 'Vaniköy – constructed by Vani Mehmed Efendi was one of the only two areas in Istanbul where

Sufis, especially *Hamzavi Melamis* never set foot. They blamed Vani Efendi for the murder of Beşir Ağa and the drowning of his disciples at Kadıköy Feneri in 1662. For this reason they cursed him and his village, and called him "Vani, the murderer".' See Baer, *Honoured by the Glory of Islam*, p. 115.
25. La'lizade, *Ṭarīḳāt-i 'Aliyye-i Bayrāmiyye*, pp. 56–7.
26. See Ilic, 'Lamekani Hüseyin Efendi'.
27. See Hafizović, 'A Bosnian Commentator on the *Fusus al-Hikam*'.
28. For more information on this figure, see Soysal, 'XVII. Yüzyılda Bir Bayrami-Melami Kutbu'.
29. See Işın, 'Melamilik'. For an evaluation of the *Hamzavī-Melāmī* effect on the leisure culture of the palace during the early eighteenth century, see Çalış-Kural, *Şehrengiz*. According to Işın and Çalış-Kural, some of the most important figures of the early eighteenth century were *Melāmi*s. 'In the early eighteenth century, Şehid Ali Paşa, the grand vizier, was the leader of *Melāmi* society. Following him the grand vizier Ibrahim Paşa, Nedim, Habeşizade Abdurrahim Efendi known as poet Rahimi, La'lizade Abdulbaki, *Reisül-Küttab* Mustafa efendi, Ahmed Arif Paşa, *Defterdār* (chief finance officer) Mehmed Paşa, historian Mehmed Raşid, Mustafa Sami, Osmanzade Taib were all melamis.' Çalış-Kural, *Şehrengiz*, p. 207.
30. Imber, 'Malamatiyya, in Ottoman Lands'.
31. Algar, '*Hamzaviye*', pp. 255–6.
32. Terzioğlu, 'Sufis in the Age of State-Building', p. 97.
33. For a detailed study of the Ottoman political transformation, see Tezcan, *The Second Ottoman Empire*.
34. For arguments of a globally conceived early modernity, see Fletcher, 'Integrative History'; Subrahmanyam, 'Connected Histories'.
35. See Terzioğlu, 'Where 'Ilm-i Ḥāl Meets Catechism', p. 96; Tezcan, *The Second Ottoman Empire*, pp. 14–23; Sariyannis, '"Mob," "Scamps" and Rebels in Seventeenth-Century Istanbul'.
36. Atayi describes his affluent residence and its popularity within the upper class through a description of his estate after his death (Atayi, *Ḥadaik*, pp. 603–4).
37. Lamekani Hüseyin and Oğlan Shaykh Ibrahim were known as *Halveti*s and operated in their own lodges. Such efforts were often seen as a form of *taqiyyah*, hiding their real identities for the sake of safety. See Kılıç, 'Bir Tarikatın Gizli Direnişi'. Regarding Oğlan Shaykh Ibrahim, Şeyhi notes that the rich surrounded his *tekke* to the extent that the poor could not find a way to get in. Şeyhi, *Vekayi*, part I, p. 553.)
38. See Terzioğlu, 'Where 'Ilm-i Ḥal Meets Catechism', p. 84; Kafadar, 'Self and Others'.
39. See, for instance, Hakiki Bey's (d. 1640) *Irşādnama*. A concise translation in English is available in Yavuz, 'The Worldview of a Sufi'.
40. He was quite successful as a cultivator of flowers and was dubbed *çiçekçibaşı* (head flower cultivator) by Ibrahim I. It is also said that his epithet, *Sarı*,

meaning blonde or yellow, referred to a special kind of tulip he was able to cultivate.

41. Sarı Abdullah produced various treatises that stand witness to his competence in Classical Sufi sources in Arabic and Persian. His *Cevāhir-i Bevāḥir-i Meṣnevi* (written between 1035 and 1041 (1625–31) and printed in Istanbul in 1288/1871) is a five-volume Turkish translation of and commentary on Rūmī's *Mesnevi*. His *Cevheretu'l-Bidāye ve Durratu'n-Nihāye* (*The Jewel of the Beginning and the Pearl of the End*) is another mystical treatise with content similar to the *Ṣemerāt*. It was written in the year 1049/1639 in celebration of Murad IV's (r. 1623–40) conquest of Baghdad. He also penned an advisory treatise for Sultan Mehmed IV: *Nasihatu'l-Mulūk Tergīben li husni's-sulūk* (*Advice to Kings Encouraging a Good Path*). It was summarised by Osmanzade Ahmed Taib Efendi (d. 1724) under the title *Telhisü'n-Neṣāyih* and was presented to Ahmed III (r. 1703–30). After retirement, Sarı Abdullah produced a collected edition of Ibn Arabi's comments regarding sainthood, the perfect human being and the *melāmetis* from his *Futūḥāt al-Makkiyya* under the title *Mirʾatu'l-Asfīyaʾ fī Ṣifatu'l- Malamatiyatu'l-Akhfīyaʾ va 'Uluv Shani'l-Evliya* (*Mirror of the Pure Ones in the Attributes of Hidden Melametis and the Great Glory of the Saints*). The text is in its original Arabic and introduced with foreword in Turkish. This book should be understood as a final product of his interest in the concept of *melāmet*. Ibn Arabi's understanding of the *melāmetiyye* as the highest level of saints, fitted perfectly with his own understanding and representation of the *Hamzaviyya* as the Melamis. An interest in Ibn Arabi's writing and heritage, I believe, becomes a hallmark among the Bayrami *Hamzavi*s after this. For more information on Ibn Arabi's understanding of the *melāmetis* within the classification of saints, see Chodkiewicz, *Seal of the Saints*; Chodkiewicz, 'Les Malamiyya dans la doctrine d'Ibn Arabi'.

42. La'lizade, *Ṭārīkāt-i 'Aliyye-i Bayrāmiyye*, pp. 43–5. Accordingly, when Abdullah was around the age of fifteen, Hüseyin Ağa took him to the order's corners at Kırkçeşme marketplace. After making sure that they had the permission of the Efendi (referring to Idris Muhtefi), twelve men (all artisans working in neighbouring shops as weavers of cloth) gathered. They asked Abdullah what his goal was. Abdullah responded, as instructed by his stepfather, that he wanted God. The elder one said, 'Then, eliminate everything other than God from your heart and turn towards Him completely. We'll see what kind of favour our *Efendi* will do.' Then those twelve men made a circle around him and collectively turned their eyes to his heart and gazed. After a certain point, Sarı Abdullah remembered losing consciousness and when he woke, seeing a light streaming from his heart. Trying to hide the light with his hands, he was assured that he was the only one who could see this light and that he should not worry about other people noticing it. Müstakimzade reports that Sarı Abdullah carried this light within his heart until he committed adultery as a result of which he lost the light and felt devastated.

After hearing about the situation, Hüseyin Ağa took him back to the corners of *Hamzavi*s in Kırkçeşme marketplace. Here Sarı Abdullah was punished according to the sharia rules (*ḥadd*- beaten for a number of times), and then he was able to feel better. He was, however, unable to perceive the light from his heart after this. Müstakimzade, 'Risale-i Bayramiyye', pp. 54b–55a.

43. La'lizade, *Ṭārīḳāt-i 'Aliyye-i Bayrāmiyye*, pp. 45–6. Accordingly, one look from Idris Muhtefi was enough to leave him perplexed and unconscious.
44. Following an embarrassing defeat in Iran, Halil Paşa was removed from his position as the grand vizier, and the two returned to Istanbul disguised as ordinary people. During the journey, they stopped at a village to spend the night. From the lady of this house, Sarı Abdullah learned that Kabayi had died a couple of days earlier. He regretted losing touch with the order and not knowing what was going on. Müstakimzade, 'Risale-i Bayramiyye', pp. 65b–66a.
45. Müstakimzade, 'Risale-i Bayramiyye', p. 67a–b. According to Safayi, Sarı Abdullah lived in the same neighbourhood as Beşir Ağa and visited him often. This started rumours that Sarı Abdullah was a *Hamzavi*, which according to Safayi, was not true. Safayi, *Tezkire-i Safayi*, p. 376.
46. *Şemerāt*, pp. 93–8.
47. Ibid., pp. 120–6.
48. Ibid., pp. 98–118.
49. For Gölpınarlı's observations on this tendency, see *Melamilik ve Melamiler*, pp. 59–65, 98–9; also see Yavuz, 'The Making of a Sufi Order', pp. 180–5.
50. See Erünsal, *XV.–XVI. Asır Bayrami-Melamiliği'nin Kaynaklarından*, p. 23. 'It is the light of the prophet that becomes manifest / And the mystery of Ali that shines today.' For this phenomenon in the sixteenth-century Ottoman context, which is also known as *ahl-al-baytism*, see Erginbaş, 'Problematizing Ottoman Sunnism'.
51. *Şemerāt*, pp. 132–3.
52. Ibid., pp. 127–8. According to this interpretation, the ecstatic Sufi Bayazid Bistami is believed to have received the esoteric teaching from Jafar al-Sadiq, the sixth imam, in the Nakşbandi genealogy. The latter, however, had died long before Bayazid was born. Sarı Abdullah acknowledges this, but solves the problem by suggesting the possibility of a spiritual transmission (*uwaysi*) between the two. It is also interesting that Sarı Abdullah sees Jafar as the main source of inspiration for Bayazid, and refuses to consider the alternative Nakşbandi tradition, which posits a link between Abu Bakr and Bayazid. For the importance of the sixth imam in the Sufi tradition, see Algar, 'Ja'far al-Ṣadeq, III. Sufism'.
53. These accusations were levelled against Ismail Ma'şuki, and can be found in *Şemerāt*, p. 6.
55. For further information on *devr* and *devriye*s, see Uçman, 'The Theory of the Dawr'.
56. *Devriye*s written in the Bayrami-*Hamzavi* tradition include those written by

From the Hamzaviyye *to the* Melāmiyye

Vizeli Alaaddin and Sarban Ahmed, see Gölpınarlı, *Kaygusuz Vizeli Alaeddin*, pp. 42, 53–6, 76–7. Idris Muhtefi's *devriye* can be found in Gölpınarlı, *Melamilik ve Melamiler*, pp. 125–6; also see Tansel, 'Oğlanlar Şeyhi İbrahim Efendi ve Devriyesi'; Sun'ullah Gaybi's (d. after 1676) *Keşfu'l-Ghita*, found in Gölpınarlı, *Melamilik ve Melamiler*, pp. 116–18.

57. In the *Sohbetname*, a collection of Oğlanlar Şeyhi İbrahim Efendi's oral teachings, we find his statement that 'In every sect [*maẓhab*], there is a profound trace from *tenasukh*,' and that Attar (d. 1220) indicated, 'Those who are the carriers of this knowledge / They are the accepters of *tenasukh* and *ittihad* [complete union with God].' For more information, see Yavuz, 'The Making of a Sufi Order', p. 177.
58. La'lizade presents the letter in an effort to underscore that Beşir Ağa was compliant with sharia and expected his followers to do the same. *Tarikat-i Bayramiyye*, p. 52.
59. *Semerāt*, pp. 10–14. Also see his point of view regarding *maskh*, a concept that signifies the appearance of a human being in an animal form after death, pp. 218–23.
60. Ibid., p. 11.
61. The following lines by Rūmī are quoted in the *Şemerāt*, pp. 13–14: 'First he appeared in the realm of inanimate; / Thence came into the world of plants and lived / The plant-life many a year, nor called to mind / What he had been, then took the onward way / To animal existence, and once more / Remembers naught of that life vegetative. / Save when he feels himself moved with desire / Towards it in the season of sweet flowers, / As babes that seek the breast and know not why. /Again the wise creator when Thou knowest / Uplifted him from animality / No man's estate, and so from realm to realm / Advancing, he became intelligent, / Cunning, and keen of wit, as he is now. / No memory of his past abides with him, / And from his present soul he shall be changed. / Though he is fallen asleep, God will not leave him, / In this forgetfulness. Awakened, he will laugh to think what troubles dreams he had, / And wonder how this happy state of being / He could forget and not receive that all / Those pains and sorrows were the effect of sleep / And guile and vain illusion. So this world / Seems lasting, though 'tis bit the sleeper's dream / Who, when the appointed day shall dawn, escapes / From dark imaginings that haunted him, / And turns with laughter on his phantom griefs / When he beholds his everlasting home' (translation Arberry, *Rumi: Poet and Mystic*, p. 187).
62. 'Terkedup namu nişanı giy melamet hırkasın / Bu melamet hırkasında nice sultan gizlidir' (Gölpınarlı, *Melamilik ve Melamiler*, p. 50). As an indication of the collision between the spiritual and the earthly dominion, *sultan* here signifies the saint.
63. Kayabaşı, 'Sarban Ahmed Divanı'nda Melamilik', p. 1145. 'Her kim bize ta'n eylerse cins-i beşerden / Hak saklasun alemde anu havf u hatardan / Her kim ki bizim ayıbımızı söyler olursa / Ya Rab pur it ağzını anun şehd u şekerden.'

64. According to Andrews, who speaks of a *melami function* against the despotic order in the Ottoman lyrical poetry, it 'represents alienations within semiotic space: casting the signifiers of the dominant order adrift, increasing ambiguity and hence the possibility of nomadic dislocations, being within an order and yet subverting it (the "hidden" secret/ treasure).' The *melami function* reinterprets everything, he says, resulting in the creation of uncertainty. These lines from Baki (d. 1600) are an example of leading the reader/listener into a state of ambiguity by turning the expectation of pursuit of happiness upside down: 'Since, for the lovers, pain and affliction are amusement and pleasure / Then what an affliction it is to fall into the pain of amusement and pleasure.' Andrews, 'Singing the Alienated "I"', p. 212.
65. Erünsal, *XV.–XVI. Asır Bayrami-Melamiliği*, p. 143; also see pp. 27–8 for the importance of adherence to sharia and that illegitimate behaviour is forbidden on the path.
66. Hakiki, *'Irşādname'*, p. 55a.
67. This narrative appears in various sources, including Askeri's *Miratu'l-'Işk* (Erünsal, *XV.–XVI. Asır Bayrami-Melamiliği*, p. 201). As Müstakimzade points out, the earliest appearance of it is in an unlikely source by the Hanafi jurist Kefevi's (d. 990/1582) *'Katā'ib A'lām al-Akhyār'*, pp. 524b–526a). Its account is fully quoted in Müstakimzade, 'Risale-i Bayramiyye', pp. 3b–5a.
68. *Şemerāt*, p. 145. For the sacrosanct hadith (sayings that were believed to have been uttered by God through the mouth of the Prophet) that is cited here, and for many others that were commonly used by Sufis, see the index in Schimmel, *Mystical Dimensions of Islam*, pp. 477–8.
69. *Şemerāt*, p. 146.
70. The title Bayramiyye is a reference to the founder of the order, Hacı Bayram. This epithet was given to him by his shaykh Hamidudin Aksarayi due to his submission just before the Muslim festival that celebrates Prophet Ibrahim's sacrifice of the lamb. The story as narrated in the Qur'an is re-enacted by the pilgrims every year in Mecca as part of inscribed rituals of the *Haj*. A disciple was expected to sacrifice himself in the path just like a lamb in the hands of Ibrahim.
71. *Şemerāt*, pp. 161–2; also see p. 121, when he uses the term to describe the troubles that Abu Hanifa, the founder of the Hanafi juristic school, went through in his own society.
72. See Massignon and Gardet, 'al-Ḥallaj'. Names and narratives of these Sufis can be found inserted within the Halveti genealogy in *Şemerāt*, pp. 175–95.
73. See Teubner, ''Ayn al-Kudat al-Hamadhani'. This well-educated shaykh was brutally executed for holding beliefs close to that of the Ismailis, the most hated heretics of the time. *Şemerāt*'s account on him is quite interesting and indicates that Sufi circles around Sarı Abdullah commonly read his works.
74. Mecdu'd-Din Bağdadi was a Kubravi shaykh who was executed due to the anger of the sultan (Muhammad Kharazmshah, r. 1200–20) upon hearing he had secretly married his mother. Although the context might have been

From the Hamzaviyye *to the* Melāmiyye

different, Majd ad-Din's name does not commonly appear in the list of Sufis who were executed for heretical beliefs. Öngören, 'Mecdüddin el-Bağdadi'.

75. Şams was the enigmatic friend of Rūmī, and was possibly killed by the latter's younger son who was bothered by their close relationship. See Schimmel, 'Shams-i Tabriz(i)'.

76. Nesimi was a brilliant poet who had a lasting influence on Sufi poetry in Anatolia. The Timurids executed him viciously for his ties with the Ḥurūfiyya. For a study of his life and poetry, see Burrill, *The Quatrains of Nesimi*.

77. This was an argument commonly advanced among the Halvetis of the seventeenth-century tradition as well. Ömer el-Fu'adi of the Şabaniyye in Kastamonu invoked it in regard to the life of his order's founder Şa'ban-i Veli. For more information, see Curry, *The Transformation of Muslim Mystical Thought*, pp. 131–3.

78. For instance, Oğlan Shaykh Ibrahim represents a different trend within the order. His negative reaction towards Abdullah Efendi is evident in an interesting episode reported by the author of the *Hediyye*: 'In a gathering where Aksarayi Oğlan Shaykh was present, Abdullah Efendi was telling stories regarding the unveilings and miraculous deeds of some ecstatics [*mecazib*]. The former, as usual in his noble manner, was sitting quietly, concentrating on his own thoughts. Although he was a wise [*'ārif*] and elegant [*zarīf*] person, Ibrahim Efendi ended up sniping at Abdullah Efendi: "What a dull idiot [*ebhel-i ğabi*] you are! In the presence of the *kutb*, you keep us busy with the nonsense sayings of some lunatics rather than trying to get him [presumably Ibrahim Efendi himself] to speak and benefit all of us"' (Türer, *Osmanlılarda Tasavvufi Hayat*, p. 455).

7

Fabricating the Great Mass: Heresy and Legitimate Plurality in Harputlu İshak Efendi's Polemics against the *Bektaşi* Order

Benjamin Weineck

Introduction

İmām ʿAlī meyḫānede mi şehīd oldı yoḳsa cāmiʿde mi?
Did Imam Ali become a martyr in a tavern or a mosque?[1]

This question is among the many provocative expressions in İshak Efendi's[2] polemical treatise (*risāle*) on the disbelief of the *Bektaşi* order that was published in the year 1291/1874. In his work *Kaşifü 'l-esrar ve dafiʿu 'l-eşrar* he sets out to polemicise against the Sufi order of the *Bektaşis*, their beliefs and ritual practices in order to illustrate their corrupted morality and to inform the 'great mass of those who are saved'[3] about their disbelief.

Accusations such as the one articulated in the quote aim at the perceived religious libertinism among the *Bektaşi*s which has been, among other topoi, one of the central aspects of anti-Sufi and anti-Shii polemics throughout Islamic history.[4] Yet the (re)activation of such polemics in the second half of the nineteenth century by an Ottoman *ʿālim* against the *Bektaşi* order of dervishes is interesting in several respects. First of all, İshak is writing against the *Bektaşi*s roughly fifty years after the order's official abolition. With the destruction of the Janissary corps on the occasion of the 'Auspicious Incident' (*vakʿa-i hayriyye*) in 1826, the *Bektaşi* order's lodges had been closed.[5] Second, up until the banning of the order, the Ottoman state had maintained an interesting relationship with the *Bektaşi*s. They were among the first Sufis who had settled in the newly conquered regions of the Balkans, and *Bektaşi*s played a prominent role in educating the levied *devşirme*-boys before they entered palace service.[6] By the sixteenth century, the *Bektaşi zāviye*s had become important instruments for the Ottoman state, as they were in charge of collecting taxes and cultivating the land.⁷ Whereas other groups of similar Sufic-Shiite belief systems, such as the *Kızılbaş*, were periodically heavily persecuted and constituted a severe problem for the Ottoman legitimacy, the *Bektaşi* order did not face such treatment and accusations. On the contrary, it seemed that the order was used as a vehicle to control the various *Kızılbaş*-Alevi communities in Anatolia. To achieve this, the *Bektaşi*s were granted a high degree of autonomy, and the privilege to appoint their own shaykhs to their *tekke*s all over Anatolia without any state intermediaries, such as the qadis, being involved.⁸

In the context of the sixteenth-century *Kızılbaş* persecution, the tendency of the Ottoman state towards articulating an increasingly strict Sunni-minded outlook has recently come to be the subject of academic interest.⁹ However, whatever the extent of this transformation, it did not disturb the relationship between the Sublime Porte and the *Bektaşi* order until 1826. Even then, the *Bektaşi* affiliation with the Janissaries was the main reason for their abolition, and not so much their non-Sunni character.¹⁰

This chapter seeks to explore the politico-theological universe of İshak Efendi as a late Ottoman *'alim*. His theological perceptions of right and wrong, and his division of the population into *küffār* and the great mass of the saved Muslims (*sevād-i a'ẓam*),¹¹ are subtly differentiated, as he discerns various formations of non-Sunni groups, like Alawis, "Nusayris" and Twelver Shiites, and compares them with the *Bektaşi*s with the intent of condemning the latter. This, in turn, shapes the scope and the degree of inclusivity in İshak's conception of the 'great mass' of saved Muslims. As such, İshak's views offer a unique perspective on the highly specific and quite well-informed perception of Muslim plurality in late Ottoman times. The final decades of the Ottoman Empire witnessed the transformation of modes of religio-political belonging in favour of a seemingly equal citizenship, pan-Islamic ideas and the unity of Muslims (*ittiḥād-i islām*).¹² Therefore, it is important to contextualise İshak Efendi's polemics on the *Bektaşi*s against the backdrop of these political transformations of the later nineteenth century. In the end, analysing specific nuances in İshak's imagination of heterodoxy may help us overcome conventional ideas of 'orthodox' ulema and 'heterodox'¹³ Sufis. Furthermore, historicising his construction, by highlighting the entanglement of political and theological discourse in İshak's work, reveals an understanding of late Ottoman Sunnism (and its constituted others) as intentionally fabricated, in continuous flux and contingent.

Georg Jacob, who edited a part of İshak's text in 1908,¹⁴ was convinced that the treatise was an important text for strengthening and further developing the study of the phenomenon of Muslim dervishes as opposed to the 'Islam of the scribes'.[15] The text, Jacob noted, 'is valuable because it can yield insight into the secret teachings of the *Bektaşi*s – teachings that only a Muslim could get in a fortunate opportunity'.[16] And as such, İshak's polemics were used by many researchers of *Bektaşi* rituals and history because sources on internal developments of the order, just like in many other Sufi traditions and less codified constellations, are scarce.[17] Yet in contemporary times, very different from those in which Jacob operated, it is imperative to approach the treatise with a different understanding. My primary interest has less to do with its content and polemics; rather, I focus more on its discursive nature. Thus, I ask questions like how the denunciation of the *Bektaşi*s as heretics equally constitutes the 'great mass of saved Muslims'? In this context, it is also worth reflecting on the degree of İshak's agency as the author of this text: where does he reproduce common topoi of anti-Sufi polemics, which are as old as, for example, as al-Ghazali's (d. 1111) treatises against Sufis and Fatimids, and where does he depart from these?[18] This final question also serves to emphasise the historicity of İshak's text and of Ottoman Sunnism alike, the meaning of which is socially fabricated in time and place, and thus constructed by means of drawing boundaries between unbelief and a legitimate plurality of the broader mass of the population.

İshak's Polemics: Topoi of Anti-Sufism in the late Ottoman Empire

İshak's *Kaşif* was printed in two different versions – a fact that has significant ramifications for the interpretation of his ideas about disbelief and inner-Islamic diversity. According to Özege, the first version is dated 1291/1874, while the second edition cannot be dated. The latter edition is also shorter and consists of only 173 pages instead of 174.[19] The importance of the differences between these two versions will become clearer as we address the broader context of the work.

The *Kaşif* is part of a bigger dispute that took place between 1871 and 1876 in the Ottoman Empire. In 1871, there were several texts published which had a *Bektaşi*-Sufi character.[20] This triggered İshak to write a *reddiye*, a refutation of the various Sufi and, and in his eyes, 'heretical' contents of these texts. İshak's *reddiye* was followed by another text written by one Ahmet Rıf'at, who rejected, in turn, the accusations against the *Bektaşi*s articulated in İshak's work.[21] According to İshak, these '*Bektaşi* publications' consisted of five books written by a certain Fazlallah Esterabadi (or Fazl-i Hurufi, as he calls him throughout his treatise) and his later disciples, in particular, a certain Fereşteoğlu among them.[22] This Fazlallah (1340–94) was known as an ascetic Sufi who had founded the Sufi school of the Ḥurūfiyya in fourteenth-century Iran.[23] According to Ḥurūfī teachings, the twenty-eight letters of the Arabic alphabet in which the Qur'an was revealed, hold an ontological status, and likewise carry a secret knowledge about the numerical value of the Arabic letters. In this context, one important aspect of Fazlallah's view is that God reveals his divine self in men through his word, as articulated in Arabic letters.

Apart from the theological rejection of the Ḥurūfī doctrine, İshak also emphasises that one of his main goals was to expose their 'blasphemous acts' (*küfriyāt*) in order to protect the community of righteous Muslims.[24] Therefore, in the first part of his *risāle* (pp. 1–31), he gives some information about Fazlallah Hurufi, how the Ḥurūfīs spread from their centre in Esterabad, Iran, to Anatolia via Fazallah's disciple, a certain 'Ali al-A'la, and how the 'simple-minded' (*cāhil ve nā-dān*) *Bektaşi*s at the convent in Hacı Bektaş fell prey to their tricks and deceit. Here, İshak identifies Fazlallah as a Qarmati and thus represents him as belonging to an Ismaili context. In İshak's view, just like the *Ḳarāmiṭa ṭā'ifesi*, Fazlallah would declare forbidden things allowed (*mübāḥ*). The accusation of *ibāḥ* was a very rampant criticism against various groups that can be found in much earlier periods; for example, we find it in al-Ghazali's polemics against the Fatimids and certain Sufi currents, which he labels as *ibāḥiye*.[25]

In the second and third chapters of his text, İshak summarises the other published books and focuses especially on Fereşteoğlu's *'Aşkname*. The *'Aşkname* was compiled in the fifteenth century and seems to be, according to Usluer, a synthesis of various texts by Fazlallah.[26] Interestingly, 90 of the 173 pages of İshak's text are devoted to the *'Aşkname* and its refutation. In the third chapter, he mentions other Ḥurūfī writings briefly and comes to the conclusion that these were quite similar to the aforementioned *'Aşkname*. Yet towards the very end, the treatise takes an interesting turn. After studying the writings of the *Bektaşi*s, İshak stresses that he realised that they were even worse than the Nusayris, a *ghulāṭ*-Shiite current that is known today as Alawis.[27] At this point, he ends his discussion of the contents of *Bektaşi* texts and commences a comparison of the *Bektaşi*s with another non-Sunni Muslim group present in the Ottoman Empire.

As it is mostly the *Cavidan*-books that are of primordial importance for İshak, his conception of the enemy is mainly based on the contents of these works. Thus, although his text claims to reveal the 'secrets of the *Bektaşi*' (*esrār-i Bektaşiyān*),[28] most of the *risāle*, in fact, deals with Ḥurūfī mysticism and the teachings of Fazlallah Esterabadi. Although it is not well known to what extent such Ḥurūfī teachings were actually incorporated into *Bektaşi* circles,[29] İshak takes the *Ḥurūfī* elements in the teachings of the *Bektaşi*s as the initial point for his polemics. As the *Kaşif* is also one of the texts that establish the close connection between *Ḥurūfiyya* and Bektaşiyya, I quote the part in which these are associated in the text in full here:

> ve ba'dehu ma'lūm ola ki ehl-i İslām'ı iżlāl ile meşġūl olan ṭevā'ifiñ eñ başlucası ṭā'ife-'i Bektaşiyān olub ḥālbuki bunlarıñ aḳvāl ve af'āllarından ehl-i İslām'dan olmadıkları ma'lūm ise de biñ ikiyüz seksän sekiz tārīḫinde bütün bütün iẓhār eylediler bunlarıñ (cāvidān) tesmīye eyledikleri kütüb altı nüsḫe olub birisi aṣl-i muẓılları olan (Fażlullāh) Ḥurūfī'niñ ve beşi ḫülefāsiniñ tertībātı olub nüsaḫ-i ḫamse-'i meẕkūrede küfürleri pek ẓāhir oldıġından beynlerinde sırran ta'līm ve ta'allüm eyleyüb ke'ennehü (Fereşte) Oġlu'nıñ ('Aşkname) ta'bīr olınan cāvidānında küfriyātını bir miḳdār mestūrāne ṭutdıġından.[30]

> And in the following, it shall be known that the most successful group that is active in deceiving the people of Islam is the group of the *Bektaşi*s. And although it is obvious from their speech and their acts that they are not Muslims, they made it all obvious in the year 1288. There are six books that they call 'Cavidan', among which is the one of the actual betrayer, Fazlallah Hurufi, while the other five are compilations by his disciples. They teach and learn these in secret because their infidelity is quite obvious in the aforementioned five books, just like they kept the disbelief in the Cavidan of Fereşteoğlu, that they call 'Aşkname, secret to some extent.

One of the central problems in the *Ḥurūfī* teachings of the *Bektaşi*s, according to İshak, is the stress on God's divine revelation in the human body or the human face. Such a revelation consists of complex hermeneutics and calculations, used by the *Ḥurūfī*s to reach the esoteric (*bāṭınī*) insight of the ontological status of God's word in the universe and its manifestation in the human face.[31] It furthermore illustrates the theological questions touched upon in the *Ḥurūfī* teachings, such as God's unity, his eternity and his transcendence. The human face appears here as the very locus of *Ḥurūfī* theophany (not pantheism, as Bausani stresses).[32]

This idea of God's manifestation in the human face, according to İshak, violates God's absolute unity and stands in stark contrast to the idea of God being transcendent and clearly separated from his creation.[33] Here, İshak draws upon an argument against this type of theophany that is also frequently brought to bear in accusations against *ḥulūl*, the appearance of God in a creature.[34] Furthermore, İshak notes that Fazlallah, mentioned by his Persian name Fazl-i Fiyaz in İshak's discourse, appears in place of God during a narration of the Prophet Muhammad's night journey to heaven (*mi'rāj*). This indicates one possible perspective on Fazlallah's role in *Hurūfī* mysticism, appearing as God himself. In other paragraphs, Fazlallah also emerges as a prophet, in line with other Qur'anic prophets, fulfilling Muhammad's mission of reminding the people of God's word and calling them to return to the right path. This was also demonstrated by *Hurūfī* numerology as it was claimed that Fazlallah personified the number thirty-two, as he was a Persian-speaker, and the Persian alphabet consists of thirty-two letters; there are four additional letters (*pe*, *če*, *že* and *gaf*) on top of the twenty-eight Arabic ones. Therefore, after Jesus, who revealed God's word with twenty-four letters (via the Greek alphabet), and after Muhammad, who spoke with the twenty-eight letters of the Arabic alphabet, it is necessary that another prophet would come to 'fulfil the religion' after them.[35]

The question of the nature of God's unity is among the central points of conflict in İshak's work. In this context, he shows that the *Bektaşi*s, alias *Hurūfī*s, depart from the central Sunni-Islamic understanding of *tevḥīd*. This dispute also becomes apparent in another aspect discussed in the *'Aşkname* upon which İshak elaborates: the teaching of God's attributes. İshak accuses the *Hurūfī*s of declaring Qur'anic verses defined as 'ambiguous' (*müteşābih*), in which God seems to have human attributes, as 'clear' ones (*muḥkem*). The interpretation of these verses[36] has been subject to scholastic and theological debate since the beginnings of Islamic theology, as it is closely linked to the question of the nature of God himself: if God has human attributes, then he cannot be absolutely divine. Declaring these ambiguous verses as having a clear meaning, according to İshak, the *Hurūfī-Bektaşi*s have set themselves apart from 'all religious scholars' and 'presume an extraordinarily silly and corrupting interpretation'.[37]

In addition to arguing against these theological aspects, İshak also addresses the methods by which the *Bektaşi*s hermeneutically reason, and spread their teachings among the common folk. On the one hand, he criticises the methodology of esoteric interpretation (*te'vīl*) that the *Bektaşi*s use in their *Hurūfī*-inspired construction of the universe. By using this very term, *te'vīl*, İshak separates the corrupted teachings of the *Bektaşi*s from the rightful Sunni ones which are to be derived from the holy scriptures by way of *tefsīr*. As Poonawala emphasises, *ta'wīl*[38] has a meaning of interpretation by one's own opinion (*tafsīr bi-'r-ra'y*) in contrast to *tafsīr bi-'l-ma'ṣur*, an interpretative process that proceeds via methods legitimated through tradition and on the basis of Qur'an and/or Sunna.[39] It is this interpretation through *ta'wīl*, for example, that enables the *Hurūfī*s to turn the ambiguous verses into clear ones, or that allows them to abandon any required religious duties (*farż*), such as prescribed daily prayers. When İshak criticises the *Bektaşi* mode of praying in silent, habitual devotions (*zikr-i dā'imī*), he also argues that using *te'vil*, the *Bektaşi*s transform the apparent, outside manifestations (*ẓāhir*) of religious duties, like daily prayers, into esoteric ones (*baṭın*).[40]

Closely related to the negligence of religious duties is another very pervasive aspect of anti-Sufi polemics: drinking wine and having unmarried intercourse. İshak argues that the 'trick' (*desīse*) used by the *Bektaşi*s in order to legitimise such acts is to declare all religiously forbidden things allowed.[41] Such a strategy is also employed when it comes to their perceived promiscuity; at this point in the work, İshak stops paraphrasing Fereşteoğlu and tells a story, which he has heard from 'a trustworthy person':[42] one night, the *Bektaşi*s gathered for the *cem* ritual, and a woman entered the *meydān*, that is, the space in the middle, where the participants of the ritual gather around. The woman was given to one of the participants, and after they withdrew to a secluded place (*ḥalvet*) until they satisfied their sensual needs (*ḥuẓūẓ-i nefsāneleri*). İshak narrates another such story in which a woman was in search of inspiration and guidance (*himmet*) through a *Bektaşi* dervish, only to have the dervish come and fulfil a lewd (i.e., unmarried) sexual act with her.[43] Interestingly, such an episode is brought up along similar lines by al-Ghazali in his polemical treatise against the Fatimids. Al-Ghazali also mentions women who, in order to get blessings, approach dervishes with sexual intentions.[44] That such a story is told similarly in different contexts indicates that such accusations are more topoi of discourse rather than actual acts.

To sum up, this bird's-eye view on the themes and topoi of İshak's polemical treatise reveals quite complex and specific theological aspects of criticism about the *Bektaşi-Ḥurūfī* concept of God's relation to his creation and his attributes. Furthermore, İshak criticises Fazlallah's allegations to be superior to Muhammad and to even appear as God himself. He also posits that the *Bektaşi*s make use of certain tricks and methods, among them the esoteric hermeneutical instrument of *te'vīl*, which urges İshak to intervene. These should be characterised as established topoi of anti-Sufi and anti-Shiite discourse.

Bektaşis, Shiis and Nusayris: Who is Worse?

İshak warns his readers that among the tricks that the *Bektaşi*s use to seduce the *ehl-i imān*, the community of faith, is to pretend to be Shiite; the *Bektaşi*s teach in their *tekke*s the *Khuṭbatu'l-bayān*, the collection of sayings of Ali. Furthermore, it is said in one of the *Cavidan*s that Fazlallah would also manifest himself in Ali so that anyone venerating Ali would also venerate Fazlallah.[45] He stresses, however, that although they pretend

Fabricating the Great Mass

to belong to the *ehl-i beyt*, it becomes apparent that they are not Shiites but 'a group of polytheists on their own'.[46]

Based on this discursive strategy, one could argue that İshak draws a line between non-Sunni currents that are to be rejected completely, and others, like the Shiites named here (i.e., Twelver Shiites), that are considered to be legitimate followers of the *ehl-i beyt*. As such, they also appear as a legitimate non-Sunni community within the wider group of the great mass of saved Muslims. Another aspect has to be taken into account that makes it difficult to come to terms with İshak's seemingly obvious relationship of 'good' Sunnis and Twelver Shiites, on the one hand, and 'bad' *Bektaşi-Hurūfī*s and their heretical teachings, on the other. As noted previously, there are two different versions of İshak's *risāle*. The differences between these two versions may be only marginal and, formally speaking, of minor significance. However, judging from their contents, they reveal some interesting deviations in perspective as the alterations are critical in interpreting İshak's construction of intra-Muslim difference, along with his register of religious differentiation and stratification.

In Özege's catalogue of printed works, there are two entries for the *Kaşif*: the first entry is the version dated to 1291/1874. This version consists of 174 pages, which we will refer to as 'A' in the following discussion. The other version, according to Özege, is a second edition (referenced as 'B' henceforth), which is undated and only 173 pages long.[47] There are three points in the text where version A speaks of 'Shiites', whereas version B uses alternative vocabulary in its place, such as *cühelā* (ignorant ones).[48] These alterations appear in the first chapter where İshak, having not yet paraphrased the *Cavidan*s, summarises the 'tricks' of the *Bektaşi*s. First, he says that one of the *Bektaşi* tricks to try to convert the Shiites is to employ the doctrine of Fazlallah by taking Ali's shape.[49] In addition to this difference between version A and B, there is another point in which A speaks of Shiites, while B replaces the term with alternate vocabulary: here, İshak stresses that the *Bektaşi*s are only keen on seducing and proselytising among the Muslims, and not among Christians or Jews; within the Muslim community, he argues, it is the people inclined to Shiism that are most likely to be ensnared by their teachings. But version B does not speak of Shiites as part of this discussion, but instead references them as 'those who tend to give way to their carnal passions'.[50] Thirdly, there is yet another similar, but not identical, alteration: there is a whole sentence omitted in version B. In version A, İshak articulates an analogy between different kinds of non-(Sunni) Muslim groups and the central figures that are venerated among them; meaning that the 'polytheists' (*müşrik*) follow

Jesus, the '(Shiite) heretics' (*rāfiżī*) follow Imam Jafar al-Sadiq just as the *Bektaşi*s venerate Hacı Bektaş.[51]

Version A	Version B
Formal differences	
Dated 1291/1874	Undated
174 pages	173 pages
Measures: 18 × 12 cm and 13.5 × 8 cm[52]	Measures: 16 × 11 cm and 14 × 8 cm
Differences in content	
şī'īleri celb içün	cühelāyı celb içün
ehl-i İslām içinde şī'īye miyāl olanları celb eylediler	ehl-i Islām içinde hevā-yı nefse miyāl olanları celb eylediler
müşrik – 'Isā	
rāfıżī – Imām Ca'fer-i Şādık	*Missing*
Bektaşi – Hacı Bektaş	

Despite these differences regarding the relationship of *Bektaşi*s and Shiites, İshak in both versions stresses that although the *Bektaşi*s pretend to be Shiites, they clearly are not.[53] However, version A stresses that Shiites, not 'ignorant people (to the true faith, i.e., Islam)', are more likely to be seduced by the *Bektaşi* teachings. As he also emphasises that *Bektaşi*s are definitely not Shiites, it can be assumed that Shiites (apparently Twelvers) are of somewhat higher rank in his stratification of different religious currents. Furthermore, the term *rāfiżī* is completely missing in version B, which is interesting in its own right as this term had been used with varying frequency as an accusation against the *Kızılbaş* in the previous centuries. The term originally stemmed from Umayyad accusations brought first against the followers of Jafar al-Sadiq, and then against the followers of Zayd b. 'Ali.[54] According to Kohlberg, it was also taken up by Shiites as an honorific term because they saw themselves as 'rejecters' (from Arabic *rafaḍa* – to reject) of injustice.[55] Later, *rāfiḍī* (or *rāfiżī* in the Persian/Ottoman rendering) was also used as a polemical term to denote any kind of heresy stemming from a Shiite milieu, and could, therefore, be applied to both *Bektaşi*s and *Kızılbaş* in Anatolia and Iran alike.[56] The omission in version B of this pejorative term suggests that this version does not draw as much attention to inner Islamic sectarian differences between Sunni and Shiites, and locates those who are too easily corrupted by the *Bektaşi*s outside the community of Sunni and Shiite Muslims (with the term *cühelā* evoking notions of pre-Islamic and not yet enlightened ignorance and disbelief). This deliberate omission, therefore, strengthens Islamic unity vis-à-vis its internal enemy, at a time where enemies from abroad in the form of (semi-)colonial incursions were testing Islamic unity.[57]

It is difficult to determine who made these subtle editorial changes in the second version. This is the very point mentioned at the beginning of this chapter, where the articulated idea of difference and plurality has to be reconciled with the author being capable of a certain degree of agency, on the one hand, and discourse, on the other, determining the implicit rules of utterance.[58] In the end, it is a methodological decision (and, in fact, a matter of political outlook) whether the argument stresses the power of the individual in shaping his text and its content, or the 'discursive structure', which in turn yields regulatory and disciplining forces that also find their expression in the specific articulations of intra-Muslim difference in this text.[59] Also, if we consider the possibility that an anonymous editor was in charge of making these subtle changes to the text, the argument still holds true: İshak as 'the author' of the text is not the only source or single agent producing its very content. There are, furthermore, political modes of belonging and rules of speech at work (which may be personified here as an anonymous editor). With the changes made to these two different versions of the text, the subject of Shiite rejection, as well as the opposing we-group, modifies its shape and its inclusivity: in version A, the Shiites are clearly among the 'great mass of the saved ones', while the term and associations with it do not show in the other version – a finding that yet again suggests the constructed nature and the historicity of legitimate plurality within this 'great mass'.

While the reasons for the differences between the versions must remain unclear, another aspect of İshak's idea of intra-Muslim difference and heresy is present in both versions. Towards the end of his *risāle*, he says that based on the contents of the *Hurūfī-Bektaşi* books, it is obvious that they are not among the *ehl-i kitāb*, like Christians or Jews, but are a group of 'polytheists', whose 'slaughter is forbidden to eat' (*zebīḥası yenmez*).[60]

As for other (Muslim) currents, he remarks that he was able to collect scriptures of various 'misguided groups' (*fırak-i żālle*) in order to study them and protect the umma from their mischievous behaviour and teachings.[61] In doing so, he initially concluded that the Nusayris were the worst of all. Yet after having studied the *Cavidan*s of the *Bektaşi*s, he discovered that the *Bektaşi*s were worse, and 'more foolish' even than the Nusayris, as they had declared Fazlallah their God, and despite him being their God, they also admitted that Timur's son could kill him.[62]

Elaborating upon the Nusayris, İshak describes what he learned from 'their books'.[63] It is not clear which books he was referring to; we can only speculate on the sources of his information. Unlike his mention of gathering information on the *Bektaşis* by talking to *Bektaşi* dervishes themselves,[64] İshak does not refer to any such oral reports from a Nusayri source. Furthermore, given the importance of keeping Nusayri teachings secret using dissimulation (*taqiyah*), it is interesting that İshak could gather any information at all. He describes part of an initiation ritual, in which a young boy is brought before an 'imam' and has to prove that he can keep a secret.[65] İshak stresses the importance among the Nusayris of keeping a secret, as he goes on to summarise the ritual and emphasises that the novice's patron would be killed if the child betrays the community's secrets.[66]

The most important texts on Nusayri rituals are the various *dastūr* that have been studied by Olsson and Friedman. Yet these texts, like the *Kitāb al-hawi fi 'ilm al-fatāwa* by Maymun al-Tabarani from the eleventh century, were rarely circulated outside Nusayri communities, and it is unlikely that İshak had access to them. Furthermore, as Friedman notes, Nusayri texts do not elaborate on what happens when a novice betrays a secret.[67] However, another testimony on Nusayri rituals can be found in the *Kitāb al-bakura as-Sulaymāniya* by the famous Nusayri renegade Sulayman al-Adani.[68] This book was printed in Beirut in 1864[69] and thus may well be one of the books İshak mentioned on the teachings of the various *fırak-i żālle* in the Ottoman realm. In this work, al-Adani described how he was threatened with death if he came to betray the secret teachings after his initiation. It is thus likely that this is the source of İshak's explanations.[70] For his part, İshak describes the ritual without using specific Nusayri vocabulary.[71] Furthermore, he does not provide any detailed description of the ritual in question or its three-step procedure, as described in Friedman's work.[72] Friedman describes how it was customary to drink wine in the first of the three steps of the initiation. Interestingly, İshak does not mention this fact, even though it could have added to his arguments for Nusayris being among the misguided heretical sects. But, on the contrary, he states that wine consumption is one of the differences between Nusayris and *Bektaşis*, and one of the reasons why *Bektaşis* were worse than the Nusayris.[73] Apart from this sketchy information about a certain Nusayri ritual, he describes their habits, the food they eat or avoid, and their habit of shaving the head as a religious duty.[74]

With regard to the role of 'Ali b. Abu Talib among the Nusayris, İshak makes various conflictive statements. According to some Nusayris, there was no (other God) but Ali, while others maintain that Ali and Muhammad were one person.[75] He also mentions other important figures in the Nusayri teachings briefly, among them the Persian companion of the Prophet Muhammad, Selman al-Farsi, who is, according to Jacob, part of the

Fabricating the Great Mass

Nusayri trinity of Ali–Muhammad–Selman.[76] Although he clearly states that the Nusayris believe that there is no God but Ali,[77] he concludes that the unbelief (*küfur*) of the Nusayris was, in comparison with the *Bektaşi*s, the better of two bad alternatives. His reasoning here remains enigmatic as he states that the Nusayris would 'not associate [whom?] with the Divine'.[78] This not only contradicts his own fact-finding but also completely ignores the central Nusayri doctrine of Ali's divinity.

Negotiating Belonging in the Late Ottoman Empire

The differences between the two versions of İshak's text and its construction of stratification between Shiites, *Bektaşi*s and Nusayris is important not only for theological purposes. At the time of İshak's activities, a transformation of religious and political belonging had already been set in motion across the Ottoman Empire. It is likely that İshak, as an Ottoman *'ālim* living and working in Istanbul, was aware of such political transformations. Reinkowski, for example, has underlined that the *Tanzīmāt* reform Edict of Gulhane, 1839, and more so the *Işlāḥāt* Edict, 1856, make use of religiously neutral vocabulary to integrate the various religious currents into the imaginary of *tebā'a* (citizenship).[79] Pistor-Hatam noted these intentions and further emphasised the increasing efforts of Ottoman–Iranian (i.e., Sunni–Shiite) reconciliation from the 1850s onward.[80] Reinkowski traced such transformed notions of order as they found their way into Ottoman documents on the Druze of Mount Lebanon back to the 1860 uprising – a finding that may also be suggestive with regard to the Nusayris, as they lived in close proximity. Moreover, we now know that the Alawis took advantage of the transformations during the *Tanzīmāt*. As Stefan Winter has shown in his recent work on the Alawis, they regularly had representatives from their community elected to the local councils (*meclis*).[81] Given these changing notions of belonging and citizenship, the Nusayri communities came to play critical roles within the Ottoman juridico-political apparatus, as opposed to the *Bektaşi*s, who since 1826 had been officially banned from joining the council of shaykhs (*meclis-i meşāyiḫ*).[82] Despite the fact that the *Bektaşi*s and Nusayris were discussed in an analogous polemical style and compared with one another in works such as Ishak's, one must not forget the different historical experiences of such socio-religious groups within the Ottoman realm, whose standing, degree of influence and political power was not determined solely by their religious identification, but more so by local, administrative necessity.

Although İshak's theological discourse may be based on some other rationale than political and administrative priorities, such a transformed notion of belonging may have influenced this *'ālim*'s ideas. His preference for the Nusayris over the officially abolished *Bektaşi*s, as well as his integration of Shiites, who he saw as being in need of protection from the proselytising *Ḥurūfī-Bektaşi*s, may hint at an implicit awareness of such political transformations. It seems these considerations also contributed to his theological understanding of the degrees of heresy, and on the explicit and implicit boundaries he draws between the umma and those who were denied membership in it. This remains speculative for the time being, as it is not clear which of the two versions of Ishak's text was the first. If version A (containing Shiites) is the earlier one, then the later removal of the term suggests removal of potentially divisive language. If version B (without the Shiites), on the other hand, was the earlier one, it indicates that their later introduction was aimed at protecting and warning the Shiite subjects of the empire against being drawn into *Bektaşi* circles – as opposed to the ignorant ones. Also, it remains unclear if it was İshak himself who was responsible for making a variable choice of words in the different versions or if it was an early form of Ottoman textual censorship that was employed here, which would become widespread and increasingly sophisticated during the course of Abdülhamid II's reign from the late 1870s onward.

Conclusion

The preceding discussion has made clear that the imagery of intra-Muslim difference and plurality is a more nuanced and complex matter which cannot possibly be grasped by simplistic dichotomies of 'orthodox' ulema working for Sunni statehood and 'heretic' or 'folk-Islamic' currents. The process of fabricating the 'great mass' and its heretical opposition was more complex and contingent than simplistic analyses will allow.

The contents of the polemical treatise sketched above make use of a ubiquitous set of topoi of disbelief and discursive tropes that one can find in other polemical writings aimed at Shiites, *Kızılbaş* or Sufis in other places and times. İshak's work also emphasises the immoral practices of the *Ḥurūfī-Bektaşi*s and highlights their theological deviance. His heavy focus on *Ḥurūfī* teachings, which he presumes to be widespread among the *Bektaşi*s, means that İshak sees the problem as precisely grounded in this very aspect of *Bektaşi*sm. That is why he can safely claim that Hacı Bektaş himself was not one of the heretics; rather, he was a good Muslim following the sharia.[83] Instead, İshak argues, his teachings became corrupted in the course of time by his disciples. Such a differentiated view on the

Fabricating the Great Mass

*Bektaşi*s, who were not all collectively to be judged as heretics, was also apparent in the course of the incidents of 1826 when a decision was eventually rendered to abolish the order along with the Janissaries. As Faroqhi[84] has stressed with reference to a document reprinted by Uzunçarşılı,[85] a lengthy debate took place over whether it would be in accordance with the sharia to close all the *Bektaşi-tekke*s without proving that all the accused acted in a way that would justify such drastic measures. The existence of such nuances, even regarding the deeply suspect *Bektaşi*s, bear witness to very thorough thinking about who belonged to the 'great mass of the saved Muslims', and who did not. Likewise, developing specific language and approaches to the *fırak-i żālle* was in order, as the state also engaged in integrating and domesticating various Sufi currents and their leaders within the administrative apparatus via the *meclis-i meşāyiḥ*. As a result, İshak's discussion of the heretical character of the Nusayris was oddly contradictory. Furthermore, the fact that he sets out to compare and stratify different 'heretical groups' suggests a nuanced, complex and non-monolithic imagined continuum of acceptable or unacceptable sectarian groups.

To conclude, leaving aside the question of İshak's ideas regarding heresy and intra-Muslim difference and the matrix informing him, there remains the theoretical consideration of whether it is possible to locate the specific articulation of difference expressed in his text within the parameters of the author's agency. In this context, it is difficult to come to terms with the exact power relations of individual intervention and structural constraints of discourse and language that are themselves the products of a broader set of social and governmental norms and sets of knowledge that emerge in chronological and geographically contingent times and places. The aim to locate the text somewhere in between these aspects helps us to rethink the theological discourse embedded in historical and social contexts. Thus, historicising of such discourses enables us to grasp the dynamic relationship between friend and foe in the context of polemical arguments, and helps us to determine the historical contingency of any 'Ottoman Sunnism', thereby clarifying a response to the question of who belongs to the 'great mass of the saved ones'.

Notes

1. İshak, *Kaşif*, p. 19. As two different versions of this text exist, I have to stress that all quotations, if not stated otherwise, are taken from the Version I called 'Version B' in the discussion.
2. Harputlu İshak Efendi (1803–92) was born in 1803 in the village Perçenç, near Harput. He completed his primary education there before he left for

Istanbul, where he obtained his licence to teach (*icāzet*) at the Sahn-i Seman Medresesi. After his graduation, İshak returned to Harput in order to teach at the Meydan Camii Medresesi where he built up a considerable network of students. After two years, he returned to Istanbul and held different teaching positions there before he was put in charge of a judge's position in Isparta and Medina. Later on, İshak also became a member of the Ministry of Endowments (*evḳāf neẓāreti*). He died in 1892 and was buried in the garden of the Fatih Camisi in Istanbul; Demirpolat, 'Artukoğullarından', pp. 677–9. İshak is also mentioned as the author of the *Kaşif* by Tāhir, *Osmanlı Müellifleri*, p. 364. He is mentioned by other biographic dictionaries as well, but not as the author of this work, for example, Süreyya, *Sicill-i Osmanī*, p. 805. On his life and works, see also Biçer, 'Harputlu İshak Efendi', pp. 255–68; Demirpolat, 'Harputlu İshak Hoca', pp. 397–412.
3. The expression is 'fırḳa'-i nāciyye olan sevād-i a'ẓam', İshak, *Kaşif*, p. 85. On the origin of this expression, see van Ess, *Der Eine und das Andere*, pp. 40–3.
4. One of the central terms in this regard is *ibāḥa* – 'to render forbidden things legal'. It was applied, for example, by al-Ghazali to the Fatimids or by different Ottoman ulema to the *Kızılbaş*, linking them to the Safavids in Iran; Pretzl, *Die Streitschrift*, p.16; Eberhard, *Osmanische Polemik*, p. 75; for a major general overview on forms, topoi and their functions within anti-Sufi and anti-Shiite polemical discourse, see de Jong and Radtke, 'Introduction', pp. 1–21.
5. The developments within the order after this incident are described by Mélikoff, 'L'ordre des Bektachi,' pp. 155–71.
6. On the intimate relationship of the Janissaries with the *Bektaşi* order, see Faroqhi, *Der Bektaschi-Orden*, pp. 91f.
7. The gradual integration of the order into the Ottoman fiscal regime and the parallel process of structural institutionalisation of the order itself was impressively studied by Steinherr, 'Les Bektachi', pp. 21–79; for the function of the Bektashi *tekke*s in the Ottoman economy, see Faroqhi, *Der Bektaschi-Orden*, pp. 48f. For very late Ottoman and early republican entanglements of the order and 'the state', see also Küçük, *The Role of the Bektāshīs*.
8. Faroqhi, 'Conflict, Accommodation and Long-Term Survival', p. 170.
9. Terzioğlu, 'How to Conceptualize Ottoman Sunnitization', pp. 301–38; Krstić, *Contested Conversions*, pp. 12–16.
10. Accusations of non-Sunnism were mentioned in this context, for example, by Es'ad Efendi in his *Üss-i za'fer*; however, research on the incidents in 1826 emphasises the primary importance of the Janissaries, which constituted a problem for the Ottoman government and its plans of transforming the military system; Heinzelmann, *Heiliger Kampf*. For Es'ad Efendi's judgement on the Bektashis, whom he called 'bu gürūh-i 'alevī ve revāfıż', see Dressler, *Writing Religion*, p. 2.
11. The term *sevād-i a'ẓam* was originally a transformation (and a widening) of

the concept '*jamā'a*'. As this *jamā'a*, the early community of Muslims grew after introducing Islam to Iranian *mawālī* and Turkish-speaking people, theologians like al-Hakim al-Samarkandi conceptualised the idea of the umma anew and used the term *sevād-i a'ẓam* instead of *jamā'a* henceforth; see Van Ess, *Der Eine und das Andere*, pp. 40f.; Madelung, *Religious Trends*, p. 20.

12. See, for example, Pistor-Hatam, 'Tanzīmāt oder ittiḥād', pp. 247–61; Landau, *The Politics of Pan-Islam*.
13. Such static thinking was, and still is, very widespread in the conceptualisations of inner Islamic difference and plurality. Dressler has stressed this problem in his various publications and urged for a strict separation of analytical meta-language and object language; Dressler, 'How to Conceptualize Inner-Islamic Plurality', pp. 241–60; Langer and Simon highlight the aspect of power in the negotiation of orthodoxy and heterodoxy in 'The Dynamics of Orthodoxy and Heterodoxy', pp. 273–88
14. Jacob, *Beiträge*; Georg Jacob (1862–1937) founded the academic discipline Turkology in Germany at the turn of the nineteenth and twentieth centuries. With the edition of İshak's *Kaşif* he also contributed to building a first body of knowledge on the *Bektaşi* order in Germany on which many Orientalists to come, such as Frederick Hasluck, referred to in their own later works.
15. Ibid., V.
16. Ibid., VI.
17. For example, Birge, *The Bektashi Order*; Browne, 'Further Notes on the Literature of the Ḥurufis', pp. 533–81. For a later example consider Trimingham, *The Sufi Orders*, p. 81. See also Clayer's recent treatment of İshak's work, and its reception in Europe by Georg Jacob, Frederick Hasluck and others significantly contributed to building up a first body of knowledge on the Bektashis in Europe; Clayer, 'Sufi Printed Matter', pp. 351–67. Cem Kara's book Grenzen überschreitende Derwische: Kulturbeziehungen des Bektaschi-Ordens 1826–1925 has appeared too recently to be included for discussion in this chapter.
18. Foucault called a literary text 'the point where the individual and the social are inverted into one another' in order to hint at the entanglement of powerful discourse, governing the rules of utterance, on the one hand, and the capacity of the individual subject, on the other, in shaping arguments and contents of any such literary work: Foucault, *The Archaeology of Knowledge*, p. 139. For Foucault, such an approach is typical for *Ideengeschichte*, that is, the 'History of Ideas', as opposed to his archaeological method. Yet here, clearly, it is the History of Ideas and not archaeology that is given preference in coming to terms with İshak's text and the relationship of its contents with the 'author as actor' and the historical social context of which he was part, and, one must stress, subject to. On the question of the agency of medieval Near Eastern historians, see Hirschler, *Medieval Arabic Historiography*.
19. Özege, *Eski Harflerle*, p. 838.

20. Among them were the *'Aşkname* of Fereşteoğlu, Nesimi's *Divan* and the *Hüsniye*, all being texts that subsequently circulated widely among *Bektaşi*s and *Alevi*s. A *tezkere* listing these publications and condemning their contents may be found in BOA (MF. MKT.) 47.022.
21. Rıf'at, *Mir'atü 'l-makāsıd*. It is unclear if Ahmet Rıf'at was *Bektaşi* himself, but in his refutation of İshak's work, he seeks to represent the *Bektaşiyye* as being in conformity with the Prophet's Sunna, and does not elaborate on specific ritual practices or wine consumption, etc. He furthermore takes up İshak's line of argument, that Hacı Bektaş himself was acting according to sharia, but some of his later followers departed from his path and inclined to *Hurūfi* or other teachings, as shown by İshak. Rıf'at's text was edited by Çift, *Gerçek Bektaşilik*; I thank Dr Cem Kara (Vienna) for pointing this out to me and sharing Rıf'at's original Ottoman text.
22. İshak, *Kaşif*, p. 3. It is assumed that the publication of these texts was possible through protection and promotion by Valide Sultan Bezmialem, Sultan Abdülmecit's wife, who seemed to be *Bektaşi* herself; Faroqhi, 'The Bektashis', p. 22.
23. On his teachings, see Bausani, 'Ḥurūfiyya', pp. 600–1. See also Usluer, who provides a genealogy of Fazlallah bearing witness to his *seyyid* descent; Usluer, *Fazlullah Esterābādī*, pp. 11f. See also Usluer, *Hurūfilik*. Ahmet Karamustafa historicises the emergence of this 'new religious movement' in the post-Mongol Near East; Karamustafa, *God's Unruly Friends*, p. 22.
24. İshak, *Kaşif*, pp. 3, 37, 172.
25. Pretzl, *Die Streitschrift*, p. 16.
26. Usluer, *Fazlullah Esterābādī*, p. 22.
27. İshak, *Kaşif*, pp. 166ff.
28. As noted in the title of the *risāle*.
29. Algar, 'The *Hurūfi* Influence on Bektashism', pp. 41–54; Birge, *The Bektashi Order*, p. 60; Browne, 'Further Notes on the Literature of the Ḥurufis', p. 537; Gölpınarlı, 'Bektaşîlîk [sic!]', p. 18. See, for an illustrative example both of Ḥurūfism and its connection to the *Bektaşi* order, the cover of Oytan's work, which displays the famous picture of a human face consisting of Arabic letters and the words 'Allah' and 'Ali' inscribed in this face; Oytan, *Bektaşiliğin İçyüzü*.
30. İshak, *Kaşif*, S. pp. 2f.; Note that Hasluck, for example, identified Fazlallah as the founder of the *Bektaşiyye*, thus being indicative of the reception of İshak's text in early European scientific work on the Anatolian religious landscape in general, and the *Bektaşi*s in particular; Hasluck, *Christianity and Islam*, p. 565.
31. For example: 'şab-i mi'rācda Muḥammad 'aleyhi 's-selām ḥażret-i aḥadiyyeti yedi ḫaṭṭ ile gördi * çār može har do abrū wa mū-ye sar * haft ḫaṭṭand az ḫodā-ye dādgar * ki bu dört 'anāṣıra żarb olınsa yiğirmi sekiz olur ḥurūf-i ḳur'an [sic!] 'adedince ki yiğirmi sekizdir pas ḳur'ānı ādam vechinde oḳudı ve Muḥammad ('m) ḥaḳḳı emred ṣūratında gördiği Fażl Fiyāż idi-ki nūr-i

Fabricating the Great Mass

vāḥid lam yazal ve lā yazāludır nūr ki ġayr-i maḥsūsdır ve kelāmdır ẓuhūr etse elbetde yedi saṭırla ẓuhūr eder*' ('In the night of his journey to heaven, Muhammad, peace be upon him, saw the Lord of Singularity with seven lines: four eyelashes, two brows each and the main hair / are seven of God, the just ruler. These multiplied with the four elements [water, fire, wind, earth] adds up to 28; when one counts the letters of the Qur'an it is also 28, thus he reads the Qur'an in human's face. And it was Fazl-i Fiyaz whom Muhammad saw as God in the face of the beardless young one who is the light of the one who did not end and does not end, who is imperceptible and who is the word. And if he reveals himself he reveals in seven lines.') İshak, *Kaşif*, p. 83.

32. Bausani, 'Ḥurūfiyya', p. 600.
33. Or in his words, 'kelime-'i tevḥīdiñ ma'nā-yi şerīfi ... nefy ile cenāb-i ḥakḳa ḥaṣr', İshak, *Kaşif*, p. 45.
34. Massignon, 'Ḥulūl', p. 571.
35. The term used is 'tekmīl-i dīn eyleyüb', İshak, *Kaşif*, p. 109.
36. Following Q 2:255, where God sits on a throne (suggesting anthropomorphic ambiguity) or Q 48:10, where God's hand is mentioned. For a discussion within Matūrīdī contexts, see Brodersen, *Der unbekannte Kalām*, p. 495.
37. Expressed as 'fevḳu'l-'āde cāhilāne ve mużıllāne te'vīle cür'et etmişdir', İshak, *Kaşif*, p. 31.
38. As Poonawala mainly discusses Arabic-speaking contexts, I quote him with the Arabic phonology of the term, while using the Ottoman-Turkish *te'vil* when referring to İshak's Ottoman usage.
39. Poonawala, 'Ta'wīl', p. 391.
40. For example, İshak, *Kaşif*, p. 32.
41. Ibid, pp. 5, 7, 9. The *Bektaşis*' latitudinarian relation to the drinking of wine in İshak's imagination is also apparent from the quote in the beginning of this chapter.
42. Ibid., pp. 29f.: he uses the phrasing 'mu'temed bir ẕātıñ rivāyetine göre'.
43. Ibid., p. 30; the phrasing is 'fa'l- i şenī' icrā eylemiş'.
44. Pretzl, *Die Streitschrift*, p. 26: 'bar sabīl-e tabrīk taqrīb mīkonand'.
45. İshak, *Kaşif*, p. 7.
46. Ibid., p. 9; phrased as 'bunlar şī'ī olmayub başlu başına bir ṭā'ife-'i müşrikīn olub'.
47. There are also differences in their measurements which I was unable to verify, as I have only copies and did not have a chance to see the original prints.
48. İshak, *Kaşif*, pp. 7–8.
49. Ibid., p. 8; phrased as 'cühelāyı celb içün ḥażret-i Ali ṣūretinde görünän yine Fażl-i Ḥurūfīdir'.
50. Ibid., p. 9; phrased as 'hevā-yi nefse miyāl olanları celb eylediler'.
51. Ibid., A, p. 24; omitted in B.
52. These represent the measurements of the pages and the text block, respectively.

53. İshak also claims that he asked one 'of the Iranian religious scholars' ('*acem 'ulemādan bir ẕāt*), Mirza Safa, about the *Bektaşi*s being Shiites. The '*alim* replied that they denied the Sharia; see İshak, *Kaşif*, p. 9. Hacı Mirza Safa was an Iranian dervish from among the retinue of the Iranian embassy in Istanbul during the time İshak was writing. He maintained relationships with both various Sufi orders in Istanbul and Iranian modernists such as Mirza Malkum Han; Algar, *Mīrzā Malkum Khān*, p. 70.
54. Kohlberg, 'al-Rāfiḍa', p. 386.
55. Ibid., p. 387a.
56. Eberhard, *Osmanische Polemik*, pp. 75, 98; see also Ocak, *Osmanlı Toplumunda Mülhidler ve Zındıklar*, p. 116.
57. For example, see Pistor-Hatam's work on Persian newspapers published in Istanbul; Pistor-Hatam, 'The Persian Newspaper', pp. 141–7. Though short-lived, this journal was one of the platforms in which the idea of Sunni and Shii, that is, of Ottoman and Iranian reconciliation, was discussed with reference to the idea of an *ittiḥād-i islām*, as noted in Pistor-Hatam, 'Tanzīmāt oder ittiḥād', *passim*. See also Baltacıoğlu-Brammer's chapter in this volume.
58. Historian Philip Sarasin calls such discursive influences 'überindividuelle Sachverhalte' ('over-subjective matters'), Sarasin, *Geschichtswissenschaft*, p. 29.
59. Already Roland Barthes, in his well-known essay 'The Death of the Author', emphasises the secret bond of capitalism's obsession with individualism 'which has attached the greatest importance to the "person" of the author'. Barthes, 'The Death of the Author', p. 143.
60. İshak, *Kaşif*, p. 166.
61. Ibid.
62. 've ṭā'ife-'i Bektaşiyān bunlardan aḥmaḳ olıyor ki Fażl-i Ḥurūfī'niñ ülūhiyyetini iddi'ā etdikleri ḥālde Timūr'ıñ oğlı ḳatl etdiğini muḳırrlardır', İshak, *Kaşif*, p. 168.
63. Ibid., p. 166.
64. See, for instance, ibid., p. 9.
65. Ibid., pp. 167f. These descriptions point to a notion of conspiracy around the Nusayris.
66. Ibid., p. 167.
67. Friedman, *Nuṣayrī-'Alawīs*, pp. 220f.
68. Ibid., p. 221.
69. Olsson, 'Gnosis', p. 177.
70. Friedmann, *Nuṣayrī-'Alawīs*, p. 221.
71. At one point, İshak speaks of *nukabā* ('elders of a community'), whereas Friedman, from the texts he is working with, only recognises its singular form *nakīb*, denoting the leader of the ritual in question. Friedman, *Nuṣayrī-'Alawīs*, p. 213; İshak, *Kaşif*, p. 167.
72. Friedman, *Nuṣayrī-'Alawīs*, p. 213.
73. İshak, *Kaşif*, p. 168.

74. Ibid.
75. Ibid., p. 167.
76. Jacob, *Beiträge*, p. 26.
77. 'ḥażret-i Ali'den başḳa ilāh yoḳdır', İshak, *Kaşif*, p. 167.
78. As İshak phrased it, 'faḳaṭ bu ṭā'ifeniñ bektaşī'den küfürleri ehven oldığı şul cihetle ki ülūhiyyete yaḳışdırmayub', ibid., p. 168.
79. Reinkowski, *Die Dinge der Ordnung*, p. 257.
80. Pistor-Hatam, 'Tanzīmāt oder ittiḥād', pp. 250f.
81. Winter, *A History of the 'Alawis*, p. 209.
82. Silverstein, 'Sufism and Governmentality', pp. 171–85.
83. İshak, *Kaşif*, p. 24.
84. Faroqhi, *Der Bektaschi-Orden*, p. 121.
85. Uzunçarşılı, *Osmanlı Devleti*, p. 569.

8

The Ottoman Policy of 'Correction of Belief(s)'

Necati Alkan[1]

Studies of so-called 'heterodox' religious groups in the late Ottoman period of Sultan Abdülhamid II (r. 1876–1909) discuss the application of 'correction of belief(s)' (*taṣḥīḥ-i i'tikād/'akāid*) to non-Sunni Islamic sects such as the Alevis (Turkish and Kurdish), the Nusayris (Alawis) in Syria or the Shiites in Iraq and the Yezidis in eastern Anatolia, among others. The Hamidian administration attempted to 'civilise' and turn them into obedient 'good' Muslims, thereby applying a 'fine-tuning' of their beliefs. This chapter will compare these policies with those of Mahmud II (r. 1808–39), who had already applied a policy of 'correction of beliefs' to the *Bektaşi* Sufi order that he persecuted as allies of the Janissaries (elite military troops) after their elimination in 1826. The chapter explores the evolution of the use of the neglected concept of *taṣḥīḥ-i i'tikād/'akāid* from the late eighteenth century until the late nineteenth century, a period that stands out for its increase in centralising policies. Conversion campaigns were carried out to enforce the 'true' Sunni belief, as defined by the Ottoman administration, to preserve or restore order in the face of threats posed by groups accused of heresy and disobedience. Therefore, whenever this chapter employs designations and terms such as 'heretical', 'heterodox', 'civilise' or any specific terminology or description that is placed within quotation marks, the intent is to express the view of self-professed Ottoman Sunnis of the Hamidian era who use them in their sources.

The Ottoman Conversion Campaigns of the Eighteenth and Nineteenth Centuries

Within Islam, groups deemed to be outside mainstream Sunnism, the 'internal others', are called *al-firaq al-ḍālla* ('misguided sects') or *ahl al-bidʻa* ('people of innovation' or 'sectarians'); these are labels that refer to conceptual trends or sects within Islam that were viewed as having deviated from the Sunni consensus. Their conflicting viewpoints are perceived as the origin of *fitna* ('sedition'), and thus a threat to the unity of the Muslim community. The most common term that has been used pejoratively by Sunnis, as applied to Shiite groups and various sects of Shiism, is *rāfiḍa/rawāfiḍ*, meaning 'rejecter(s)'.[2] In the Ottoman Empire, followers of Shiʻa Islam and various sects such as the Nusayris, Alevis and *Bektaşi*s were called *rāfiżi/revāfıż*, or *ehl-i rafż*.[3]

Studies of so-called 'heretical' religious groups (*fırak-ı żālle*) in the late Ottoman period discuss the application of 'correction of belief(s)' (*taṣḥīḥ-i iʻtikād/ʼakāid*)[4] towards groups with Shiite leanings, and sometimes those who were regarded as nominal Sunni Muslims.[5] This Islamic concept (derived from *taṣḥīḥ al-iʻtiqād* in Arabic) is not mentioned in the Qur'an, but it is discussed in books about the principles of Islam. It is linked to the Qur'anic dictum of 'commanding right and forbidding wrong', and concerns the rectification of the religious beliefs of the Muslim individual and his relation to social and political life.[6]

Sultan Abdülhamid II dispatched itinerant imams or Sunni missionaries (*dāi-misyoner*) who were trained to propagate the Hanafi version of Sunni Islam in the Ottoman Empire. They carried out active missionary work in the name of the sultan. Based on petitions of governors in various provinces, he also commissioned the construction of mosques and religious schools (*medrese*s) as a measure to educate and 'civilise' these people and make them obedient and 'good' Muslims. Many official documents at the *Başbakanlık Osmanlı Arşivi* (BOA, Prime Ministerial Ottoman Archives, Istanbul) provide evidence for this. The recent discussions on 'Ottoman Sunnitisation' and 'confessionalisation'[7] have overlooked *taṣḥīḥ-i iʻtikād/ʼakāid*.

It is not clear exactly when the Ottomans first applied *taṣḥīḥ-i iʻtikād/ʼakāid* as a political tool. The earliest reference I was able to locate in Ottoman sources where the ulema had an active role was the educative measures applied to the 'disobedient' Abkhaz and Circassian tribes (*Abaza ve Çerkes*) in Soğucak/Anapa in the Caucasus towards the end of the eighteenth century. According to the Ottoman chronicler Ahmed Lutfi, Circassians and Abkhaz lived in a 'state of savagery' (*ḥālet-i vaḥşiyāne*). He writes that most of them belonged to a Zoroastrian creed called 'Şāsı'[8] that was engaged in pillage and theft, and they were 'deprived of the glory of Islam' (*şeref-i islāmiyetden bī-behre*). Ferah Ali Paşa (d. 1785),[9] who was assigned as governor of that region, had spread the 'lights of Islam' there.[10] Mustafa Nuri Paşa[11] (d. 1890) noted in his chronicle that since the time of Ferah Ali, the tribes had been entering the fold of Islam and civilisation (*dā'ire-i dīn-i mübīn ü medeniyyete idhāl olunmakda*).[12]

In the early nineteenth century, the issue of the conversion of Caucasian tribes re-emerged and Çeçenzade Hasan Paşa (d. 1831),[13] governor-general of Trabzon and military commander at Anapa in 1826–7, took responsibility and went to the notables and tribal chiefs in the Crimea. He took with him imperial orders along with manuals of faith and instructions as to 'command right and forbid wrong' and 'correct the beliefs' (*emr-i bi'l-ma'rūf ve nehyi 'ani'l-münker ve ilm-i ḥāl ve taṣḥīḥ -i 'aḳāidi muḥtevī fermānlar*), and reform these people by appointing and sending a mufti and sixteen judges from among the ulema to them.[14] An Ottoman imperial document about Hasan Paşa from late 1826 states that 'some tribes have abandoned the *şazz* innovation which was a Zoroastrian custom' (*Mecusī adeti olan şazz bid'atını terk edüb*), meaning that they left 'what is contrary to general rule'.[15] It is perhaps telling that the efforts of Hasan Paşa occurred during the reign of Mahmud II (r. 1808–39), who became sultan of the Ottomans after a violent power struggle between his predecessor Selim III (r. 1789–1807) and the Janissary elite troops as a response to military/political reforms that were commenced by the sultan and intended to establish a 'new order'.

Although this chapter primarily approaches the issue of 'correction of belief(s)' in relation to Islamic sectarianism, it is worthwhile to dwell on this early case study, because it demonstrates that the modern bureaucrats of the nineteenth-century Ottoman state interpreted the spreading of Islam in those non-Islamic regions in the eighteenth century retrospectively as the cause of 'civilisation' (*medeniyet* or *temeddün* in Turkish). The use of these terms to mean 'civilisation' was coined in the late nineteenth century, and became watchwords of modernisation attempts.[16] They were also used in conjunction with *taṣḥīḥ-i i'tiḳād/'aḳāid* and education (*ma'ārif*) aimed at 'heretical' groups: they needed to abandon their old ways of nomadism and savagery and be brought into the 'circle of civilisation'.[17]

Even though attempts to modernise the empire had already begun by the late eighteenth century, it was in the nineteenth century that the Ottomans developed a more centralised administration after the reforms of the *Tanẓīmāt* ('reordering') were introduced through two edicts in 1839 and 1856. In the next decades, the constitution was proclaimed (in 1876) and it introduced a parliament as a reaction to the bureaucratic-authoritarian *Tanẓīmāt* rule.[18] The constitution was short-lived and was practically abolished by Abdülhamid II in 1878, who then established his own style of despotism. At the same time, the Ottoman state found that its policies of centralisation inadvertently often proved to be destabilising and attempted to confront this problem with a 'fine-tuning'[19] of its population. It seems that 'fine-tuning' becomes important in times of crisis or emergency, the most important aspect of which is 'that it is a process through which the legitimation ideology of the state is promoted, and state policy is imposed on society'. It also involves 'the process of making state policy'.[20] While Selim Deringil discusses 'correction of belief(s)' as part of the 'fine-tuning' efforts of Abdülhamid II and his creation of a state ideology, I argue that we can also apply this to the centralising policies of Mahmud II that took place earlier in a time of crisis.

Correcting the Beliefs of the Bektaşis after 1826

In the first half of the nineteenth century, *taṣḥīḥ-i i'tiḳād/'aḳāid* was applied by Sultan Mahmud II (r. 1808–39) on a large scale to the *Bektaşi* Sufi order as part of his reforms. *Bektaşi*sm[21] is a Sufi order that was established in Anatolia during the fifteenth century by Balım Sultan (d. 1519)[22] and named after Hacı Bektaş Veli (d. 1270). *Bektaşi*sm was widely spread among the Turkish nomadic tribes of central Anatolia that originally came from Azerbaijan and Iran. Hacı Bektaş was a Sufi saint who became one of the main spiritual leaders of Alevism,[23] a mystical branch of Shi'a Islam.[24] Despite the fact that some of his beliefs run somewhat contrary to mainstream Sunni Islam, Hacı Bektaş was revered in the Ottoman Empire and is still held in high esteem in Turkey today.[25]

Bektaşi dervishes had participated in the conquest and conversion to Islam of Christian domains by the early Ottomans and were deeply involved in the Ottoman army. For unknown reasons, the Janissary corps were placed under the spiritual guidance of the *Bektaşi*s; thus, the Janissaries were sometimes called *Ocak-ı Bektaşiyan*, 'the hearth of the *Bektaşi*s'. Because of the association of the *Bektaşi*s with the Janissaries and the protection they received from the Ottoman state, *Bektaşi*sm was a tolerated sectarian group. Initially, they were given the mission of preventing sympathisers of the Safavid ruler Isma'il I (r. 1501–24) of Iran who had infiltrated Ottoman domains[26] from fleeing to Safavid-controlled territories. Due to their support of these efforts, *Bektaşi*sm came to be domesticated by the Ottomans.[27]

The *Bektaşi*s were closely linked to the Janissaries, and their involvement in opposition to Sultan Selim III in the early nineteenth century was the cause of their subsequent abolition by Mahmud II, as he persecuted them as allies of the Janissaries.[28] Mahmud II sought to perpetuate the 'New Order' his predecessor Selim III had initiated, but he was convinced that military reforms alone were not sufficient. Traditional historiography holds that since Mahmud knew that the Janissaries and other conservative groups had revolted after the introduction of Selim III's innovations, he acted prudently and gathered loyal ministers, the people's 'natural leaders among the ulema' and soldiers around him ahead of time, who could act immediately against any revolt. Mahmud pursued an unprecedented propaganda campaign against the 'degenerated' Janissaries, who came to be defined as the enemies of the state.[29]

After the Janissaries ostensibly accepted the fatwa of the *Şeyhülislam* Mehmed Tahir Efendi (d. 1838)[30] regarding the creation and education of a new troop, they revolted against the sultan for the last time a few days later on 15 June 1826. Mahmud II was prepared and crushed the Janissary revolt in their barracks, with contemporary accounts reporting that thousands of Janissaries were killed and many more fled. This bloody campaign, called *Vak'a-i Hayriyye* ('Auspicious Event'), entailed the wiping out of even the name Janissary and the persecution of anyone who had associated with them, such as the *Bektaşi* order of dervishes.[31]

Despite these tensions, initially Selim III protected the *Bektaşi* order and tried to win them over to support his reforms, but without success. The *Bektaşi*s, in turn, had supported the Janissaries in their opposition to the sultan. They took part in an action against Alemdar Mustafa Paşa, a notable from the Balkans who marched to Istanbul with his troops to try to save the life of Selim III. While Alemdar Mustafa Paşa was not successful in preserving the reign of Selim III, he was able to install Mahmud II as a new sultan. The *Bektaşi*s were subsequently persecuted due to their involvement in the revolt against both the former sultan and Alemdar Mustafa Paşa, with a focus on their supposed propagation of heresy among the people.[32] This implies that persecutions of the *Bektaşi*s began immediately after the restoration of order in 1808. But the complete persecution of the *Bektaşi* presence and destruction of the Janissaries could not be achieved until after 1826. Mahmud II was aware of early Janissary revolts and he was cautious in his actions towards both groups before 1826. The early persecutions of *Bektaşi*s may have affected the order's power between the 1808 restoration and the Auspicious Event in 1826.

Based on Baki Tezcan's argument,[33] we can infer that the ensuing persecution of the *Bektaşi*s was a political tactic aimed at supporting the centralisation politics and reforms of Mahmud II. Anyone who had supported the Janissaries was chastised severely. Hence, the sultan punished with death or exiled *Bektaşi* leaders and their followers, and closed, converted or destroyed their convents because he regarded the *Bektaşi*s as a possible opposition to his policies of centralisation. To build a centralised state, Mahmud needed to eliminate the Janissaries and their allies.[34]

Moreover, it appears that Mahmud did this as much to appease various Sunni ulema, who detested the *Bektaşi*s, as a trade-off to acquire their consent for his reforms of the Ottoman military and society in general. To achieve this, Mahmud needed an ideological source of support, and he employed Sunni Islam as a means of propaganda. Eager to win wider support for his reforms, he commissioned Sahaflar Şeyhizade Es'ad Efendi[35] as an official chronicler to write a treatise titled *Üss-i Zafer* ('The Foundation of Victory').[36] It is an apologetic work that deals with the events of 1241 AH (i.e., the numerical value of the words *Üss-i Zafer*),[37] meaning 1826, the year in which the Janissary corps was abolished. The work was published just two years after the incident. Apart from being a chronicle of the *Vak'a-i Hayriyye*, Es'ad Efendi engages in periodic digressions from the chronicle's narrative to provide comments that he calls *istitrād* ('excursion'), which are aimed at supporting the reasons for the elimination of the Janissaries and the prohibition of *Bektaşi*sm. They constitute the core of an ideological argument as to why Mahmud II was required to commence military reforms and create a new army. Es'ad calls Mahmud 'the renewer of the religion and the state' (*müceddid-i din ü devlet*) and 'the cause of repose and peace' (*bāis-i asayiş ü rahat*), who wanted to exalt the Word of God (*i'lā-yı kelimetullah*). Es'ad maintains that according to a hadith of the Prophet Muhammad, God sends a 'renewer of religion' (*mujaddid*) at the beginning of every century when unrest and rebellions occur, and a mighty person appears to restore order. These arguments are expressed in a deeply religious context to win over devout Sunni leadership to Mahmud II's Westernising reforms. As a conclusion for his argument, Es'ad states there were much unrest and rebellion that heralded the coming of Mahmud II, who was born in 1199, at the beginning of the thirteenth Islamic century. During that time, the disorder was rampant, for the Janissaries had revolted and the heretical *Bektaşi*s supported them. Therefore, Es'ad says, it was 'as clear and evident as the sun at midday' that Mahmud was the 'renewer of religion and helper of the Muslims' (*müceddid-i din ve mu'in-i müslimīn*) for that century.[38]

The *Bektaşi* order was prohibited at a consultative meeting for which Mahmud assembled the *şeyhülislam* ('grand mufti'), his prime minister and leaders of Sunni Sufi orders such as the *Nakşbendi*s and the *Halveti*s.[39] An imperial decree subsequently confirmed their decision.[40] The chronicler Ahmet Lutfi wrote that Mahmud abolished the Janissaries because they had become disorganised and defective, like the 'people of error', by which he meant the *Bektaşi*s, who had strayed from the Islamic sharia. The sultan therefore reformed this 'gang' (*gūruh*) of the *Bektaşi*s in his capacity as 'God's representative on earth who was commissioned with commanding good' (*emr-i bi'l-ma'rūf ile me'mūr halīfe-i rūy-ı zemīn*).⁴¹

It is interesting that the imperial decree mentions that those *Bektaşi*s who chose to follow the Sunna thereafter would be spared, and the state had always shown reverence to Hacı Bektaş, the founder of *Bektaşi*sm.⁴² Mahmud II conceived of the original *Bektaşi*sm as an order that had followed Sunnism and the sharia. He differentiated between this original *Bektaşi*sm and the *Bektaşi*sm of contemporary times, called *zamane Bektaşilik*. This 'contemporary *Bektaşi*sm' was corrupted by people who claimed to be *Bektaşi*s, but did not adhere to the sharia, were lawless like the Janissaries, and had become heretical in their beliefs.⁴³ According to Mahmud, the decline of *Bektaşi*sm, which he otherwise spoke of as one of the 'exalted orders' (*turuk-ı 'Aliyye*), had gone hand in hand with the decline of the Janissary corps since the two institutions had become allied.⁴⁴

The sultan decreed that *Bektaşi* convents in Istanbul that were more than sixty years old were either to be demolished, their possessions confiscated, or turned into mosques or *medrese*s, thus carrying out a transformation or conversion of their sacred spaces.⁴⁵ Because of their closeness to the sultan, the shaykhs of the *Nakşbendi* order were often assigned to look after the convents. Most importantly, as part of the Sunnitisation of the *Bektaşi*s, a *Nakşbendi* shaykh took over the central Hacı Bektaş Veli convent in central Anatolia. The *Nakşbendi* shaykhs, who replaced *Bektaşi* shaykhs in other convents often came from the *Halidiyye/Khalidiyya* suborder of the revivalist and sharia-based *Müceddīdī/Mujaddīdī* branch, whose founder Shaykh Khalid had emphasised a strong fulfilment of sharia and the revival of the Sunna. He had urged his followers in Ottoman domains who had been active since the early nineteenth century that they should 'rectify the beliefs' (*tashīh al-i'tiqād*) of the Muslims.⁴⁶ The active role the *Khalidiyya* played during this period implies an 'orthodox trend' in Istanbul that was utilised by Mahmud II to get support against groups that were deemed disobedient, such as the *Bektaşi*s. The views of Shaykh Khalid and his later supporters may have diverged a bit due to greater integration into Ottoman state centralisation programmes.

While some *Bektaşi* leaders who had supported the Janissaries in their last revolt were killed and others exiled to remote places and placed under surveillance, some others were seen as having 'corrected their beliefs' and became obedient Sunnis, and were then released from exile, according to archival evidence about *Bektaşi*s. The indoctrination of *Bektaşi*s with Sunni beliefs occurred in localities that were 'abodes of the ulema' (*makarr-ı ulema*), that is, strongholds of religious scholars,

Ottoman Policy of 'Correction of Belief(s)'

such as Kayseri, Hadim (Konya), Bursa, Manisa, Birgi and other places.[47] It appears that by using *makarr-ı ulema* as locations for the reform of individuals deemed to be deviant, the Ottoman administration intended to impose the opposite of what they deemed 'heretical' or unwanted, in other words 'Sunni orthodoxy'.

Whereas the main reason for the prohibition of *Bektaşi*sm was their close relationship with the Janissaries, the state's suppression of the order was grounded in religious ideology, arguing that the *Bektaşi*s were not following sharia.[48] In the decree prohibiting *Bektaşi*sm in Istanbul and the edicts the sultan sent to the provinces, the sultan almost entirely refrained from mentioning the name '*Bektaşi*', instead he used *gürüh-ı mekrūha* ('despised gang'), *gürüh-ı melāhide* ('gang of disbelievers'), *gürüh-ı Alevi ve revāfız* ('gang of Alevis and Shiite heretics'),[49] *gürüh-ı ibāhiye* ('gang of the libertines') or *erbāb-ı rafz ve ilhad* ('people of heresy and unbelief').[50]

In Istanbul, the convents were closed down by distinguished members of the *ilmiye*, the religious establishment, and officers from the Imperial Gate (*kapıcıbaşı*). They would secretly go to the convent and raid it, arrest the shaykhs and their followers, and then seal the doors. The arrested persons were brought to the *Cebehane* ('Ammunition House'). Each *Bektaşi* in Istanbul was brought to the presence of the *şeyhülislam*, who would ask questions to determine their knowledge of Islam. Some passed the test and were released; others were not deemed to be credible, but escaped death and were exiled instead. Apparently, some shaykhs saved their lives by resorting to taqiyah or dissimulation as a legitimate form of defence. It was demanded that the exiled *Bektaşi*s were put under constant surveillance in order to make them follow sharia rules and prevent misguided behaviour; in short, they should be Sunnitised.[51] The persecution of the *Bektaşi*s was extensive; everyone who was even accused of being a *Bektaşi*, even if they actually were not, was still arrested and exiled. Ahmed Cevdet Paşa lists in his *History* names of men who were innocent of the charge of being *Bektaşi*s, but who were nevertheless sent into exile.[52]

What were the measures that constituted the *tashīh-i i'tikād/'akāid* of the *Bektaşi*s? And after how many years were *Bektaşi* leaders and followers released because of good conduct? There are many cases based on archival evidence; this chapter will present a few that can give us an idea of how 'correction of belief(s)' was carried out.

In a document from January 1828 (1243) a certain İsmail and Nazif from the Asian Istanbul suburb of Üsküdar were mentioned as 'having gone astray in the path of contemporary *Bektaşi*sm' (*zamane Bektaşiliği yoluna saparak*) and had behaved in a way that went against the exalted sharia. In order to discipline them, they were sent to Güzelhisar (Aydın), which was an 'abode of the ulema' (*makarr-ı ulema*). There the mufti, various ulema and madrasa teachers taught them the glorious way of the Sunna congregation (*tarīk-i nāciyye olan ehl-i sünnet ve cemāat*). After being indoctrinated (*telkīn*) they left 'their heretic path and accepted the straight path' (*tarīk-i melāḥideden udūl, rāh-ı müstakīmi kabul*) and so 'corrected their beliefs'. They had also performed their ritual prayers on time with the community of believers. While being on the right course, Nazif died, and İsmail stayed behind in a bad financial condition. Because his wife and children lamented his wretched condition and it was observed that İsmail was disciplined and pulled himself together (*ıslāh-ı nefs*), they pleaded for his release. In this case, we see that a *Bektaşi* was already released after one year or so.[53]

Another case is that of Dellāl ('broker') Ahmed who worked at the *Saraçhane* ('saddlery') and Çedikçi ('slipper-maker') Hafız Hüseyin from Istanbul, who were accused of being *Bektaşi*s and had 'gone astray on the path of contemporary *Bektaşi*sm' (*zamane Bektaşiliği yoluna saparak*). They were exiled in 1826 by imperial order to Bayındır (Izmir), and ordered to be chastised so that they might 'rehabilitate themselves' (*ıslāḥ-ı nefs*) accordingly, because they had opposed sharia and 'treaded the dark path of unbelief and heresy'. This had been previously investigated by the *şeyhülislam*, and an imperial decree set forth the conditions of their exile as a measure of discipline. According to this 'benevolent decree' the convicts were sent into exile under the supervision of a *çavuş* ('guard' or 'sergeant') and were not to be forgiven unless they 'corrected their beliefs and improved themselves'. They were cautioned and advised that they should 'be caused to renounce their superstitious beliefs in word and deed' (*i'tikadāt-ı bātıla kālen ve kalben yed-i keff ile ve ferāgat etdirderek*) according to the obligations of sharia. For this they had to stay in a chamber in the *Fetvāhāne* ('office of the mufti'), were consistently reminded about actions contrary to sharia, and stayed in their place of exile for about six or seven years performing their ritual prayers and fasting. Eventually, they heeded the cautions and gave up their previous beliefs (*i'tikād-i sābıkalarından ferāgat etmiş*) and followed the path of the Sunna and the righteous companions of the Prophet by 'correcting their beliefs'. The mufti, the *medrese* teachers, the ulema, the imams, the preachers and other Muslims attested in a legal proceeding that the two exiles had disciplined themselves (*terbiye-i nefs*), followed the way of sharia and left their previous 'wretched' condition. As a result, they were worthy to be forgiven, and their records in the *Bāb-ı Āsafī* ('the office of the prime minister') were deleted. All present in this assembly had signed and sealed the petition asking for the release of the two men.[54]

Ottoman Policy of 'Correction of Belief(s)'

As a rule, officials residing in places along the exile route were advised to ensure that no problems occurred. Also, local officials such as the *naib* ('judge of lower rank') and the mufti had the duty of ensuring that the exiles reached their destination. The mufti was commissioned to guarantee that the *Bektaşi*s abandoned their old beliefs and rehabilitated themselves by word and deed. The common duty of the *naib* and the mufti was to prevent the exiles from actions contrary to religion (Islam), and not to release them until they rehabilitated themselves.[55]

Even many decades after 1826 when *Bektaşi*sm was prohibited, there was much state-sponsored propaganda against the *Bektaşi*s. In the same negative way that Es'ad Efendi spoke of them, others also reviled them, saying that the *Bektaşi*s were heretics, did not heed sharia, that they were immoral, womanisers or that some *Bektaşi*s held drinking parties with women in their convents.[56] They would then go among the people and spread their unbelief. As late as the 1890s and even the 1910s, we have reports and accounts describing the *Bektaşi*s as 'irreligious' and as needing rehabilitation.[57]

Despite the rigid and long-lasting persecution by the state, there were counter-measures to which the *Bektaşi*s resorted in order to escape persecution and survive. They would, for example, change their attire and headdress; Cevdet Paşa notes that because of this, there remained no one who could be identified as '*Bektaşi*'. Es'ad Efendi, Cevdet Paşa and other official historians recorded that the *Bektaşi*s hid their beliefs, and sought to pass as Sunnis when the *şeyhülislam* questioned them. Others chose to become *Nakşbendi*s and escaped exile or came back from their exile as *Nakşbendi*s. Yet others sought refuge in convents of other Sufi orders, mostly *Mevlevi*, but they were cautioned not to wear their *Bektaşi* attire. There was also a mutual exchange of ideas between the *Bektaşi*s and other orders. It is said that *Bektaşi*s have influenced Sufi orders such as the *Mevlevi*s, *Sa'di*s and *Rufai*s. There were, for example, *Mevlevi* shaykhs who wore the *Bektaşi* headgear or acquired licences (*icāzet*) for the two orders at the same time due to *Bektaşi* presence in their lodges. Official documents also mention *Bektaşi*s who, after seeking refuge in Sunni orders, are said to have caused unrest until the beginning of the twentieth century.[58]

Despite all the persecution and propaganda against the *Bektaşi*s, many of them had already been released from exile during the reign of Mahmud II, and some convents even resumed their activities. In the years following the death of Mahmud in 1839, the prohibition was not as strictly enforced. During the time of Sultan Abdülmecid (r. 1839–61) the state was more lenient towards *Bektaşi*s, and Sultan Abdülaziz (r. 1861–76) even allowed the *Bektaşi*s to rebuild convents and hold gatherings. Also, from the reign of Abdülmecid onward, the *Bektaşi*s could publish their works openly. In this way, they actively promoted themselves in order to have a positive effect on public opinion.[59]

The Ottoman state's attitude towards *Bektaşi*sm from the reign of Mahmud II onward was ambivalent. The state-sponsored 'correction of beliefs' of the *Bektaşi*s during the reign of Mahmud II was not effective because most of the *Bektaşi*s knew how to hide their beliefs and escaped persecution. *Bektaşi* leaders later sent petitions during the Hamidian era, asking for official recognition of their order, which was declined on the ground that Mahmud II had forbidden the brotherhood. For this reason, the *Bektaşi*s went on to reopen their convents as *Nakşbendi* convents.[60] The official prohibition, which had pushed the *Bektaşi*s into hiding, lasted until the end of the empire, but the *Bektaşi*s were visible and active throughout the final century of the empire. Yet, in contrast to the Nusayis who took advantage of the transformations during the *Tanzīmāt* period, the *Bektaşi*s were disadvantaged. With all this in mind, we have to remember the different historical circumstances and experiences of such socio-religious groups deemed as 'heretical' by official Ottoman Sunnism.[61]

What all this tells us is that the *Bektaşi*s were silenced by Mahmud II as a potential source of opposition against the politics of centralisation, as were anti-reform ulema, notables and Janissaries, who had come to control public opinion in Istanbul and 'sought to control the state and negotiated different agendas of order, reform, and restoration'. In the eighteenth century, these groups as provincial actors and the centre participated in the rule of the empire together.[62] It seems that the Ottoman polity, which had been a 'vertical empire' in which the imperial elite kept its power through a hierarchical system, turned into a 'horizontal and participatory empire'. Now there were new mechanisms formed by provincial communities in public administration where their leaders became active participants in governance. Yet within this larger process of the modernisation and centralisation of the Ottoman state, as it resumed its old vertical structure in the nineteenth century,[63] powerful independent and semi-independent groups could not co-exist with a centralising state agenda.[64]

'Fine Tuning' during the **Tanzīmāt** *and the Reign of Abdülhamid II*

Despite the atmosphere of proclaimed religious tolerance in the Ottoman capital with the *Tanzīmāt* reforms, the situation in the eastern provinces was quite different. A major example was the conflict between Sunni

Ottoman Policy of 'Correction of Belief(s)'

Ottomans and their Shiite subjects in Iraq. Shiite clerics were actively proselytising, not only among Sunni tribes but also Ottoman officials.[65] Despite the European-oriented military and administrative reforms that had been initiated since the late eighteenth century, 'many of the reformers turned at the same time to what they believed to be the Ottoman heyday, the sixteenth century, and its Sunnitization of the state'.[66] They aimed to indoctrinate 'heretical' sects with the 'orthodox' doctrines of the Hanafi legal school. This was done through *taṣḥīḥ-i i'tikād/'akāid*, in other words, a 'fine-tuning' of religious beliefs of those who had inherited their conceptions of Islam from their ancestors, and were Muslims in name only.[67] This 'fine-tuning' also intersected with the conversion of non-Muslims like those in the tribes in the Caucasus, as mentioned previously. Among these were the Kurdish Yezidis, who will be addressed subsequently.

There seems to have been no tangible efforts to 'correct the beliefs' on a large scale during the reigns of sultans Abdülmecid and Abdülaziz. Whereas until the proclamation of the second *Tanẓīmāt* Edict in 1856, Sunni Islam was of vital concern for the sultan and the Sublime Porte, in the two following decades, there was an internal ideological clash fostered by European influence.[68] Yet as much as European ideals became widespread in the Ottoman Empire, a widely-felt need for Muslim unity against the Christian 'infidels' developed. A vital concern during the reign of Abdülaziz seems to have been how to bring about reconciliation among the soldiers who belonged to different non-Sunni Islamic sects. In an article titled *İhtiyacāt-ı Askeriye* ('Military Necessities') that was published in the Ottoman newspaper *Hakayīk el-Vekayi'* in 1871[69] and written in the context of jihad ('holy war') against 'infidels and dissenters' (*küffār ve buğāt*), the author highlights that religiously educated persons called *dāi* or 'missionary', should be thoroughly trained and sent to the regions where the followers of these sects live. There they should teach Sunni Islam, and the 'sound faith' (*'akīde-i ṣaḥīḥe*). This, in turn, would eliminate the causes of divisions within Islam and ultimately unite the soldiers:

> The Ottoman State accepts soldiers from among the Muslims in Rumelia and Anatolia. Just as the Rafızis ['heretics', meaning the Alevis in this context] have been spreading in Rumelia recently, there are miscellaneous Islamic sects that are outside Sunni Islam (*hāric-i ehl-i sünnet bir takım mezāhib-i müteferrika-ı İslāmiye*), such as the 'Alevis' in Anatolia 'who ascribe divinity to [Imam] Ali and are called *Kızılbaş*' (*Kızılbaş ta'bīr olunan ve Hazret-i Ali'ye ulūhiyet isnād eyleyen Aleviyyūn*),[70] the Yezidis in Kurdistan and the Druze, Nusayris, Metawalis, Wahhabis, Shi'is, Zaydis, Isma'ilis and Rafızis in the Arab regions. Although most of the members of these sects [among the soldiers] confirm and acknowledge the glory of martyrdom and holy war [for Islam], there cannot

Ottoman Sunnism

be a union of hearts (*ittiḥād-ı ḳulūb*) due to such divisions; and because these persons will consider the other sects an enemy and look at each other with hate and animosity (*yekdiğerini düşmān-ı mezheb add ederek naẓār-ı nefret ve husūmet ile göreceği cihetle*), it is imperative to strive to wipe out the causes for such divisions within Islam for the sake of unifying the hearts of the soldiers.

This union can be achieved by appointing preachers (*hoca*) who are well-versed in religious sciences and partake of the intellectual disciplines ('*ulūm-i diniyede māhir ve fünūn-ı aḳliyeden behremend*), and can convince their antagonists (*ḥıṣmını ilzāma muḳtedīr*) in the regions where the followers of these sects live. And these learned personages who spread the true faith are called *dāi* in our language, which is the equivalent of 'missionary' (*misyoner*) in Europe. Even if there are found enough zealous men, who will be commissioned to spread the true faith and go to distant lands, choose of one's own accord the burden of the voyage and bear such a sacrifice for the sake of religion, the number of such volunteers will not be sufficient even under a special order.

These *dāi*s were envisioned as being trained so that they were acquainted with the books of the respective Islamic sects and able to write refutations (*reddiye*) of them, and well-versed in preliminary sciences (*muḳaddemāt-ı fünūn*) such as geography and mathematics. They were to receive a salary during their two years of education, and schools were to be built in Istanbul and other regions where they could study the 'exalted sciences' ('*ulūm-i āliye*), that is, the Islamic branches of knowledge. These missionaries should not only be active in Istanbul, but be sent to other Ottoman domains where these 'harmful sects' (*mezāhib-i saḳīme*) were present, and they were even envisioned as being sent to distant Islamic lands and other countries with Muslim communities in order to correct the beliefs of the people, and safeguard Islam and fortify its pillars (*erkān-ı İslāmiyetin ḥifẓ ve teşyīdi*). The outcome of appointing such missionaries would be the union of hearts worthy of the Muslims in the 'well-protected' Ottoman domains.[71]

In contrast to this comparatively neutral description of soldiers belonging to non-Sunni sects, a more severe portrayal of the Alevi soldiers in the Ottoman army came from the late Ottoman jurist and writer Mehmed Arif (d. 1897). He states in his memoirs *Başımıza Gelenler* ('What we went through')[72] about the Ottoman–Russian War of 1877/8 that the reason for the corruption of the Ottoman Muslim soldiers' hearts was that they did not belong to one religious (legal) school (*mezheb*). In his opinion, one-fourth of the troops consisted of individuals who were on different paths, being Shiites, *Bektaşi*s and some akin to polytheism (*putperestliğe şebīh*) far outside Sunni Islam; others were serving a 'special composite creed' (*i'tiḳād-ı mürekkeb ve mahṣuṣ*) consisting of all these beliefs. Mehmed

Arif urged the Sublime Porte to categorically suppress the ignorance of these various groups with severe and effective measures (*bu cāhillerin izāle-i cehāletleri emrinde tedābir-i şedīde ve müessire*), in order to ensure an important part of the defence against 'our enemies'. He attached utmost importance to the educative role of the officers (*żābiṭ*) in times of war because, through their staunchness, the soldiers would not desert the army, even if their hearts were full of satanic delusions. Mehmed Arif's description of these 'heretics' can be seen as part of the Ottoman bureaucratic discourse of the later nineteenth century that sought to report instances of religious deviance to Istanbul.

The fight against all forms of 'ignorance' was the aim of the Ottomans in later decades as well, especially during the latter part of the reign of Abdülhamid II, when Sunni Islam was politicised to serve an imperial ideology known as the 'Union of Islam' (*İttiḥād-ı İslām* or pan-Islam). The aim was to strengthen the position of the sultan as caliph, to prevent the empire from falling apart, and thus to stabilise the state structure.[73] Many bureaucrats composed and sent 'memoranda' (*lāyiḥa*) to Istanbul about political, economic, administrative or military shortcomings in the Ottoman domains while recommending solutions and reforms. Many of these petitions were observations about the hinterland, a *terra incognita*, about peoples who were regarded as 'backward'. Many of the memoranda were concerned with importing central authority or strengthening it in the midst of 'disobedient peoples' (*ahāli-i gayr-i mutīa*) in the borderlands of the empire. This was equally true for tribes in the Balkans, the Arab provinces and the Kurds in the east. Not only should the tribes be settled, but at the same time, it was necessary to prevent alliances between tribes, weaken the position of their leaders and ultimately abolish their supremacy. According to the modern and rationalist imperial administration of the nineteenth century, the *lāyiḥa*s depicted the social, cultural, economic and religious conditions of the peoples in those critical regions at the Ottoman 'frontier' and at the same time proposed that 'rebellious and savage tribes' or 'disobedient people' needed to be 'civilised' (*temdīn*), their 'savagery abolished' (*izāle-i vaḥşet*) and their superstitious and wrong 'beliefs corrected' (*taṣḥīḥ-i i'tiḳād*).[74]

Most of the late Ottoman memoranda, as in the case of the 'Dersim question'[75] concerning Kurdish tribes, are not written from an objective point of view: they are based on the personal observations of the writers, represent the perspectives of people who were oppressed by others, or are manipulative reports of notables who wanted to discredit other tribes. Despite this, some petitions are quite genuine, albeit they were written in an 'Ottoman orientalist' fashion. What is striking about the memoranda is that they do not talk about the state and tribes in a dichotomy of 'good' and 'bad'. The relations between the two were too complex and multi-layered to speak from the viewpoint of consistent states of conflict or reconciliation, and were contingent upon specific times and spaces. To preserve hegemony in the region, certain tribes allied with external powers, such as the state, against other tribes, following the maxim of 'my enemy's enemy is my friend'. The Ottoman state sometimes relied on tribes as potential allies for the realisation of centralist reforms. At a time when the Ottoman Empire was losing territories in the Balkans, it was in need of the incomes from other regions in Anatolia, the Arab provinces and North Africa; to preserve this, the state applied its centralist policies to the unsettled peoples of these regions.[76] If we take into consideration the forced population movements and reform policies after the beginning of the *Tanẓīmāt* period in Anatolia and the Arab provinces, the 'Dersim question' does not stand as an isolated event of this sort. As Türkyılmaz observes: 'This ethnographic curiosity was new and full of prejudices against this community [*Kızılbaş*]. It was not just the secular bureaucracy but the religious cadres that also thought it was their duty to help the state in its struggle against the enemies of the religion.'[77]

Among the *lāyiḥa*s sent to Istanbul, Syria and Iraq were prominently represented. The famous Süleyman Hüsnü Paşa (d. 1892),[78] one of the main actors in the deposition of Sultan Abdülaziz in 1876, wrote an extensive and detailed report/petition (twenty-four pages) in 1892 from his political exile in Iraq.[79] It relates to measures that he proposed to integrate diverse 'heretical' groups – including the Wahhabis, Twelver Shiites (Usuli, Akhbaris and Shaykhis), Aliyullahis, Yezidis, Sabians[80] and the Babis (Baha'is)[81] – into the official belief structure. He offers a breakdown of the complex ethnic (Turks, Kurds and Arabs) and religious elements in the provinces of Mosul, Basra and Baghdad, and then comments as follows: 'As can be seen from the above, the elements belonging to the official faith and language of the state are in a clear minority, whereas the majority falls to the hordes of the opposition.'[82] He remarks that the conversion and guidance to Islam through correction of beliefs of 'misguided sects' such as the various Shiite branches, Wahhabis, Yezidis and Babis is quite easy (*ihdā ve irşād ile taṣḥīḥ-i 'aḳīdeleri pek kolay*), and presents this as a most appropriate and utterly blessed service to the caliph of all Muslims.[83] The remedy would be systematic propaganda and 'correction of beliefs' of deviant sects. Süleyman Hüsnü advanced the idea that the Ottoman state should sponsor the writing of a book called *Book of Beliefs* (*Kitābü'l-'Aḳāid*), consisting of fifteen chapters, each addressing one group. It should be a specific rebuttal used 'to correct the beliefs of misguided

Islamic sects' (*fırak-ı żālle-i İslāmiye'nin 'akīdelerini taṣḥīḥan*). For this, a 'missionary society' (*dāiyān cemiyeti, dāi-misyoner cemiyeti*) consisting of well-trained ulema should be formed, and they should scrutinise the 'unsound beliefs' (*'akāid-i sakīme*) of these sects. After two or three years of training, they would be awarded the title *dāi ilā'l-hakk misyoner*[84] ('missionary calling to the Truth') and commissioned to correct the beliefs of misguided Islamic sects.[85] As Deringil has noted, '[r]eligious uniformity was thus seen as a means by which normative standards of behavior could be imposed on the population'.[86] This was an urgent necessity since those who adhered to the official Sunni Hanafi School were in the minority among the Sunnis of Iraq. Altogether the inhabitants consisted of twenty different religious groups speaking one or more of the four languages: Kurdish, Turkish, Arabic and Armenian.

In line with other writers' proposals during that time, in Süleyman Paşa's view, the cure for the problem of religious heresy was proper education. By bringing back primary and secondary schooling into the Sunni Hanafi fold, all would be saved: 'The spread of education will instill the love of religion (*din*), country (*vatan*), and nationality (*milliyet*), as well as strengthening the salutary allegiance of the people to our Master the Caliph of all Muslims. Whereas the persistence of ignorance will only increase and intensify disunity and disintegration.'[87] It is noteworthy that Süleyman Hüsnü Paşa talks here about novel ideas such as loyalty to the 'country' and 'nationality' at the same time as he invokes the classic Islamic idea of allegiance to the caliph. Moreover, he appropriates the European idea of missionary activity at a time when it had become an aspect of political power.[88]

It appears that as a result of petitions such as that of Süleyman Hüsnü it became the practice after 1892 during the Hamidian reign that Sunni preachers and missionaries were allowed to practise with a diploma only after a four-year period; specialised in correcting wrong beliefs, these individuals were then ready to take up their 'teaching posts' at schools (*medreses*) in the provinces among 'marginals'.[89]

Protestant Missionaries among the Nusayris

This kind of 'civilising mission' was extended to all ethnic and religious groups in the 'Ottoman Wild East' in what is called an era of 'Ottoman colonialism';[90] those regions needed to obey the sultan as the only authority. Being regarded as nominal Muslims, the Nusayris – Arabic-speaking members of an esoteric sect with roots in Shi'a Islam in south Turkey and Syria – were the target of various hostile Ottoman policies.

The ill-treatment of the Nusayris by the majority of the population and the authorities in the nineteenth century had aroused the compassion of Protestant missionaries who tried to win their souls. The Protestant missionary movement was initiated for religious purposes first, in the form of the evangelisation of the world.

For the American Protestant missionaries of the American Board of Commissioners for Foreign Missions (ABCFM), the Nusayris were 'a wretched and degraded people ... for whom no evangelical exertions have been made',[91] and who were constantly oppressed by an unjust Ottoman government.[92] Missionary schools were eventually established to educate those 'who are destitute of the knowledge of Christianity'.[93] Besides nominal Christians and Jews, this included 'heterodox' sects such as the Nusayris. But only a few Nusayris converted to Protestantism; by 1911, a missionary wrote that the schools they established in Nusayri villages did not yield much fruit, although a few Nusayris did convert to Protestantism. Efficient work was hindered by the 'persistent and determined opposition' of the Ottoman government over the two previous decades, and the outcome was that 'the darkness of ignorance, superstition, and paganism still broods like a deadly miasma over the land, paralyzing the hearts and souls of men and casting over them the lethargy of spiritual death'.[94]

On the whole, the missionary project failed, not only in Syria but elsewhere in the Ottoman domains. A few schools of the Syrian mission were closed down in the late 1880s and early 1890s,[95] at the height of Sultan Abdülhamid II's reign. Mehmed Ziya Bey,[96] the local governor (*mutaşarrıf*) of Latakia from 1885 to 1892, as the local representative of the Ottoman government, is reported to have barred Protestant missionary work. Writing in November 1891, a missionary in Latakia stated that he 'is doing all he can to hinder our work, seizing Mission property ... turning our teachers out of doors and threatening them if they will not leave our employ'.[97] The missionaries protested the closing of the schools, saying that it was illegal because the Nusayris were 'pagans' and not Muslims.[98]

After decades of Ottoman oppression under the rule of several governors until the 1880s, efforts were subsequently made to improve the condition of the Nusayris;[99] however, this was done not out of sheer benevolence, but as a calculated part of the centralisation policy of Abdülhamid II. Ismail Kemal Bey, governor-general of Beirut from 1890 to 1892, writes that he was struck by the injustices done to the Nusayris when he was inspecting the hinterland of Latakia, and so he introduced measures to appease them.[100]

The Latakia region was to be a 'high-profile case' for carrying out the Ottomans' 'benevolent reforms'.[101] Their 'imperial reformation' in this period was not aimed at bringing liberty to subjects, but at tightening the state's grip on them even further and firmly bring them under the central power.[102] In order to prevent missionary work among heterodox sects, Abdülhamid II's regime produced counter-propaganda through the establishment of Muslim schools and mosques in non-Sunni areas. These were means of a 'civilising mission' by which 'heretics' could be converted to Sunni Islam. A policy of reward and punishment, a 'carrot or stick' method was applied.[103] Though sometimes brutal methods and systematic repression were used 'to correct the ignorance and heresy of these people', often education and persuasion were applied as a 'defensive weapon' against the imminent threat to the unity and integrity of the Ottoman Empire posed by these so-called unorthodox communities.[104] It appears that this sometimes worked, as groups of these marginal elements periodically converted to Hanafi Sunnism willingly in response to Christian missionary activities. They would ask to be converted to the Hanafi School and request that schools and mosques be built in their district. Mehmed Ziya Bey warned Istanbul that if the Ottoman state left the Nusayris in a state of ignorance, this would only profit the missionaries, 'who have already gone so far as to pay regular salaries to the Nusayri leaders'. Therefore, the sultan should respond to the Nusayris' wish to become Muslims and prove to the foreigners that their government is able to take care of them.[105]

Being a functionary of the Ottoman state and a devoted servant of Abdülhamid, Mehmed Ziya's version of the story is that several religious heads and secular leaders of the Nusayris approached him, and told him that in early times they had been pious Muslims, but that in the course of time had strayed far from the right path because of ignorance. Now they wanted to awake from their 'slumber of negligence' (*ḥāb-ı gaflet*) and see how the 'matchless' Sultan Abdülhamid, like 'a second Conqueror' (*Fātiḥ-i sānī*),[106] had spread sciences (*'ulūm*), education (*ma'arif*) and justice (*'adālet*) in the Ottoman Empire and so 'revived the people' (*ahāliyi iḥyā eylemiş*). The Nusayri leaders expressed pride in being attached to the sultan, wanted to return to Islam and the Hanafi School, and benefit from the sciences, education and the new just order. Since they had 'desired salvation' (*necāt bulmak*), the governor promised them instruction in the religion of Islam, sciences and education by carrying out the necessary measures, such as the construction of schools and mosques and providing introductory textbooks about Islamic principles.[107] Schools and mosques were built in Nusayri towns and villages, but were then abandoned after the death of Mehmed Ziya.[108] They were used as storage rooms and stables.[109] 'The result has been', according to one missionary, 'that a generation has grown up in ignorance.'[110] And as Martin Kramer put it, mosques had been built in Nusayri areas 'almost as talismans to ward off the foreign eye'.[111]

There was a wide range of concepts and terms used in the Hamidian period to discuss this 'civilising mission'. For instance, the Yezidi tribes in Şeyhan who 'corrected their beliefs' (*tashīh-i 'akāid*) and the children of Shiites in villages near Mosul who accepted the Hanafi doctrine needed copies of the Qur'an, books to teach them the Arabic alphabet and Islamic principles (1892);[112] the Yezidis of Mosul wanted to 'correct the belief and the doctrine' (*tashīh-i i'tikād ve mezheb*) and convert to Sunni Islam (1892);[113] the beliefs of heretical groups in Iraq needed to be corrected (*tashīh-i akīde*);[114] the Nusayri population of Latakia accepted the Hanafi creed through 'correction of the religion and change of the belief' (*tashīh -i dīn ve tebdīl-i i'tikād*);[115] following the 'correction of the religion and belief' (*tashīh-i dīn ve i'tikād*) of the Nusayris in the Nusayriyya mountains near Latakia, a mosque and a school needed to be constructed;[116] in order to prevent the mischief and the deception of the *Kızılbaş* and other 'ignorant ones' (*cehele*), some precautionary measures were proposed to 'reform the beliefs' (*ıslāh-ı 'akāid*) of those groups.[117] In order to 'purify the minds' of the Alevis in Dersim, the state spoke of *tasfīye-i ezhān*,[118] and bringing heretics and nomadic people back to a civilised life required the 'wiping out of savagery' (*izāle-i vahşet*).[119] Describing the state these people were to be found, officials used, for example, *fazīha-yı cāhilāne* ('ignorant wickedness'),[120] and labelled their faith as *i'tikād-ı bātila* ('superstitious belief')[121] or *tarīk-i gayr-ı meşru* ('unlawful path').[122] Representatives of the Ottoman state used this vocabulary to describe people who needed to be 'civilised' or whose religious beliefs required 'fine-tuning'. They viewed these groups as having inherited their understanding of Islam from their ancestors and saw them as Muslims in name only. All of this was reflective of the Hamidian era, where the Ottoman state was trying to consolidate its power and political legitimacy in the empire's 'Wild East', a project that has been labelled as a form of Ottoman 'colonialism/orientalism'[123] or 'Ottoman borrowed colonialism'.[124]

Conclusion

This chapter has demonstrated that the concept of *tashīh-i i'tikād/'akāid* had become a political tool across the nineteenth century aimed at turning so-called 'heretics' into obedient Sunni subjects. As early as the late eighteenth century, the Ottomans applied a policy of 'correction of belief(s)' as a measure to 'civilise' what they considered to be heretical groups or disobedient borderland tribes, such as the Circassians. This reached a climax after 1826, with the draconian ban on the *Bektaşi* order and the attempt to Sunnitise its followers in the wake of the centralisation policies of Mahmud II. In the following decades, especially during the *Tanẓīmāt*, the state became somewhat more lenient towards these groups, and there was a strategy of attempting to unite the various non-Sunni sects for military purposes. With the rule of Abdülhamid II, the concept was applied differently once again, this time in the context of a 'civilising mission', again for the centralisation of the sultan's powers. This was also intended to protect various non-Sunni groups from the conversion campaigns of Christian missionaries. Even if Abdülhamid's strategy of incorporating heretical groups did not really win them over, 'it isolated them successfully from the ABCFM'.[125]

In earlier centuries, efforts to consolidate Ottoman Sunnism were carried out in the context of the Qur'anic dictum of 'commanding right and forbidding wrong'.[126] Efforts aimed at correcting the beliefs of Muslims and non-Muslims alike by the Ottoman state and ulema in the eighteenth and nineteenth centuries need to be seen in the context of the centralisation of the state and its attempt to 'civilise' people it deemed as being outside the scope of official Ottoman Islam, by which it meant Hanafi Sunnism. What is distinctive to the Hamidian period, as opposed to the earlier efforts of Mahmud II, is that the whole policy of reforms was subordinated to a more strongly felt need for 'unity among the Muslim population of the Empire'.[127]

Notes

1. This study was written within the context of my research project 'The Nusayris in the Late Ottoman State, 1840–1918', generously supported by the DFG (German Research Foundation, research No. FR 1536/5-1) and kindly supervised by Prof. Dr Patrick Franke (head of the Department of Islamic Studies, Universität Bamberg, Germany). I am grateful to the Gerda Henkel Stiftung for its financial support of my project in 2015. My study developed from two papers titled 'The Ottoman Policy of "Correction of Beliefs" towards the *Bektaşis* after the *Vaka-i Hayriye* in 1826' and 'The Ottoman Concept of "Correction of the Belief": its Roots and Application', presented, respectively, at the 22nd International Conference of the German Middle East Studies Association (DAVO) in Bochum, Germany, 24–26 September 2015 and the third annual conference of the British Association for Islamic Studies (BRAIS), 11–12 April 2016, London. I should like to thank the participants for their questions and comments. My heartfelt thanks are due to Patrick Franke for his constant encouragement and criticism. I am also grateful to Rossitsa Gradeva (American University in Bulgaria),

Rıza Yıldırım (Emory University), Baki Tezcan (University of California, Davis), Todd Lawson (University of Toronto) and the anonymous reviewers for their valuable comments. Finally, I am beholden to Vefa Erginbaş, the editor of this volume, who kindly accepted my chapter and made critical remarks together with John Curry (University of Nevada, Las Vegas).
2. Kohlberg, 'al-Rāfiḍa'.
3. Pakalın, 'Rafizi'; Öz, 'Rāfızīler''
4. Also 'rectification of belief(s)'.
5. See Selim Deringil's various works: Deringil, 'The Struggle against Shiism', pp. 45–62; Deringil, 'The Invention of Tradition', pp. 3–29; Deringil, *The Well-Protected Domains*; Deringil, 'From Ottoman to Turk', pp. 217–26; Deringil, ' "There Is No Compulsion in Religion"', pp. 547–75; Deringil, 'Conversion and Ideological Reinforcement', pp. 419–43; Deringil, 'Redefining Identities', pp. 107–30; Deringil, *Simgeden Millete*. For other similar studies, see Somel, *The Modernization of Public Education*; Gölbaşı, 'The Yezidis and the Ottoman State', Gölbaşı, '"Heretik" aşiretler ve II. Abdülhamid rejimi', pp. 87–156; Gölbaşı, '"Devil Worshippers"', pp. 133–55; Türkyılmaz, 'Anxieties of Conversion', who does not explicitly refer to *taṣḥīḥ-i i'tiḳād/'aḳāid*.
6. For this, see Cook, *Commanding Right and Forbidding Wrong*; Cook, *Forbidding Wrong in Islam*.
7. Krstić, *Contested Conversions*; Terzioğlu, 'How to Conceptualize Ottoman Sunnitization', pp. 301–38; Terzioğlu, 'Where 'Ilm-i Ḥal Meets Catechism', pp. 79–114; Tulasoğlu, 'Türk-Sünnī', pp. 165–83; Burak, 'Faith, Law and Empire', pp. 1–23.
8. I was not able to find information about this creed, unless Lutfi wrongly attributed it to Zoroastrianism.
9. Yağcı, 'Ferah Ali Paşa'.
10. *Vak'anüvis Ahmed Lutfî Tarihi*, 1:170; Natho, *Circassian History*, p. 137.
11. Kurt, 'Muṣṭafā Nūrī'.
12. Mustafa Nuri Paşa, *Netāyicü'l-Vukū'āt*, p. 414.
13. Süreyya, *Sicill-i Osmanī*, 2:636.
14. *Vak'anüvis Ahmed Lutfî Tarihi*, 1:170.
15. BOA, HAT 1103/44569H, in Tosun, 'Çeçenzade Hasan Paşa'; for *şazz*, see at: http://www.luggat.com/%C5%9Fazz/1/1, both last accessed 21 December 2016.
16. Schaebler, 'Civilizing Others', pp. 17–18; İhsanoğlu, *Osmanlı Devleti ve Medeniyeti Tarihi*, vol. 2, pp. 201–2.
17. Deringil, *The Well-Protected Domains*, pp. 19, 41, 73, 102, 103.
18. Koçunyan, *Negotiating the Ottoman Constitution*; Devereux, *The First Ottoman Constitutional Period*.
19. The idea of 'fine tuning' in imperial structures comes from Faruk Birtek; Deringil, *The Well-Protected Domains*, p. x, 10, fn. 50.
20. Deringil, *The Well-Protected Domains*, pp. 8–10.

21. Zarcone, 'Bektaşiyye'.
22. Ocak, 'Balım Sultan'.
23. Dressler, 'Alevīs'.
24. For a critique of the term 'heterodox' with regard to the Alevis, see Karolewsksi, 'What is Heterodox about Alevism?', pp. 434–56.
25. For an in-depth study about who can be called 'Bektaşi' in the Ottoman Empire/Turkey, see Yıldırım, 'Bektaşi kime derler?', pp. 23–58.
26. *Kızılbaş* 'is used loosely to denote a wide variety of extremist Shii sects that flourished in Anatolia and Kurdistan from the late seventh/thirteenth century onwards. The common characteristic was the wearing of red headgear. In its specific sense, *Kızılbaş* was a term of opprobrium applied by the Ottoman Turks to the supporters of the Ṣafawid house'; see 'Kîzîl-bāsh', *Encyclopaedia of Islam*, 2nd edn (Brill online), available at: http://dx.doi.org/10.1163/1573-3912_ei2glos_SIM_gi_02456, last accessed 10 April 2018. See also Baltacıoğlu-Brammer's chapter in this volume.
27. Yıldırım, 'Bektaşi kime derler?' p. 37; Zarcone, '*Bektaşiyye*'; Faroqhi, 'Conflict, Accommodation and Long-Term Survival', pp. 177–78; Varol, *Islahat, Siyaset, Tarikat*, pp. 29–30.
28. An important study of *Bektaşi*sm in the nineteenth century is Soyyer, *19. Yüzyılda Bektaşilik*.
29. Shaw and Shaw, *History of the Ottoman Empire*, vol. 2, p.19.
30. İpşirli, 'Kadızāde Mehmed Tāhir'.
31. Aksan, *Ottoman Wars*, pp. 306–25.
32. Esʿad Efendi, *Üss-i Zafer* (Latinised) p. 204; Uzunçarşılı, *Kapıkulu Ocakları*, vol. 1, p. 566 and fn. 1; Uzunçarşılı, *Alemdar Mustafa Paşa*, p. 168; Mutlu, *Yeniçeri*, pp. 24–5, fn. 60; Çataltepe, *19. Yüzyıl Başlarında*, pp. 245–6; Maden, 'Yeniçerilik-Bektaşilik', p. 186.
33. Tezcan, 'The New Order', pp. 76–7; Tezcan, *The Second Ottoman Empire*, pp. 191–226. For similar ground-breaking research about radical social and political changes in the Ottoman Empire '[d]uring the age of revolutions between 1760 and 1820', see Yaycıoğlu, *Partners of the Empire*, p. 1.
34. Tulasoğlu, 'Türk-Sünnī', pp. 169–70.
35. Yılmazer, 'Esad Efendi'.
36. Esʿad Efendi (Sahaflar Şeyhizâde), *Üss-i Zafer* (Istanbul 1243/1828); based on the pagination of this first edition, a Latinised edition was published; *Üss-i Zafer (Yeniçeriliğin Kaldırılmasına Dair)*, edited by Mehmet Arslan (2005); for an elaboration of *Üss-i Zafer*, see Heinzelmann, 'Die Auflösung der Janitscharentruppen', pp. 653–75.
37. Heinzelmann, 'Die Auflösung der Janitscharentruppen', p. 654.
38. *Üss-i Zafer*, pp. 177–8, Heinzelmann, 'Die Auflösung der Janitscharentruppen', p. 656. See also Glassen, 'Krisenbewusstsein und Heilserwartung', pp. 167–79; Abu-Manneh, 'The Naqshbandiyya-Mujaddidiyya in the Ottoman Lands', pp. 1–36.
39. Algar and Nizami, 'Naḳshbandiyya'.

40. BOA, HAT, 290/17351; *Üss-i Zafer*, pp. 208–9; Ahmed Cevdet Paşa, *Tarih-i Cevdet*, vol. 12, pp. 181–2; Ayar, *Bektaşilik'te Son Nefes*, pp. 38–40; Varol, *Islahat, Siyaset, Tarikat*, pp. 45–7.
41. *Vak'anüvis Ahmed Lutfî Tarihi*, vol. 1, p. 110.
42. Ayar, *Bektaşilik'te Son Nefes*, p. 39.
43. BOA, HAT 290/17351; Ayar, *Bektaşilik'te Son Nefes*, pp. 36–7, 134 fn. 92; Soyyer, *19. Yüzyılda Bektaşīlik*, p. 70.
44. BOA, HAT 290/17351; Ayar, *Bektaşilik'te Son Nefes*, p. 134.
45. See Baer, *Honoured by the Glory of Islam*, pp. 6, 13.
46. See Abu-Manneh, 'The Naqshbandiyya-Mujaddidiyya in the Ottoman Lands', p. 13; Abu-Manneh, 'The Naqshbandi-Mujaddidi', pp. 59–71; Foley, 'Hagiography, Court Records, and Early Modern Sufi Brotherhoods', pp. 50–67.
47. BOA, C.ZB, 34/1680; C.ZB, 17/843; BOA, HAT 512/25094-D, E, F and G; BOA, HAT 290/17351; BOA, C.DH 125/6218; *Üss-i Zafer*, pp. 211–12; *Vak'anüvis Ahmed Lutfî Tarihi*, vol. 1, p. 151; Maden, *Bektaşī Tekkelerinin Kapatılması*, p. 99; Varol, *Islahat, Siyaset, Tarikat*, pp. 45–7.
48. *Üss-i Zafer*, pp. 213–21; Maden, 'Hacı Bektaş Veli Tekkesinde Nakşi Şeyhler', p. 160.
49. This is one of the early uses of the term 'Alevi' in the nineteenth century in the Ottoman context; see Dressler, *Writing Religion*, pp. 2–3. For another mention of 'Alevi' in 1871, see below.
50. BOA, C.ADL, 29/1734; BOA, HAT, 290/17386; BOA, Mühimme-i Asakir Defteri, No. 26, pp. 89–90, 108–10, 192–4; Es'ad Efendi, *Üss-i Zafer*, pp. 213–21; Maden, 'Hacı Bektaş Veli Tekkesinde Nakşi Şeyhler', p. 175 fn. 1; Maden, *Bektaşī Tekkelerinin Kapatılması*, pp. 170–1.
51. Ayar, *Bektaşilik'te Son Nefes*, p. 42; Soyyer, *19. Yüzyılda Bektaşilik*, pp. 67, 72.
52. Ayar, *Bektaşilik'te Son Nefes*, pp. 43–4.
53. BOA, C.ZB, 17/843, 21 C 1243
54. BOA, HAT 512/25094-E, 25 Rebiülevvel 1249 (12 August 1833); BOA, HAT 512/25094-E, 25 Rebiülevvel 1249 (12 August 1833); BOA, HAT 512/25094-G, 27 Rebiülevvel 1249 (14 August 1833); see full text in Ayar, *Bektaşilik'te Son Nefes*, pp. 147–8.
55. Maden, *Bektaşi Tekkelerinin Kapatılması*, p. 99.
56. DH.MKT. 1487/38, 8 Cemaziyelahir 1305/21 February 1888; DH.MKT. 1975/31, 25 Zīlhicce 1309/20 July 1892; DH. MKT. 1983/15, 11 Muharrem 1310/5 August 1892; for other details, see Weineck, 'Fabricating the Great Mass', Chapter 7, above.
57. Maden, *Bektaşi Tekkelerinin Kapatılması*, pp. 196–7.
58. Ibid., pp. 197–200.
59. Ibid., pp. 214–15.
60. Ibid., p. 214.
61. Weineck, 'Fabricating the Great Mass', Chapter 7, above.

62. Yaycıoğlu, *Partners of the Empire*, ch. 3.
63. Ibid., p. 2.
64. Üstün, 'Rethinking *Vaka-i Hayriyye*', p. 41; for the relations of the Janissaries with economic, social and religious groups, see Chapter 2.
65. Deringil, 'The Struggle against Shiism'; Nakash, 'The Conversion of Iraq's Tribes to Shiism', pp. 443–63; Litvak, *Shi'i Scholars of Nineteenth-Century Iraq*, pp. 128–34, 140–2; Çetinsaya, 'The Caliph and Mujtahids', pp. 561–74; Yaslıçimen, 'Saving the Minds and Loyalties of Subjects', pp. 63–108.
66. Kieser, *Nearest East*, p. 36.
67. Deringil, *The Well-Protected Domains*, pp. 68–92; Ortaylı, '19. yüzyılda heterodox dinî gruplar', pp. 156–61; Ortaylı, 'Alevîlik, Nusayrîlik ve Bâbıâlî', pp. 161–9.
68. For Sunni orthodox trends in the *Tanẓīmāt* period, see Abu-Manneh, 'The Naqshbandiyya-Mujaddidiyya in Istanbul', pp. 99–114; Abu-Manneh, 'The Porte and the Sunni-Orthodox Trend', pp. 125–40.
69. *Hakayık el-Vekayi'*, No. 416, 6 Ramazan 1288/18 November 1871, pp. 2–3; this is part of an instalment published before and after this issue. I could not find the name of the author.
70. It is interesting to note that this is one example of the use of the term 'Alevi' for '*Kızılbaş*' in the late Ottoman period, despite Dressler's assertion that 'it is important to emphasize that in the late Ottoman period there was as of yet no necessary connection between the terms Alevi and *Kızılbaş* established'; Dressler, *Writing Religion*, p. 3. Another much earlier example from the early sixteenth century is when an official Ottoman chronicler called the *Bektaşi* poet Hayretî as belonging to the 'Alevi school/sect' (*alevi mezheb*); see Sohrweide, 'Der Sieg der Safaviden in Persien', p. 164, fn. 437; Tatcı, 'Hayretî'. For a discussion of the use of 'Alevi' in late nineteenth-century Ottoman dictionaries and encyclopaedias, see Zimmermann, 'Aleviten in osmanischen Wörterbüchern', pp. 179–204.
71. For the use of *ittiḥād-ı ḳulūb* among the soldiers during the reign of Mahmud II, see *Üss-i Zafer* (Latinised), pp. 11, 46, 99 (*ittifāḳ-ı ḳulūb*); Sungu, 'Mahmut II.nin Bir Hattı', p. 181; see also *Vak'a-Nüvîs Es'ad Efendi Tarihi*, p. 574.
72. Mehmed Arif, *Başımıza Gelenler*, pp. 393–5; Latinised modern Turkish edition, *Başımıza Gelenler*, vol. 3, pp. 784–7; drawn to my attention by Veysel Şimşek.
73. Duguid, 'The Politics of Unity', pp. 139–55; Landau, *The Politics of Pan-Islam*, pp. 9–79; Karpat, *The Politicization of Islam*.
74. Gündoğdu and Vural, *Dersim'de Osmanlı Siyaseti*, pp. 11–13.
75. Dersim is present-day Tunceli.
76. Gündoğdu and Vural, *Dersim'de Osmanlı Siyaseti*, pp. 13–15.
77. Türkyılmaz, 'Anxieties of Conversion', pp. 267–8.
78. He was the author of *Hiss-i İnkılāb*, a detailed account of the deposition

of Sultan Abdülaziz; in English by Devereux, 'Süleyman Pasha's "The Feeling of the Revolution"', pp. 3–35.
79. BOA, YEE 9/34, 9 Ramazan 1309/7 April 1892. For the whole issue, see Deringil, 'Legitimacy Structures', pp. 348–9; Deringil, 'The Struggle against Shiism', pp. 53–54; Deringil, *The Well-Protected Domains*, p. 49; Çetinsaya, *Ottoman Administration of Iraq*, pp. 108–9. For a summary and the style of the petition, see Özbilgen, *Osmanlının Balkanlardan Çekilişi*, pp. 264–7.
80. Followers of the ancient religion of Sabianism usually traced to John the Baptist; for the Sabians of Iraq in the late Ottoman period, see Güner, 'Irak Sābiīlerine Dair', pp. 3–28.
81. For the Babis and Baha'is in the late Ottoman Empire, see Alkan, *Dissent and Heterodoxy*.
82. BOA, YEE 9/34, p. 1: 'İşte bu taksimat devletin mezheb ve lisan-ı resmiyesine intisabı olan fırkaların akalliyet mikdarını ve muhalif güruhun ağlabiyet nüfusunu nazarlarda pek vazıh olarak tebyin eder'; quoted in Deringil, *The Well-Protected Domains*, p. 49.
83. BOA, YEE 9/34, p. 1.
84. Deringil misread this as *dāi-ul-hak-misyoner*; see Deringil, 'The Struggle against Shiism', p. 53; Deringil, 'Legitimacy Structures', p. 349.
85. BOA, YEE 9/34, p. 3.
86. Deringil, 'The Struggle against Shiism', p. 53.
87. BOA, YEE 9/34, p. 4; quoted in ibid.
88. Deringil, 'The Struggle against Shiism', p. 54.
89. Deringil, *Well-Protected Domains*, pp. 75–84.
90. Deringil, '"They Live in a State of Nomadism and Savagery"', pp. 311–42.
91. Salibi and Khoury, *The Missionary Herald*, vol. 2, p. 292 (1831).
92. Lyde, *The Asian Mystery*, pp. 208–10.
93. Salibi and Khoury, *The Missionary Herald*, vol. 3, p. 65 (1836).
94. Balph, 'Among the Nussairyeh', p. 184.
95. Richter, *A History of Protestant Missions*, p. 214; Douwes, 'Knowledge and Oppression', p. 166.
96. The Circassian Ziyāeddin Mehmed Efendi; Süreyya, *Sicill-i Osmanī*, vol. 5, p. 1717.
97. *Herald of Mission News* 1892/3 (*Journal of the Reformed Presbyterian Church*), p. 26.
98. Tibawi, *American Interests in Syria*, p. 262; Deringil, *The Well-Protected Domains*, p. 83.
99. Hanssen, *Fin de siècle Beirut*, pp. 68–9.
100. Ismail Kemal Bey, *The Memoirs*, pp. 199–200.
101. Hanssen, *Fin de siècle Beirut*, p. 68.
102. Fortna, *Imperial classroom*, pp. 50–60; Makdisi, *Artillery of Heaven*, p. 208.
103. Deringil, *The Well-Protected Domains*, pp. 101–2; Ceylan, 'Carrot or Strick?', pp. 169–86.

104. Deringil, 'The Invention of Tradition'; Somel, *The Modernization of Public Education*, pp. 222–3. For the conversion policies among the Yezidis, see Gölbaşı, 'The Yezidis and the Ottoman State'; Gölbaşı, '"Heretik" aşiretler ve II. Abdülhamid rejimi'.
105. BOA, İ.MMS. 114/4687, 13 Haziran 1306/26 June 1891, quoted in Deringil, 'The Invention of Tradition', p. 15; about the 're-education' of the Alawis, see Winter, *A History of the 'Alawis*, pp. 220–38.
106. *Fātiḥ* is the title of the Ottoman sultan Mehmed II, who had conquered Constantinople in 1453.
107. BOA, İ.MMS. 113/4821, No. 7, 9 Mayıs 1306/21 May 1890; see also BOA, DH.MKT. 1823/38, 21 Şaban 1308/31 March 1891. The same was to be carried out for the Nusayris in Antakya and its environs; see BOA, DH.MKT. 1958/80, 12 Zīlkāde 1309/8 June 1892; BOA, DH.MKT. 2049/13, 18 Receb 1310/5 February 1893; BOA, DH.MKT. 31/9, 11 Rebiüssani 1311/22 October 1893.
108. BOA, MF.MKT. 77/10, 1 Şaban 1312/28 January 1895, states that primary (*ibtida'i*) schools were abandoned.
109. Wajdi, *Dā'irat al-ma'ārif*, s.v. 'Nuṣayriyya' (quoting an article from the Egyptian newspaper *al-Ahrām*), vol. 10, p. 252; Moosa, *Extremist Shiites*, p. 279; Douwes, 'Knowledge and Oppression', p. 168. Still, around the same time and later in 1904 we see reports of Nusayris in Antakya asking for conversion and for schools: BOA, İ.MF. 2/1311/R-1, 8 Ramazan 1311/15 March 1894; BOA, DH.MKT 866/56, 18 Ramazan 1822/26 November 1904.
110. Balph, 'Among the Nussairyeh', p. 182.
111. Kramer, *Arab Awakening*, p. 191.
112. BOA, Y.MTV. 68/90.
113. BOA, DH.MKT. 2012/117; for an Ottoman 'colonial' exposé about the Yezidis, see Mustafa Nuri Paşa's *Abede-i İblis*; translated into German and annotated by Menzel, *Die Teufelsanbeter*, pp. 90–211.
114. BOA, Y.A. HUS. 260/130, 28 Şevval 1309/25 May 1892.
115. BOA, ŞD. 2280/40.
116. BOA, İ.MMS. 113/4821.
117. BOA, BEO 2250/168719.
118. BOA, DH.MKT 74/10.
119. BOA, Y.PRK.BŞK 19/27; DH. MKT. 1555/58.
120. BOA, Y.PRK.KOM. 7/59.
121. BOA, Y.A.RES 51/9.
122. BOA, Y.A.RES. 60/27; for the last five references, see Özdemir, 'Alevilik ve Ehl-i Hak (Yaresan)', p. 255.
123. Makdisi, 'Ottoman Orientalism', pp. 768–96; for the conversion campaigns, see Deringil, *The Well-Protected Domains*, pp. 68–92; Somel, 'Osmanlı Modernleşme Döneminde', pp. 178–201; see further Herzog and Motika, 'Orientalism "alla turca"', pp. 139–95.

124. Deringil, '"They Live in a State of Nomadism and Savagery"', p. 312.
125. Kieser, *Nearest East*, p. 56.
126. Cook, *Commanding Right and Forbidding Wrong*.
127. Duguid, 'The Politics of Unity', p. 139.

9

Some Reflections on the Fluidity of Orthodoxy and Heterodoxy in an Ottoman Sunni Context

John J. Curry

Throughout their histories, there has been a strong tendency within religious traditions to differentiate between true and false doctrine and praxis, and Muslim communities were no exception. As a result, Muslim authors from the earliest periods of their recorded history have regularly produced arguments aimed at either defining themselves as falling within the orbit of the Muslim community and therefore 'acceptable', or defining others as 'heterodox' or 'heretical', thereby excluding them as outsiders to the community liable to persecution. These attempts at defining or policing the boundaries between legitimate and illegitimate thought and praxis were dramatically heightened by the modern intellectual movement of the Enlightenment, which placed definition and taxonomy at the heart of an attempt to create a universally applicable understanding of the world and its peoples. Ironically, despite its ostensibly secular perspective, this process of ordering, and its origins in a peculiar European historical context, has heightened perceptions of sectarian difference well beyond what peoples of earlier historical eras would have recognised.[1] Thus, as historians have grown in theoretical sophistication, a more cautious approach to this process of categorisation has developed that forces us to interrogate our sources, and question whether or not fixed categories of orthodoxy versus heterodoxy – or even a continuum between them – can be clearly defined.

In its lengthy and multiple historical trajectories dating from its origins in the fourteenth century to its collapse in the early twentieth century, the historiography of the Ottoman Empire is deeply intersected with questions about the relationship between orthodox and heterodox forms of belief. The supporters of the early Ottoman enterprise were a mixture of different groups whose religious beliefs and orientations varied widely – indeed, not all of them may have been Muslim. Furthermore, they lacked interest in maintaining firm boundaries between themselves and others, a characteristic of early Ottoman *ghaza* that Cemal Kafadar described as 'metadoxy', or a lack of interest in defining others as orthodox or heterodox. This proved useful to the early Ottoman enterprise, and allowed for a process of being able to quickly transform contemporary enemies into tomorrow's allies.[2] The slow development of a more traditional-minded ulema class in the Ottoman context well into the fifteenth century, and a stronger predilection towards charismatic, or even 'shamanic', Sufi leadership has also led some observers to claim varying degrees of 'heterodoxy' as a defining trait of early Ottoman society. But with the expansion of the Ottoman state across three continents, and the need for stronger governing institutions to consolidate and manage these vast dominions, the extent to which the early sectarian fluidity of the Ottoman state could flourish increasingly came under challenge.

The growing extent and imperial pretensions of the Ottoman ruling house gave rise to a desire to increase the convergence of the Ottoman state and learned hierarchy. As Guy Burak has noted, this created an extended project that aimed to establish an Ottoman Hanafi *madhhab* as an official school in the empire.[3] The implications of the Ottoman state taking an official stand on matters that were previously construed to be primarily the purview of the religious elites suggest a turn towards establishing a state-sanctioned definition of orthodoxy, with its corollary restriction of sectarian possibilities. However, the Ottomans never fully succeeded in making their version of Hanafism universal across the empire, especially in Egypt, one of its largest and most important provinces, and the pilgrimage cities in Arabia.[4] Moreover, no pre-modern empire could fully enforce its will outside the immediate orbit of its centres of power, so the idea of a universal system of Islamic law, fused with the imperial orders of the Ottoman ruling house, remained more of an idealised conception than a fully-realised system.

But another driver of Ottoman moves towards constraining their sectarian diversity emerged concurrently from the eastern borderlands of the empire. The rapid rise of the Safavid leadership, and its incorporation of various elements of Shiism, Sufism and messianic pretensions, culminated in the rapid emergence of Shah Isma'il's dominions at the beginning of the sixteenth century. The potential appeal of the Safavid ideology to both nomadic peoples and rural Sufi groups that still inhabited vast swathes of Ottoman territory would eventually cause Ottoman leaders and thinkers to harden the boundaries between accepted and proscribed forms of religious observance. With the obvious threat posed by the Şahkulu uprisings of 1511–12, the newly enthroned Selim I, following a track already laid out by the intellectual work of his younger brother Korkud prior to his accession, supported ulema attempts to define the Safavids and their *Kızılbaş* supporters as heretics, and embarked on a bloody campaign of eradication throughout Anatolia.[5] Moreover, this abrupt hardening of confessional lines did not limit itself strictly to Safavid Shiism or messianic groups – it also targeted Sufi orders such as the *Halvetiyye* and *Bayramiyye*, bringing both their orthodoxy and loyalty into question.[6]

Ultimately, these tensions proved to be short-lived, and a reconciliation was made between most Sufi orders and the Ottoman ruling classes. By the latter half of the sixteenth century, as a recent study has argued, Ottoman religious leaders and intellectuals had revived the idea of the Ottoman sultanate as a caliphate, albeit with a strong Sufi mystical component that relieved the potential tensions between the religious authority of Sufi groups and the political authority of the sultan.[7] The concurrence reached a point where Sultan Murad III (r. 1574–95) even pledged his allegiance to a prominent Sufi adviser and guide, envisioning himself as a Sufi devotee who could harness the powers of the divine to advance his reign.[8] But conflicts over the boundaries of Ottoman Islam had not been silenced, and they re-emerged with a vengeance with the onset of multiple environmental and political disasters that threw the empire into crisis during the seventeenth century. While the resurgence of religious controversy is often credited to the figure of Kadızade Mehmed (d. 1635) and the growing power and visibility of the *Kadızadeli* movement that bears his name, it is now clear that the ideas that drove the movement had been fermenting for quite some time, especially in the provincial centres of the empire.[9] The major achievement of Kadızade Mehmed and his subsequent followers was to attract the interest of prominent Ottoman leadership figures, who recognised ways by which the movement could be used to achieve the goal of re-establishing stability and order. This meant that while the *Kadızadelis* could never aspire to full control of imperial policy and institutions, they attracted sufficient interest and support from sultans such as Murad IV (r. 1623–40) and Mehmed IV (r. 1648–87) to be able to place passionate debates about the orthodoxy and heterodoxy of their fellow subjects to the forefront of public consciousness. Moreover, they did not just restrict their activities to the Muslim community, as the Jewish Sabbatean movement was directly targeted, and widespread attempts to convert Christians were also undertaken by the court of Mehmed IV.[10] But in a rapid reversal, the leadership of the movement abruptly lost their legitimacy with the second Ottoman defeat at Vienna, and were increasingly restricted to the provincial regions of the empire, as evidenced by their brief re-emergence in Cairo in 1711.[11] Yet the tensions they initiated continued to linger well into the eighteenth century, with the result being that they lent a much more conservative cast to Ottoman religious life. Moreover, in some urban centres in the Arab provinces, their influence may have lingered to the point where they may have inspired a nascent Wahhabi movement a century later.[12]

The reassertion of a tolerant approach to religious diversity and difference in the wake of the *Kadızadeli* movement's decline, as long as various groups demonstrated their loyalty to the Ottoman state, largely held during the course of the eighteenth century.[13] However, the growing weakness of the Ottoman Empire by the end of the eighteenth century, followed by its attempts to reform and restructure its institutions in the face of growing European imperialism, raised a new set of tensions regarding confessional boundaries. The uncomfortable marriage between European influences and traditional Ottoman institutions throughout the period heightened sectarian and confessional tensions. As Ali Yaycıoğlu has recently pointed out, the conflict over Westernisation and its discontents unleashed during events such as the Patrona Halil Rebellion of 1730, followed by the reactions against the 'New Order' programme initiated by Selim III, cannot be read simply as a religious reaction to Europeanisation, as Ottoman religious leaders often based their opposition more on the degree to which they preferred to preserve existing privileges and institutions, rather than on any knee-jerk reaction to the legitimacy of interaction with non-Muslim or heterodox groups.[14] While much of the literature on these subjects, and the *Tanzīmāt* period that followed, focuses on the fraying of the historical tolerance of Muslim communities for their non-Muslim counterparts, Muslim sectarian communities were also deeply affected by the changes. The suppression of the Janissary corps may have been primarily due to the threat they posed to the centralising authority of the Ottoman state, but the justifications for their destruction often took sectarian form, focusing on their relationship with *Bektaşi*sm, a Sufi order that was abruptly re-defined as 'heterodox'. Furthermore, the growing highlighting of an Islamic consciousness, be it through the Young Ottomans and the Islamic Constitutional movement, or the pan-Islamic programme of Abdülhamid II, raised questions over how Islam was to be reformed, or how far an Islamic unity was perceived to extend.

This brief historical sketch does not intend to be comprehensive; rather, it aims to demonstrate the difficulty historians would have in articulating the contours of a clearly defined 'Ottoman Sunnism' throughout the six centuries of Ottoman imperial history, or which groups might lie inside or outside its confines. Therefore, the chapters in this edited volume, all of which carry out an interrogation of what exactly 'Ottoman Sunnism', 'orthodox', 'heresy' or 'sectarian' entailed in the various historical periods of the Ottoman Empire, are welcome interventions that aim to develop a more nuanced understanding of the fluctuating boundaries between orthodoxy and heterodoxy. They force us to accept the inherently unstable nature of these definitions, which rarely took on a permanent form, even in cases in which our basic instincts would suggest obvious assumptions.

In the first selection of this volume, Rıza Yıldırım argues that the problem with defining changes in Ottoman religio-political life as 'confessionalisation' in a broadly comparative sense with European trends during the early modern period is that the Ottoman – or perhaps even the Muslim – version of this trend preceded that time frame by at least a century, and perhaps more. While he does not take issue with the possibility of comparative work on processes of confessionalisation across the Eurasian world, for him, the roots of 'confessionalisation' in an Islamic context were laid during the formative medieval period of Islamic civilisation, not during the early modern period. What made Islamic history distinct, in his view, was that these trends were dramatically interrupted by the Turco-Mongol irruptions of the eleventh to the fifteenth centuries, which destabilised and de-centred the Perso-Islamic caliphal systems and their institutional religious infrastructure. As a result, the Ottoman form of 'confessionalisation', for Yıldırım, is actually a 're-confessionalisation' process – the Ottomans did not create new confessions, in contrast to the divergence of Protestant sects that emerged in the Western European context. Instead, the revival of an older process of confessionalisation marked a growing ability of Ottoman political leaders to further intersect and blur the lines between state and religious institutions. The result was the Ottoman success in integrating the legal apparatus of sultanic *ḳānūn* into the Muslim sharia. As a result, Yıldırım argues, this process of re-confessionalisation was fairly advanced by the time that Europeans initiated their own processes of confessionalisation.

Yıldırım's chapter makes a good case for disentangling elements of the confessionalisation paradigm in European and Islamic contexts. Yet it also opens the way to further questions and historiographical debate. In Yıldırım's view, the process of confessionalisation in the Ottoman Muslim context was in place by the time these processes began to emerge in Europe in the mid-sixteenth century. However, this also excludes the emergence of equally transformative religious movements, such as the *Kadızadeli* movement (and thinkers that laid the framework for it, such as Birgivi Mehmed) that began to emerge by the end of the sixteenth century. While Yıldırım's points about the Muslim head start on the confessionalisation process are well-founded, we might also ask whether the

Ottoman process of confessionalisation was made up of multiple phases with concerns that diverged from those of European Christianities, as the subsequent chapter by Yasir Yılmaz in this volume suggests. In this case, Yıldırım has identified the foundations of a confessionalisation process in Ottoman Sunnism – but not necessarily its conclusion.

I am also struck by the overlap between Yıldırım's carefully constructed description of the evolution of Muslim thinkers towards the ultimate Ottoman fusion of sultanate and caliphate, and the recent work of Hüseyin Yılmaz, who laid out a similar set of arguments in his *Caliphate Redefined*. However, there is one key divergence between their two approaches. Whereas Yıldırım focuses on the persecution or restraining of Sufi groups as part and parcel of the Ottoman process of confessionalisation, Yılmaz argues instead that Ottoman thinkers developed a political theory that fused together elements of later medieval Sufi mystical thought with the temporal power of the Ottoman sultanate, which allowed the Ottoman rulers to acquire power not just over the ulema, but the entire range of religious functionaries. Moreover, this was often done with the connivance of key Sufi figures who helped to outline these theories of Ottoman sultanate-as-caliphate.[15] Untangling the nature of the Ottoman confessionalisation process may require that we rethink the boundaries between who was a Sufi, an *'ālim*, or other types of Ottoman intellectuals, broadly speaking, for they were just as likely to overlap in their views or fall into conflicting positions amongst themselves in the debates of their time, rather than remain within boundaries that allow us to conveniently categorise them.

Ayşe Baltacıoğlu-Brammer's study of the use of the term '*Kızılbaş*' in Ottoman sources seeks to further complement the nature of confessionalisation, in reference to the sectarian divisions that marked the sixteenth-century Ottoman and Safavid domains. The emergence of the Safavids as a political and dynastic ruling house capable of challenging Ottoman power and legitimacy was an abrupt historical shift, and Baltacıoğlu-Brammer shows how Ottoman sources showed no real awareness of any *Kızılbaş* group prior to the rebellions that brought Bayezid II's reign to an end in 1511–12. Yet by rejecting the historiographical foundations of the Turkish nationalist period, which held that the *Kızılbaş* were basically Turks who invariably acted as traitors towards the Ottoman state by siding with its enemies, she also argues that the period of Ottoman intolerance towards *Kızılbaş* groups was brief, and largely confined to the reign of Selim I, with a more pragmatic strategy quickly emerging thereafter. While it is true that sources created by the official Ottoman religio-political hierarchy often give an impression of an uncompro-

Fluidity of Orthodoxy and Heterodoxy

mising intolerance towards the *Kızılbaş*, be they Ottoman or foreign, records originating from other parts of Ottoman government and society paint a very different picture. By the mid-sixteenth century, Ottoman official sources had begun to distinguish clearly between *Kızılbaş* who were law-abiding and posed no threat to state hegemony, and those who migrated to Safavid domains or supported Safavid causes. Moreover, as the position of the *Kızılbaş* declined vis-à-vis the consolidating Safavid state of the early seventeenth century, the term's meaning shifted into an even more vague usage, largely aimed at various groups with Shiite tendencies among its Ottoman subjects. This suggests that if Yıldırım's 're-confessionalisation' was in fact complete by the latter half of the sixteenth century, it was not one in which the lines between confessions were drawn particularly clearly, as the Ottoman state's primary concerns did not encompass a ruthless enforcement of religious homogeneity save in certain specific situations, such as Selim I's brutal repression of Safavid threats to Ottoman power in Anatolia.

Baltacıoğlu-Brammer's chapter reminds us that we should be cautious about according too much universality to the pronouncements of prominent leaders at the top of the religious hierarchy in the Ottoman context. While the edicts of prominent jurists played an important role in laying out ideological guidelines and an ideal approach to the enforcement of religious norms, the reality that Ottoman statesmen and functionaries faced across their vast imperial domains often called for a different set of approaches. Despite the best efforts of anti-Safavid propagandists, difficult campaigns to the east, combined with harsh policies against Anatolian populations, however heterodox they were perceived to be, often proved far less popular than campaigns against non-Muslim unbelievers in Europe. It is no accident that Suleyman I quickly turned his attention westward at the start of his reign, earning even a guardedly positive mention from the later Safavid chronicler Eskandar Monshi Beg in the process.[16] Thus, the rapid growth of qualifiers in various Ottoman state records distinguishing between *Kızılbaş* who challenged Ottoman authority and *Kızılbaş* who did not was probably inevitable.

Furthermore, I would add to Baltacıoğlu-Brammer's analysis that we must couple this situation with the growing impact of the ecological–political crises introduced in the latter half of the sixteenth century, in which concerns about upholding rudimentary political stability and guaranteeing the fiscal survival of the Ottoman house trumped any attempt to enforce ideological rigour.[17] Even the subsequent resurgence of the Safavids under 'Abbas I in the early seventeenth century and the Ottoman response of Murad IV did not put significant focus on the *Kızılbaş* as the primary issue. This was because they had lost their privileged position in the Safavid power structure by the 1590s and, therefore, Ottomans discussing this seventeenth-century conflict did not emphasise the kind of fifth-column loyalties deemed to be existential threats during Selim I's reign a century earlier. In fact, the peaceful surrender of the Safavid commander Emirgün led to his becoming a drinking companion of Murad IV in the Ottoman capital, rather than to his detention or execution.[18] And as Baltacıoğlu-Brammer points out, in the wake of the 1639 peace treaty, the term was rarely used in any consistent fashion thereafter.

Vefa Erginbaş further complicates our ideas of a confessionalising Ottoman state in the sixteenth century by pointing out the continued reverence of the Ottoman ruler Murad III for the *ahl al-bayt*, the family of the Prophet Muhammad and his descendants via Ali b. Abu Talib. In so doing, he invokes the late Shahab Ahmed's ideas of 'coherent contradiction', where Ahmed had pointed out that juristic or legalistic visions of what Islam should be do not necessarily square with the full range of discourses or motivations that make up Muslim societies at any given time or place. To demonstrate the degree to which *ahl al-bayt* reverence had penetrated Ottoman cultural life, he focuses on the Ottoman Sultan Murad III's production of an extensive illustrated work based on the writings of a fourteenth-century author, Mustafa Darir, and his little-known and now partially lost primary source for the work, the biography of the Prophet and his companions by al-Bakri. Erginbaş' painstaking reconstruction of the content of Mustafa al-Darir's work shows that he eschewed much of the traditional sources for prophetic biography, such as the eighth/ninth-century Ibn Ishaq and his redactor Ibn Hisham, and instead drew more heavily on al-Bakri, despite the fact that the latter displayed strong Alid proclivities. While al-Bakri did not frame his narrative through the use of full-blown Shiite ideological tropes, such as cursing the first three caliphs, it is also clear that Ali b. Abu Talib is granted an exalted status over the other early Muslim caliphs in the narrative, and he is able to perform supernatural feats. The narratives are also more closely tied to the frontier narratives that marked the Ottomans' origins, which had been consolidated as a genre nearly a half-century prior to Murad III's reign. Therefore, Erginbaş argues, the revival of this type of genre probably had a good deal to do with its reverential and legendary treatment of Ali b. Abu Talib, which would have squared well with his devotion to various figures in the Halveti Sufi order, who located the origins of the doctrine and praxis of their *silsila* in the mystical teachings first laid down by Ali.[19] This demonstrates that at even at the highest levels of the Ottoman court and imperial hierarchy, no form of staunch Sunni orthodoxy had evolved to the point where it could exercise a stranglehold capable of excluding works deemed to have questionable elements.

Yet Erginbaş' chapter still leaves us with a number of questions as to Murad III's motivations in directing royal patronage towards the propagation of this text. This will likely require further research, but a few preliminary thoughts come to mind. The inclination of Murad III towards the shaykhs of the Halveti order, along with a need for the Ottoman state to secure the loyalty of former Safavid subjects in the newly-conquered regions of the Caucasus and southwestern Persia after the campaigns of the 1580s, are good potential explanations for why Murad III may have been drawn to this particular text. However, the timing of the text's production also raises questions: after all, it was produced not during the Ottoman–Safavid war of 1578–90, when such concerns would have been paramount, but in the final year of Murad III's reign. In fact, he did not live to see its completion, and the work was posthumously presented to his son Mehmed III instead. Thus, a case could be made that the implicit endorsement of the Alid content of Mustafa Darir's work may have had additional motivations, in addition to having appeal to a ruler who envisioned himself as taking up the spiritual mantle of a Sufi order tied to Alid origins. When we look at the immediate context for the book's emergence, the political event dominating imperial policy at the time would have been the onset of the conflict with the non-Muslim Habsburgs, which had begun in earnest by 1593. Given the immediate onset of difficulties for the Ottoman military during that conflict, and its intersection with the growing general seventeenth-century ecological, military and social crisis, a work that glorified the exploits of the early Muslims in an epic cycle, which featured a framing that appealed to more Alid themes, may have appealed to Ottoman military cadres, given the heavy *Bektaşi* influence in the Janissary corps. Yet whatever the motivations, it is clear that the *ahl al-bayt*ism that imbued Mustafa Darir's work proved to be no obstacle to a broad Ottoman embrace of the popular narratives that emerged out of the later medieval context.

Yasir Yılmaz also takes issue with an overly-broad use of the confessionalisation paradigm in comparative historical perspective. Using the oft-utilised comparison between the Ottoman, Russian and Habsburg empires in the early modern context of world history, he argues for a more cautious approach to each of the three empires, and to better define exactly how we should compare or contrast the historical experience of the three polities. This does not mean we should avoid comparative work altogether; rather, we should avoid the growing trap of trying to define the Ottoman Empire as being encompassed within the framework of events taking place in the very different cultural and religious spheres of European states, be they the Catholic context of the Austrian Habsburgs or the Eastern Orthodox evolution of Russia.

It is true that the three empires were all affected by key events during the early modern era, most notably the aforementioned seventeenth-century crisis of ecology and climate that led to the collapse of a number of states and societies across the globe.[20] But as Yılmaz points out, attempts to discuss other possible similarities, such as growing tensions and overlaps between religious and political authorities, often defined in the framework of confessionalisation, fail to recognise the very different religio-political contexts and outcomes that marked the three empires. In the case of the Ottomans, Yılmaz suggests that the *Kadızadeli* movement lacked an idea of separation between the religious and political spheres that came to develop in the Russian and Habsburg cases; as a result, the dynamic of the political elites gaining a decisive authority over the religious leadership could not emerge – at least not in the same fashion. Moreover, the lack of any significant property or wealth under the control of *Kadızadeli* figures meant their power could extend only as far as the Ottoman political authorities recognised it as a useful tool in preserving the political stability and power of its own elites. If that dynamic failed to hold at any point in the course of events, then the representatives of the *Kadızadeli* movement could be, and were, rapidly suppressed. In contrast, the attempt by the Russian Orthodox patriarchate under a series of activist leaders to subordinate the political authority of the tsars to the church failed, and they instead found that the state became the guarantor and upholder of church doctrines, paving the way for Peter the Great's strengthening of the Russian imperial autocracy. As for the Habsburgs, the construction of their empire had been built out of dynastic marriage politics and a weak vertical integration between provincial aristocracy and the political centre, which the Protestant upheaval successfully exploited to weaken the empire. The Thirty Years War, which for Yılmaz represents the Habsburg attempt to fuse together the imperial state with Catholic leaders to roll back the tide, led to Habsburg defeat. But a carefully crafted alliance between royal power and Catholic symbols of authority persisted long after, making it the state that had the strongest alliance between religious and political leadership due to the heartfelt commitment of the Catholic monarchs and their societies to this relationship. In the end, Yılmaz stresses that we can compare these three case studies effectively – but more in terms of their very different outcomes in resolving the religio-political tensions that set all three of them on very different trajectories from that point forward.

Yılmaz's analysis aims at identifying the ways in which religious tensions differed in terms of structure and outcomes during the seventeenth century; this is a welcome contribution, as previous studies have neglected the role played by religious leadership or reduced it to the role of a handmaiden of state interests.[21] However, the comparison he has produced underscores the need for a deeper inquiry into the ultimate outcomes of the *Kadızadeli* movement. While the leadership of the movement can be construed as having failed by the end of the seventeenth century, with its discrediting at the gates of Vienna in 1683, the conservative influences it introduced may have persisted well beyond that point. There are signs of a more sharia-conscious piety among various Sufi orders as a reaction to the *Kadızadeli* movement even after its decline, suggesting that even the opponents of the movement lacked full immunity from the ideas they introduced.[22] Furthermore, I wonder whether the power of the Ottoman state to control religious groups might be overstated in the wake of these events. For example, the rebellion against the Ottoman sultan in 1703 had a strong ulema component to it that made up part of an oligarchy that dramatically circumscribed the power of the Ottoman sultan.[23] Rebel ulema also re-emerged during the subsequent Patrona Halil rebellion of 1730 that deposed Sultan Ahmed III, with signs that their religious arguments were adopted by the broader mass of the population to advance their own grievances and goals during the conflict that followed.[24] Is it possible to argue that the processes of political–religious unification that gave the state a certain ascendancy over religious institutions (whatever the differing context for this evolution), as Yılmaz describes in the Russian and Habsburg cases, simply could not be replicated so easily in Ottoman political and religious culture, even well into the nineteenth century?

Betül Yavuz tackles the interesting case of the *Hamzaviyye* branch of the *Bayrami* Sufi order, and its distinct evolution in the Ottoman context. Unlike many of the other major Sufi orders that underwent a transformation during the first two or three centuries of Ottoman rule to adapt themselves to an emerging Ottoman form of Sunni Hanafi culture, the *Hamzaviyye* branch only saw this process emerge during the tumultuous years of the seventeenth century. A new generation of enterprising *Hamzavi* leaders and thinkers restructured the doctrine and praxis of the order away from its origins in the mixture of messianic, popular and anti-imperial movements from the fourteenth to the sixteenth centuries, and sought to re-orient itself in a more socially acceptable set of ideas without necessarily abandoning some of its most distinctive practices. Focusing on a pivotal period of change that came to be encapsulated in the *Ṣemerātu'l-fu'ād* of Sarı Abdullah, a work produced in the mid-seventeenth century, Yavuz provides us with a window on how the *Hamzavi* order underwent a process of self-transformation that led it to become very influential among a number of Ottoman statesmen, and later known as the *Melāmi-Bayrami* order. Through a careful reading of Sarı Abdullah's work, Yavuz demonstrates how key concepts in the order changed over time, which allowed the followers of the *Hamzaviyye* to legitimise themselves and transform their public image. Controversial concepts such as *devr*, which could be seen as advocating the heretical concept of transmigration of souls or reincarnation, were reconfigured to reflect more the Sufi progress towards the status of the perfected man. Furthermore, the concept of *melāmet* evolved from its original idea of incurring society's condemnation as a sign of one's spiritual superiority, to the more modest concept of taking up everyday occupations in the marketplace and not flaunting one's spiritual credentials to the general public.

Yavuz locates this very transformation in the context of changes in Ottoman society and culture that marked the seventeenth century, in the form of growing marketplace culture and public spaces that changed Ottoman life more broadly.[25] Noting that Sarı Abdullah was initiated into the order via his family connections to prominent *Hamzavi* leaders who worked in the markets of Istanbul, and reflective of a more urbane and intellectualised form of religious expression, she makes a convincing case that the *Şemerāt* marked a turning point as to how the *Hamzavi* branch of the order became 'Ottomanised'. However, in a direct challenge to the confessionalisation paradigm, she points out that this transformation did not mean that the followers of the *Hamzaviyye* abandoned their core traditions. They never adopted the practice of founding Sufi lodges, preferring to receive visitors and devotees in their homes or market shops, and they resisted abandoning their veneration of the *ahl al-bayt*, to the point where they argued that the *Nakşibendi* were mistaken in claiming Abu Bakr as the foundational origin of the principles of their order! Nevertheless, these novel ideas proved to be no obstacle to the rehabilitation of this *Bayrami* branch, for its followers achieved significant recognition in the form of a number of prominent Ottoman statesmen who espoused its teachings by the early eighteenth century.

This overview of the transformation of the *Hamzavi/Bayrami* order in Istanbul by the end of the seventeenth century does raise questions about the degree to which the emerging *Kadızadeli* movement and its influence played a role in the adaptive strategies on display in the work of Sarı Abdullah. Yavuz's discussion hints at the persecutions that *Hamzavi* shaykhs faced, culminating in the execution of Beşir Ağa at the hands of Fazıl Ahmed Paşa and Vani Mehmed Efendi in 1662. It would be useful to identify how the intellectual apparatus developed by Sarı Abdullah would

Fluidity of Orthodoxy and Heterodoxy

compare to other figures who had to confront the height of *Kadızadeli* power in the latter half of the century, such as the extensive study of Niyazi-i Misri's writings by Derin Terzioğlu, or studies on *Mevlevi* doctrinal works during the seventeenth century.[26] Unfortunately, few studies exist of the intellectual production of various Sufi figures outside the field of religious studies in Turkish institutions, as historians tend to be more drawn to the narrative structures of the hagiographical writings. The careful positioning taken by Sarı Abdullah in his writings suggest that more such work needs to be done in the future.

The volume concludes with two entries from the nineteenth-century context of Ottoman history, which demonstrates that the lines between an Ottoman orthodoxy and the nebulous world beyond it remained ill-defined throughout the entire course of its history. Benjamin Weineck carefully dissects İshak Efendi's *Kāşifü'l-esrār*, a work that targeted the *Bektaşi* order with charges of heresy, but in a way that proves to be quite revealing in regard to shifts in the late Ottoman understanding of the degrees to which the term could be employed. The work raises questions about why an Ottoman intellectual would target the *Bektaşi* order nearly fifty years after their ostensible abolition – how did the historical context of late Ottoman times inform the concerns of this work? While these questions cannot be answered with full certainty due to the uncertain dating and provenance of one of the surviving two texts of the work, Weineck makes a good case that the most likely scenario was that as time passed, the work was subtly altered to further blur sectarian difference in the Muslim community. In attacking *Bektaşi* Sufism as offshoots of more extreme Alid movements such as the fourteenth-century *Ḥurūfi* movement, and even reaching back to the tenth-century Qarmatian Isma'ili movement, İshak Efendi carefully distinguished them from other groups, such as Twelver Shiites and the Nusayris, who were deemed more tolerable. Weineck then demonstrates that the real rationale behind this taxonomy and its hierarchical organisation of religious sectarianism within the Ottoman domains was not primarily concerned with enforcing clear boundaries between orthodoxy and heterodoxy. Instead, Ottoman thinkers like İshak Efendi were willing to tolerate sectarian groups who proved to be willing to uphold the Ottoman state in a period when its influence was shrinking rapidly. The work subtly evolved further in later eras to support the pan-Islamic goals of the Abdülhamidian period, even going as far as to elide clear references to Twelver Shiites from the work altogether, in favour of vague language that simply referred to groups who were 'in error'. In sum, as with other periods in Ottoman history, it seemed that support of the imperial state and its interests easily trumped concerns about religious orthodoxy. The reason that the *Bektaşi* continued to be excluded were grounded in concerns about their attempts to re-emerge into the mainstream of Ottoman society by the second half of the nineteenth century, coupled with a failure to make a case for working their way back into the state's good graces and institutional apparatus.

Despite the gap in time periods, Weineck's chapter has clear lines of intersection with that of Baltacıoğlu Brammer. Both studies demonstrate a certain continuity in Ottoman thinking about religious sectarian groups. By using the yardstick of loyalty to the state – or a need to keep wavering groups within the Ottoman fold given potential external threats – Ottoman functionaries, be they İshak Efendi or sixteenth-century scribes, carefully distinguished between groups that needed to be suppressed and those that called for more pragmatic approaches. In fact, they raise real questions about the nature of Ottoman 'confessionalisation'. Rather than seeing greater religious control over various sectarian populations, backed by the power of the state to ensure a more homogeneous set of beliefs and practices, we instead see the emergence of a certain laxness towards sectarian difference, as long as the state's interests were not threatened. This, to me, explains the odd references to the Qarmatian Isma'ili movements of early medieval times as the ostensible 'source' for *Bektaşi* beliefs. The historical links posited by İshak Efendi are clearly tendentious, but the reason for them becomes clearer once we recognise that the real point of intersection is the Qarmatian rebellion against the late Abbasid caliphate. After all, another contemporary author, Eyüb Ṣabri Paşa (d. 1890), even likened the emergence of the puritanical Wahhabi movement to that of the Qarmatians, even as they directly targeted Shiite shrines for destruction![27] The key point for these late nineteenth-century observers was probably not that the doctrines of the groups were identical, it was that they shared the characteristic of defying state authority and wreaking destruction on fellow Muslims.

Necati Alkan's chapter has multiple fortuitous intersections with those of both Weineck and Baltacıoğlu-Brammer. Like Baltacıoğlu-Brammer, Alkan focuses on the development and evolution of a specific term employed by the Ottomans to address the issue of sectarian difference, a process called *taṣḥīḥ-i i'tikād*, or 'correction of belief'. First emerging in the eighteenth century as a concept evolving out of the Qur'anic dictum to 'command the right and forbid the wrong', the Ottomans employed this conceptual terminology in different ways over the course of the empire's final century and a half. It first appeared in the context of Ottoman attempts to stabilise the borderland regions of the empire in the late eighteenth century. Following claims that the Circassian and Abkhazian tribes of the Caucasus region were still following a variant of Zoroastrianism, in addition to disrupting the security of the Ottoman borderlands, Ottoman governors began to suggest sending various kinds of Sunni missionaries and scholars to these regions to teach the basics of Islam, thereby making these unruly frontier groups into supportive Muslim allies. But as Alkan demonstrates, these types of initiative quickly intersected with the struggles of Mahmud II to marginalise and destroy the *Bektaşi*sm of the Janissaries in the run-up to the 1826 'Auspicious Incident'. The final decade of Mahmud II's reign generated multiple records that show how Ottoman ulema and administrators sought to capture former *Bektaşi*s and exile them to strongholds of Sunni orthodox piety, thereby 'correcting their beliefs' and reintegrating them into the Sunni fold. After Mahmud II's death, however, these efforts waned to the point where the *Bektaşi* order was able to tacitly re-emerge under the guise of being *Nakşibendi*s, particularly after the latter order was placed in charge of many of the former *Bektaşi* institutions.

During the *Tanzīmāt* period, the idea of 'correction of beliefs' took on a broader application. Recognising that a substantial part of the Ottoman population was composed of various sectarian groups, many of whom were Muslim in name only, Ottoman thinkers began to call for a missionary proselytisation of these different groups. A primary Ottoman concern in this regard was military in nature; they wanted to unify all the different Ottoman soldiers militarily under the single aegis of Sunni Islam to improve their effectiveness. At this point, the Ottoman view of sectarian difference was not outright negative – rather, they viewed these groups as potential allies if they could be coaxed into more orthodox positions. But by the Abdülhamid II period, in the wake of catastrophic military defeats, the problem of sectarianism had come to be viewed as a liability that needed to be actively suppressed, not just won over. Defining such groups as lacking 'civilisation' or being in a 'savage' state, the late Ottoman state sought to use carrot-and-stick tactics to both suppress groups who would not cooperate with them, while cooperating with groups who were willing to be won over and drawn closer to the state. Interestingly, when Protestant missionaries sought to evangelise groups that were assumed to be 'heretical' and outside the Sunni fold (and therefore fair game), the Ottoman state responded by defining these groups as Muslims and off-limits, even if they were in need of 'correction', and successfully suppressed many of the Protestant attempts at converting them.

This all points to a process whereby the idea of 'correction of beliefs' eventually became intertwined with Ottoman ideas borrowed from the European Enlightenment about the hierarchies between 'civilised' and 'savage' peoples, and made the suppression or incorporation of sectarian groups a key part of the process of spreading Ottoman 'civilisation' to the imperial borderlands. In fact, Alkan's overview of the concept of *taṣḥīḥ-i i'tiḳād* and its implications of bringing 'civilisation' to the 'barbarians' of the borderlands invites fruitful comparisons with the nineteenth-century history of Latin American states, in which the transforming leaders and intellectuals of the urban centres portrayed themselves as waging a similar struggle against the peoples of their hinterlands.[28] However, in contrast to the anti-clericalism that sometimes marked the thinking of the liberal elites in Latin America, it is striking that Ottoman thinkers framed this dichotomy in the form of religious reform that just happened to intersect with the pacification and centralisation goals of the Ottoman state. Of course, this illustrates the very different goals of the two elites – one wanted to draw their states firmly into the fold of European modernisation, whereas the other wanted to avoid being swallowed up by it and to maintain their religious and cultural distinctiveness. Nevertheless, Ottoman bureaucrats and statesmen found themselves operating within the same rhetorical frames built out of the Enlightenment as their counterparts in other parts of the world – and, as Alkan points out, confronted by the same limitations at the local level that prevented them from fully realising their goals. One is struck by the degree to which local actors could manipulate and exploit the state's desires to arrogate resources and support to their own position, a phenomenon that has been noted in other nineteenth-century Ottoman contexts as well.[29]

In the end, we might be forgiven for espousing a cynical point of view about the nature of Ottoman religiosity, reducing it merely to its intersection with the pragmatic concerns that marked state and society at any given moment in historical time. As these studies have all shown, attempts to retreat into essentialist categories as a shortcut to defining the position of the sectarian diversity of the empire are ill-advised. But I think it would also be a mistake to simply dismiss the deeply-held religious convictions of the various Ottoman actors who have crossed our paths in this volume as props for the pursuit of material concerns. Most Ottomans throughout the fourteenth to nineteenth centuries would not have recognised the distinction between religious and secular spheres that modern Enlightenment positions assume in the modern era. Rather, they assessed their contemporary situation and the issues that confronted them, and reacted to it through their own interpretations of religious texts, beliefs, doctrines and praxis to create an ever-evolving set of novel responses that were informed by the broader trajectory of events. As these studies have shown, sometimes broader historical patterns can emerge from individual

Fluidity of Orthodoxy and Heterodoxy

periods, such as a primary concern for loyalty to the Ottoman state as a condition for toleration, whereas in other moments, such as Selim I's war with the Safavids or the *Kadızadeli* upsurges of the seventeenth century, dramatic departures from historical norms could ensue, with long-lasting effects. It is only through the careful sifting of these historical moments that we can move closer to realising a true definition of what 'Ottoman Sunnism' meant to its practitioners – and, indeed, those who may have thought of themselves as alternatives to it.

Notes

1. See, for example, the recent discussion of Dominguez, 'Introduction: Religious Toleration', pp. 273–87.
2. For the fluidity of religious engagements in the early Ottoman period and their interpretation as a form of 'metadoxy', see Kafadar, *Between Two Worlds*, pp. 65–90.
3. Burak, *The Second Formation of Islamic Law*.
4. Hathaway, *The Chief Eunuch*, pp. 197–203.
5. Al-Tikriti, 'Şehzade Korkud'; Sohrweide, 'Der Sieg der Safawiden in Persien', pp. 95–223.
6. Curry, *The Transformation of Muslim Mystical Thought*, pp. 72–4, 273–5; Yavuz, 'The Making of a Sufi Order', pp. 99–114.
7. Extensive documentation of this politico-religious trend in sixteenth-century Ottoman intellectual and political culture is detailed in Yılmaz, *Caliphate Redefined*, esp. chs 2 and 5.
8. For more on Murad III's engagement with multiple *Halveti* Sufis from different branches, see Curry, 'The Meeting of the Two Sultans', pp. 223–42.
9. Curry, *The Transformation of Muslim Mystical Thought*, p. 206 n. 22, pp. 229–32; Zilfi, *Politics of Piety*, pp. 143–6.
10. For the *Kadızadeli* intersection with the Sabbatean movement, see Şişman, *The Burden of Silence*; for more on Mehmed IV's targeting of non-Muslim communities for highly public conversion ceremonies, see Baer, *Honoured by the Glory of Islam*.
11. Peters, 'The Battered Dervishes', pp. 93–115.
12. For the growing conservatism of Ottoman ulema circles after the seventeenth century, see Zilfi, *Politics of Piety*, pp. 232–5; for possible links between post-*Kadızadeli* figures and Wahhabism, see Currie, '*Kadızadeli* Ottoman Scholarship', pp. 265–88.
13. See, for example, the public nature of these assertions of support for the Ottoman state by various religious groups, organised into a hierarchy, in Zilfi, *Politics of Piety*, pp. 183–6.
14. Yaycıoğlu, 'Guarding Traditions and Laws', pp. 1542–603.
15. See, for example, the discussion of Sufi contributors to the theory of an

Ottoman caliphate by thinkers such as Hüseyin b. 'Abdullah el-Şirvani, Mevlana 'Isa and the Halveti Shaykh 'Ali Dede in Yılmaz, *Caliphate Redefined*, pp. 257–76.
16. See ibid., pp. 252–3; Iskandar Munshi Beg (d. 1633/4), *The History of Shah 'Abbas*, vol. 1, pp. 72–3.
17. As detailed extensively in White, *The Climate of Rebellion*.
18. Finkel, *Osman's Dream*, p. 216.
19. For the connection of the *Halveti silsile* and teachings with Ali b. Abu Talib, see Curry, *The Transformation of Muslim Mystical Thought*, pp. 23–8; on Murad's intersections with Halveti ideas, see Curry, 'Meeting of the Two Sultans'.
20. On the increasingly globalised approach to the miseries of the seventeenth century, see Parker, *Global Crisis*.
21. See, for instance, the remarks of Barkey, *Empire of Difference*, pp. 104–8.
22. See, for example, Terzioğlu, 'Sunna-minded Sufi Preachers', pp. 241–79. For the potential impact of *Kadızadeli* persecutions on Halveti orders in Istanbul, see Curry, 'Defending Islamic Mysticism', pp. 311–99.
23. Abou-el-Haj, *The 1703 Rebellion*.
24. Konrad, 'Coping with "the Riff-Raff"', pp. 363–98.
25. For more on this broader transformation, see Grehan, 'Smoking and "Early Modern" Sociability', pp. 1352–77.
26. Terzioğlu, 'Sufi and Dissident'; on the Mevlevi context, see Ambrosio, 'İsma'il Rusuhi Ankaravi', pp. 191–4.
27. Interestingly, this work, published in 1879, seeks to place the Wahhabi movement in the same camp as the Qarmati movement; see Eyüb Sabri Paşa, *Tarih-i Vehhābiyan*, pp. 22–4.
28. It would be interesting to compare the contexts of Sarmiento, *Facundo* and da Cunha, *Backlands*.
29. An extensive documentation of this phenomenon in diverse frontier zones can be found in Blumi, *Rethinking*.

Bibliography

Abisaab, R. J., *Converting Persia: Religion and Power in the Safavid Empire* (London: I. B. Tauris, 2004).
Abou el-Haj, R. A., 'Aspects of the Legitimation of Ottoman Rule as Reflected in Preambles of Two Early Liva Kanunnameler', *Turcica* 21–3 (1991): 372–83.
Abou-el-Haj, R. A., *The 1703 Rebellion and the Structure of Ottoman Politics* (Leiden: Nederlands Instituut vor heet Nabije Oosten, 1984).
Abu Husayn, A., 'The Shiites in Lebanon and the Ottomans in the 16th and 17th Centuries', in *Convegno sul Tema: La Shī'a nell'Impero Ottomano* (Roma: Accademia Nazionale dei Lincei, 1993), pp. 107–19.
Abu-Manneh, B., *Studies on Islam and the Ottoman Empire in the 19th Century (1826–1876)* (Istanbul: Isis Press, 2001).
Abu-Manneh, B., 'The Naqshbandi–Mujaddidi and the Bektaşi Orders in 1826', in B. Abu-Manneh (ed.), *Studies on Islam and the Ottoman Empire in the 19th Century (1826–1876)* (Istanbul: Isis Press, 2001), pp. 59–71.
Abu-Manneh, B., 'The Naqshbandiyya-Mujaddidiyya in Istanbul in the Early Tanzimat Period', in B. Abu-Manneh (ed.), *Studies on Islam and the Ottoman Empire in the 19th Century (1826–1876)* (Istanbul: Isis Press, 2001), pp. 99–114.
Abu-Manneh, B., 'The Porte and the Sunni-Orthodox Trend in the Later Ottoman Period', in B. Abu-Manneh (ed.), *Studies on Islam and the Ottoman Empire in the 19th Century (1826–1876)* (Istanbul: Isis Press, 2001), pp. 125–40.
Abu-Manneh, B., 'The Naqshbandiyya–Mujaddidiyya in the Ottoman Lands in the Early 19th Century', *Die Welt des Islams*, NS, 22/1–4 (1982): 1–36.
Ágoston, G., 'Military Transformation in the Ottoman Empire and Russia, 1500–1800', *Kritika: Explorations in Russian and Eurasian History* 12/2 (2011): 281–319.
Ágoston, G., 'A Flexible Empire: Authority and its Limits on the Ottoman Frontiers', *International Journal of Turkish Studies* 9/1–2 (2003): 15–31.
Ahmed, S., *What is Islam?: the Importance of Being Islamic* (Princeton, NJ: Princeton University Press, 2015).
Ahmad, S. B., 'Conversion from Islam', in C. E. Bosworth et al. (eds), *The*

Islamic World from Classical to Modern Times: Essays in Honor of Bernard Lewis (Princeton, NJ: Darwin Press, 1989), pp. 3–25.

Ahmed, Shahab and Nenad Filipovic, 'The Sultan's Syllabus: a Curriculum for the Ottoman Imperial Medreses Prescribed in a Fermān of Qānūnī Süleymān, dated 973 (1565)', *Studia Islamica* 98/9 (2004): 183–218.

Ahmed Cevdet Paşa, *Tarih-i Cevdet*, 12 vols (Istanbul: Matbaa-i Osmaniye, 1309/1891–2).

Ahmed Lutfi Efendi, *Vak'anüvis Ahmed Lutfī Tarihi*, 8 vols (Istanbul: Tarih Vakfı/Yapı Kredi Yayınları, 1999).

Ahmet Rıf'at, *Mir'atü 'l-makasıd fi def'i 'l-mefasid* (İstanbul, 1293/1876).

Akçay, G., 'Bir Propaganda Aracı Olarak Divan Şiiri: Kızılbaş Örneği', *Gazi Üniversitesi Türk Kültürü ve Hacı Bektaş Veli Araştırma Dergisi* 79 (2016): 197–215.

Aksan, V. H. 'Mobilization of Warrior Populations in the Ottoman Context, 1750–1850', in Erik J. Zürcher (ed.), *Fighting for a Living: a Comparative History of Military Labour 1500–2000* (Amsterdam: Amsterdam University Press, 2013), pp. 331–51

Aksan, V. H., *Ottoman Wars 1700–1870: an Empire Besieged* (London: Routledge, 2007).

Aksan, V. H. and D. Goffman (eds), *Early Modern Ottomans: Remapping the Empire* (New York: Cambridge University Press, 2007).

al-Bakri, Abi al-Hasan bin 'Abdullah, *Al-Anwār fī mawlid al-Nabī Muḥammad* (Al-Kuwayt: Maktabat al-Alfayn, 1986).

al-Bakri, Abi al-Hasan bin 'Abdullah, *Al-Anwār wa-maṣbāḥ al-surūr wa-al-afkār aw-dhikr nūr Muḥammad al-Muṣṭafá al-Mukhtār* (Miṣr: Maktabat wa-Matba'at Muṣṭafá al-Bābī al-Ḥalabī wa-Awlāduh, 1939).

Algar, H., 'Ja'far al-Ṣadeq, III.Sufism', *Encyclopedia Iranica*.

Algar, H., 'Malamatiyya', *Encyclopedia of Islam*, 2nd edn (Brill online).

Algar, H., 'Hamzavīye: A Deviant Movement in Bosnian Sufism', *Islamic Studies* 36/2–3 (1418/1997): 243–61.

Algar, H., 'The Hurufi Influence on Bektashism', in Alexandre Popovic and Gilles Veinstein (eds), *Bektachiyya: Études sur l'Ordre Mystique des Bektachis et les Groups Relevant de Hadji Bektach* (Istanbul: Les Éditions Isis, 1995), pp. 39–54.

Algar, H., 'Hurufi Influence on Bektashism', *Révue des Études Islamiques* 60 (1992): 41–54.

Algar, H., *Mirza Malkum Khan: a Study in the History of Iranian Modernism* (Berkeley: California University Press, 1973).

Algar, H. and K. A. Nizami, 'Naḵs̲h̲bandiyya', *Encyclopedia of Islam*, 2nd edn (Brill online), last accessed 10 April 2018.

Alkan, N., *Dissent and Heterodoxy in the Late Ottoman Empire: Reformers, Babis and Baha'is* (Istanbul: Isis Press, 2008)

Alkan, N., 'Fighting for the Nuṣayrī Soul: State, Protestant Missionaries and the 'Alawīs in the Late Ottoman Empire', *Die Welt des Islams* 52/1 (2012): 23–50.

Bibliography

Al-Tabari, *The History of al-Tabari, vol. 14: The Conquest of Iran A.D. 641–643/ A.H. 21–23*, ed. and trans. G. R. Smith (Albany, NY: State University of New York Press, 1994).

Al-Tabari, *The History of al-Tabari, vol. 9: The Last Years of the Prophet: The Formation of the State* A.D. *630–632/*A.H. *8–11*, trans. I. Q. Husayn (Albany, NY: State University of New York Press, 1990).

Al-Tikriti, N., 'Ibn Kamal's Confessionalism and the Construction of an Ottoman Islam', in Christine Isom-Verhaaren and Kent F. Schull (eds), *Living in the Ottoman Realm: Empire and Identity, 13th to 20th Centuries* (Bloomington: Indiana University Press, 2016), pp. 95–107.

Al-Tikriti, N., 'Kalam in the Service of State: Apostasy and Defining of Ottoman Islamic Identity', in Hakan Karateke (ed.), *Legitimizing the Order: the Ottoman Rhetoric of State Power* (Leiden: Brill, 2005), pp. 131–49.

Al-Tikriti, N., 'Şehzade Korkud (ca. 1468–1513) and the Articulation of Early 16th Century Ottoman Religious Identity', PhD dissertation, University of Chicago, 2004.

Ambros, E., *Candid Penstrokes: the Lyrics of Me'ālī, an Ottoman Poet of the 16th Century* (Berlin: K. Schwarz, 1982).

Ambrosio, A. F., 'İsma'il Rusuhi Ankaravi: an Early Mevlevi Intervention into the Emerging Kadızadeli-Sufi Conflict', in John J. Curry and Erik S. Ohlander (eds), *Sufism and Society: Arrangements of the Mystical in the Muslim World 1200–1800* (London: Routledge, 2012), pp. 183–97.

Amoretti, B. S., 'Religion in the Timurid and Safavid Periods', in Peter Jackson (ed.), *The Cambridge History of Iran*, 7 vols (Cambridge: Cambridge University Press, 1986), vol. 6, pp. 610–55.

Andrews, Walter G., 'Singing the Alienated "I": Guattari, Deleuze and Lyrical Decodings of the Subject in Ottoman Poetry', *Yale Journal of Criticism* 6/2 (1993): 191–219.

Anonymous, 'İhtiyacāt-ı Askeriye', *Hakayık el-Vekayi'* 416 (6 Ramazan 1288/18 November 1871), pp. 2–3.

Arberry, R. A., *Rumi: Poet and Mystic (1207–1273)* (London: Allen and Unwin, 1950).

Arjomand, S. A., *The Shadow of God and the Hidden Imam: Religion, Political Order and Societal Change in Shi'ite Iran from the Beginning to 1890* (Chicago: University of Chicago Press, 1984).

Arjomand, S. A., 'Religious Extremism (Ghuluww), Sufism and Sunnism in Safavid Iran: 1501–1722', *Journal of Asian History* 15/1 (1981): 1–35.

Aşıkpaşazade, *Aşıkpaşazade Tarihi* [Osmanlı Tarihi (1285–1502)], ed. Necdet Öztürk (Istanbul: Istanbul Bilgi Sanat, 2013).

Atayi, Nev'izade, *Ḥadaik al-Ḥakaik fi Takmilat al-Shakaik*, published by Abdülkadir Özcan, as vol. 2, *Şakaik-i Nu'maniyye ve Zeyilleri* (Istanbul: Çağrı Yayınları, 1989).

Atçıl, A., *Scholars and Sultans in the Early Modern Ottoman Empire* (Cambridge: Cambridge University Press, 2017).

Atçıl, A., 'The Safavid Threat and Juristic Authority in the Ottoman Empire during the 16th Century', *International Journal of Middle East Studies* 49 (2017): 295–314.

Atçıl, A., 'The Route to the Top in the Ottoman *Ilmiye* Hierarchy of the Sixteenth Century', *Bulletin of the School of Oriental and African Studies (BSOAS)* 72/3 (2009): 489–512.

Atsız, Nihal, *Osmanlı Tarihleri I* (Istanbul, Türkiye Yayınevi, 1949).

Ayar, M., *Bektaşilik'te Son Nefes: Yeniçeriliğin Kaldırılmasından Sonra Bektaşilik* (Istanbul: Giza, 2009).

Aytekin, A., 'Bābertī', *Diyanet Islam Ansiklopedisi* (Istanbul: Turkiye Diyanet Vakfi, 1991), vol. 4, pp. 377–8.

Azamat, Nihat, 'Idris-i Muhtefi', *Diyanet Islam Ansiklopedisi*.

Azamat, Nihat, 'Sarı Abdullah Efendi', *Diyanet Islam Ansiklopedisi*.

Babayan, K., *Mystics, Monarchs, and Messiahs: Cultural Landscape of Early Modern Iran* (Cambridge, MA: Harvard University Press, 2002).

Babayan, K., 'The Safavid Synthesis: From Qizilbash Islam to Imamite Shi'ism', *Iranian Studies* 27/1–4 (1994): 137–61.

Babinger, F., 'Anadolu'da İslamiyet (İslam Tedkikatının Yeni Yolları)', trans. Ragıp Hulusi, *Darülfünun Edebiyat Fakültesi Mecmuası* 2/3 *Temmuz* 1338 [1922]: 188–221.

Babinger, F., 'Der Islam in Kleinasien. NeueWege de Islamforschung', *Zeitschrift der Deutschen Morgenländischen Gesellschaft* 76/1 (1922): 126–52.

Babinger, F., *Osmanli Tarih Yazarlari ve Eserleri*, trans. Coşkun Üçok (Ankara: Kültür Bakanlığı, 1992).

Baer, M. D., 'Book Review: *Contested Conversions to Islam: Narratives of Religious Change in the Early Modern Ottoman Empire* by Tijana Krstić', *Journal of Islamic Studies* 23/3 (2012): 391–4.

Baer, M. D., *Honoured by the Glory of Islam: Conversion and Conquest in Ottoman Empire* (Oxford: Oxford University Press, 2008).

Balcı, Tamer, 'The Rise and Fall of Nine Lights', *Politics, Religion, and Ideology* 12/2 (2011): 145–60.

Balcı, Tamer, 'From Nationalization of Islam to Privatization of Nationalism: Islam and Turkish National Identity', *History Studies* 1/1 (2009): 82–107.

Balph, J. M., 'Among the Nussairyeh', *Olive Trees (Journal of the Reformed Presbyterian Church)* 8 (1912): 180–5.

Baltacı, C., *XV–XVI. Yüzyıllarda Osmanlı Medreseleri*, 2 vols (İstanbul: Marmara Üniversitesi İlahiyat Fakültesi Vakfı, 2005).

Baltacıoğlu-Brammer, A., 'Safavid Conversion Propaganda in Ottoman Anatolia and the Ottoman Reaction, 1440s–1630s', PhD thesis, the Ohio State University, 2016.

Baltacıoğlu-Brammer, A., 'The Formation of *Kızılbaş* Communities in Anatolia and Ottoman Responses, 1450s–1630s', *International Journal of Turkish Studies* 20/1–2 (2014): 21–48.

Bibliography

Bang, P. and C. Bayly (eds), *Tributary Empires in Global History* (Basingstoke: Palgrave Macmillan, 2011).

Barkan, Ö. L., 'Caractère religieux et charactère séculier des institutions ottomanes', in Jean-Louis Bacqué-Grammont and Paul Dumont (eds), *Contributions à l'histoire économique et sociale de l'Empire ottoman* (Leuven: Peeters, 1983), pp. 11–58.

Barkan, Ö. L., *Kanunlar* (İstanbul: Burhaneddin Matbaası, 1943).

Barkan, Ö. L., 'Osmanlı imparatorluğunda bir iskan ve kolonizasyon metodu olarak vakıflar ve temlikler. I. İstilā devirlerinin kolonizatör Türk dervişleri ve zāviyeler', *Vakıflar dergisi* 2 (1942): 279–353.

Barkey, K., *Empire of Difference: the Ottomans in Comparative Perspective* (Cambridge: Cambridge University Press, 2008).

Barkey, K. and Rudi Batzell, 'Comparisons across Empires: the Critical Social Structures of the Ottomans, Russians and Habsburgs during the Seventeenth Century', in Peter F. Bang and C.A. Bayly (eds), *Tributary Empires in Global History* (New York: Palgrave Macmillan, 2011), pp. 227–61

Başbakanlık Osmanlı Arşivleri (BOA), Bab-i Ali Evrak Odası (BEO), 2250/168719.

BOA, Cevdet Tasnifi Adliye (C.ADL), 29/1734.

BOA, Cevdet Tasnifi Dahiliye (C.DH.), 125/6218.

BOA, Cevdet Tasnifi Zabtiye (C.ZB), 34/1680.

BOA, Cevdet Tasnifi Zabtiye (C.ZB), 17/843.

BOA, Cevdet Tasnifi Zabtiye (C.ZB.), 17/843, 21 C 1243.

BOA, Dahiliye Nezareti Mektubi Kalemi (DH.MKT.), 1487/38, 8 Cemaziyelahir 1305/21 February 1888.

BOA, Dahiliye Nezareti Mektubi Kalemi (DH.MKT.), 1823/38, 21 Şaban 1308/31 March 1891.

BOA, Dahiliye Nezareti Mektubi Kalemi (DH.MKT.), 1975/31, 25 Zālhicce 1309/20 July 1892.

BOA, Dahiliye Nezareti Mektubi Kalemi (DH. MKT.), 1983/15, 11 Muharrem 1310/5 August 1892.

BOA, Dahiliye Nezareti Mektubi Kalemi (DH.MKT.), 1958/80, 12 Zīlkāde 1309/8 June 1892.

BOA, Dahiliye Nezareti Mektubi Kalemi (DH.MKT.), 2049/13, 18 Receb 1310/5 February 1893.

BOA, Dahiliye Nezareti Mektubi Kalemi (DH.MKT.), 31/9, 11 Rebiüssani 1311/22 October 1893.

BOA, Dahiliye Nezareti Mektubi Kalemi (DH.MKT.), 866/56, 18 Ramazan 1822/26 November 1904.

BOA, Dahiliye Nezareti Mektubi Kalemi (DH.MKT), 74/10.

BOA, Dahiliye Nezareti Mektubi Kalemi (DH. MKT.), 1555/58.

BOA, Dahiliye Nezareti Mektubi Kalemi (DH.MKT.), 2012/117.

BOA, Hatt-ı Hümayun Tasnifi (HAT), 1654/4 (1014/1605).

BOA, Hatt-ı Hümayun Tasnifi (HAT), 1446/ 21 (1015/1606).

BOA, Hatt-ı Hümayun Tasnifi (HAT), 1654/4 (1014/1605).
BOA, Hatt-ı Hümayun Tasnifi (HAT), 1103/44569H.
BOA, Hatt-ı Hümayun Tasnifi (HAT), 290/17351.
BOA, Hatt-ı Hümayun Tasnifi (HAT), 290/17386.
BOA, Hatt-ı Hümayun Tasnifi (HAT), 512/25094-D, E, F and G.
BOA, Hatt-ı Hümayun Tasnifi (HAT), 512/25094-E, 25 Rebiülevvel 1249 (12 August 1833).
BOA, Hatt-ı Hümayun Tasnifi (HAT), 512/25094-G, 27 Rebiülevvel 1249 (14 August 1833).
BOA, İbnülemin Tasnifi Maliye (İE. ML),11/952 (1042/1632).
BOA, İrade Meclis-i Mahsus (İ.MMS.), 114/4687, 13 Haziran 1306/26 June 1891
BOA, İrade Meclis-i Mahsus (İ.MMS.), 113/4821, 9 Mayıs 1306/21 May 1890.
BOA, İrade Şurayı Devlet (İ.ŞD.), 2280/40.
BOA, İ.MF. 2/1311/R-1, 8 Ramazan 1311/15 March 1894
BOA, Maarif Nezareti Mektubi Kalemi (MF. MKT.), 47.022.
BOA, Maarif Nezareti Mektubi Kalemi (MF.MKT.), 77/10, 1 Şaban 1312/28 January 1895.
BOA, Mühimme Defterleri (MD), vol. 1, Nos 70, 86 and 409, 961–2/1553–4.
BOA, MD, vol. 2, No. 1841, 24 Safer 964/ 26 December 1556.
BOA, MD, vol. 3, No. 172, 10 Muharrem 967/12 October 1559.
BOA, MD, vol. 3, No. 1295, 966–8/1558–60.
BOA, MD, vol. 9, No. 230, 22 Şaban 977/29 January 1570.
BOA, MD, vol. 10, No. 279, 979/1571.
BOA, MD, vol. 12, Nos. 822, 832 and 833.
BOA, MD, vol. 14, No. 311, 14 Safer 978/18 July 1570.
BOA, MD, vol. 14, No. 488, 12 Ramazan 978/7 February 1571.
BOA, MD, Vol. 25, No. 1627 (17 Sefer 982 / June 7, 1574).
BOA, MD, vol. 29, Nos 488 and 489, 14 Zilkade 989/11 December 1581; Nos 490, 491 and 500, 14 Zilhicce 989/9 January 1582.
BOA, MD, vol. 31, No. 66, 28 Ramazan 985/8 December 1577.
BOA, MD, vol. 33, No. 413, 8 Zilkade 985/16 January 1578.
BOA, MD, vol. 35, No. 816, 26 Şaban 986/28 October 1578.
BOA, MD, vol. 58, No. 206 (17 Cemaziyelevvel 993/17 May 1585.
BOA, MD, vol. 62, No. 27 (2 Sefer 995/11 January 1587.
BOA, MD, vol. 63, No. 52, 23 Sefer 996/22 January 1588.
BOA, MD, vol. 67, No. 180, 21 Rebiülevvel 999/21 January 1591.
BOA, Mühimme-i Asakir Defteri, No. 26, pp. 89–90, 108–10, 192–4.
BOA, Sadaret Hususi Maruzat Evrakı (Y.A. HUS.), 260/130, 28 Şevval 1309/25 May 1892.
BOA, Sadaret Resmi Maruzat Evrakı (Y.A.RES), 51/9.
BOA, Sadaret Resmi Maruzat Evrakı (Y.A.RES.), 60/27
BOA, Yıldız Esas Evrakı (Y.EE), 9/34, 9 Ramazan 1309/7 April 1892.
BOA, Yıldız Mütenevvi Maruzat Evrakı (Y.MTV.), 68/90.
BOA, Yıldız Perakende Evrakı Başkitabet Dairesi Maruzatı (Y.PRK.BŞK), 19/27

Bibliography

BOA, Yıldız Perakende Evrakı Komisyanlar Maruzatı (Y.PRK.KOM.), 7/59.

Barthes, R., 'The Death of the Author', in Stephen Heath (ed.), *Image, Music, Text* (London: Fontana, 1977), pp. 142–8.

Bartov, O. and Eric D. Weitz (eds), *Shatterzone of Empires: Coexistence and Violence in the German, Habsburg, Russian, and Ottoman Borderlands* (Bloomington, IN: Indiana University Press, 2013).

Bashir, S., 'The Origins and Rhetorical Evolution of the Term Kızılbaş in Persianate Literature', *Journal of the Economic and Social History of the Orient* 57 (2014): 364–91.

Bashir, S., *Fazlullah Astarabadi and the Hurufis* (Oxford: Oneworld, 2006).

Bashir, S., *Messianic Hopes and Mystical Visions: the Nurbakhshiyya Between Medieval and Modern Islam* (Columbia, SC: University of South Carolina Press, 2003).

Bashir, S., 'Deciphering the Cosmos from Creation to Apocalypse: the Hurufiyya Movement and Medieval Islamic Esotericism', in Abbas Amanat and Magnus Bernhardson (eds), *Imagining the End: Visions of Apocalypse from the Ancient Middle East to Modern America* (London: I. B. Tauris, 2002), pp. 168–84.

Bashir, S., 'Enshrining Divinity: the Death and Memorialization of Fazlallah Astarabadi in Hurufi Thought', *Muslim World* 90/3–4 (2000): 289–308

Bashir, S., 'Between Mysticism and Messianism: the Life and Thought of Muhammad Nurbakš (d. 1464)', PhD dissertation, Yale University, 1997.

Bausani, A., 'Ḥurūfiyya', *Encyclopedia of Islam*, 2nd edn (Brill online, 1971), vol. 3, pp. 600–1.

Bausani, A., 'Religion Under the Mongols', in J. A. Boyle (ed.), *The Cambridge History of Iran*, vol. 5 (Cambridge: Cambridge University Press, 1968), pp. 538–49.

Beldiceanu-Steinherr, I., 'Les Bektachi à la lumière des recensements ottoman (XVe–XVIe siècles)', *Wiener Zeitschrift für die Kunde des Morgenlandes* 81 (1991): 21–79.

Berkes, N., *The Development of Secularism in Turkey* (New York: Routledge, [1964] 1998).

Biçer, R., 'Harputlu İshak Efendi'nin Kelāmī Görüşleri', in Fikret Karaman (ed.), *Dünü ve Bügünüyle Harput (Sempozyum: 24–27 Eylül 1998, Elazığ* (Elazığ: Türkiye Diyanet Vakfı Elazığ Şubesi, 1999), pp. 255–68.

Bilge, M., *İlk Osmanlı Medreseleri* (İstanbul: İstanbul Üniversitesi Edebiyat Fakültesi Yayınları, 1984).

Birdal, M. S., *The Holy Roman Empire and the Ottomans: From Global Imperial Power to Absolutist States* (New York: I. B. Tauris, 2011).

Bireley, R., *Ferdinand II, Counter-Reformation Emperor, 1578–1637* (New York: Cambridge University Press, 2014).

Bireley, R., *The Jesuits and the Thirty Years' War: Kings, Courts, and Confessors* (Cambridge: Cambridge University Press, 2003).

Bireley, R., *Religion and Politics in the Age of the Counterreformation: Emperor*

Ferdinand II, William Lamormaini, S.J., and the Formation of Imperial Policy (Chapel Hill, NC: University of North Carolina Press, 1981).

Birge, J. K., *The Bektashi Order of Dervishes* (London: Luzac, [1937] 1994).

Blumi, Isa, *Rethinking the Late Ottoman Empire: a Comparative Social and Political History of Albania and Yemen, 1878–1918* (Istanbul: Isis Press, 2003).

Boettcher, S. R., 'Confessionalization: Reformation, Religion, Absolutism, and Modernity', *History Compass* 2 (2004): 1–10.

Bogatyrev, S., 'Ivan IV (1533–1584)', in Maureen Perrie (ed.), *The Cambridge History of Russia, vol. 1: From Early Rus' to 1689* (Cambridge: Cambridge University Press, 2008), pp. 240–63.

Bossy, J., *Christianity in the West, 1499–1700* (Oxford: Oxford University Press, 1985).

Brady, Jr, T. A., 'Confessionalization: the Career of a Concept', in John M. Headley, Hans J. Hillerbrand and Anthony J. Papals (eds), *Confessionalization in Europe, 1555–1700: Essays in Honour and Memory of Bodo Nischan* (Farnham: Ashgate, 2004), pp. 1–20.

Breebaart, D. A. and D. K. Chakrabarti, 'The Fütüvvet-nāme-i kebīr: a Manual on Turkish Guilds', *Journal of the Economic and Social History of the Orient* 15/1 (1972): 203–19.

Bremer, T., *Cross and Kremlin: a Brief History of the Orthodox Church in Russia*, trans. Eric W. Gritsch (Grand Rapids, MI: Eerdmans, 2013).

Brodersen, A., *Der unbekannte Kalām. Theologische Positionen der frühen Matūrīdīya am Beispiel der Attributenlehre* (Berlin: Lit-Verlag, 2014).

Brown, P., 'How Muscovy Governed: Seventeenth-Century Russian Central Administration', *Russian History* 36/4 (2009): 459–529.

Browne, E. G., 'Further Notes on the Literature of the Hurufis and Their Connection with the *Bektaşi* Order of Dervishes', *Journal of the Royal Asiatic Society of Great Britain and Ireland* (1907): 533–81.

Browne, E. G., 'Some Notes on the Literature and Doctrine of the Hurufi Sect', *Journal of the Royal Asiatic Society of Great Britain and Ireland* (1898): 61–94.

Brüning, A., 'Confessionalization in the Slavia Orthodoxa (Belorussia, Ukraine, Russia)? Potential and Limits of a Western Historiographical Concept', in Thomas S. Bremer (ed.), *Religion and the Conceptual Boundary in Central and Eastern Europe: Encounters of Faiths* (Basingstoke: Palgrave Macmillan, 2008), pp. 66–97

Bulliet, R. W., 'The Shaikh al-Islām and the Evolution of Islamic Society', *Studia Islamica* 35 (1972): 53–67.

Burak, G., *The Second Formation of Islamic Law: the Hanafi School in the Early Modern Ottoman Empire* (New York: Cambridge University Press, 2015).

Burak, G., 'Faith, Law, and Empire in the Ottoman Age of Confessionalization (Fifteenth–Seventeenth Centuries): The Case of "Renewal of Faith"', *Mediterranean Historical Review* 28/1 (2013): 1–23.

Bibliography

Burrill, K. R. F., *The Quatrains of Nesimi: Fourteenth-Century Turkic Hurufi* (The Hague: Mouton, 1972).
Bushkovitch, P., *Peter the Great: the Struggle for Power, 1671–1725* (Cambridge: Cambridge University Press, 2001).
Bushkovitch, P., *Religion and Society in Russia: the Sixteenth and Seventeenth Centuries* (New York: Oxford University Press, 1992).
Çakmak, Y. and İ. Gürtaş (eds), *Kızılbaşlık, Alevilik, Bektaşilik: Tarih-Kimlik-Ritüel* (Istanbul: İletişim, 2015).
Calder, N., *Islamic Jurisprudence in the Classical Era*, ed. Colin Imber (Cambridge: Cambridge University Press, 2010).
Calder, N., 'The Limits of Islamic Orthodoxy', in Farhad Daftary (ed.), *Intellectual Traditions in Islam* (New York: I. B. Tauris, 2000), pp. 66–86.
Çalış-Kural, B. D., *Şehrengiz: Urban Rituals and Deviant Sufi Mysticism in Ottoman Istanbul* (Farnham: Ashgate, 2014).
Carlson, T. A., 'Safavids before Empire: Two 15th-Century Armenian Perspectives', *IJMES* 49 (2017): 286.
Çataltepe, S., *19. Yüzyıl Başlarında Avrupa Dengesi ve Nizam-ı Cedit Ordusu* (Istanbul: Göçebe Yayınları, 1997).
Çavuşoğlu, M., *Yahya Bey Divanı (tenkitli basım)* (İstanbul: İstanbul Üniversitesi Yayınları, 1977).
Çavuşoğlu, S., 'The *Kadızadeli* Movement: An Attempt of Şeri'at-Minded Reform in the Ottoman Empire', PhD thesis, Princeton University, 1990.
Çerçi, F. (ed.), *Mustafa Ali'nin Künhü'l Ahbarın'da II. Selim, III. Murat ve III. Mehmet Devirleri* (Kayseri: Erciyes Üniversitesi Yayınları, 2000).
Çetinsaya, G., *Ottoman Administration of Iraq, 1890–1908* (London: Routledge, 2006).
Çetinsaya, G., 'The Caliph and Mujtahids: Ottoman Policy towards the Shiite Community of Iraq in the Late Nineteenth Century', *Middle Eastern Studies* 41/4 (2005): 561–74.
Ceylan, E., 'Carrot or Strick? Ottoman Tribal Policy in Baghdad, 1831–1876', *International Journal of Contemporary Iraqi Studies* 3/2 (2009): 169–86.
Chabbi, J., 'Remarques sur le Développement Historique des Mouvements Ascétiques et Mystiques au Khurasan', *Studia Islamica* 46 (1977): 5–72.
Chodkiewicz, M., 'Les Malamiyya dans la doctrine d'Ibn Arabi', in Nathalie Clayer, Alexandre Popovic and Thierry Zarcone (eds), *Melamis-Bayramis: Études sur Trios Movements Mystiques Musulmans* (Istanbul: Les Éditions Isis, 1998), pp. 15–27.
Chodkiewicz, M., *Seal of the Saints, Prophethood and Sainthood in the Doctrine of Ibn 'Arabi*, trans. Liadain Sherrard (Cambridge: Islamic Texts Society, 1993).
Clayer, N., 'Sufi Printed Matter and Knowledge about the Bektaşi Order in the Late Ottoman Period', in Rachida Chih, Rüdiger Seesemann and Catherine Mayeur-Jaouen (eds), *Sufism, Literary Production and Printing in the 19th Century* (Würzburg: Ergon, 2015), pp. 351–67.

Clayer, Nathalie, Alexandre Popovic and Thierry Zarcone (eds), *Melamis-Bayramis: Études sur Trios Movements Mystiques Musulmans* (Istanbul: Les Éditions Isis, 1998).

Cook, M., *Commanding Right and Forbidding Wrong in Islamic Thought* (Cambridge: Cambridge University Press, [2000] 2004).

Cook, M., *Forbidding Wrong in Islam* (Cambridge: Cambridge University Press, 2003).

Coreth, A., *Pietas Austriaca: Austrian Religious Practices in the Baroque Era*, trans. William David Bowman (West Lafayette, IN: Purdue University Press, 2004).

Crummey, R. O., 'Past and Current Interpretations of Old Belief', in Georg B. Michels and Robert L. Nichols (eds), *Russia's Dissident Old Believers: 1650–1950* (Minneapolis: Mediterranean and East European Monographs, 2009), pp 36–52.

Crummey, R. O., 'The Orthodox Church and the Schism', in Maureen Perrie (ed.) *From Early Rus' to 1689*, The Cambridge History of Russia, vol. 1 (Cambridge: Cambridge University Press, 2008), pp. 618–29.

Currie, J. M. D., 'Kadızadeli Ottoman Scholarship, Muhammad Ibn 'Abd al-Wahhāb, and the Rise of the Saudi State', *Journal of Islamic Studies* 26/3 (2015): 265–88.

Curry, J. J., '"The Meeting of the Two Sultans": Three Mystics Negotiate with the Court of Murad III', in John J. Curry and Erik S. Ohlander (eds), *Sufism and Society: Arrangements of the Mystical in the Muslim World, 1200–1800* (London: Routledge, 2012), pp. 223–42.

Curry, J. J., *The Transformation of Muslim Mystical Thought in the Ottoman Empire: the Rise of the Halveti Order, 1350–1650* (Edinburgh: Edinburgh University Press, 2010).

Curry, J. J. 'Defending Islamic Mysticism in an Age of Transformation: the Foundation and Development of the Şa'baniyye Branch of the Halveti Order in the Ottoman Empire as Reflected in Its Hagiographical Writings, 1500–1750', unpublished PhD dissertation, the Ohio State University, 2005).

Curry, J.J. and Eric S. Ohlander (eds), *Sufism and Society: Arrangements of the Mystical in the Muslim World, 1200–1800* (London: Routledge, 2012).

Da Cunha, E., *Backlands: the Canudos Campaign*, trans. Elizabeth Lowe (New York: Penguin, 2010).

Dağlı, Murat, 'The Limits of Ottoman Pragmatism', *History and Theory* 52/2 (2013): 194–213.

Dalkıran, S., 'İran Safavi Devletini'nin Kuruluşuna Şii İnançların Etkisi ve Osmanlı'nın İran'a Bakışı', *Atatürk Üniversitesi İlahiyat Fakültesi Dergisi* 18 (2002): 49–96.

Dalsar, F., *Türk Sanayi ve Ticaret Tarihinde Bursa'da İpekçilik* (İstanbul: Sermet Matbaası, 1960).

Dankoff, R., *An Ottoman Mentality: The World of Evliya Çelebi* (Leiden: Brill, 2006).

Bibliography

Darling, L. T., *A History of Social Justice and Political Power in the Middle East: the Circle of Justice from Mesopotamia to Globalization* (London: Routledge, 2013).
De Groot, A. H., 'Murad III', *Encyclopedia of Islam*, 2nd edn (Brill online), vol. 7, 595–7.
De Jong, F. and B. Radtke (eds), 'Introduction', in *Islamic Mysticism Contested: Thirteen Centuries of Controversies and Polemics* (Leiden: Brill, 1999), pp.1–21.
Demir, A., 'Kanunī Sultan Süleyman'ın Terk-i Salāt Edenlerle İlgili Fermanı', *Tarih İncelemeleri Dergisi* 2 (1984): 46–53.
Demir, M. and M. Özafşar, 'Vehb bin Münebbih', *Diyanet Islam Ansiklopedisi* (Istanbul: Turkiye Diyanet Vakfı, 2009), vol. 42, pp. 608–10.
Demirpolat, E., 'Artukoğullarından Cunhuriyet'e Kadar Harputlu Müellifler', in Enver Çakar (ed.), *Geçmişten Geleneğe Harput Sempozyumu, Elazığ, 23–25. Mayıs 2013, Bildiriler*, Cilt 2 (Elazığ: Fırat Üniversitesi Harput Uygulama ve Araştırma Merkezi, 2013), pp. 667–96.
Demirpolat, E., 'Harputlu İshak Hoca'nın Hayatı ve Eserleri', *Selçuk Üniversitesi Sosyal Bilimleri Enstitüsü Dergisi* Sayı 9 (2003): 397–412.
Demirtaş, F., 'Celāl-Zāde Mustafa Çelebi, Tabakātü'l-Memālik ve Derecātü'l-Mesālik', PhD dissertation, Erciyes Üniversitesi, 2009.
Deringil, S., *Conversion and Apostasy in the Late Ottoman Empire* (Cambridge: Cambridge Universty Press, 2012).
Deringil, S., *Simgeden Millete: II. Abdülhamid'den Mustafa Kemal'e Devlet ve Millet* (Istanbul: İletişim, 2007).
Deringil, S., 'Redefining Identities in the Late Ottoman Empire: Policies of Conversion and Apostasy', in A. Miller and A. J. Rieber (eds), *Imperial Rule* (Budapest: Central European University Press, 2004), pp. 107–30.
Deringil, S., '"They Live in a State of Nomadism and Savagery": the Late Ottoman Empire and the Post-Colonial Debate', *Comparative Studies in Society and History* 45/2 (2003): 311–42.
Deringil, S., 'Conversion and Ideological Reinforcement: the Yezidi Kurds', in Mercedes García-Arenal (ed.), *Conversions islamiques: Identités religieuses en Islam méditerranéen* (Paris: Maisonneuve et Larose, 2001), pp. 419–43.
Deringil, S., '"There Is No Compulsion in Religion": On Conversion and Apostasy in the Late Ottoman Empire: 1839–1856', *Comparative Studies in Society and History* 42/3 (2000): 547–75.
Deringil, S., 'From Ottoman to Turk: Self-Image and Social Engineering in Turkey', in Dru C. Gladney (ed.), *Making Majorities: Constituting the Nation in Japan, Korea, China, Malaysia, Fiji, Turkey, and the United States* (Stanford, CA: Stanford University Press, 1998), pp. 217–26.
Deringil, S., *The Well-Protected Domains: Ideology and the Legitimation of Power in the Ottoman Empire, 1876–1909* (London: I. B. Tauris, 1998).
Deringil, S., 'The Invention of Tradition as Public Image in the Late Ottoman

Empire, 1808 to 1908', *Comparative Studies in Society and History* 35/1 (1993): 3–29.

Deringil, S., 'Legitimacy Structures in the Ottoman State: the Reign of Abdulhamid II (1876–1909)', *International Journal of Middle East Studies* 23/3 (1991): 345–59.

Deringil, S. 'The Struggle against Shiism in Hamidian Iraq: a Study in Ottoman Counter Propaganda', *Die Welt des Islams*, NS, 30/1–4 (1990): 45–62.

Devereux, R., 'Süleyman Pasha's "The Feeling of the Revolution"', *Middle Eastern Studies* 15/1 (1979): 3–35.

Devereux, R., *The First Ottoman Constitutional Period* (Oxford: Oxford University Press, 1964).

Dominguez, J. P., 'Introduction: Religious Toleration in the Age of Enlightenment', *History of European Ideas* 43/4 (2017): 273–87.

Douwes, D., 'Knowledge and Oppression: the Nusayriyya in the Late Ottoman Period', *Convegno sul tema La Shia nell'impero ottomano* (Roma: Accademia nazionale dei Lincei, Fondazione Leone Caetani, 1993), pp. 149–69.

Dressler, M., 'Alevīs', *Encyclopedia of Islam*, 3rd edn (Brill online).

Dressler, M., *Writing Religion: the Making of Turkish Alevi Islam* (New York: Oxford University Press, 2013).

Dressler, M., 'How to Conceptualize Inner-Islamic Plurality/Difference: "Heteredoxy" and "Syncretism" in the Writings of Mehmet F. Köprülü (1890–1966), *British Journal of Middle Eastern Studies* 37/3 (2010): 241–60.

Dressler, M., 'Inventing Orthodoxy: Competing Claims for Authority and Legitimacy in the Ottoman–Safavid Conflict', in Hakan T. Karateke and Maurius Reinkowski (eds), *Legitimizing the Order: the Ottoman Rhetoric of State Power* (Leiden: Brill, 2005), pp. 151–73.

Duffy, E., *The Stripping of the Altars: Traditional Religion in England, 1400–1580* (New Haven, CT: Yale University Press, 1992).

Duguid, S., 'The Politics of Unity: Hamidian Policy in Eastern Anatolia', *Middle Eastern Studies* 9/2 (1973): 139–55.

Dursteler, E., *Venetians in Constantinople: Nation, Identity, and Coexistence in the Early Modern Mediterranean* (Baltimore, MD: Johns Hopkins University Press, 2006).

Düzdağ, M. E., *Şeyhülislam Ebussuud Efendi Fetvaları* (İstanbul: Enderun, 1972).

Eberhard, E., *Osmanische Polemik gegen die Safawiden in 16. Jahrhundert nach arabischen Handschriften* (Freiburg: Klaus Schwartz Verlag, 1970).

El Shamsy, A., 'The Social Construction of Orthodoxy', in Timothy J. Winter (ed.), *The Cambridge Companion to Classical Islamic Theology* (Cambridge: Cambridge University Press, 2008), pp. 97–117; reprinted in Maribel Fierro (ed.), *Orthodoxy and Heresy in Islam*, vol. 1 (London: Routledge, 2013), pp. 257–74.

Emre, S., 'Crafting Piety for Success: Gülşeniye Literature and Culture in the Sixteenth Century', *Journal of Sufi Studies* 1 (2012): 31–75.

Ergene, B., *Local Court, Provincial Society, and Justice in the Ottoman Empire:*

Bibliography

Legal Practice and Dispute Resolution in Çankırı and Katamonu (1652–1744) (Leiden: Brill, 2003).

Erginbaş, V., 'Reading Ottoman Sunnism through Islamic History: Approaches toward Yazid bin Muawiya in the Ottoman Historical Writing', in Tijana Krstić and Derin Terzioğlu (eds), *Rethinking Ottoman Sunnitization, 1450s–1700* (Leiden: Brill, forthcoming).

Erginbaş, V., Review, 'Shahab Ahmed: What is Islam: the Importance of Being Islamic', *Journal of Ottoman and Turkish Studies Association* 5/1 (2018).

Erginbaş, V., 'Problematizing Ottoman Sunnism: Appropriation of Islamic History and Ahl al-Baytism in Ottoman Literary and Historical Writing in the Sixteenth Century', *Journal of Economic and Social History of Orient* 60/5 (2017): 614–46.

Erginbaş, V., 'The Appropriation of Islamic History and Ahl al-Baytism in the Ottoman Historical Writing', unpublished PhD dissertation, the Ohio State University, 2013.

Erkan, M., 'Darir', *Diyanet Islam Ansiklopedisi* (Istanbul: Turkiye Diyanet Vakfi, 1993), vol. 8, pp. 498–99.

Erkan, M., 'Siretü'n Nebi (Tercümetü'ż Żarir)', unpublished PhD dissertation, Ankara University, 1986.

Erünsal, İ., *XV.–XVI. Asır Bayrami-Melamiliği'nin Kaynaklarından Abdurrahman el-Askeri'nin Mir'atu'l-Işk'ı* (Ankara: Türk Tarih Kurumu, 2003).

Es'ad Efendi, *Üss-i Zafer* (Istanbul: Matbaa-i Āmire, 1243/1828).

Es'ad Efendi, *Fatāvā-i Es'ad Efendi*, Suleymaniye Library, MS Kasidecizade 277.

Esad Efendi, *Üss-i Zafer (Yeniçeriliğin Kaldırılmasına Dair)*, ed. M. Arslan (Istanbul: Kitabevi, 2005).

Esad Efendi, *Vak'a-Nüvīs Es'ad Efendi Tarihi*, ed. Z. Yılmazer (Istanbul: OSAV, 2000).

Eşrefoğlu Rūmī, *Müzekki'n-nüfūs*, ed, Abdullah Uçman (Istanbul: İnsan Yayınları, 2013).

Eyüb Sabri Paşa, *Tarih-i Vehhābiyan* (İstanbul: Bedir, 1992).

Faroqhi, S., *Pilgrims and Sultans: the Hajj under the Ottomans, 1517–1683* (London: I. B. Tauris, 1994).

Faroqhi, S., 'Conflict, Accommodation and Long-Term Survival: the Bektaşi Order and the Ottoman State', *Revue des Études Islamiques*, 60 (1992), special issue: *Bektachiyya*, Alexandre Popovic and Gilles Veinstein (eds), pp. 167–84.

Faroqhi, S., 'Conflict, Accommodation and Long-term Survival: the Bektaşi Order and the Ottoman State', in Alexandre Popović (ed.), *Bektachiyya: Études sur l'ordre mystique de Bektachis et les groups relevant de Haji Bektach* (Istanbul: Isis, 1992), pp. 162–80.

Faroqhi, S., 'The Bektashis: a Report on Current Research', in *Bektachiyya: Études sur l'ordre mystique de Bektachis et les groups relevant de Haji Bektach, Revue des Études Islamiques* 60 (Istanbul: Isis, 1992), pp. 9–29.

Faroqhi, S., *Der Bektaschi-Orden in Anatolien (vom späten 15. Jahrhundert bis 1826)* (Vienna: Verlag der Österreichischen Akademie der Wissenschaft, 1981).

Fażlallāh b. Rūzbihān Khunjī-Iṣfahānī, *Tarīkh-i 'ālam-ārā-yi Amīnī*, ed. M. A. 'Āshiq (Tehran: Mīrās̱ Maktūb, 2003).

Felek, Ö., '(Re)creating Image and Identity: Dreams and Visions as a Means of Murad III's Self-Fashioning', in Özgen Felek and Alexander D. Knysh (eds), *Dreams and Visions in Islamic Socities* (Albany, NY: State University of New York Press, 2012), pp. 249–72.

Finkel, C., *Osman's Dream: the History of the Ottoman Empire 1300–1923* (New York: Basic Books, 2005).

Fisher, C. G., 'A Reconstruction of the Pictorial Cycle of the *Siyar-i Nabī* of Murād III', *Ars Orientalis* 14 (1984): 75–94.

Fisher, C. G., 'The Pictorial Cycle of the *Siyer-i Nebi*: A Late Sixteenth-Century Manuscript of the Life of Muhammad', PhD dissertation, Michigan State University, 1981.

Fleischer, C. H., 'Ancient Wisdom and New Sciences: Prophecies at the Ottoman Court in the Fifteenth and Sixteenth Centuries', in Massumeh Farhad and Serpil Bağcı (eds), *Falnama: the Book of Omens* (Washington, DC: Arthur M. Sackler Gallery, Smithsonian Institution, 2009), pp. 232–43.

Fleischer, C. H., 'Shadows of Shadows: Prophecy and Politics in 1530s Istanbul', *International Journal of Turkish Studies* 13/1–2 (2007): 51–62.

Fleischer, C. H., 'Mahdi and Millennium: Messianic Dimensions in the Development of Ottoman Imperial Ideology', in Kemal Çiçek et al. (eds), *The Great Ottoman-Turkish Civilization*. 3 vols (Ankara: Yeni Türkiye, 2000), vol. 3, pp. 42–54.

Fleischer, C. H., 'The Lawgiver as Messiah: the Making of the Imperial Image in the Reign of Suleyman', in Gilles Veinstein (ed.), *Soliman le magnifique et son temps* (Paris: La Documentation Française, 1992), pp. 159–77.

Fleischer, C. H., *Bureaucrat and Intellectual in the Ottoman Empire: The Historian Mustafa Ali, 1541–1600* (Princeton, NJ: Princeton University Press, 1986).

Flemming, B., 'Literary Activities in Mamluk Halls and Barracks', in Myriam Rosen-Ayalon (ed.), *Studies in Memory of Gaston Weit* (Jerusalem: Hebrew University of Jerusalem, 1977), pp. 251–71.

Fletcher, J., 'Integrative History: Parallels and Interconnections in the Early Modern Period, 1500–1800', *Journal of Turkish Studies* 9 (1985): 37–57.

Foley, S., 'Hagiography, Court Records, and Early Modern Sufi Brotherhoods: Shaykh Khalid and Social Movement Theory', in J. Curry and E. S. Ohlander (eds), *Sufism and Society* (London: Routledge, 2012), pp. 50–67.

Fortna, B. C., *Imperial Classroom: Islam, the State, and Education in the Late Ottoman Empire* (Oxford: Oxford University Press, 2002).

Foucault, M., *The Archaeology of Knowledge and the Discourse of Language* (New York: Pantheon, 1972).

Frary, L. J. and M. K. Kozelsky, *Russian–Ottoman Borderlands: the Eastern*

Bibliography

Question Reconsidered (Madison, WI: University of Wisconsin Press, 2014).

Freeze, G. L., 'Handmaiden of the State? The Church in Imperial Russia Reconsidered', *Journal of Ecclesiastical History* 36/1 (1985): 82–102.

Friedman, Y., *The Nuṣayrī-'Alawīs: an Introduction to the Religion, History, and Identity of the Leading Minority in Syria* (Leiden: Brill, 2010).

García-Arenal, M. (ed.), *Conversions islamiques: Identités religieuses en Islam méditerranéen* (Paris: Maisonneuve et Larose, 2001).

Gerber, H., *State, Society, and Law in Islam: Ottoman Law in Comparative Perspective* (Albany, NY: State University of New York Press, 1994).

Gibb, E. J., *History of Ottoman Poetry* (London: Luzac, 1958).

Gibb, H. A. R., 'Lutfī Paşa on the Ottoman Caliphate', *Oriens* 15 (1962): 287–95.

Gladney, D. C. (ed.), *Making Majorities: Constituting the Nation in Japan, Korea, China, Malaysia, Fiji, Turkey, and the United States* (Stanford: Stanford University Press, 1998).

Glassen, E., 'Krisenbewusstsein und Heilserwartung in der islamischen Welt zu Beginn der Neuzeit', in Ulrich Haarmann et al. (eds), *Die islamische Welt zwischen Mittelalter und Neuzeit: Festschrift für Hans Robert Roemer zum 65. Geburtstag* (Wiesbaden: Setiner, 1979), pp. 167–79.

Goffman, D., *The Ottoman Empire and Early Modern Europe* (New York: Cambridge University Press, 2002).

Gölbaşı, E., '"Devil Worshippers" Encounter the State: "Heterodox" Identities, State Building and the Politics of Imperial Integration in the Late Ottoman Empire', in A. Sipahi, D. Derderian and Y. T. Cora (eds), *The Ottoman East in the Nineteenth Century: Societies, Identities and Politics* (London: I. B. Tauris, 2016), pp. 133–55.

Gölbaşı, E., '"Heretik" aşiretler ve II. Abdülhamid rejimi: Zorunlu askerlik meselesi ve ihtida siyaseti odağında Yezidiler ve Osmanlı idaresi', *Tarih ve Toplum – Yeni Yaklaşımlar* 9 (2009): 87–156.

Gölbaşı, E., 'The Yezidis and the Ottoman State: Modern Power, Military Conscription, and Conversion Policies, 1830–1909', MA thesis, Boğaziçi Universitesi, 2008.

Goldstone, J. A., 'The Problem of the "Early Modern" World', *Journal of the Economic and Social History of the Orient* 41/3 (1998): 249–84.

Gölpınarlı, A., *Melamilik ve Melamiler* (Istanbul: Milenyum Yayınları, 2006).

Gölpınarlı, A., *Hurufîlik Metinleri Kataloğu* (Ankara: Türk Tarih Kurumu Basımevi, 1973).

Gölpınarlı, A., 'Bektaşîlîk, Hurufîlik ve Faḍl Allah'ın oldürülmesine düşürülen üç tarih', *Şarkiyat Mecmuası* 5 (1964): 15–22.

Gölpınarlı, A., *Kaygusuz Vizeli Alaaddin* (Istanbul: Remzi Kütüphanesi, 1932).

Gorski, P. D., 'Historicizing the Secularization Debate: Church, State, and Society in Late Medieval and Early Modern Europe', *American Sociological Review* 65 (2000): 138–67.

Grabill, J. L., *Protestant Diplomacy and the Near East: Missionary Influence on American Policy, 1810–1927* (Minneapolis: University of Minnesota Press, 1971).

Gradeva, R., 'A Kadi Court in the Balkans: Sofia in the Seventeenth and Early Eighteenth Centuries', in Christine Woodhead (ed.), *The Ottoman World* (London: Routledge, 2012), pp. 57–71.

Graf, T. P., *The Sultan's Renegades: Christian-European Converts to Islam and the Making of the Ottoman Elite, 1575–1610* (Oxford: Oxford University Press, 2017).

Grehan, J., *Twilight of the Saints* (Oxford: Oxford University Press, 2014).

Grehan, J., 'Smoking and "Early Modern" Sociability: the Great Tobacco Debate in the Ottoman Middle East (Seventeenth to Eighteenth Centuries)', *American Historical Review* 111/5 (2006): 1352–77.

Griffel, F., 'Toleration and Exclusion: al-Shafi'i and al-Ghazali on the Treatment of Apostates', *Bulletin of the School of Oriental and African Studies* 64/3 (2001): 342–5.

Gündoğdu, C. and G. Vural, *Dersim'de Osmanlı Siyaseti: İzāle-i Vahşet, Tashīh-i İtikād ve Tasfiye-i Ezhān* (Istanbul: Kitap Yayınevi, 2013).

Gülten, Sadullah, 'Some Considerations on Usage of the Word Alawite in the Ottoman State' *Alevilik Araştırmaları Dergisi* 6/11 (2016): 27–41.

Güner, S., 'Irak Sābiīlerine Dair Bir Asayiş Dosyası (1873–1898)', *Cumhuriyet Tarihi Araştırmaları Dergisi* 9/18 (2013): 3–28.

Güneş Yağcı, Z., 'Ferah Ali Paşa'nın Soğucak Muhafızlığı (1781–1785)', PhD dissertation, Ondokuz Mayız Üniversitesi, 1998.

Gürkan, E. S., 'Mediating Boundaries: Mediterranean Go-Betweens and Cross-Confessional Diplomacy in Constantinople, 1560–1600', *Journal of Early Modern History* 19/2–3 (2015): 107–28.

Gürtunca, M. F., *Siyer-i Nebi*, 6 vols (Istanbul: Doğuş, 2004).

Hafizović, R., 'A Bosnian Commentator on the *Fusus al-Hikam*', *Journal of the Muhyiddin Ibn 'Arabi Society* 47 (2010): 87–107.

Hagen, G., 'Heroes and Saints in Anatolian Turkish Literature', *Oriente Moderno* 89/2 (2009): 349–61.

Hagen, G., 'Afterword'. in Robert Dankoff, *An Ottoman Mentality: the World of Evliya Çelebi* (Leiden: Brill, 2006), pp. 215–56.

Hagen, G., 'Ottoman Understandings of the World in the Seventeenth Century', in Robert Dankoff, *Evliya Çelebi: An Ottoman Mentality*, 2nd edn (Leiden: Brill, 2006), pp. 207–48.

Hagen, G., 'Some Considerations about the Tergüme-i Darir ve taqdimetü z-zahir, based on Manuscripts in German Libraries', *Journal of Turkish Studies/Türklük Bilgisi Araştırmaları* 26 (2002): 323–37.

Hakiki, '*Irşadname*', Süleymaniye Library, Mihrişah Sultan 203, pp. 43a–58b.

Hallaq, W. B., *Shariah: Theory, Practice, and Transformation* (Cambridge: Cambridge University Press, 2009).

Hallaq, W. B., *The Origin and Evolution of Islamic Law* (Cambridge: Cambridge University Press, 2005).

Bibliography

Hallaq, W. B. 'Apostasy', *Encyclopedia of the Qur'ān* (Brill online, 2001), vol. 1, pp. 119–22.
Hanssen, J., *Fin de siècle Beirut: the Making of an Ottoman Provincial Capital* (Oxford: Oxford University Press, 2005).
Haririzade, Seyyid Mehmed Kemaleddin, *Tibyān Vesāilu'l-Ḥaḳāiḳ fī Beyān Selāsilu'l-Ṭarāiḳ*, 3 vols, Süleymaniye Library, Ibrahim Efendi 430, 431, 432.
Hartmann, R., 'As-Sulami's Risalat al-Malamatija', *Der Islam* 7 (1918): 157–203
Hasluck, Frederick, *Christianity and Islam under the Sultans*, vol. 2 (Oxford: Clarendon Press, 1929).
Hathaway, J., *The Chief Eunuch of the Ottoman Imperial Harem: From African Slave to Power-Broker* (Cambridge: Cambridge University Press, 2018).
Huart, Cl. and Kathleen Burrill, 'Ṣarı 'Abd Allah Efendi', *Encyclopedia of Islam*, 2nd edn (Brill online).
Heffening, W., 'Murtadd', *Encyclopedia of Islam*, 2nd edn (Brill online, 1993), vol. 7, p. 635.
Heinzelmann, T., *Heiliger Kampf oder Landesverteidigung? Die Diskussion um die Einführung der allgemeinen Militärpflicht im Osmanischen Reich 1826–1856* (Frankfurt: Lang, 2004).
Heinzelmann, T., 'Die Auflösung der Janitscharentruppen und ihre historischen Zusammenhänge: Sahhaflarşeyhizade Mehmed Esad Efendis *Üss-i Zafer*', *Asiatische Studien: Zeitschrift der Schweizerischen Asiengesellschaft* 54/3 (2000): 653–75.
Hellie, R., 'The Expanding Role of the State in Russia', in Jarmo Kotilaine and Marshall Poe (eds), *Modernizing Muscovy: Reform and Social Change in Seventeenth-Century Russia* (London: Routledge Curzon, 2004), pp. 27–53
Herzog, C. and R. Motika, 'Orientalism "alla turca": Late 19th/Early 20th Century Ottoman Voyages into the Muslim "Outback"', *Die Welt des Islams*, NS, Ottoman Travels and Travel Accounts from an Earlier Age of Globalization, 40/2 (2000): 139–95.
Heyd, U., *Studies in Old Ottoman Criminal Law*, ed. V. L. Ménage (Oxford: Clarendon Press, 1973).
Heyd, U., 'Some Aspects of the Ottoman *Fetvā*', *BSOAS* 32 (1969): 35–56.
Heyd, U. (trans.), *Ottoman Documents on Palestine, 1552–1615: a Study of the Firman According to the Mühimme Defteri* (Oxford: Clarendon Press, 1960).
Hirschler, K., *Medieval Arabic Historiography: Authors as Actors* (London: Routledge, 2006).
Hodgson, M. G. S., 'Ghulat', *Encyclopedia of Islam*, 2nd edn (Brill online).
Hodgson, M. G. C., *The Venture of Islam: Conscience and History in a World Civilization, vol. 2: The Expansion of Islam in the Middle Periods* (Chicago: University of Chicago Press, 1974).
Holbrook, V. R., 'Ibn Arabi and Ottoman Dervish Traditions: the Melami Supra-Order. Part Two', *Journal of the Muhyiddin Ibn 'Arabi Society* 12 (1992): 15–33.

Holbrook, V. R., 'Ibn Arabi and Ottoman Dervish Traditions: the Melami Supra-Order', *Journal of the Muhyiddin Ibn 'Arabi Society* 9 (1991): 18–35.
Howard, D. A., *A History of the Ottoman Empire* (Cambridge: Cambridge University Press, 2017).
Ibn Ishaq, *Sīrāṭ Rasūl Allāh (The Life of Muhammad)*, ed. Alfred Guillame (Oxford: Oxford University Press, 1955).
İhsanoğlu, E. (ed.), *Osmanlı Devleti ve Medeniyeti Tarihi*, 2 vols (Istanbul: IRCICA, 1998).
Ilic, S., 'Lamekani Hüseyin Efendi', *Diyanet Islam Ansiklopedisi*.
Imber, C. H., 'Malamatiyya, in Ottoman Lands', *Encyclopedia of Islam*, 2nd edn (Brill online).
Imber, C. H., 'Frozen Legitimacy', in Hakan Karateke (ed.), *Legitimizing the Order: the Ottoman Rhetoric of State Power* (Leiden: Brill, 2005), pp. 99–107.
Imber, C., *Ebu's-su'ud: the Islamic Legal Tradition* (Stanford, CA: Stanford University Press, 1997).
Imber, C. H., 'Ideals and Legitimation in Early Ottoman History', in Metin Kunt and Christine Woodhead (eds), *Suleyman the Magnificent and His Age: the Ottoman Empire in the Early Modern World* (Harlow: Longman, 1995), pp. 147–53.
Imber, C., 'Persecution of Ottoman Shiites according to Mühimme Defterleri 1565–1585', *Der Islam* 56 (1979): 245–73.
İnalcık, H., *Devlet-i Aliyye: Tagayyür ve Fesad (1603–1656), vol. 2: Osmanlı İmparatorluğu Üzerine Araştırmalar* (İstanbul: Türkiye İş Bankası Kültür Yayınları, 2014).
İnalcık, H.,, 'How to Read 'Ashik Pasha-zade's History', in *Essays in Ottoman History* (Istanbul: Eren, 1998), pp. 139–56.
İnalcık, H., 'State and Ideology under Sultan Suleyman I', in *The Middle East and the Balkans under the Ottoman Empire: Essays on Economy and Society* (Bloomington, IN: Indiana University Turkish Studies, 1993), pp. 70–96.
İnalcık, H., 'Islamization of Ottoman Laws on Land and Land Tax', in Christa Fragner and Klaus Schwarz (eds), *Osmanistik-Turkologie-Diplomatik* (Berlin: Klaus Schwarz Verlag, 1992), pp. 101–18.
İnalcık, H., 'Military and Fiscal Transformation in the Ottoman Empire, 1600–1700', *Archivum Ottomanicum* 6 (1980): 282–337.
İnalcık, H., *The Ottoman Empire: the Classical Age, 1300–1600* (New York: Praeger, 1973).
İnalcık, H., 'Suleyman the Lawgiver and Ottoman Law', *Archivum Ottomanicum* 1 (1969): 105–38.
Ingrao, C. W., *The Habsburg Monarchy, 1618–1815* (Cambridge: Cambridge University Press, 1994).
Ingrao, C. W. and Yasir Yılmaz, 'Ottoman vs. Habsburg: Motives and Priorities', in Plamen Mitev, Ivan Parvev, Maria Baramova and Vania Racheva (eds), *Empires and Peninsulas: Southeastern Europe between Karlowitz and the Peace of Adrianople, 1699–1829* (Berlin: LIT Verlag, 2010), pp. 5–17.

Bibliography

İpşirli, M., 'Kadızāde Mehmed Tāhir', *Türkiye Diyanet Vakfı İslam Ansiklopedisi (TDVİA)*, 24: 97–8, available at: http://www.islamansiklopedisi.info.

Ishak Efendi, *Kaşifü 'l-esrar ve dafi'u 'l-eşrar* (İstanbul: Yahya Efendi Matba'ası, 1291/1874).

Işın, Ekrem, 'Idris-i Muhtefi' *Dünden Bugüne Istanbul Ansiklopedisi*.

Işın, Ekrem, 'Melamilik', *Dünden Bugüne Istanbul Ansiklopedisi*.

Işın, Ekrem, 'Melamiyye (Ikinci devre Melamileri, Bayramiler)', *Diyanet Islam Ansiklopedisi*.

Iskandar Munshi Beg (d. 1633/4), *The History of Shah 'Abbas the Great: Tarikh-e alamara-ye 'Abbasi* (Boulder, CO: Westview Press, 1978).

Ismail Kemal Bey, *The Memoirs of Ismail Kemal Bey*, ed. S. Story (London: Constable, 1920).

Isutzu, T., *The Concept of Belief in Islamic Theology* (Yokohama: Yurindo, 1965).

Jackson, S. A., *Islamic Law and the State: the Constitutional Jurisprudence of Shihāb al-Dīn al-Qarāfī* (Leiden: Brill, 1996).

Jacob, G., *Beiträge zur Kenntnis des Derwisch-Ordens der Bektaschis* (Berlin: Mayer & Müller, 1908).

Jennings, R. C., 'Kadi, Court, and Legal Procedure in 17th c. Ottoman Kayseri', *Studia Islamica* 48 (1978): 133–72.

Johansen, B., 'Apostasy as Objective and Depersonalized Fact: Two Recent Egyptian Court Judgments', *Social Research* 70/3 (2003): 687–708.

Johansen, B., 'Secular and Religious Elements in Hanafite Law: Function and Limits of the Absolute Character of Government Authority', in Ernst Gellner and J. C. Vatin (eds), *Islam et politique au Maghreb* (Paris: Editions du CNRS, 1981), pp. 281 303.

Kafadar, C., *Between Two Worlds: The Construction of the Ottoman State* (Berkeley: University of California Press, 1995).

Kafadar, C., 'Self and Others: the Diary of a Dervish in Seventeenth-Century Istanbul and First-Person Narratives in Ottoman Literature', *Studia Islamica* 69 (1989): 121–50.

Kafesoğlu, İ., *Türk-İslam Sentezi* (İstanbul: Aydınlar Ocağı, 1985).

Kandemir, M. Y., 'Ka'b el-Ahbar', *Diyanet Islam Ansiklopedisi* (Istanbul: Turkiye Diyanet Vakfi, 2001), vol. 24, pp. 1–3.

Karakaya-Stump, A., *Vefailik, Bektaşilik, Kızılbaşlık: Alevi Kaynaklarını, Tarihini ve Tarihyazımını Yeniden Düşünmek* (Istanbul: Bilgi Univeristy, 2015).

Karakaya-Stump, A., 'The Wafā'iyya, the Bektashiyye and Genealogies of "Heterodox" Islam in Anatolia: Rethinking the Köprülü Paradigm', *Turcica* 44 (2012/13): 279–300.

Karakaya-Stump, A., 'Documents and Buyruk Manuscripts in the Private Archives of Alevi Dede Families: An Overview', *British Journal of Middle Eastern Studies* 37/3 (2010): 273–86.

Karamustafa, A. T., *Sufism: the Formative Period* (Berkeley: University of California Press, 2007).

Karamustafa, A. T, *God's Unruly Friends: Dervish Groups in the Islamic Later*

Middle Period, 1200–1550,, 2nd edn (Salt Lake City: University of Utah Press, 1994; Oxford: One World, 2006).

Karamustafa, A. T., 'Origins of Anatolian Sufism', in Ahmet Yaşar Ocak (ed.), *Sufism and Sufis in Ottoman Society: Sources, Doctrine, Rituals, Turuq, Architecture, Literature and Fine Arts, Modernism* (Ankara: Turkish Historical Society, 2005), pp. 67–95.

Karataş, H., 'The Ottomanization of the Halveti Sufi Order: a Political Story Revisited', *Journal of the Ottoman and Turkish Studies Association* 1/1–2 (2014): 71–89.

Karolewsksi, J., 'What is Heterodox about Alevism? The Development of Anti-Alevi Discrimination and Resentment', *Die Welt des Islams* 48 (2008): 434–56.

Karpat, K. H., *The Politicization of Islam: Reconstructing Identity, State, Faith, and Community in the Late Ottoman State* (Oxford: Oxford University Press, 2001).

Katz, M. H., *The Birth of the Prophet Muhammad: Devotional Piety in Sunni Islam* (London: Routledge, 2007).

Kayabaşı, B., 'Sarban Ahmed Divanı'nda Melamilik', *Turkish Studies* 5/1 (2010): 1123–46.

Kefevi, Maḥmud b. Suleyman, 'Katā'ib A'lam al-Akhyār min Fuqahā Madhhab al-Nu'mān al-Mukhtār', Suleymaniye Library, Asır Efendi 263.

Kemalpaşazade, *Tevârih-i Al-i Osman*, Defter VIII, published by Ahmet Uğur in his *The Reign of Sultan Selim I in the Light of the Selim-nāme Literature* (Berlin: Klaus Schwarz Verlag, 1985).

Kermeli, E., 'The Tobacco Controversy in Early Modern Ottoman Christian and Muslim Discourse', *Hacettepe Üniversitesi Türkiyat Araştırmaları Dergisi* 11/21 (2014): 121–35.

Khoury, R. G., 'Wahb b. Munabbih', *Encyclopedia of Islam* (Brill online), vol. 11, pp. 34–6.

Kieser, H. L., *Nearest East: American Millennialism and Mission to the Middle East* (Philadelphia, PA: Temple University Press, 2010).

Kılıç, M., 'Ebu'l-Hayr Abdulmecid b. Muharrem es-Sivasi'nin (971–1049/1563–1639) Fatiha Tefsiri'nin Tahkiki', MA thesis, Marmara University, 2005.

Kılıç, R., 'Bir Tarikatin Gizli Direnişi: Bayrami-Melamileri veya *Hamzaviler*', *Tasavvuf* 10 (2003): 52–72.

Kliuchevskii, V. O., *A Course in Russian History: the Seventeenth Century* (Armonk, NY: Routledge, 1994).

Knysh, A., '"Orthodoxy" and "Heresy" in Medieval Islam: an Essay in Reassessment', *Muslim World* 83/1 (1993): 48–67.

Koç, Y., 'Early Ottoman Customary Law: the Genesis and Development of Ottoman Codification', in Walter Dostal and Wolfang Kraus (eds), *Shattering Tradition: Custom, Law and the Individual in the Muslim Mediterranean* (London: I. B. Tauris, 2005), pp. 75–121.

Koçunyan, A., *Negotiating the Ottoman Constitution: 1856–1876* (Leuven: Peeters, 2018).

Bibliography

Kohlberg, Ethan, 'al-Rāfiḍa', *Encyclopedia of Islam*, 2nd edn (Brill online, 1993), vol. 8, pp. 386–9.

Kollmann, N. S., *The Russian Empire 1450–1801* (Oxford: Oxford University Press, 2017).

Konrad, F., 'Coping with "the Riff-Raff and the Mob": Representations of Order and Disorder in the Patrona Halil Rebellion (1730)', *Die Welt des Islams* 54 (2014): 363–98.

Köprülüzāde, M. F., *Anadolu'da İslamiyet*, ed. Hasan Aksakal (Istanbul: Alfa, 2017).

Köprülüzāde, M. F., 'Anadolu'da İslamiyet: Türk İstilasından Sonra Anadolu Tarihi Diniyesine Bir Nazar ve Bu Tarihin Menbaları-Mabadı', *Darülfünun Edebiyat Fakültesi Mecmuası*, 2/4 *Eylül* 1338/1920: 281–311.

Köprülüzāde, M. F., 'Anadolu'da İslamiyet (Türk İstilasından Sonra Anadolu Tarihi Diniyesine Bir Nazar ve Bu Tarihin Menbaları-mābadı)', *Darülfünun Edebiyat Fakültesi Mecmuası* 2/5 *Teşrin-i Sani* 1338/1920: 385–420.

Köprülüzāde, M. F., 'Anadolu'da İslamiyet (Türk İstilasından Sonra Anadolu Tarihi Diniyesine Bir Nazar ve Bu Tarihin Menbaları-mābadı)', *Darülfünun Edebiyat Fakültesi Mecmuası* 2/6 *Kānun-ı Sani* 1339/1921: 457–86.

Kramer, Martin, *Arab Awakening and Islamic Revival: the Politics of Ideas in the Middle East* (London: Routledge, 2008).

Krstić, T., 'State and Religion, "Sunnitization" and "Confessionalism" in Süleyman's Time', in P. Fodor (ed.), *Szigetvar 1566: Proceedings of the Commemorative Conference on the Siege of Szigetvar and Suleyman the Magnificent's and Miklos Zrinyi's Death* (Budapest: Hungarian Academy of Sciences, 2018).

Krstić, T., 'From *Shahāda* to *'Aqīda*: Conversion to Islam, Catechization, and Sunnitization in Sixteenth-Century Ottoman Rumeli', in A. C. S. Peacock (ed.), *Islamisation: Comparative Perspectives from History* (Edinburgh: Edinburgh University Press, 2017), pp. 296–314.

Krstić, T., *Contested Conversions to Islam: Narratives of Religious Change in the Early Modern Ottoman Empire* (Stanford, CA: Stanford University Press, 2011).

Krstić, T., 'Illuminated by the Light of Islam and the Glory of the Ottoman Sultanate: Self-Narratives of Conversion to Islam in the Age of Confessionalization', *Comparative Studies in Society and History* 51/1 (2009): 35–63.

Krstić, T. and D. Terzioğlu (eds), *Rethinking Ottoman Sunnitization, 1450s–1700* (Leiden: Brill, forthcoming).

Küçük, H., *The Role of the Bektashis in Turkey's National Struggle* (Leiden: Brill, 2002).

Kurt, Y., 'Muṣṭafā Nūrī', available at: http://www.ottomanhistorians.uchicago.edu.

Kurz, M. (ed.), *Das Osmanische Reich und die Habsburgermonarchie: Akten des Internationalen Kongresses zum 150-jährigen Bestehen des Instituts für*

Österreichische Geschichtsforschung; Wien, 22.–25. September 2004 (Vienna: Oldenbourg, 2005).

Kütükoğlu, B., *Osmanlı-İran Siyasi Münasebetleri* (Istanbul: İstanbul Fetih Cemiyeti, 1993).

Landau, J. M., *The Politics of Pan-Islam: Ideology and Organization* (Oxford: Oxford University Press, 1990).

Langer, R. and Udo Simon, 'The Dynamics of Orthodoxy and Heterodoxy: Dealing with Divergence in Muslim Discourses and Islamic Studies', *Die Welt Des Islams* 48 (2008): 273–88.

Langer, R. et al. (eds), *Ocak und Dedelik: Institutionen religiösen Spezialistentums bei den Aleviten* (Frankfurt: Peter Lang, 2013).

La'lizade A., *Tārīḳat-i 'Aliyye-i Bayrāmiyye'den Taife-i Melamiyye'nin 'An'ane-i Iradetleri ve Keyfiyyet-i Sohbetleri ve Aşk-i Muhabbetullaha Cumleden Ziyade Rağbetleri Beyanındadır* (Istanbul: Mihran Matbaası, 1296/1879).

Le Gall, D., *A Culture of Sufism: Naqshbandis in the Ottoman World (1450–1700)* (New York: State University of New York Press, 2005).

Lewis, G. L., 'Ahmadi, Tadj Al-Din Ibrahim B. Khidr', *Encyclopedia of Islam*, 2nd edn (Brill online), vol. 1, pp. 299–300.

Litvak, M., *Shi'i Scholars of Nineteenth-Century Iraq: the Ulema' of Najaf and Karbala'* (Cambridge: Cambridge University Press, 1998).

Lobachev, S. V., 'Patriarch Nikon's Rise to Power', *The Slavonic and East European Review* 79/2 (2001): 290–307.

Loewen, A., 'Proper Conduct (Adab) is Everything: The Futuwwat-nāmah-i Sulṭānī of Husayn Va'iz-i Kashifi', *Iranian Studies* 36/4 (2003): 543–70.

Louthan, H., *Converting Bohemia: Force and Persuasion in the Catholic Reformation* (Cambridge: Cambridge University Press, 2009).

Lugal, N. and A. Erzi, *Fatih Devrine Ait Münşeat Mecmuası* (İstanbul: İstanbul Matbaası, 1956).

Lyde, S., *The Asian Mystery: Ansaireeh or Nusairis of Syria* (London: Longman, 1860).

MacCulloch, D., *The Reformation: a History* (London: Penguin, 2005).

MacCulloch, D., M. Laven and E. Duffy, 'Recent Trends in the Study of Christianity in Sixteenth-Century Europe', *Renaissance Quarterly* 59 (2006): 697–731.

MacHardy, K. J., *War, Religion and Court Patronage in Habsburg Austria: the Social and Cultural Dimensions of Political Interaction, 1521–1622* (Basingstoke: Palgrave Macmillan, 2003).

Madelung, W., *Religious Trends in Early Islamic Iran* (Albany, NY: Persian Heritage Foundation, 1988).

Madelung, W., 'Early Doctrine Concerning Faith as Reflected in the "Kitāb al-Īmān" of Abū al-Qāsim b. Sallām (d. 224/839)', *Studia Islamica* 32 (1970): 233–54.

Maden, F., 'Yeniçerilik-Bektaşilik İlişkileri ve Yeniçeri İsyanlarında *Bektaşiler*', *Türk Kültürü ve Hacı Bektaş Velī Araştırma Dergisi* 73 (2015): 173–202.

Bibliography

Maden, F., *Bektaşi Tekkelerinin Kapatılması (1826) ve Bektaşiliğin Yasaklı Yılları* (Ankara: Türk Tarih Kurumu, 2013).
Maden, F., 'Hacı Bektaş Veli Tekkesinde Nakşi Şeyhler ve Sırrı Paşa'nın Lāyıhası', *Türk Kültürü ve Hacı Bektaş Velī Araştırma Dergisi* 59 (2011): 159–80.
Makdisi, U., *Artillery of Heaven: American Missionaries and the Failed Conversion of the Middle East* (Ithaca, NY: Cornell University Press, 2009).
Makdisi, U., 'Ottoman Orientalism', *American Historical Review* 107/3 (2002): 768–96.
Mandaville, J. E., 'Usurious Piety: The Cash Waqf Controversy in the Ottoman Empire', *International Journal of Middle East Studies* 10/3 (1979): 289–308.
Marin, I., *Contested Frontiers in the Balkans: Ottoman and Habsburg Rivalries in Eastern Europe* (London: I. B.Tauris, 2012).
Markiewicz, C., 'Europeanist Trends and Islamicate Trajectories in Early Modern Ottoman History', *Past & Present* 239/1 (2018): 265–81.
Martin, B. G., 'A Short History of the Khalwati Order', in Nikki R. Keddie (ed.), *Scholars, Saints, and Sufis: Muslim Religious Institutions since 1500* (Berkeley: University of California Press, 1972).
Massignon, L., 'Ḥulūl'. *Encyclopaedia of Islam*, 2nd edn (Brill online, 1971), vol. 3, pp. 570–71.
Massignon, L. and L. Gardet, 'al-Ḥallaj', *Encyclopedia of Islam*, 2nd edn (Brill online).
Matthee, R. P., *The Politics of Trade in Safavid Iran: Silk for Silver, 1600–1730* (Cambridge: Cambridge University Press, 1999).
Mazower, M., *Salonica, City of Ghosts: Christians, Muslims and Jews, 1430–1950* (New York: Alfred Knopf, 2005).
Mazzaoui, M. M., *Origins of the Ṣafawids: Shīism, Ṣūfism, and the Ġulāt* (Wiesbaden: F. Steiner, 1972).
McChesney, R. D., *Waqf in Central Asia: Four Hundred Years in the History of a Muslim Shrine, 1480–1889* (Princeton, NJ: Princeton University Press, 1991).
Mehmed Amiki, 'Eyyuhe'l-Veled', Süleymaniye Library, Halet Efendi 764.
Mehmed Arif, *Başımıza Gelenler* (Cairo: Matbaatü'l-Maarif, 1321/1903).
Mehmed Arif, *Başımıza Gelenler* (Latinised modern Turkish edn), 3 vols (Istanbul: Tercüman, n.d.)
Mehmed Nazmi Efendi, *Osmanlılar'da Tasavvufi Hayat-Halvetilik Örneği-Hediyyetü'l- İhvan*, ed. O. Türer (Istanbul: Insan Yayınları, 2005).
Mélikoff, I., *Hadji Bektach: un mythe et ses avatars: genèse et évolution du soufisme populaire en Turqui* (Leiden: Brill, 1998).
Mélikoff, I., *Sur les traces du soufisme turc: recherches sur l'Islam populaire en Anatolie* (Istanbul: Editions Isis, 1992).
Mélikoff, I., 'L'ordre des Bektachi après 1826', *Turcica. Révue des Études Turques* 15 (1983): 155–71.
Melis, N., 'A Seventeenth-Century Hanafi Treatise on Rebellion and Jihād in the Ottoman Age', *Eurasian Studies* 11/2 (2003): 215–26.

Melvin-Khouski, M., 'Ibn Turka', *Encyclopedia of Islam*, 3rd edn (Brill online).
Meyer, J. H., *Turks across Empires: Marketing Muslim Identity in the Russian–Ottoman Borderlands, 1856–1914* (Oxford: Oxford University Press, 2014).
Meyer, M. and Konstantin Zhukov, 'The Present State of Ottoman Studies in Saint Petersburg and Moscow', *Turkish Historical Review* 5/1 (2014): 115–27.
Michels, G. B., *At War with the Church: Religious Dissent in Seventeenth-Century Russia* (Stanford, CA: Stanford University Press, 2000).
Miller, A. and Alfred J. Rieber (eds), *Imperial Rule* (Budapest: Central European University Press, 2004).
Minadoi, G. T., *The History of the Warres between the Turkes and Persians*, trans. Abraham Harthwell (Tehran: Islamic Revolution Publications and Educational Organization, 1976).
Minorsky, V., 'Shaykh Bali-Efendi on the Safavids', *Bulletin of the School of Oriental and African Studies* 20 (1957): 437–50.
Mir-Kasimov, O., *Words of Power: Hurufi Teachings between Shi'ism and Sufism in Medieval Islam* (London: I. B. Tauris, in Association with the Institute of Ismaili Studies, 2015).
Moin, A., *The Millennial Sovereign: Sacred Kingship and Sainthood in Islam* (New York: Columbia University Press, 2012).
Moosa, Matti, *Extremist Shiites: the Ghulāt Sects* (Syracuse, NY: Syracuse University Press, 1988).
Morimoto, K., 'How to Behave toward *Sayyid*s and *Sharif*s: a Trans-Sectarian Tradition of Dream Accounts', in K. Morimoto (ed.), *Sayyids and Sharifs in Muslim Societies: the Living Links to the Prophet* (London: Routledge, 2012), pp. 15–36.
Murphey, R., 'Continuity and Discontinuity in Ottoman Administrative Theory and Practice during the Late Seventeenth Century', *Poetics Today* 14 (1993): 419–43.
Mustafa Nuri Paşa, *Abede-i İblis* (Istanbul: Matbaa-i İctihad, 1328/1910).
Mustafa Nuri Paşa, *Die Teufelsanbeter oder ein Blick auf die widerspenstige Sekte der Jeziden: Ein Beitrag zur Kenntnis der Jeziden*, trans. T. Menzel, in Hugo Grothe (ed.), *Meine Vorderasienexpedition 1906 und 1907: Die fachwissenschaftlichen Ergebnisse*, vol. 1.1 (Leipzig: Hiersemann, 1911), pp. 90–211.
Mustafa Nuri Paşa, *Netāyicü'l-Vukū'āt: Kurumlarıyla Osmanlı Tarihi I–IV*, ed. Y. Kurt (Ankara: Birleşik Yayınevi, 2008).
Müstakimzade, Sadeddin Süleyman, 'Risale-i Melamiyye-i Bayramiyye', Istanbul University Library, Ibnul Emin 3357.
Mutlu, Ş. (ed.), *Yeniçeri Ocağının Kaldırılışı ve II. Mahmud'un Edirne Seyahati: Mehmed Daniş Bey ve Eserleri* (Istanbul: Edebiyat Fakültesi Basımevi, 1994).
Nakash, Y., 'The Conversion of Iraq's Tribes to Shiism', *International Journal of Middle East Studies* 26/3 (1994): 443–63.
Nasr, S. H., 'Shi'ism and Sufism: Their Relationship in Essence and in History', *Religious Studies* 6/3 (1970): 229–42.

Bibliography

Natho, K. I., *Circassian History* (Bloomington, IN: Xlibris, 2009).
Necipoğlu, G., *The Age of Sinan: Architectural Culture in the Ottoman Empire* (Princeton, NJ: Princeton University Press, 2005).
Neşri, Mehmed, *Kitāb-ı Cihan-nümā, Neşrī Tarihi*, trans. Faik Reşit Unat and Mehmed A. Köymen, 2 vols (Ankara: Türk Tarih Kurumu Basımevi, 1949).
Nizri, M., *Ottoman High Politics and the Ulema Household* (Basingstoke: Palgrave Macmillan, 2014).
Norris, H. T., 'The Hurufi Legacy of Fadlullah of Astarabad', in Leonard Lewisohn (ed.), *The Heritage of Sufism*, vol. 2 (Oxford: Oneworld, 1999), pp. 87–97.
Ocak, A. Y., 'Balım Sultan', in *Türkiye Diyanet Vakfı İslam Ansiklopedisi (TDVİA)*, vol. 5, pp. 17–18, available at: http://www.islamansiklopedisi.info.
Ocak, A. Y., *Perspectives and Reflections on Religious and Cultural Life in Medieval Anatolia* (Istanbul: Isis Press, 2012).
Ocak, A. Y., *Osmanlı Toplumunda Tasavvuf ve Sufiler: Kaynaklar, Doktrin, Ayin ve Erkān, Tarikatlar, Edebiyat, Mimari, Güzel Sanatlar, Modernism* (Ankara: Türk Tarih Kurumu Yayınları, 2005).
Ocak, A. Y., 'Islam in the Ottoman Empire: a Sociological Framework for a New Interpretation', *International Journal of Turkish Studies* 9/1–2 (2003): 183–98.
Ocak, A. Y., *Alevi ve Bektaşî inançlarının İslam öncesi temelleri* (Istanbul: Iletisim, 2000).
Ocak, A. Y., *Türkler, Türkiye ve İslam* (İstanbul: Iletisim, 1999).
Ocak, A. Y., *Osmanlı Toplumunda Zındıklar ve Mülhidler (15. ve 17. Yüzyıllar)* (Istanbul: Tarih Vakfı Yurt Yayınları, 1998).
Ocak, A. Y., 'XVI–XVII. Yüzyıllarda Bayrami Melamileri ve Osmanlı Yönetimi', *Belleten* 61 (1997): 93–110.
Ocak, A. Y., *Türkiye'de tarihin saptırılması sürecinde Türk Sūfīliğine bakışlar: Ahmed-i Yesevī, Mevlānā Celāleddin-i Rūmī, Yunus Emre, Hacı Bektaş-ı Velī, ahīlik, Alevīlik-Bektaşīlık: yaklaşım, yöntem ve yorum denemeleri* (Istanbul: Iletisim, 1996).
Ocak, A. Y., *Kültür Tarihi Kaynağı Olarak Menakıbnameler (Metodolojik Bir Yaklaşım)* (Ankara: Türk Tarih Kurumu, 1992).
Ocak, A. Y., *Osmanlı İmparatorluğu'nda marjinal Sūfīlik: Kalenderīler: XIV–XVII. Yüzyıllar* (Ankara: Türk Tarih Kurumu Basımevi, 1992).
Ocak, A. Y., 'Kanuni Sultan Süleyman Devrinde Osmanlı Resmi Düşüncesine Karşı Bir Tepki Hareketi: Oğlan Şeyh Ismail-i Maşuki', *Osmanlı Araştırmaları* 10 (1990): 49–58.
Ocak, A. Y., *Islam-Türk inançlarında Hızır yahut Hızır-İlyas kültü* (Ankara: Türk Kültürünü Araştırma Enstitüsü, 1985).
Ocak, A. Y., *XIII. Yüzyılda Anadolu'da Baba Resūl (Babaīler) İsyanı ve Anadolu'nun İslamlaşması tarihindeki yeri* (Istanbul; Dergah, 1980).
Öçal, Ş., *Kemal Paşazade'nin Felsefi ve Kelami Görüşleri* (Ankara: Kültür Bakanlığı, 2000).
Olsson, T., 'The Gnosis of Mountaineers and Townspeople: the Religion of the Syrian Alawites, or the Nuṣayrīs', in E. Özdalga and C. Raudevere (eds),

Alevi Identity: Cultural, Religious and Social Perspectives (London: Routledge Couzon, 2003), pp. 167–83.

Öngören, Reşat, 'Mecdüddin el-Bağdadi', *Diyanet Islam Ansiklopedisi*.

Orbay, A. (ed.), *The Sultan's Portrait: Picturing the House of Osman* (Istanbul: Isbank, 2000).

Oren, M., *Power, Faith and Fantasy: America in the Middle East, 1776 to the Present* (New York: Norton, 2007).

Ortaylı, İ., 'Alevīlik, Nusayrīlik ve Bābıālī', in *Batılılaşma Yolunda* (Istanbul: Merkez Kitaplar, 2007), pp. 161–9.

Ortaylı, İ., '19. yüzyılda heterodox dinī gruplar ve Osmanlı idaresi', in *Batılılaşma Yolunda* (Istanbul: Merkez Kitaplar, 2007), pp. 156–61.

Oytan, M. T., *Bektaşiliğin İçyüzü* (Istanbul: Demos Yayınları, 2007).

Öz, Baki, *Alevilik ile İlgili Osmanlı Belgeleri* (Istanbul: Can, 1996).

Öz, M., 'Rāfızīler', *Türkiye Diyanet Vakfı İslam Ansiklopedisi* (*TDVİA*), 34 (2018): 396–7, available at: http://www.islamansiklopedisi.info.

Özbilgen, E., *Osmanlı'nın Balkanlar'dan Çekilişi: Süleyman Hüsnü Paşa ve Dönemi* (Istanbul: İz, 2006).

Özcan, A. (ed.), *Kānūnnāme-i Āl-i Osman* (İstanbul: Kitabevi, 2003).

Özdemir, A. R., 'Alevilik ve Ehl-i Hak (Yaresan): Benzerlikler ve Farklılıklar', *Alevilik Araştırmaları Dergisi/Journal of Alevi Studies* 10 (2015): 253–85.

Özege, S., *Eski Harflerle Basılmış Türkçe Eserler Kataloğu* (Istanbul: Fatih Yayınevi Matbaası, 1973).

Özel, O., *The Collapse of Rural Order in Ottoman Anatolia: Amasya 1576–1643* (Leiden: Brill, 2016).

Özel, O., 'The Reign of Violence: The Celalis, c. 1550–1700', in Christine Woodhead (ed.), *The Ottoman World* (London: Routledge, 2011), pp. 184–202.

Öztürk, N., 'Islamic Orthodoxy among the Ottomans in the Seventeenth Century with Special Reference to the Qadi-Zade Movement', unpublished PhD dissertation, University of Edinburgh, 1981.

Pakalın, M. Z., *Osmanlı Tarih Deyimleri ve Terimleri Sözlüğü*, 3 vols (Istanbul: Milli Eğitim, 1983).

Pancaroğlu, O., 'The Itinerant Dragon-Slayer: Forging Paths of Image and Identity in Medieval Anatolia', *Gesta* 43/2 (2004): 151–64.

Paret, R., *Die Legendare Maghazi-Literatur, Arabische Dichtungen uber die Muslimischen Kriegszuge zu Muhammeds Zeit* (Tubingen: J. C. B. Mohr, 1930).

Parker, G., *Global Crisis: War, Climate Change and Catastrophe in the Seventeenth Century* (New Haven, CT: Yale University Press, 2013).

Parker, G. and Lesley M. Smith (eds), *The General Crisis of the Seventeenth Century* (London: Routledge, 1978).

Pavlov, A. P., 'Fedor Ivanovich and Boris Godunov (1584–1605)', in Maureen Perrie (ed.), *The Cambridge History of Russia, vol. 1: From Early Rus' to 1689* (Cambridge: Cambridge University Press, 2008), pp. 245–64.

Peacock, A. C. S. and S. N. Yıldız (eds), *Islamic Literature and Intellectual Life in Fourteenth- and Fifteenth-Century Anatolia* (Würzburg: Ergon, 2016).

Bibliography

Peacock, A. C. S., B. De Nicola and S. N. Yıldız (eds) *Islam and Christianity in Medieval Anatolia* (Farnham: Ashgate, 2015).

Pellat, C., 'al-Baṣra', *Encyclopedia of Islam*, 2nd edn (Brill online).

Peters, R., 'What does It Mean to be an Official Madhhab? Hanafism and the Ottoman Empire', in Peri Bearman, Rudolph Peters and Frank E. Vogel (eds), *The Islamic School of Law: Evolution, Devolution, and Progress* (Cambridge, MA: Harvard Series in Islamic Law, 2005), pp. 147–58.

Peters, R. 'The Battered Dervishes of Bab Zuwayla: a Religious Riot in Eighteenth-Century Cairo', in Nehemia Levtzion and John O. Voll (eds), *Eighteenth-Century Renewal and Reform in Islam* (Syracuse, NY: Syracuse University Press, 1987), pp. 93–115.

Peters, R. and G. J. J. De Rries, 'Apostasy in Islam', *Die Welt des Islam* 17/1–4 (1976/7): 1–25.

Pfeifer, H., 'Encounter after the Conquest: Literary Salons in Sixteenth-Century Ottoman Damascus', *International Journal of Middle East Studies* 47/2 (2015): 219–39.

Pfeiffer, J., 'Confessional Ambiguity vs. Confessional Polarization: Politics and the Negotiation of Religious Boundaries in the Ilkhanate', in Judith Pfeiffer (ed.), *Politics, Patronage, and the Transmission of Knowledge in 13th–15th Century Tabriz* (Leiden: Brill, 2014).

Pfeiffer, J., 'Confessional Polarization in the 17th Century Ottoman Empire and Yūsuf ibn Ebī 'Abdü'd-Deyyān's Keşfü'l-Esrār fī ilzāmi'l-Yehūd ve'l-ahbār', in Camilla Adang and Sabine Schmidtke (eds), *Contacts and Controversies between Muslims, Jews and Christians in the Ottoman Empire and Pre-Modern Iran* (Würzburg: Ergon, 2010), pp. 15–55.

Philliou, C., 'Communities on the Verge: Unravelling the Phanariot Ascendancy in Ottoman Governance', *Comparative Studies in Society and History* 51/1 (2009): 151–81.

Pistor-Hatam, A., 'Tanzīmāt oder ittiḥād? Zwei Konzepte Osmanisch-Persischer Einigung', *Turcica. Révue des Études Turques* 27 (1995): 247–61.

Pistor-Hatam, A., 'The Persian Newspaper *Akhtar* as a Transmitter of Ottoman Political Ideas', in Thierry and Fariba Zarinebaf-Shahr (eds), *Les Iraniens d'Istanbul* (Istanbul: Institut Français de Recherches en Iran, 1993), pp. 141–7.

Poe, M., 'The Central Government and its Institutions', in Maureen Perrie (ed.), *The Cambridge History of Russia, vol. 1: From Early Rus' to 1689* (Cambridge: Cambridge University Press, 2008), pp. 435–63.

Poonawala, I., 'Ta'wīl', *Encyclopedia of Islam*, 2nd edn (Brill online, 2000), vol. 10, pp. 390–2.

Pretzl, O., *Die Streitschrift des Ġazālī gegen die Ibāḥīja* (Munich: Verlag der Bayerischen Akademie der Wissenschaften, 1933).

Rafeq, A. K., 'The Opposition of the Azhar 'Ulemā to Ottoman Laws and its Significance in the History of Ottoman Egypt', in *Études sur les villas du Proche-Orient XVIe–XIXe Siècle: Homage à André Raymond* (Damascus: Institute français d'études arabes de Damas, 2001). pp. 43–54.

Reinhard, W., 'Gegenreformation als Modernisierung', *Archiv für Reformationsgeschichte* 68 (1997): 226–52.

Reinkowski, M., *Die Dinge der Ordnung. Eine vergleichende Untersuchung über die osmanische Reformpolitik des 19. Jahrhunderts* (Munich: Oldenbourg, 2005).

Repp, R. C., 'Qānūn and Sharī'a in the Ottoman Context', in Aziz al-Azmeh (ed.), *Islamic Law: Social and Historical Contexts* (London: Routledge, 1988), pp. 124–45.

Repp, R. C., *The Mufti of Istanbul: a Study in the Development of the Ottoman Learned Hierarchy* (London: Ithaca Press, 1986).

Reynolds, M. A., *Shattering Empires: the Clash and Collapse of the Ottoman and Russian Empires 1908–1918* (Cambridge: Cambridge University Press, 2011).

Richter, J., *A History of Protestant Missions in the Near East* (London: Oliphant, 1910).

Robarts, A., *Migration and Disease in the Black Sea Region: Ottoman–Russian Relations in the Late Eighteenth and Early Nineteenth Centuries* (London: Bloomsbury Academic, 2016).

Rosenthal, F., 'Al-Bakri', *Encyclopedia of Islam*, 2nd edn (Brill online), vol. 2, pp. 964–5.

Roshwald, A., *Ethnic Nationalism and the Fall of Empires: Central Europe, the Middle East and Russia, 1914–23* (London: Routledge, 2000).

Ross, E. D., 'The Early Years of Shāh Ismaʻīl, Founder of the Safavi Dynasty', *Journal of the Royal Asiatic Society of Great Britain and Ireland* 2 (1896): 249–340.

Rothman, E. N., 'Dragomans and "Turkish Literature": the Making of a Field of Inquiry', *Oriente Moderno* 93/2 (2013): 390–421.

Rubin, U., 'Nur Muhammadi', *Encyclopedia of Islam*, 2nd edn (Brill online), vol. 8, p. 125.

Rubin, U., *The Eye of the Beholder: the Life of Muhammad as Viewed by the Early Muslims, a Textual Analysis* (Princeton, NJ: Darwin Press, 1995).

Rubin, U., 'Pre-existence and Light: Aspects of the Concept of Nur Muhammad', *Israel Oriental Studies* 5 (1975): 62–119.

Ṣafayi, M., *Tezkire-i Ṣafayi*, ed. Pervin Çapan (Ankara: Atatürk Kültür Merkezi Başkanlığı Yayınları, 2005).

Safi, O., *The Politics of Knowledge in Premodern Islam: Negotiating Ideology and Religious Inquiry* (Chapel Hill: University of North Carolina Press, 2006).

Şahin, H., 'Mutasavvıf Bir Osmanlı Bürokratı: La'lizade Abdülbaki Efendi', *Türklük Araştırmaları Dergisi* 18 (2006): 101–22.

Şahin, İ. and F. Emecen (eds), *II. Bayezid Dönemine Ait 906/1501 Tarihli Ahkam Defteri* (İstanbul: Türk Dünyası Araştırmaları Vakfı, 1994).

Şahin, K., 'From Frontier Principality to Early Modern Empire: Limitations and Capabilities of Ottoman Governance', in William Caferro (ed.), *The Routledge History of the Renaissance* (London: Routledge, 2017), pp. 321–36.

Bibliography

Şahin, K., *Empire and Power in the Reign of Süleyman: Narrating the Sixteenth-Century Ottoman World* (Cambridge: Cambridge University Press, 2013).

Salibi, K. and Yusuf K. Khoury (eds), *The Missionary Herald: Reports from Syria 1819–1870*, 5 vols (Beirut: Royal Institute for Inter-Faith Studies, 1997).

Sarasin, P., *Geschichtswissenschaft und Diskursanalyse* (Frankfurt: Suhrkamp, 2003).

Saray, M., *Türk – İran Münasebetlerinde Şiiliğin Rolü* (Ankara: Türk Kültürünü Araştırma Enstitüsü Yayınları, 1990).

Sariyannis, M., '"Mob", "Scamps" and Rebels in Seventeenth-Century Istanbul: Some Remarks on Ottoman Social Vocabulary', *International Journal of Turkish Studies* 11/1–2 (2005): 1–15.

Sarmiento, D. F., *Facundo: Civilization and Barbarism*, trans. Kathleen Ross (Berkeley: University of California Press, 2004);

Sarı Abdullah, *Şemerātu'l-Fuad fi'l-Mebde' ve'l-Me'ad* (Istanbul: Matba'a-yi Amire, 1288/1871).

Sarı Abdullah, 'Cevheretu'l-Bidaye ve Durratu'n-Nihaye', Istanbul University Library, TY 3792.

Sarı Abdullah, 'Mir'atu'l-Aṣfīya' fī Ṣifati'l-Malamatiyyati'l-Akhfīya' va 'Uluv Şani'l- Evliya', Süleymaniye Library, Halet Efendi 296.

Sarı Abdullah, 'Nasiḥatu'l- Muluk Tarġīben li Ḥusni's-Suluk', Süleymaniye Library, Hekimoğlu Ali Paşa 679.

Sato, T., *State and Rural Society in Medieval Islam: Sultans, Muqta's and Fallahun* (Leiden: Brill, 1997).

Sato, T., *The Syrian Coastal Town of Jabala: Its History and Present Situation* (Tokyo: Institute for the Study of Languages and Cultures of Asia and Africa, 1988).

Savaş, Saim, *XVI. Asırda Anadolu'da Alevilik* (Istanbul, Vadi, 2002).

Schaebler, B., 'Civilizing Others: Global Modernity and the Local Boundaries (French/German/Ottoman and Arab) of Savagery', in Birgit Schaebler and Leif Stenberg (eds), *Globalization and the Muslim World: Culture, Religion, and Modernity* (Syracuse, NY: Syracuse University Press, 2004), pp. 3–31.

Scherberger, M., 'The Confrontation between Sunni and Shi'i Empires: Ottoman–Safavid Relations between the Fourteenth and the Seventeenth Century', in Ofra Bengio and Meir Litvak (eds), *The Sunna and Shi'a in History: Division and Ecumenism in the Muslim Middle East* (New York: Palgrave, 2011), pp. 51–67.

Schilling, H., 'Confessionalization: Historical and Scholarly Perspectives of a Comparative and Interdisciplinary Paradigm', in John M. Headley, Hans J. Hillerbrand and Anthony J. Papalas (eds), *Confessionalization in Europe, 1555–1700: Essays in Honour and Memory of Bodo Nischan* (Farnham: Ashgate, 2004), pp. 21–36.

Schilling, H., 'Confessional Europe', in Thomas A. Brady, Heiko A Obermon and James D. Tracy (eds), *Handbook of European History, 1400–1600: Late Middle Ages, Renaissance and Reformation, vol. 2: Visions, Programs and Outcomes* (Leiden: Brill, 1995), pp. 641–81.

Schilling, H., 'Confessionalization in the Empire: Religious and Societal Change in Germany between 1555 and 1620', in Heinz Schilling (ed.), *Religion, Political Culture and the Emergence of Early Modern Society: Essays in Germany and Dutch History* (Leiden: Brill, 1992), pp. 205–45.

Schilling, H., *Konfessionskonflikt und Staatsbildung* (Gütersloh: Gütersloher Verlag, 1981).

Schimmel, A., 'Shams-i Tabriz(i)', *Encyclopedia of Islam*, 2nd edn (Brill online).

Schimmel, A., *Mystical Dimensions of Islam* (Chapel Hill: University of North Carolina Press, 1975).

Schimmel, A., 'The Ornament of Saints: the Religious Situation in Pre-Safavid Times', *Iranian Studies* 7 (1974): 88–111.

Schmitz, M., 'Ka'b al-Ahbar', *Encyclopedia of Islam*, 2nd edn (Brill online), vol. 4, pp. 316–17.

Selaniki, Mustafa, *Tārih-i Selānikī* (İstanbul, 1281).

Şem'dani-zade Fındıklı Süleyman Efendi, *Mür'i't-Tevarih*, ed. Münir Aktepe (İstanbul: Edebiyat Fakültesi Matbaası, 1980).

Şener, Cemal and Ahmet Hezarfen (eds), *Osmanli Arşivi'nde, Muhimme ve Irade defterleri'nde, Aleviler-Bektasiler: 130 adet orjinal belge* (Istanbul: Karacaahmet Sultan Kultur Dernegi, 2002).

Sertoğlu, M., 'İstanbul'da Gizli Idris', *Türk Kültürü* 279 (1986): 437–41.

Shaw, S. and E. K. Shaw, *History of the Ottoman Empire and Modern Turkey, vol. 2: Reform, Revolution, and Republic: the Rise of Modern Turkey 1808–1975* (Cambridge: Cambridge University Press, 1977).

Sheikh, M., *Ottoman Puritanism and its Discontents: Ahmad Al-Rumi Al-Aqhisari and the Qadizadelis* (Oxford: Oxford University Press, 2016).

Shoshan, B., *Popular Culture in Medieval Cairo* (Cambridge: Cambridge University Press, 1993).

Silverstein, B., 'Sufism and Governmentality in the Late Ottoman Empire', *Comparative Studies of South Asia, Africa and the Middle East* 29/2 (2009): 171–85.

Sipahi, A., D. Derderian and Y. T. Cora (eds), *The Ottoman East in the Nineteenth Century: Societies, Identities and Politics* (London: I. B. Tauris, 2016).

Şişman, C., *The Burden of Silence: Sabbatai Sevi and the Evolution of the Ottoman-Turkish Dönmes* (New York: Oxford University Press, 2015).

Sohrweide, H., 'Der Sieg der Safaviden in Persien und seine Rückwirkungen auf die Schiiten Anatoliens im 16. Jahrhundert', *Der Islam* 41 (1965): 95–223.

Somel, S. A., *The Modernization of Public Education in the Ottoman Empire, 1839–1908: Islamization, Autocracy and Discipline* (Leiden, Brill, 2001).

Somel, S. A., 'Osmanlı Modernleşme Döneminde Periferik Nüfus Grupları', *Toplum ve Bilim* 83 (1999/2000): 178–201.

Soysal, A. A., 'XVII. Yüzyılda Bir Bayrami-Melami Kutbu: Oğlan(lar) Seyh(i) Ibrahim Efendi', unpublished PhD dissertation, Hacetepe University, 2005.

Soyyer, A. Y., *19. Yüzyılda Bektaşīlik* (Istanbul: Frida Yayınları, 2012).

Bibliography

Spielman, J. P., *The City and the Crown: Vienna and the Imperial Court, 1600–1740* (West Lafayette, IN: Purdue University Press, 1993).

Stewart, D., 'The Ottoman Execution of Zayn al-Dīn al-'Āmilī,' *Die Welt des Islams* NS The Dynamics of Orthodoxy and Heterodoxy in Islam 48/3–4 (2008): 289–347.

Stewart, D., 'The Doctorate of Islamic Law in Mamluk Egypt and Syria', in Jospeh E. Lowry, Devin J. Stewart and Shawkat M. Toorawa (eds), *Law and Education in Medieval Islam: Studies in Memory of Professor George Makdisi* (Cambridge: E. J. W. Gibb Memorial Trust, 2004), pp. 45–90.

Strauss, G., *Luther's House of Learning: Indoctrination of the Young in the German Reformation* (Baltimore, MD: Johns Hopkins University Press, 1978).

Strohmeyer, A. and N. Spannenberger (eds), *Frieden und Konfliktmanagement in interkulturellen Raumen: Das Osmanische Reich und die Habsburgermonarchie in der Fruhen Neuzeit* (Stuttgart: Franz Steiner, 2013).

Subrahmanyam, S., 'Turning the Stones Over: Sixteenth-Century Millenarianism from the Tagus to the Ganges', *Indian Economic and Social History Review* 40/2 (2003): 129–61.

Subrahmanyam, S., 'Connected Histories: Notes towards a Reconfiguration of Early Modern Eurasia', *Modern Asian Studies* 31/3 (1997): 735–62.

Süleyman Hüsnü Paşa, *Hiss-i İnkılâb Yahud Sultan Abdülazizin Hal'i ile Sultan Murad-i Hamisin Cülusu* (Istanbul: Tanin Matbaası, 1326/1910).

Süleymaniye Manuscript Library, Özel Collection, Doc. No. 626.

Sungu, İ., 'Mahmud II'nin İzzet Molla ve Asākir-I Mansūre Hakkında Bir Hattı', *Tarih Vesikaları* 3/1 (1941): 162–83.

Sun'ullah Efendi, *Fetāvā*, Suleymaniye Library, MS Resid Efendi 269.

Süreyya, M., *Sicill-i Osmanī 3* (Istanbul: Numune Matbaacılık, 1996).

Sviri, S., 'Ḥakim Tirmidhi and the *Malamati* Movement in Early Sufism', in Leonard Lewisohn (ed.), *The Heritage of Sufism*, vol. 1 (Oxford: Oneworld, 1999), pp. 583–613

Tāhir, Bursalı Mehmet, *Osmanlı Müellifleri. 1.* Cild. (Istanbul: Meral Yayıncılık, 1972).

Tanındı, Z., *Siyer-i Nebi: İslam Tasvir Sanatında Hz. Muhammed'in Hayatı* (Istanbul: Hürriyet Vakfı Yayınları, 1984).

Tansel, F. A., 'Oğlanlar Şeyhi İbrahim Efendi ve Devriyesi', *Ankara Üniversitesi İlahiyat Fakültesi Dergisi (AÜİFD)* 17 (1969): 187–99.

Tansel, S., *Yavuz Sultan Selim* (Ankara: Milli Eğitim Bakanlığı Yayınları, 1969).

Tatcı, M., 'Hayretī', *Türkiye Diyanet Vakfı İslam Ansiklopedisi (TDVİA)*, vol. 17, pp. 61–2, available at: http://www.islamansiklopedisi.info.

Tek, A. (ed.), *Melamet Risaleleri: Bayrami-Melamiliği'ne Dair* (Bursa: Emin Yayınları, 2007).

Tek, Abdurrezzak, 'Mustakimzade Süleyman Sadeddin'in Risale-i Melamiyye-i Bayramiyye Adlı Eserinin Metni ve Tahlili', MA thesis, Uludağ University, 2000.

Tekindag, Ş., 'Yeni Kaynak ve Vesikaların Işığı Altında Yavuz Sultan Selim'in İran Seferi', *Tarih Dergisi* 22 (1968): 53–6.
Telci, C., 'Hamza Bali ve Hamzavīlere Dair', *Prilozi* 46 (1997): 115–29.
Terzioğlu, D., 'Where 'Ilm-i Ḥāl Meets Catechism: Islamic Manuals of Religious Instruction in the Ottoman Empire in the Age of Confessionalization', *Past & Present* 220/1 (2013): 79–114.
Terzioğlu, D., 'How to Conceptualize Ottoman Sunnitization: a Historiographical Discussion', *Turcica* 44 (2012/13): 301–38.
Terzioğlu, D., 'Sufis in the Age of State-building and Confessionalization', in Christine Woodhead (ed.), *The Ottoman World* (London: Routledge, 2012), pp. 86–103.
Terzioğlu, D., 'Sunna-minded Sufi Preachers in the Service of the Ottoman State: the *Nasīhatnāme* of Hasan Addressed to Murad IV', *Archivum Ottomanicum* 27 (2010): 241–79
Terzioğlu, D., 'Sufi and Dissident in the Ottoman Empire: Niyazī-i Misrī (1618–1694)', unpublished PhD dissertation, Harvard University, 1999.
Teubner, J. K., ''Ayn al-Kudat al-Hamadhani', *Encyclopedia of Islam*, 2nd edn (Brill online).
Tezcan, B., 'The New Order and the Fate of the Old: the Historiographical Construction of an Ottoman Ancien Régime in the Nineteenth Century', in Peter Bang and Christopher Bayly (eds), *Tributary Empires in Global History* (Basingstoke: Palgrave Macmillan 2011), pp. 74–95.
Tezcan, B., *The Second Ottoman Empire: Political and Social Transformation in the Early Modern World* (Cambridge: Cambridge University Press, 2010).
Tezcan, B., 'Ottoman Mevali as "Lords of the Law"', *Journal of Islamic Studies* 20/3 (2009): 383–407.
Thomas, K., *Religion and the Decline of Magic* (London: Weidenfeld and Nicolson, 1971).
Tibawi, A., *American Interests in Syria: a Study of Educational, Literary and Religious Work* (Oxford: Clarendon Press, 1966).
Toledano, E., 'Turkish Nationalism and Islamic Faith-Based Politics: Historical and Contemporary Perspectives', in Anita Shapira, Yedidia Z. Stern and Alexander Yakobson (eds), *The Nation State and Religion: the Resurgence of Faith* (Brighton: Sussex Academic Press, 2013), pp. 101–18.
Tosun, M. D., 'Çeçenzade Hasan Paşa'nın Abaza ve Çerkes Kabileleri ile İlişkileri', available at: https://muratdursuntosun.wordpress.com/2014/04/03/cecenzade-haci-hasan-pasanin-abaza-ve-cerkes-kabileleri-ile-iliskileri.
Trimingham, J. S., *The Sufi Orders in Islam* (Oxford: Oxford University Press, [1978] 1998).
Tulasoğlu, G., 'Türk-Sünnī Kimlik İnşasının II. Mahmud Dönemindeki Kökenleri Üzerine', in Yalçın Çakmak and İmran Gürtaş (eds), *Kızılbaşlık, Alevilik, Bektaşilik: Tarih-Kimlik-Ritüel* (Istanbul: İletişim, 2015), pp. 165–83.
Tuna, M. Ö., *Imperial Russia's Muslims: Islam, Empire and European Modernity, 1788–1914* (Cambridge: Cambridge University Press, 2015).

Bibliography

Türkyılmaz, Z., 'Anxieties of Conversion: Missionaries, State and Heterodox Communities in the Late Ottoman Empire', unpublished PhD disseration, University of California Los Angeles, 2009.

Uçman, A., 'The Theory of the *Dawr* and the *Dawriya*s in Ottoman Sufi Literature', in Ahmet Yaşar Ocak (ed.), *Sufism and Sufis in Ottoman Society* (Ankara: Türk Tarih Kurumu, 2005), pp. 445–75.

Uğur, A., *The Ottoman 'Ulema in the mid-17th Century: an Analysis of the Vakā'ü'l-fuzalā of Mehmed Seyhī Efendi* (Berlin: Klaus Schwartz, 1986).

Üsküdarli Haşim Baba, 'Esraru'l-Ilahiyyun ve Eṭvaru'l-Melamiyyun', Süleymaniye Library, Reşid Efendi 784.

Usluer, F., *Fazlullah Esterābādī. Cāvidān-Nāme. Dürr-i Yetim İsimli Tercümesi* (Istanbul: Kalbalcı Yayınevi, 2012).

Usluer, F., *Hurufilik* (Istanbul: Kabalcı Yayınevi, 2009).

Üstün, İ. S., 'Heresy and Legitimacy in the Ottoman Empire in the Sixteenth Century', unpublished PhD dissertation, University of Manchester, 1991.

Üstün, K., 'Rethinking *Vaka-i Hayriyye* (Auspicious Event): Elimination of the Janissaries on the Path of Modernization', PhD dissertation, Bilkent University, 2002.

Uzunçarşılı, İ. H., *Osmanlı Devleti'nin İlmiye Teşkilatı* (Ankara: TTK, 1965).

Uzunçarşılı, İ. H., *Osmanlı Devleti teşkilātından Kapukulu Ocakları I: Acemi Ocağı ve Yeniçeri Ocağı* (Ankara: Türk Tarih Kurumu, 1944).

Uzunçarşılı, İ. H., *Osmanlı Tarihi, vol. II: Istanbul'un Fethinden Kanuni Sultan Süleyman'in Ölümüne Kadar* (Ankara: Türk Tarih Kurumu, 1943).

Uzunçarşılı, İ. H., *Meşhur Rumeli Āyanlarından Tirsinikli İsmail, Yılık Oğlu Süleyman Ağalar ve Alemdar Mustafa Paşa* (İstanbul: Maarif Matbaası, 1942).

Van Ess, J., *Der Eine und das Andere. Beobachtungen an islamischen häresiographischen Texten.*, vol. 1 (Berlin: Walter de Gruyter, 2011).

Van Ess, J., *Theologie und Gesellschaft I'm 2. und 3. Jahrhundert Hidschra. Eine Geschichte des religiösen Denkens im frühen Islam*, vol. 2 (Berlin: Walter de Gruyter, 1991–7).

Varol, M., *Islahat, Siyaset, Tarikat: Bektaşiliğin Ilgası Sonrasında Osmanlı Devleti'nin Tarikat Politikaları* (Istanbul: Dergâh, 2013).

Vassaf, O. H., *Sefine-i Evliya*. 6 vols (Istanbul: Kitabevi, 2006).

Vicdani, Sadık, *Tomar-i Ṭuruk-u'Aliyye* (Istanbul: Evkaf-ı Islamiye Matbaası, Matba'a-yi Amire, 1338–40/1920–2).

Vocelka, K., 'The Counter-Reformation and Popular Piety in Vienna: a Case Study', in C. Scott Dixon, Dagmar Freist and Mark Greengrass (eds), *Living with Religious Diversity in Early-Modern Europe* (Farnham: Ashgate, 2009), pp. 127–37.

Vovchenko, D., *Containing Balkan Nationalism: Imperial Russia and Ottoman Christians, 1856–1914* (Oxford: Oxford University Press, 2016).

Wajdi, M. F., *Dā'irat al-maʿārif li-qarn al-ʿashrūn*, 10 vols (Beirut: Dar al-fikr, 1971).

Watt, W. M., *The Formative Period of Islamic Thought* (Oxford: Oneworld, [1973] 1998).
Werner, E., *Büyük Bir Devletin Doğuşu – Osmanlılar*, trans. Yılmaz Öner (Istanbul: Alan Yayınları, 1988).
White, S., *The Climate of Rebellion in the Early Modern Ottoman Empire* (Cambridge: Cambridge University Press, 2011).
Winkelbauer, T., *Ständefreiheit und Fürstenmacht: Länder und Untertanen des Hauses Habsburg im konfessionellen Zeitalter*, vol. 2: *Österreichische Geschichte (1522–1699)* (Vienna: Ueberreuter, 2003).
Winter, S., *A History of the 'Alawis: From Medieval Aleppo to the Turkish Republic* (Princeton, NJ: Princeton University Press, 2016).
Winter, S., 'The *Kızılbaş* of Syria and Ottoman Shiism', in Christine Woodhead (ed.), *The Ottoman World* (London: Routledge, 2011), pp. 171–83.
Winter, S., *The Shiites of Lebanon under Ottoman Rule, 1516–1788* (Cambridge: Cambridge University Press, 2010).
Winter, M., 'Ottoman Qādīs in Damascus in 16th–18th Centuries', in Ron Shaham (ed.), *Law, Custom, and Statute in the Muslim World: Studies in Honor of Aharon Layish* (Leiden: Brill, 2007), pp. 87–109.
Woods, J., *The Aqquyunlu: Clan, Confederation, Empire*, rev. and expanded edn (Salt Lake City: University of Utah Press, 1999).
Yahyā Efendi, *Fetāvā*, Suleymaniye Library, MS Ayasofya 1569.
Yananlı, R. (ed.), *Oğlan Şeyh İbrahim Efendi Külliyatı* (Istanbul: Kitabevi, 2008).
Yaslıçimen, F., 'Saving the Minds and Loyalties of Subjects: Ottoman Education Policy Against the Spread of Shiism in Iraq During the Time of Abdülhamid II', *Divan: Disiplinlerarası Çalışmalar Dergisi* 21/41 (2016): 63–108.
Yavuz, F. Betul, 'The Worldview of a Sufi in the Ottoman Realm: Hakiki and His Book of Guidance', in Hani Khafipour (ed.), *Empires of the Near East and India: Source Studies of the Safavid, Ottoman, and Mughal Literate Communities* (Columbia: Columbia University Press, 2019), pp. 00–00.
Yavuz, F. B., 'The Making of a Sufi Order between Heresy and Legitimacy: Bayrami-Malamis in the Ottoman Empire', unpublished PhD dissertation, Rice University, 2013.
Yaycıoğlu, A., 'Guarding Traditions and Laws – Disciplining Bodies and Souls: Tradition, Science, and Religion in the Age of Ottoman Reform', *Modern Asian Studies* 52/5 (2018): 1542–603.
Yaycıoğlu, A., *Partners of the Empire: the Crisis of the Ottoman Order in the Age of Revolutions* (Stanford, CA: Stanford University Press, 2016).
Yazıcı, T., 'Gölpınarlı, Abdulbaki', *Encyclopedia Iranica*, vol. XI, fasc. 1, pp. 100–1.
Yıldırım, R., 'The Rise of the Safavids as a Political Dynasty: the Revolution of Shah Ismail, the Founder of the Safavid State', in Rudi Matthee (ed.), *The Safavid World* (New York: Routledge, forthcoming), pp. 00–00.

Bibliography

Yıldırım, R., *Aleviliğin Doğuşu Kızılbaş Sufiliğinin Toplumsal ve Siyasal Temelleri 1300–1501* (Istanbul: İletişim, 2017)
Yıldırım, R., 'Sunni Orthodoxy vs. Shi'ite Heteredoxy? A Reapprasial of Islamic Piety in Medieval Anatolia', in A. C. S. Peacock, B. De Nicola, and S. N. Yıldız (eds), *Islam and Christianity in Medieval Anatolia* (Farnham: Ashgate, 2015), pp. 287–308.
Yıldırım, R., 'Anadolu'da İslāmiyet: Gaziler Çağında (XII.–XIV. Asırlar) Türkmen İslām Yorumunun Sünnī-Alevī Niteliği Üzerine Bazı Değerlendirmeler', *Osmanlı Araştırmaları/Journal of Ottoman Studies* 43 (2014): 93–124.
Yıldırım, R., 'Shī'itisation of the Futuwwa Tradition in the Fifteenth Century', *British Journal of Middle Eastern Studies* 40/1 (2013): 53–70.
Yıldırım, R., 'Beylikler Dünyasında Kerbela Kültürü ve Ehli-i Beyt Sevgisi: 1362 Yılında Kastamonu'da Yazılan bir Maktel'in Düşündürdükleri', in Halil Çetin (ed.), *Kuzey Anadolu'da Beylikler Dönemi Sempozyumu Bildiriler* (Çankırı: Çankırı Karatekin Üniversitesi Yayınları, 2012), pp. 344–72.
Yıldırım, R., 'Büyüklüğün Büyümeye Set Çekmesi: Fuat Köprülü'nün Türkiye'de Yesevilik Araştırmalarına Katkısı Üzerine Bir Değerlendirme', in Yahya Kemal Taştan (ed.), *Mehmet Fuat Köprülü* (Ankara: Kültür ve Turizm Bakanligi, 2012), pp. 357–98.
Yıldırım, R., 'Bektaşi kime derler? Bektaşi kavramının kapsamı ve sınırları üzerine tarihsel bir analiz denemesi', *Türk Kültürü ve Hacı Bektaş Veli Araştırma Dergisi* 55 (2010): 23–58.
Yıldırım, R., 'Turcomans between Two Empires: the Origins of the *Kızılbaş* Identity in Anatolia (1447–1514)', PhD dissertation, Bilkent University, 2008.
Yılmaz, H., *Caliphate Redefined: the Mystical Turn in Ottoman Political Thought* (Princeton, NJ: Princeton University Press, 2018).
Yılmaz, H., 'The Sultan and the Sultanate: Envisioning Rulership in Age of Süleymān the Lawgiver (1520–1566)', PhD dissertation, Harvard University, 2004.
Yılmaz, Y., 'Nebulous Ottomans vs. Good Old Habsburgs: A Historiographical Comparison', *Austrian History Yearbook* 48 (2017): 173–90.
Yılmazer, Z., 'Esad Efendi, Sahaflar Şeyhizāde', *Türkiye Diyanet Vakfı İslam Ansiklopedisi* (*TDVİA*), vol. 11, pp. 341–45, available at: http://www.islamansiklopedisi.info.
Zarcone, T., '*Bektaşiyye*', *Encyclopedia of Islam*, 3rd edn (Brill online), last accessed 9 March 2017.
Zarinebaf-Shahr, F., 'Kızılbaş "Heresy" and Rebellion in Ottoman Anatolia During the Sixteenth Century', *Anatolia Moderna* 7 (1997): 1–15.
Zilfi, M. C., 'The Ottoman Ulema', in Suraiya N. Faroqhi (ed.), *Cambridge History of Turkey, vol. 3: The Later Ottoman Empire, 1603–1839* (Cambridge: Cambridge University Press, 2006), pp. 209–95.
Zilfi, M., *The Politics of Piety: the Ottoman Ulema in the Post-Classical Age (1600–1800)* (Minneapolis, MN: Bibliotheca Islamica, 1988).

Zilfi, M. C., 'The *Kadızadeli*s: Discordant Revivalism in Seventeenth-Century Istanbul', *Journal of Near Eastern Studies* 45/4 (1986): 251–69.

Zilfi, M. C., 'Elite Circulation in the Ottoman Empire: Great Mollas of the Eighteenth Century', *Journal of the Economic and Social History of the Orient* 26/3 (1983): 318–64.

Zimmermann, J., 'Aleviten in osmanischen Wörterbüchern und Enzyklopädien des späten 19. Jahrhunderts', in Robert Langer et al. (eds), *Ocak und Dedelik: Institutionen religiösen Spezialistentums bei den Aleviten* (Frankfurt: Peter Lang, 2013), pp. 179–204.

Index

Abbas I, Shah, 31, 63, 70n, 199
Abdülaziz, Sultan, 175–6, 177, 180
Abdülhamid II, Sultan
  censorship, 158
  'civilising mission'. 185
  'correction of belief(s)'. 166–9
  missionaries, 182–3
  pan-Islamic programme, 196, 205
  sectarianism, 207
  'Union of Islam'. 179
Abdülmecid, Sultan, 175–6, 177
Abkhaz tribe, 167, 206–7
Abu Bakr (caliph), 129, 204
Adolphus, Gustavus (Swedish king), 106
Ağa, Beşir, 124, 130, 139–40n, 139n, 204
ahl-al-baytism, 21, 72–3, 80, 84, 200, 201
Ahmed, Shahab, 3, 71–2, 200
Ahmed Paşa, Fazıl, 96, 204
Aksarayi, Hamiduddin, 132
Akşemseddin, 132
al-Akhbar, Ka'b, 87n
Alevism, 169, 178, 184, 189n
Alexis (Alexei) Mikhailovich, Tsar, 100–1, 102
Algar, Hamid, 125
al-Ghazali, 29–30, 32, 78, 148, 149, 152
Ali, Ferah Paşa, 167–8
Ali, Mustafa, 82, 83, 89n
Ali, Paşmakçızade Seyyid, 125
Ali Efendi, Kınalızade, 26
Ali Paşa, Sehid, 124, 125, 140n
Alid Sufism, 2, 21, 71–89, 129, 201
Alkan, Necati, 166–192, 206–8
Amasya peace treaty, 61

American Board of Commissioners for Foreign Missions (ABCFM), 182, 185
Anapa, 167, 168
Anatolia
  ahl-al-baytism, 73
  Bektaşi order, 147, 169
  Birgivi, Mehmed 94
  Darir, 74–5
  Halveti/Safavid tradition, 132
  Hamzaviyye, 135
  Hanafi *madhhab*, 24
  Ḥurūfīs, 149
  Kızılbaş, 48, 54, 60, 63, 187n, 195
  pīrs, 124
  rāfıḍī, 154
  religious texts, 31
  Safavid Empire, 58, 61, 65n, 71, 199
  Safavid propaganda, 50–1
  Tanẓīmāt reform, 180
  Turkoman tribes, 35
Andrews, Walter G., 144n
anti-Sufism, 148–52
al-Anwār wa'l Misbah, 76
apostasy, 28–32, 44n
Arab provinces, 179, 180, 194, 196
Ardabil, 51–2, 57, 64n
Arif, Mehmed, *Başımıza Gelenler*, 178–9
Aşıkpaşazade, 51–2
Assembly of the Land, 99
Atayi, Nev'izade, 36, 139n, 140n
Atçıl, Abdurrahman, 23, 67n, 85n, 109–10
'Auspicious Incident', 146, 170, 207

Austria, 96, 202
　Inner, 91, 104

b. Abdülkerim, Ali, 53
b. Abu Talib, Ali, 78–80
　ahl-al-baytism, 72–3, 200
　Atayi, 139n
　Battle of Siffin, 77
　Darir, 83
　Fazlallah Esterabadi, 153
　futuwwah, 85n
　as the Ghazi, 80–2
　Haydar, 64n
　Hutbatu'l-bayan, 152
　Nusayris, 156–7
　Semerāt, 129
　Sunnitisation, 21
b. 'Ali, Zayd, 154
b. Ata, Wasil, 77
b. Munabbih, Wahb, 87n
Babayan, K., 70n
Babinger, Franz, 1
al-Babirti, Akmal al-Din Muhammad b. Muhammad Mahmud, 74–5
Baer, Marc David, 21
Baghdad, 58, 68n, 180
al-Bakri, Abu Hasan
　Sirāt, 75–7, 78, 83, 87n, 200
　used by Darir, 79, 81
　used by Shiites, 87–8n
Bali, Hamza, Bali Efendi, Sheikh Bali, 56, 125, 128
Balıkesir, 94
Balım Sultan, 169
Balkans
　Bektaşi order, 146
　'correction of belief(s)', 179
　Hamzaviyye, 135
　Hanafi *madhhab*, 24
　'ilm-i hāls, 19
　Kızılbaş, 61
　loss of territories from, 180
　Mustafa Paşa, 170
　pīrs, 124
Baltacıoğlu-Brammer, Ayşe, 47–70, 198, 199, 200, 206
Banu Nakha, 79
Barkan, Ö. L., 44n
Barkey, Karen, 108–9
Barquq (Mamluk Sultan), 74–75
Bashir, Shahzad, 64n
Basra, 77, 180
Battle of Chaldiran, 48, 67n

Battle of Lützen, 106
Battle of Siffin, 77
Battle of White Mountain, 103, 105–6
Batzel, Rudi, 108–9
Bayezid II, 66n, 198
Bayram, Hacı, 132, 144n
Bayramiyye Sufi order, 121, 133, 135, 195, 203, 204
Bektaşi order, 152–7
　'correction of belief(s)', 166, 169–76, 185
　Hurūfis, 158
　Hutbatu'l-bayan, 152
　Janissary corps, 2, 196, 201
　Mahmud II, 207
　polemics against, 146–65, 205–6
Bektaşi/Alevi Islam, 2, 130
Bohemia, 105–6, 113
Bohemian Protestants, 104–5
Book of Beliefs, 180–1
Bosnia, 125
Bossy, John, 16
Burak, Guy, 20, 30, 31, 42n, 50, 194
Bursa, 55

Cafer Pasha, 61
Cairo, 74, 76, 195
cash waqfs, 37
Catholic Union, 104
Catholicism, 18, 91, 103–7, 202
Caucasus, 68n, 167–8, 177, 201, 206–7
Cavidan-books, 149–50, 153, 155
Celal, 61
Celali Rebellions, 61, 108, 115
Çeşmi Efendi, 70n
Cevdat Paşa, Ahmed, 173, 175
　History, 173
Charles V (Habsburg), 104
Christianity, 77, 96, 98–103, 181–4, 195, 198
　Orthodox, 90–120
　see also Catholicism; Protestantism
Circassian tribe, 167, 184, 206–7
Çivizade, Mufti, 37
'coherent contradiction', 3, 72, 75, 200
'Confessional Age' of Europe, 15–16
'confessional ambiguity', 85n
confessionalisation, 17–21, 90–120
　debate (in the Ottoman Empire), 3–4, 12–21
　Erginbaş and, 20–1
　Eurasian trend, 3
　Mediterranean, 38–9

Index

paradigm, 14–17
and state power, 40n
and Sunnitisation, 71
Yıldırım and, 197–8
Constantinople, 70n, 116
convent-masjids, 34–5
Coreth, Anna, 103
'correction of belief(s)', 166–92, 206–8
Council of a Hundred Chapters, 98
Crummey, Robert O., 91, 100, 114
Curry, John, 83, 86n, 193–210
Cyprus, 57, 68n, 96

dāis, 178
al-Darir, Mustafa, 200, 201
  Siret, 71–89
dastūr, 156
Dede, Emir, 132–3
Deringil, Selim, 169, 181
Dersim, 184
'Dersim question', 179–80
devr, 130, 204
Diyarbekir, 59
Don Cossack revolts, 115
Dressler, M., 161n, 189n
Duffy, E., 16

Ebussuud
  Atçıl, 85n
  Birgivi and, 94
  fatwas, 30, 33–7
  ḳānūn, 28
  Ḳānūnnāme of Buda, 36–7
  Kızılbaş, 56–8
  legislative activities, 17–18
  sharia law, 27, 45n
  Suleyman I, 36–7
Edict of Gülhane, 157
Edict of Restitution, 106
ehl-i sünnet ve'l cemaat, 2
Egypt, 29, 42n, 74, 194
  Fatimid Ismai'ili state, 29
Emirgün, 200
Erginbaş, Vefa, 1–11, 20–1, 49, 63–4, 71–89, 200–1
Erzurum, 57, 74, 96
Es'ad Efendi, 171, 175
  Üss-i Zafer, 171
Eşrefoğlu Abdullah Rûmî, *Müzekki'n-nüfūs*, 66n
Estrabadi, Fazlallah, 148–52, 153, 155, 162n
Europeanisation, 196, 208

Faroqhi, S., 159
Fatimids, 148, 149, 152
fatwas (fetvās), 30–1, 33–5, 37, 56–7, 67n, 170
Felek, Özgen, 83–4
Ferdinand I (Habsburg), 104
Ferdinand II (Habsburg), 91, 104, 105–6, 109
Ferdinand III (Habsburg), 91, 106–7
Fereşteoğlu, 149, 152
  'Aşkname, 149, 151
Ferhad Paşa, 124–5
Feyzullah Efendi, Grand Mufti, 112, 114
Filaret, Patriarch, 99–100, 101, 112
Firak-i zalle (dalle) al-firaq al-dalla, 166, 181
Fleischer, Cornell, 36, 40n
Foucault, Michel, 161n
Frederick V of Palatinate, 105
Friedman, Y., 156, 164n

Gabor Bethlen (of Hungary), 105
Germany, 106–7, 113
Germogen, Patriarch, 99, 112
ghaza ideology, 37, 44n, 194
ghazawat, 78–9
ghulāt, 122, 137n, 149
Godunov, Boris, 98–9, 99
Gorski, P. D., 16
Graf, Tobias, 110
Greek Orthodox Church, 101
Greek Phanariots, 110
Grehan, James, *Twilight of the Saints*, 85n

Habsburgs, 71, 90–120, 201–3
Hacı Bektaş convent, 149
Hacı Bektaş-i Veli, 158, 169, 172
Hagen, Gottfried, 81–2, 82, 86n
Haḳayīk el-Vekayi' (newspaper), 177–8
Halil Paşa, 127, 142n
Halveti Sufi order
  confessionalisation, 195
  Curry on, 83
  Mahmud II, 171
  Martin on, 85–6n
  Murad III, 201
  Sari Abdullah on, 128, 133
  Veli, 132
Hamza, Mufti, 30
Hamzaviyye, 121–45, 203–4
Hanafi Sunnism
  'civilising mission', 185
  culture, 2, 203

Hanafi Sunnism (*cont.*)
  doctrine, 20, 167, 184
  madhhab, 22, 24–8, 42n, 50, 194
  School, 181, 183
  School of law, 20, 177
  tradition, 29
Hasan, Uzan, 51, 58–9
Hasan Paşa, Çeçenzade, 168
Haydar, Shaykh, 47, 51–2, 64n
heresy, 146–65
heterodoxy, 193–210
Heyd, Uriel, 25, 26, 28
Holy Roman Empire, 91, 103–4, 106
House of Osman, 111
Howard, Douglas, 111
Hulviyāt-i Shāhī, 35
Hungary, 105, 113
Hurūfī-Bektaşis, 158
Hurūfīs, 123, 138n, 149–51, 205
Hüseyin, Lamekani, 124–5, 140n

Ibn 'Arabi, 129
Ibn Ishaq, 75, 81, 83, 88n, 200
  Sirāṭ, 75–7, 78, 83
Ibn Kamal, 20, 30
Ibn Khaldun, 26
Ibn Taymiyya, 78
Ibrahim, Oğlan Şeyh, 92, 124, 140n, 145n
  Sohbetname, 143n
Idris Muhtefi, 124, 125–6, 127, 128
Idris, Şeyh Ali, 139n
İhtiyacāt-i Askeriye (article), 177–8
'ilm-i hāls, 19–20, 41n
Imami Shiism, 48, 70n
Imamism, 63
Imber, Colin, 25, 36–7, 44n, 45n, 124–5
İnalcık, H., 35, 45n
Iran
  Hurūfīs, 149
  Kızılbaş, 54
  rāfiḍī, 154
  Safavid Empire, 54–5, 60, 62
  Shiite Safavid Empire, 67n
Iraq
  'correction of belief(s)', 184
  Kızılbaş, 54, 60, 62, 63
  layihas, 180
  Safavid Empire, 50
  Sunnism, 181
Irşadname, 131–2
Isa, Mevlana, 34
Isfahan, *Tarekh-e Alam Ara-ye Amini*, 47
İshak Efendi, Harputlu, 146–65, 159–60n

Kaşifü 'l-esrar ve dafi'u 'l-eşrar, 146, 148, 150, 153, 161n, 205–6
Işlāḥāt Edict, 157
Islamic Constitutional movement, 196
Ismai'ili Shiism, 21
Ismail, Shah, 47, 51–3, 62, 194–5
Ismail I, 84
Istanbul
  Bektaşi order, 172–3, 176
  Birgivi in, 94
  dāis, 178
  Hamzaviyye, 204
  Hamzaviyye to the *Melāmiyye*, 121–45
  İshak Efendi, 157
  Janissary corps, 170
  Kadızadeli movement, 90, 93, 96
  Kızılbaş, 49, 53, 55, 55–6, 60–1, 67n
  layihas, 180
  mosques, 34
  Nusayris, 183
  Safavid Empire, 50
  Safavid propaganda, 58–9
Ivan IV (of Russia), 98

Jacob, Georg, 147–8, 161n
Janissary corps, 93
  'Auspicious Incident', 146
  Bektaşi order, 2, 159, 169–73, 196, 201
  junta, 93
  Mahmud II, 166, 176, 207
  Selim III, 168
Jeremiah of Constantinople, Patriarch, 98
Jesuits, 104, 105–6, 119n
Jews, 77, 78, 87n
  Sabbatean movement, 195
Junayd, Shaykh, 50–2, 66n

Kabayi, Hacı, 124, 127, 139n
Kadizade Mehmed, 195
Kadızadeli movement, 92–8
  and anti-Sufism, 117n
  confessionalisation, 197
  and court, 109, 111–12
  decline, 196
  Istanbul, 138n
  Krstić, Tijana, 19, 137–8n
  preachers, 108
  religion and politics, 202–5
  and Russian Orthodox Church, 90, 100–1, 112, 114
  Sunnitisation, 71
  support from Sultans, 195
  Terzioğlu, Derin, 125

Index

Kafadar, Cemal, 194
ḳānūn, 25, 26–8, 38, 197
Ḳānūnname-i Cedid, 37
Karaki, Ali, 17–18
Karaman, 75
Katz, Marion Holmes, 78
Kemal Bey, Ismail, 182
Kemalpaşazade, 36, 53–4, 56, 57
Khalid, Shaykh, 172
Khalidiyya, 172
Khunji, Fadlullah Ruzbihan, *Tarekh-e Alam Ara-ye Amini*, 47
Kırşehir (Anatolia), 61
Kızılbaş, 5, 47–70, 187n, 198–200
   Alevism and, 189n
   as the 'enemy in the East', 62
   fatwas, 30
   as 'heretic followers of the Safavid Shah', 55–9
   Kamal's treatise on, 20
   as negative label, 49–50
   as 'peaceful subjects of the Empire', 59–62
   persecution of, 147
   polemics against, 158
   rāfiḍī, 154
   as 'rebellious heretics', 48
   'red crown', 47–8, 53, 64n
   Safavid Empire, 2
   as Safavid threat, 53–4
   Türkyılmaz, 180
   ulema, 195
Kızılbaş-Alevi communities, 147
Kliuchevskii, Vasily, 101, 102, 114–15
Kohlberg, Ethan, 154
Köprülü, Fuad, *Islam in Anatolia*, 1
Korkud, Prince, 30, 195
Kramer, Martin, 183–4
Krstić, Tijana, 17–19, 21, 137–8n
Kurdistan, 187n
Kurds, 177, 179

La'lizade, A., 124
Lamormaini, William, 104, 105–6
Latakia, 182–3, 184
layihas, 179–80
Leopold I (Habsburg), 91, 107
Lufti, Ahmed, 167, 171
Lutfi Paşa, 66n
Lutheranism, 14–17
   Small Catecism, 17
   see also Protestantism

MacHardy, Karin, 111, 119n
Mahmud II, 166, 168–72, 175–6, 185, 207
al-Majlisi, Baqir, 87–8n
Makarii (Macarius), 98
al-Mansur, Ali, 74
Martin, B. G., 85–6n
Maşuki, İsmail, 131, 123, 126
Matthee, Rudi, 70n
Matthias (Habsburg), Letter of Majesty, 104
Maximilian II (Habsburg), 104
Me'ālī, 59
Mediterranean, 12–13, 18, 20, 39, 91, 116
Mehmed, 'Vani', 92, 96, 204
Mehmed Efendi, Bigivi, 94, 95
Mehmed Efendi, Kadızade, 92–8
Mehmed Efendi, Üstüvani, 92, 95–6
Mehmed II
   Friday mosques, 35
   law code, 23
   penal codes, 32–3
   Tursun Bey, 25
   ulema, 36
   and Uzan Hasan, 51
   waqfs, 41n
Mehmed III, 201
Mehmed IV, 92, 96, 195
Mehmed Paşa, Köprülü, 95–6, 97, 127
Mehmet II, 33
melāmet, 131–5, 136–7n
   Melāmis, 7, 121–2, 140n, 141n
   poetical works, 126
   Yavuz, 204
melāmī function, 144n
Melāmī-Bayrami order, 204
Melāmiyye, 121–45
memoranda, 179–80
'metadoxy', 194
Metropolitan Iov, 98
Mevlana Jalal al-Din Rumi, 74–6, 75, 143n
   Mesnevi, 75, 127
Mevlevi order, 75, 127, 175, 205
Mikhail Feodorovich (Tsar), 99–100
Minadoi, Giovanni Tommaso, 64n
Mir'atu'l-'Isk, 131
Mısri, Niyazi-i, 205
al-Mısri, Ẓu'n-Nun, 134
missionaries, 166–9, 167, 181–4, 207
Monastery Chancellery, 101
Mongol invasions, 6, 73
Mongol period, 22, 25, 122
Mongol polity, 4, 19
Moscow, 90, 99

251

mosques, 34–5, 36, 95, 172, 183–4
Mosul, 59, 180, 184
muftis, 23, 25
Murad III, 34, 73, 82, 83–4, 89n, 127, 195, 200–1
Murad IV, 70n, 92, 93–5, 195, 199–200, 200
Muscovite Church, 99
Mustafa II, 37
Mustafa Paşa, Alemdar, 170
Mustafa Paşa, Grand Vizier Kara, 96

Nakşbandiyye, 128–9, 133, 171–2, 175–6, 204, 207
Necipoğlu, G., 34–5
Neronov, Ivan, 102
Nesimi, 145n
'New Order' programme, 168–9, 196
Nikon, 101–2, 112–13, 114
  Refutation, 102
Nizri, Michael, 112
Nuri Paşa, Mustafa, 167–8
Nusayris, 2, 149, 152–8, 176, 181–4, 205

Ocak, A. Y., 2
Old Believers, 102
Olsson, T., 156
Orthodox Christianity, 90–120
Orthodoxy, 122–3, 193–210
Oruç Bey, *Tevarih-i Ali Osman*, 51–2, 66n
Osman II, 93
Özege, S., 148, 153
Özel, Oktay, 108

Pancaroğlu, Oya, 88–9n
Patrona Halil Rebellion, 196, 203
Peace of Augsburg, 115–16
Peace of Prague, 106
Peace of Westphalia, 107
Peter the Great (of Russia), 112–13, 114, 202
Peters, R., 24
Petrovich, Avvakum, 102
Pfeiffer, Judith, 85n
Philliou, Christine, 110
pietas Austriaca, 103, 107, 113
pīrs, 123, 123–4, 124, 126, 127, 131
Pistor-Hatam, A., 157, 164n
Poland, 99
polemics, 146–65
'polytheists', 79, 87n, 153–4, 155
Poonawala, I., 151
Prague Castle defenestrations, 105

Protestant Reformation, 14–17, 103–4, 113
Protestant Union, 104
Protestantism, 91, 103–7, 181–4, 197, 202, 207
  Bohemian, 104–5
  Calvinism, 14
  Reformation Europe, 19–20, 39

qadis, 23, 24
Qur'an
  Ali in, 80
  apostasy, 30
  Arabic letters in, 149
  Bayram, 144n
  Birgivi and, 94–5
  'command the right and forbid the wrong', 172, 185, 206
  'correction of belief(s)', 167
  Fazlallah Esterabadi, 151
  Hanafi Sunnism, 184
  Ibn Ishaq, 75–7
  and Jews, 87n
  Kızılbaş, 53
  Mehmet II, 33
  sharia law, 26
  text debated, 18
  and the Torah, 78

rāfiḍī (rafizi, revafiz, ehl-i rafz, erbab-i rafz ve ilhad), 154, 167, 173
're-confessionalisation', 12–46, 197, 198
reddiye, 148, 178
Reformation Europe, 19–20, 39; *see also* Protestantism
Regensburg Diet, 104
Reinhard, Wolfgang, 14–15
Reinkowski, M., 157
'religion and state' order, 12–46
'renewal of faith' legal concept, 20, 31
Repp, R. C., 27
Ridda wars, 32
Rıf'at, Ahmet, 148, 162n
risale, 149, 155
Rosenthal, Franz, 76
Ross Anonymous, 64n
Rothman, Nathalie, 110
Rtishchev, F. M., 101
Rudolf II (Habsburg), 104
Rumelia, 33
Rumi *see* Mevlana Jalal al-Din Rūmī
Rūmī (or Anatolian), 74–6
Russian Empire, 90–120, 201–3

Index

Russian Orthodox Church, 98–103
Russian Patriarchate, 98–9
Russian Tsardom, 98–103
Rüstem Pasha, Grand Vizier, 56

Sabri Paşa, Eyüb, 206
Sadeddin, Hoca, 82
al-Sadiq, Jafar, 78, 154
Safa, Hacı Mirza, 163–4n
Safavid Empire
   Ismail, 194–5
   Kızılbaş, 2, 47, 199–200
   Krstić, 17–18
   Murad III, 201
   propaganda, 50, 57–8
   Selim I, 209
   Shiite, 52
   Terzioğlu, 19
Safi, Shaykh, 66n
Şahkulu uprisings, 194–5
   Shah Kulu Rebellion, 47–8, 52, 66n
Sarban, Ahmed, 126, 131
Sari Abdullah
   Bayazid, 142n
   Hamzaviyye, 126, 135
   La'lizade, 141–2n
   pīrs, 124
   Şemerāt, 143n, 144n
   Şemerātu'l-fu'ad, 121–2, 126–35, 203–5
   treatises, 141n
Sarıgürz, Nureddin Hamza, 53, 57
   fatwa, 53–4
Şāsı, 167
Savaş, Saim, 68–9n
Schilling, Heinz, 14–16
Şehrizor (Kirkuk), 58–9
Selim I
   Kızılbaş, 52–3, 62, 198–9
   Safavid Empire, 47–8, 200, 209
   ulema, 84, 194–5
Selim II, 26
Selim III, 168, 169–70, 170, 196
şeyhülislams, 56, 125, 170, 171
al-Shafi'i, 29
sharia law, 22, 24–8, 36–8, 172, 197
Shchelkalov, A. Ia., 98
Sheikh, Mustapha, 117n
Shiism
   ahl-al-baytism, 72–3
   al-Bakri, 76–7, 87n, 87–8n
   Ali, 78–80, 200
   anti, 21, 66n

apostasy, 32
Bektaşi order, 146–7, 149, 152–8, 163–4n
confessional ambiguity, 85n
Iran, 66n
İshak, 8
Kızılbaş, 5, 47–52, 57–8, 62–4, 67n, 187n, 199
'light of Muhammad', 78
rāfiḍī, 167
Safavid Empire, 31, 47, 50–2, 194–5
Siret, 82–4
and Sufism, 122
Sunni-Shiite conflict, 32
Twelver (imami), 64n, 69n, 72–3
Shoshan, Boaz, 76, 78, 87–8n
sipahis, 93–4
Sirāṭ, 87n
   al-Bakri, 75–7, 78, 83, 87n
   Ibn Ishaq, 75–7, 78, 83
Siret, Darir, 71–89
siyāsa, 26, 43n
Stanislaus Kostka (saint), 103
Stewart, Devin, 42n
Stoglav Church Council, 101, 116
Sublime Court, 33
Sublime Porte, 147, 177, 179
Şüca Dede, 83, 84
Sufism, 2
   ahl-al-baytism, 6, 19, 73
   Ali, 21, 200–1
   of Ardabil, 47, 52
   Bayazid, 142n
   Bektaşi order, 146–52, 159, 166, 169, 175, 205
   confessionalisation, 198
   convent-masjids, 34–5
   convents, 138n
   Directorate of Religious Affairs, 72
   Hamzaviyye, 121–7, 139–40n, 203–4
   heterodoxy, 194–6
   Kadızadeli movement, 95–7, 117n, 203
   Kızılbaş, 64n
   melāmet, 7, 131–5, 136–7n
   Mevlevi order, 75
   Murad III, 83, 89n
   Şemerāt, 127–35, 141n, 144n
   Safi, 65n
Süleyman Hüsnü Paşa, 180–1
Süleyman I
   Ebussuud, 28
   Kızılbaş, 56, 62

Süleyman I (*cont.*)
  law code, 32–3
  mosques, 34
  'religion and state' order, 36–8
  sharia law, 26
  'social disciplining', 36
Süleyman the Lawgiver, 36, 94, 115
Sultan Ahmed (Blue) Mosque,
  Hippodrome Square, 93–4
Sunnification campaign, 71–2, 171
Sunni–Shiite sectarian dispute, 21, 32
Sunnitisation, 19, 21, 177
Sun'ullah Efendi, 31
Sweden, 106–7
Syria, 2, 42n, 180, 181–2
  greater, 54, 60, 68n

al-Tabarani, *Kitab al-bakura as-Sulaymaniya*, 156
al-Tabari, 79
Tahir Efendi, Mehmed, 170
Tahmasb, Shah, 115
Talikizade, 37
Tansel, S., *Yavuz Sultan Selim*, 66n
Tanzīmāt Edict, 177
Tanzīmāt reform, 157, 168, 176–81, 185, 196, 207
taqiyah, 57, 125, 156, 173
Terzioğlu, Derin, 3, 18–20, 40n, 125, 205
Tezcan, Baki, 108, 112, 170
Thirty Years War, 91, 115, 119n, 202
Thomas, Keith, 16
al-Tikriti, Nabil, 20, 30
Time of Troubles, 98–9, 108, 112, 116
Timurids, 122, 138n
Torah, 78
Trabzon, 67n, 168
Treaty of Amasya, 115
Treaty of Constantinople, 61, 68n
Treaty of Zuhab, 63, 70n
Turkish–Islamic Synthesis (Türk–İslam Sentezi), 1
Turko-Mongolian polity, 34, 35, 37–8, 39
Türkyılmaz, Zeynep, 180
Tursun Bey, 25
Twelve Shiite Imams, 21, 47, 72, 129
Twelver Buyid dynasty, 29

Twelver Shiism, 21, 58, 70n, 153, 154, 205

ulema, 23–4, 41n, 44n
  al-Ghazali, 29–30
  Bektaşi order, 172–3
  Circassian tribe, 167
  Güzelhisar, 174
  Imber, 36–7
  Mahmud II, 171, 176, 207
  missionaries, 181
  Patrona Halil Rebellion, 203
  state-sponsored, 30–2
  Sunnification campaign, 71–2
  Sunnitisation, 84
Ulozhenie law code, 101
'Union of Islam', 179
Usluer, F., 149
Uzunçarşılı, I. H., 159

Vani Efendi, 139–40n
Veled, Sultan, 75
Veli, Hacı Bayram, 132
Vienna, 96, 103–4, 107, 195, 203
Viller, Bartholomew, 104
Vonifat'ev, Stefan, 101

Wahhabi movement, 206
waqfs, 37, 41n
Weineck, Benjamin, 146–65, 205–6
White, Sam, 108
Winter, Stefan, 49, 68n, 157

Yahya Bey, Taşlıcalı
  kasides, 62
Yahya Efendi, 31
Yavuz, F. Betül, 121–45, 203–4
Yaycıoğlu, Ali, 196
Yazidis (Yezidis) 2, 8, 166, 177, 180, 184, 186n, 191n
Yıldırım, Rıza, 12–46, 66n, 73, 197–9
Yılmaz, Hüseyin, *Caliphate Redefined*, 198
Yılmaz, Yasir, 90–120, 201–3

Zealots of Piety, 100–1
Ziya Bey, Mehmed, 182, 183
Zoroastrians, 167–8, 207

EU representative:
Easy Access System Europe
Mustamäe tee 50, 10621 Tallinn, Estonia
Gpsr:requests@easproject.com